D1603647

NEGOTIATION WITHIN DOMINATION

Mesoamerican Worlds: From the Olmecs to the Danzantes

General Editors: Davíd Carrasco and Eduardo Matos Moctezuma

Editorial Board: Alfredo López Austin, Anthony Aveni, Elizabeth Boone, William Fash, Charles H. Long, Leonardo López Luján, and Eleanor Wake

NEGOTIATION
within
DOMINATION

New Spain's Indian Pueblos Confront the Spanish State

edited by
Ethelia Ruiz Medrano *and* **Susan Kellogg**

UNIVERSITY PRESS OF COLORADO

© 2010 by the University Press of Colorado

Published by the University Press of Colorado
5589 Arapahoe Avenue, Suite 206C
Boulder, Colorado 80303

 The University Press of Colorado is a proud member of
the Association of American University Presses.

The University Press of Colorado is a cooperative publishing enterprise supported, in part, by Adams State College, Colorado State University, Fort Lewis College, Mesa State College, Metropolitan State College of Denver, University of Colorado, University of Northern Colorado, and Western State College of Colorado.

∞ The paper used in this publication meets the minimum requirements of the American National Standard for Information Sciences—Permanence of Paper for Printed Library Materials. ANSI Z39.48-1992

Library of Congress Cataloging-in-Publication Data

Negotiation within domination : New Spain's Indian pueblos confront the Spanish state / edited by Ethelia Ruiz Medrano and Susan Kellogg.
   p. cm.
Includes bibliographical references and index.
ISBN 978-1-60732-032-6 (hardcover : alk. paper) — ISBN 978-1-60732-033-3 (e-book) 1. Indians of Mexico—Government relations—History. 2. Indians, Treatment of—Mexico—History. 3. Government, Resistance to—Mexico. 4. Mexico—Ethnic relations. 5. Mexico—History—Spanish colony, 1540–1810. 6. Spain—Colonies—America—Administration. I. Ruiz Medrano, Ethelia. II. Kellogg, Susan.
 F1231.N45 2010
 972'.02—dc22
                              2010029943
Design by Daniel Pratt

19   18   17   16   15   14   13   12   11   10   10 9 8 7 6 5 4 3 2 1

Chapter 6 includes parts of chapter 3, "Reform, Resistance, and Rhetoric," and chapter 6, "Bourbon Officials," from *The Art of Being In-Between*, by Yanna Yannakakis, copyright 2008, Duke University Press. All rights reserved. Used by permission of the publisher.

To the memory of Luis Reyes and Thelma Sullivan, for their dedication to the study of Nahuatl, their intellects, and their kind hearts.

They are both much missed.

Contents

Tables and Map

BRIAN OWENSBY

Foreword

What makes for domination? More concretely, what made for domination in a place without a standing army or an established constabulary in which the dominators were outnumbered, at times ten to one and never less than three-to-one, by the dominated during nearly three centuries of intimate interaction? The first of these questions is largely an abstract and theoretical one, born of contemporary political and scholarly discussions seeking to understand power relations against the backdrop of an idealized and often postponed Enlightenment egalitarianism. The second is a historical question regarding the centuries-long encounter between Europeans and indigenous peoples that began with the "discovery" of America in the late fifteenth century.

Negotiation within Domination seeks to tack back and forth between these two questions, emphasizing the latter. This volume's central point is to ask how we may understand domination not so much theoretically but as a tangible experience of human entanglement in a context of social, political, economic, and cultural inequality. As various chapters make clear, whatever domination consisted of in viceregal New Spain, it was never total. Coercion and the threat of coercion hung over all relations among people differentially situated in the colonial social order, but violence was never the mainspring of human interaction. And while there was a consensual aspect to dealings among Spaniards, Indians, Africans, and *Castas* (people of mixed race), there was never a static sense of unselfconscious ascendancy by Spaniards or of resigned acquiescence by others. Rather, as the essays in this volume insist, negotiation counterbalanced domination, reflecting the fact that social relations cannot be reduced to the mastery of overlords and the subjection and victimization of subalterns.

From the perspective of our own ideological prejudices, an obvious question follows from this approach. Why would the foremost empire of its day, the world-girding Spanish dominions, permit its subjects to negotiate the terms of their submission? A partial answer lies in the fact that we have simply failed to understand the Spanish empire of the sixteenth and seventeenth centuries on its own terms and have refused to consider how imaginatively those who lived within it responded to their circumstances. Instead, we have supposed that the early-modern Spanish empire *must* have been like later European empires of the late eighteenth and, especially, the nineteenth centuries, in which the domination was more directly coercive, more naked and rawer.[1]

This is a distortion of historical vision, one this volume contributes to identifying and correcting by boring to the bedrock of social and political life to examine how negotiation was not only permitted but encouraged by Spanish officialdom and embraced by the king's most vulnerable vassals— Indians and Indian pueblos. It does so by paying close attention to legal practice and culture. As an emerging literature has begun to show, the law represented a privileged space of interaction among various groups of actors in viceregal Mexico, a space of critical engagement that demanded that royal appointees, local power holders, and ordinary people recognize and respond to each others' presence in the articulation of power.[2] Put another way, and flirting with anachronism, the approach of this emerging literature, and of this volume, is one that sees in law a form of *political* engagement among people who stood in very different places in New Spain's social order.[3]

Above all, this requires that we take legal processes seriously on their own terms. Anyone who has ever been to archives in Mexico City, Seville, and numerous Mexican towns and cities knows how much legal documentation there is. Anyone who has ever encountered the *cedularios* (legal compilations) read Solórzano Pereira's *Política Indiana*, or perused the *Recopilación* of 1680 understands that law played a special role in the organization of Spain's New World dominions. One of the great puzzle-ments of Latin America's colonial historiography is that this embarrass-ment of riches has only recently begun to receive the attention it deserves. *Negotiation within Domination* represents a vital contribution to bringing this wealth to light.

As with virtually all historical thinking, words and categories must allow for new perspectives and at the same time tether new ideas to rec-ognized scholarly reflection. By counterposing *negotiation* to *domination*, these essays express a tension that establishes a nuanced middle ground of dialogue among disparate parties rather than a simplistic story of direct confrontation and coercion. Taken together, the chapters suggest that colonial Mexico was characterized by a culture of legal-political partici-pation at all levels of a dynamic, hierarchical social order. This was not a result of negotiation pure and simple, for all meaningful conversations among historical actors are framed by expectations shared, or at least rec-ognized as mutually impinging. As the chapters demonstrate, negotiation happened when Indian *pueblos* (communities) and individuals litigated over identities, communities, customs, resources, rights, and autonomy by using procedures and practices defined by Spanish law and its philosophi-cal underpinnings.

Attention to these underpinnings hints at an answer to why negotia-tion could give voice to those who lived under domination in the colo-nial context—why, broadly speaking, Indian litigants could negotiate through the law. Covarrubias's *Tesoro de la lengua castellana o española* (1611 and 1674) has as a first definition for "dominación" the word "imperio." "Imperio," in turn, is defined in terms of the legitimate rule of a lord, or as Covarrubias notes, quoting Marcello Amiano, "the beneficial adminis-tration and care of others" (*imperium nil alius est quam cura salutis alienae*). The entry for "dominio" indicates that "beneficial" implied the king's obligation to counterbalance the "force of the powerful and the greedy" (*la fuerza de los poderosos y codiciosos*).[4] In short, the legitimate authority of Spanish monarchs, and so of their laws, rested on acknowledging power differentials among the king's various subjects. Law and its processes were a primary means by which this recognition was made real in everyday life. By juxtaposing this understanding to domination, with its contemporary resonances of overweening power, we can check anachronism and per-haps glimpse how negotiation between Spaniards and Indian pueblos was implicit in the philosophical foundations of Spanish legality and ideas of legitimate rule.

At the highest level of generality, one of the great virtues of this col-lection is the idea that the political problems of indigenous people in New

Spain were perhaps not so different from those who live in supposedly modern and consensual—that is, not colonial—societies. What scholars have tended to forget in distinguishing between "modern" democratic societies and those other societies characterized as colonial is that all who live under the rule of another or others face similar challenges in figuring an individual or collective stance vis-à-vis power and the powerful. The conceit of modern, liberal conceptions of law has been that impersonal legal processes, whose legitimacy is premised on a radical separation of law and politics dating to the Enlightenment, actually created a sphere where competing interests were bracketed and subdued to more orderly, nonpolitical processes. This is not the place to pursue the issue to any depth, although there is a growing sense that this model is itself in crisis.[5]

These essays remind us that perhaps especially in situations of recognized inequality—as opposed to the liberal refusal to see actual inequality as anything other than the symptom of an ever-postponed egalitarian utopia—law has been a means by which power was contested, channeled, restrained, and at times even stalemated, although never defeated. This may be the larger lesson of the legal engagements of Indians and their pueblos in viceregal Mexico. Perhaps better than most, Indian litigants understood, and to this day still understand, that power and differential access to power is at issue in any system of law. This may be one reason "justicia" remained a touchstone for litigants throughout the period. Individuals and pueblos understood that substantive justice—the king's always-contested obligation to protect the weak from the powerful—over and against mere procedural correctness made the law a countervailing power. Indeed, insistence that *justice* could speak to power was perhaps the very essence of law as *political* participation in colonial Mexico, particularly during the Hapsburg period. As this volume hints, this ideal may have lost much to more instrumental and exclusionary notions of law and legality that emerged under the Bourbons in the eighteenth century and undergirded the nation-building projects of nineteenth-century Latin American elites. That is another story worth telling.

NOTES

1. See, e.g., Ranajit Guha, *Dominance without Hegemony: History and Power in Colonial India* (Cambridge, MA: Harvard University Press, 1998).

2. Woodrow Borah, *Justice by Insurance: The General Indian Court of Colonial Mexico and the Legal Aides of the Half Real* (Berkeley: University of California Press, 1983); Susan Kellogg, *Law and Transformation of Aztec Society, 1500–1700* (Norman: University of Oklahoma Press, 2000); Charles Cutter, *Legal Culture in Northern*

New Spain (Albuquerque: University of New Mexico Press, 2001); Brian Owensby, *Empire of Law and Indian Justice in Colonial Mexico* (Stanford, CA: Stanford University Press, 2008).

3. William Taylor, "Between Global Processes and Local Knowledge: An Inquiry into Early Latin American Social History, 1500–1800," in *Reliving the Past: The Worlds of Social History*, ed. O. Zunz and W. Taylor (Chapel Hill: University of North Carolina Press, 1985).

4. See entries for "dominación," "imperio," and "dominio" in Sebastián de Covarrubias Orozco, *Tesoro de la lengua castellana o española* (1611), http://www.cervantes virtual.com/servlet/SirveObras/80250529545703831976613/index.htm.

5. Boaventura de Sousa Santos, *Toward a New Common Sense* (Evanston, IL: Northwestern University Press, 2003).

Acknowledgments

This book has been long in the making, and the editors thank the contributors for their efforts and patience. Ethelia Ruiz Medrano expresses gratitude to the Dirección de Estudios Históricos del Instituto Nacional de Antropología e Historia, Susan Kellogg, Guilhem Olivier, and Aurora Olivier for their confidence and support. Susan Kellogg expresses gratitude to the Department of History at the University of Houston; Ethelia Ruiz for her efforts and wisdom; Susan Deeds, Lorena Lopez, and William Walker for friendship and many kindnesses; and Seth and Sean Mintz for their love, humor, and great articles from the Internet (with a special shout out to Sean for help with computer advice and the bibliography).

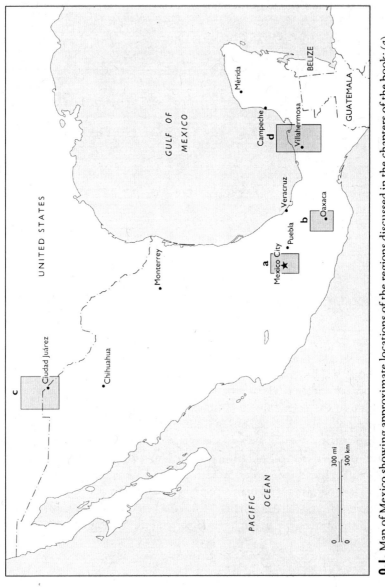

0.1. Map of Mexico showing approximate locations of the regions discussed in the chapters of the book: (*a*) Chapters 2–4; (*b*) Chapters 5–6; (*c*) Chapter 7; and (*d*) Chapter 8.

NEGOTIATION WITHIN DOMINATION

SUSAN KELLOGG

Introduction—Back to the Future

Law, Politics, and Culture in Colonial
Mexican Ethnohistorical Studies

Historians who surveyed the schools of interpretation within North American scholarship on colonial Spanish America in the 1980s described how social history, history from the bottom up, emerged out of institutional and political history.[1] But because all social groups exist within and make use of dense networks of meaning, less than ten years later, a more cultural history—focused on images, mentalities, and the deconstruction of both colonial and scholarly representations of people, places, and processes of change—emerged.[2] As issues of representation, memory, and the cultural meanings of hierarchy, hegemony, and power surged to the fore, scholars such as Edward Said and Ranajit Guha wrote evocatively and provocatively about the construction and consciousness of dominators and those who were dominated in the Middle East and South Asia, respectively. Such interests inevitably brought historians back to the study of political and legal institutions.[3] These institutions played important, if not determinative, roles in structuring everyday life in racially and class-stratified colonial societies in many parts of the world.

I

Inspired by books that have taken up these questions in the Latin American context, such as *Reclaiming the Political in Latin American History*, edited by Gilbert M. Joseph, and Peter Guardino's *The Time of Liberty*, the essays in this volume turn to earlier periods of time and focus intensively on indigenous interaction with imperial legal and political institutions in colonial New Spain.[4] Collectively, they ask, was the colonial political-legal domain simply an instrument of domination or did councils, courts, and legal personnel allow for or adjust to the assertion of agency? While the authors find a nuanced middle ground, they place a special emphasis on the role of indigenous efforts at negotiation in the emergence of a colonial legal culture during the sixteenth century and show that legal culture changed and adapted to different regions, environments, cultures, and new patterns of governance in the eighteenth.[5]

Many forces shaped this legal culture—political, social, cultural, textual, material, even environmental. Charles Cutter has defined it as a highly flexible set of practices (and, I would add, meanings), the roots of which may be found in the judicial free will (*arbitrio judicial*) held by officials high and low, whether judges of the Real Audiencia (known as *oidores*) or local officials, *alcaldes*, and in the "convergence of written law, *doctrina* (the opinions of jurists), custom, and *equidad* (a communally defined sense of fairness)."[6] The essays included here, by both Mexican and North American scholars, focus on the roles played by a variety of indigenous cultures and communities in the emergence, functioning, and local varieties of this culture over space, across time, and in combination with the extreme regional diversity that constituted the viceroyalty of New Spain.

While many North American scholars, beginning with Charles Gibson, have contributed in meaningful ways to the study of both the impact of the Spanish colonial project on native people and the ways these people not only reacted to but shaped that project, Mexican ethnohistorians also took up these very important questions. The work of Luis Reyes, for example, with his deep knowledge of the Nahuatl language and Nahua culture, was particularly important. His scholarship bridged the earlier emphasis on the study of pre-Hispanic peoples either archaeologically or through Spanish- and indigenous-language texts and the later emphasis on colonial indigenous peoples who drew upon, yet simultaneously reshaped, earlier cultural traditions. He, James Lockhart, and numerous others contributed studies that not only advance our understanding of regionally and culturally specific responses to the Spanish presence but also help to create a usable, practical rendering of the past with implications for the present by showing, for example, that indigenous languages not only were preserved but were viewed by the institutions of colonial governance as legitimate forms of communication, even in the legal arena. This scholarship establishes that while colonial rule led to many negative consequences for native peoples, resistance occurred, and cultural vitality and creativity existed and have a lengthy history.[7] While noting that Mesoamerican native peoples engaged in significant acts of resistance and rebellion, this vitality and creativity help explain why communities and individuals often turned to negotiation to deal with conflicts and ameliorate the conditions and consequences of colonial rule. The negotiating pattern had consequences for the development of colonial New Spain's and, later, Mexico's legal system as well as for indigenous-state relations.[8]

Thus, even when writing about the earliest part of the colonial past, ethnohistorians are providing reconstructions and interpretations of that past that help explain the legal, political, and economic contexts in which today's indigenous people define themselves and their political projects. Ethnohistorical studies often involve the realm of law simply because large numbers of natives interacted with colonial courts and legal personnel, thereby leaving an extensive documentary trail. But this pattern of interaction developed primarily because an important function of law in both empires and nation-states is to furnish an institutionalized means through which political and economic power, the search for such power, or conflicts over it can be expressed, negotiated, and controlled. Indigenous individuals and communities were thus led to seek out legal practitioners and institutions to deal with the myriad of political, economic, and social problems set in motion by the arrival of new populations with very different customary practices relating to land, labor, governance, and legal practices. By defining rights and providing a context through which conflicts over competing interests can be mediated and sometimes resolved, empires and states provide forms of conflict resolution between individuals and/or groups and institutions. Yet forms of conflict resolution may themselves help shape states and their political formations at particular times.[9]

This collection of essays reveals that the forms of conflict resolution, as these evolved through dialogue, negotiation, resistance, and conflict between indigenous people and the representatives and institutions of the Spanish Crown, indeed shaped aspects of colonial governance from the sixteenth through the eighteenth centuries. At the same time, the growing dependence of indigenous communities and people on colonial legal institutions for dispute resolution affected political power and officeholding within native communities and the construction and reconstruction of ethnicity in many regions. Given the array of legal compilations that councils and officeholders had to draw upon and given that bureaucrats and councils carried both administrative and judicial responsibilities,

3

competing jurisdictions and overlapping laws led litigants, almost inevitably, in both Spain and New Spain to seek to exploit the system to their advantage.[10] The issues of political authority and legitimacy, land tenure and inheritance, and rights to and abuse of labor became sources of grave conflict within indigenous communities and between indigenous individuals and communities and Spaniards. In the words of Woodrow Borah, "litigation before Spanish courts and petitions for administrative review and protection became the principal means of carrying on the long series of disputes unleashed by the conquest over land, status, and virtually all other relationships."[11]

The right of native peoples to access legal authorities and institutions grew out of medieval elements of Spanish law granting protection to *miserables* (or the poor and wretched) in combination with the need to adjudicate the new kinds of disputes to which Borah referred as well as the Crown's tendency to use law as a means of establishing its authority in the America.[12] It is also true that the ability of the Crown to assert authority—whether by Isabella in the Caribbean and early sixteenth-century New Spain or the Hapsburgs in later sixteenth-century New Spain and Peru—lay in part in the willingness of the indigenous population to accept that authority. Use of indigenous intermediaries as negotiators, an example of the transactional "go-betweens" described so ably by Alida Metcalf for colonial Brazil, became crucial to Crown authority early on, whether these were the sixteenth-century Tlaxcalan nobles as described in Jovita Baber's essay or the eighteenth-century *apoderados* (individuals empowered by local community councils, *cabildos*, to oversee cases through the early states of litigation) as described by Yannakakis. Bourbon governance, less flexible, more concerned with hierarchy and order, was more authoritarian and thus less dependent on negotiation as a means of consolidating or reinforcing authority. Nevertheless, Bourbons, like the Hapsburgs before them, had to accept the reality of the size of indigenous populations and the force of "customary" practices (by this time, most often a hybrid and flexible mix of indigenous and Spanish traditions in response to changing colonial conditions). Ultimately, Bourbon rulers did not so much try to do away with negotiation as they tried to limit and reserve it for use in peripheral areas where their authority was not as secure.[13]

The first group of essays emphasizes the political maneuverings of native communities as they dealt with governmental institutions and governing officials, sometimes at the highest levels. The chapters by Baber, Ruiz Medrano, and Osowski show how indigenous leaders in the central region influenced Spanish policies, creating and using the room to strategize, maneuver, and negotiate even as such policies created limits on that maneuvering. A second set of articles, by Romero Frizzi and Yannakakis, focuses on law, politics, and cultural practices internal to Oaxacan communities. They examine how communities and leaders operated in judicial settings while developing innovative ways to function as part of those processes and helping to fashion a colonial legal culture. The final essays look at indigenous groups and colonial governance on the northern and southern peripheries of New Spain in the eighteenth century. Both Velasco Ávila and Chávez-Gómez illustrate ways the Bourbon Crown faced at least three challenges in these regions: from other imperial powers; from the more mobile ways of life that characterized both areas; and the Crown's own weakness in dealing with threats arising out of competition among imperial powers and the cultural diversity of native peoples.

R. Jovita Baber's essay about the dealings of Tlaxcalan nobles as they pursued the status and title of "Loyal and Noble City of Tlaxcala" argues that their legal efforts not only helped the Tlaxcalan nobility gain certain privileges and protection for themselves but in so doing influenced the development of the imperial bureaucracy during the sixteenth century. She shows that leading figures among the Tlaxcalan nobility succeeded in obtaining a royal order prohibiting Tlaxcala and its native population from being granted as an *encomienda* (grant of tribute and labor). The order proved helpful as the nearby city of Puebla de los Angeles was founded because it provided a basis for the Crown to place Tlaxcala under its jurisdiction rather than Puebla's. This status allowed the Tlaxcalans, in Baber's view, a large degree of self-rule, which helped them defend themselves in a series of disputes over boundaries between communities, disputes that involved both native leaders of other communities as well as Spaniards who had taken up residence in the area.

Baber demonstrates that while the formation of more compact territories has traditionally been seen as a process imposed by Spaniards, conflicts between indigenous communities (some reflecting long-standing tensions probably predating the colonial era) played a role in setting boundaries between communities.[14] Community representatives skillfully negotiated new legal, political, and economic terrains and, in the process, provided a model, the author argues, that the Crown used to create other "self-governing" municipalities. Yet this model of self-governance ultimately strengthened the monarchy in its battle to assert royal power against local Spaniards who sought influence and power outside the Crown-sanctioned bureaucracy as that bureaucracy was emerging in the mid- to late sixteenth century.

Attempts by indigenous leaders in mid-sixteenth-century Mexico City to negotiate with a Spanish Crown that was building and asserting its power is an issue taken up by Ethelia Ruiz Medrano in another essay that focuses on indigenous strategies in the political arena. Drawing from her detailed knowledge of early colonial politics, particularly the conflicts and intrigues among elite Spaniards of the mid-sixteenth century in New Spain's capital city, Ruiz Medrano chronicles several episodes that took place from 1564 to 1566 in which a group of *encomenderos* (those who held the right to labor and tribute known as encomienda) sought to break away from royal control and crown the second Marqués del Valle, Martín Cortés, king of New Spain. On one occasion, a dinner held by the encomendero Alonso de Ávila Alvarado, he and his guests dressed themselves as Mexica nobles, with Ávila dressing as Motecuhzoma and offering his crown to Cortés. The oidores of the Real Audiencia (Royal Court) had other ideas, however, and not only had members of the conspiracy arrested but later beheaded.

While in large measure a struggle over political power, conflict over control of resources—especially indigenous labor and the tribute that labor created—fueled disagreements between the Crown and encomenderos and between Archbishop Montúfar and the Franciscan friars and their elite indigenous allies. The latter were fighting the imposition of a new tribute system, one that the descendants of the pre-Hispanic nobility well understood would weaken them economically and politically. The friars and, more importantly, the indigenous nobility were not without supporters of high status and influence, including Bartolomé de las Casas. However, not even las Casas could challenge the growing power of Philip II, as both Martín Cortés and Don Luis de Santa María Cipac, the last direct descendant of the Mexica ruling dynasty to serve as governor of Mexico Tenochtitlan, would, to their sorrow, learn.

The establishment of a more absolutist royal power, although spelling the end for the political power of most ancient royal lines and houses, did not mean the end of indigenous political influence, as Edward Osowski shows in his essay on Indian government in eighteenth-century Mexico City. Discussing the period between Semana Santa and the festival of Corpus Christi, whereas Ruiz Medrano found Spaniards dressed as Indians, Osowski finds Nahuas and Afro-Mexicans dressed as Roman soldiers and so deeply involved in the ritual practices that made up the celebration of Corpus Christi that he argues that Europeans depended on "indigenous leaders to deliver community participants . . . necessary for the symbols [of a conquering Catholicism] to work." He describes the sources of indigenous power that underlay the native ability to negotiate and shape local expressions of imperial rule. These included the long-standing practices based on which Spanish authorities depended on native leaders and institutions, especially the indigenous *cabildos* (city or town councils) of Mexico

City and Tlatelolco, to provide resources; the actual resources of labor and goods necessary to build the arches; the commerce between Indians and non-Indians that underlay festival practices such as the renting and wearing of centurion costumes; and the legal resources inherent in the General Indian Court, or the Juzgado General de Indios, upon which the indigenous population could call if need be.

These resources allowed native leaders to defend their customary roles and practices when—in the late eighteenth century—Bourbon officials, especially the viceroys Bucareli and the second Revillagigedo, attempted to reform such practices to prevent labor abuses and to strengthen the role of the Spanish cabildo at the expense of indigenous cabildos. While indigenous legal rights played a role in Indian ability to withstand reform pressures coming both from the *visitador general* (general inspector), José de Gálvez, and viceroy Revillagigedo, their economic power and the way they helped underwrite a festival economy from which non-native craftsmen and merchants profited also was an important factor.

While Baber and Osowski emphasize the ability of native communities to create some space for self-rule, María de los Ángeles Romero Frizzi, like Ruiz Medrano, points out that such efforts often carried significant costs. Analyzing conflicts among eighteenth-century Zapotec communities of the Sierra Norte area of Oaxaca, she finds energy and a will to protect community landholdings (an effort with echoes even today, she points out, in the solutions sought by native communities to contemporary agrarian problems). But before turning to particular conflicts, Romero Frizzi discusses the problems inherent in using texts that are a product of the complicated and multilayered conjunction of two legal, cultural, and linguistic systems. The documents, written in both Zapotec and Spanish, nonetheless allow the detailed reconstruction of Zapotec social organization. Conflicts within *yetze* (a quasi-kinship system with hierarchical elements) gave rise to household and community fragmentation, leading to migration, a pattern that predated the arrival of the Spanish. In the pre-Hispanic era, such events were recorded both orally and in written form in *lienzos* (pictorial genealogies) and screenfold manuscripts. In the colonial era, the *títulos primordiales* (primordial titles) served this function and had both a legal and, Romero Frizzi argues, a sacred character.

Through the lens of a case that began in 1715, involving the communities of Tanetze and Juquila, Romero Frizzi examines how the colonial legal system served as a kind of filter through which indigenous custom became reinterpreted. The lengthy litigation led to the production of mountains of paper and the multiplication of fees. Neither local-level nor higher-level judges ever acquainted themselves with Juquila's documentation in

Zapotec (and translated into Spanish) that explained the community's political history in quite culturally specific and sacred terms. Nor did they seem to recognize the system of mutual aid, *guelaguetza*, by which Tanetze further justified its demands for payments from Juquila. In 1725, the Real Audiencia in Mexico City decreed that the lands of the two communities at issue would be split in half, a sentence promulgated by lower-level judges ten years earlier but never carried out. While the failure to impose the decision in 1715 might be read simply as a weakness of the Spanish judicial system, that failure related fundamentally to a complex and ever more bureaucratic legal system that promoted lengthy court cases. The length and indeterminacy of cases reinforced the power of the Spanish judicial system in indigenous communities, a power that, as Romero Frizzi shows, led Zapotec leaders to collaborate in the weakening of traditional legal and political norms.

Although Baber argues that indigenous nobles could serve as effective advocates who sometimes acted as legal innovators and Romero Frizzi notes their creativity and energy, the latter sees them also as tragic figures, because their efforts so often came at the cost of loss of sovereignty and the modification of cultural traditions. Yanna Yannakakis also explores questions of cultural loss in an essay that scrutinizes native deployment of the Spanish concept of *costumbre* (custom) in another eighteenth-century case that involved the Zapotec community San Juan Tanetze. Describing the religiously and politically fraught atmosphere of the Villa Alta region in the early years of that century, Yannakakis focuses on the efforts of the community of San Juan Yae to attain *cabecera* (head town) status and end its dependent relationship on Tanetze. Reminding us how important it is *not* to see indigenous communities as unified actors but instead to examine *who* within communities pursued *which* ends, Yannakakis highlights the roles played by apoderados, who were accountable to communities, or at least their collective leadership as represented in the cabildos. She argues that the apoderados brought local elites and Spanish lawyers together. The latter, along with the apoderados, crafted legal strategies for the community. Each side in the lawsuit deployed the notion of costumbre, of course in ways designed to aid each side's argument. One side of litigants defined costumbre as a set of political rights emerging out of a far distant past and emphasized the egalitarian relations among villages in the region. The other promoted a more hierarchical version of intercommunity relations, a model that squared with desires of both church and state to impose a more hierarchical political structure.

The judges of the Real Audiencia did not allow for multiple definitions or uses of the concept of costumbre. Instead they interpreted it as a set of vertical relations among communities as implied by the *cabecera-sujeto* (head town–dependent town) model of governance imposed across Spanish America. They saw the concept as something for which evidence could be found in documents, not in the everyday political relations among localities. As the Bourbon state increasingly concentrated political and legal power in the king and his ministers, local practices and rhetorics, whether in Spain or the Americas, lost autonomy and legitimacy. Nevertheless, however compromised such autonomy became, it did not altogether die out, and clashes within and between indigenous communities based on the conflict between those who prize cultural autonomy and those who seek to use relationships with the national government to their own or community advantage continue even today.

While Bourbon officials tried to deny autonomy and weaken the ability of native communities to negotiate, neither ever disappeared completely, and as Cuauhtémoc Velasco Ávila's essay shows, negotiation even became the preferred mode for regularizing relations between native peoples and the Spanish in parts of the northern borderlands in the late eighteenth century. Even though Spanish officials such as Hugo O'Conor, *comandante inspector* (commandant inspector) of the northern border from 1771 to 1776, abhorred what he and others viewed as the ferocity of groups such as the Comanches and Apaches, the inability of the Spanish to subdue such groups was readily apparent to both sides. Thus, officials from O'Conor on set about to use time-honored European traditions of inducing groups to trade and enter into political alliances based on negotiations as well as playing groups off against each other. Velasco Ávila describes the efforts made by an array of officials as they bowed to the reality of the size, power, and forms of leadership and political practice (something Velasco sensitively details in careful readings of officials' correspondence) of these and other groups and sought more stable and predictable relations through peaceful means.

But Velasco Ávila also reminds us of the ripple effect that such agreements had, as word of the Comanche negotiations induced other groups like the Utes to make peace. He also notes the complexity of negotiations because of differences of approach to diplomacy within the Spanish and Indian sides. Such was especially the case with the Mescalero Apaches about whom Spanish officials could not agree upon a unified approach and who were themselves divided into independent bands that, on occasion, suffered from their own internal divisions. The cross-ethnic discussions were not conversations between equals. Instead they became the means through which Spain asserted sovereignty over native peoples as a form of forced dependency. Even though reservations were not the outcome for northern native peoples of what became the nation of Mexico, at least not in the Mexican period, greater dependence (which some might prefer to call economic integration) and second-class citizenship became the norm for New Spain's indigenous groups as the eighteenth century gave way to the nineteenth.

If Velasco Ávila only alludes to the complex imperial political geography of empire at the edges of northern New Spain, this competitive geography and its consequences for ethnogenesis among Maya groups of southern Mesoamerica, particularly the Lacandon, is discussed in detail by José Manuel A. Chávez-Gómez. His article depicts how both Mayas and Spaniards responded to the small but active British presence in the seventeenth- and eighteenth-century Tabasco region.[15] The essay details the movements of Mayas from both Campeche and the Yucatán, some of whom moved into the forested areas of the central Petén during these centuries, others of whom moved north into the province of Tabasco, where they began to develop trade relations with various English settlements forming as the English desire to explore the rivers and estuaries of this coastal region and participation in piracy increased. Searching for *palo de tinte* (logwood), English filibusters then began to move away from the coast into the forests.

Their movement set off great concern among Spanish officials of the Yucatán because the government was having obvious difficulty maintaining control over parts of the region. Early in the eighteenth century, for example, a Spanish expedition set out to capture so-called apostate Mayas who had fled the northeastern Yucatecan community of Atasta and interrogate them about the developing Anglo-Maya political economy. The judicial proceeding that followed shows the ways that Maya community leaders used a discourse relating to political exploitation, the spread of disease, and loyalty to the Catholic faith to account for their presence and way of life, which included trade with the British. Indigenous witnesses downplayed the depth of the developing economic relationship, and Spanish authorities, rather than heavily penalize the Maya captives, mediated between the local and the imperial and provided resources so that the Mayas could secure their community. Colonial authorities paired that response with a plan to find and root out the English presence militarily, which the Spanish succeeded in doing, at least for the short term.

As this last essay and the others in the volume demonstrate, indigenous peoples of colonial Mexico negotiated with representatives and institutions of what became an imperial state. Although those negotiations—legal, political, and cultural—helped shape certain aspects of colonial rule and preserved some geographic and cultural space for autonomy, such interactions also often led to the creation or reinforcement of various forms of dependency. Yet because the past is always in some sense part of the future, these negotiating processes also helped to protect languages, lands, and retention of cultural beliefs and practices.

The past is also part of the future in historiography. Many forces led to the emergence, first, of social history and, then, cultural history and influenced both the Mexican and North American scholarship represented in this volume. For social history, these forces include transnational intellectual trends such as the rise and impact of the demographic studies of the so-called Berkeley School, the application of Marxist theoretical concepts, as well as the development of dependency theory. North of the border, the political and social trends associated with protests against the Vietnam War and liberation movements seeking to empower African Americans, Mexican Americans, and women that grew out of or developed alongside the student and antiwar movements also influenced the turn to ethnohistory as a more important topic within colonial history. In Mexico, trends such as the slow disintegration of the PRI, the student movement and the 1968 massacre at Tlatelolco, and especially the increasingly apparent contradictions between the ideology of *indigenismo* (positively valuing the *idea* of indigenous culture and history) and the actual treatment and condition of contemporary indigenous peoples underlay the desire to understand the material conditions, power relations, and changing cultural practices associated with the imposition of Spanish rule over Mexico's large and diverse indigenous population.[16]

Mexican scholars were responding to political and cultural changes in their country by questioning conceptualizations of the pre-Hispanic past and the impact of Spanish rule and native responses to it. Scholars on both sides of the border thus became more concerned with epistemology and the politics of representations. These themes underlie historical writings such as the essays in this volume. They constitute "usable scholarship" that might provide a resource for contemporary or future native peoples as they seek to redefine and revitalize their identities and assert rights relating to language and religion, ownership of lands and natural resources, rights of self-determination and self-government, and protection of cultural and intellectual property.[17]

NOTES

1. I acknowledge helpful insights and suggestions from Ethelia Ruiz, John Hart, Rebecca Horn, Matthew Restall, and Yanna Yannakakis. For historiographical essays tracing the rise of social history approaches and some of the consequences,

see Benjamin Keen, "Main Currents in United States Writings on Colonial Spanish America, 1884–1984," *Hispanic American Historical Review* 65, no. 4 (1985):657–682; William B. Taylor, "Between Global Process and Local Knowledge: An Inquiry into Early Latin American Social History, 1500–1900," in *Reliving the Past: The Worlds of Social History*, ed. Olivier Zunz (Chapel Hill: University of North Carolina Press, 1985), 115–189; John Kicza, "The Social and Ethnic Historiography of Colonial Latin America: The Last Twenty Years," *William and Mary Quarterly*, 3rd ser., 44, no. 3 (1988):453–488; Steve J. Stern, "Feudalism, Capitalism, and the World-System in the Perspective of Latin America and the Caribbean," *American Historical Review*, 93, no. 4 (1988):829–872; and Enrique Florescano, *El nuevo pasado mexicano* (México DF: Cal y Arena, 1991), chap. 2. A special 1972 issue of *Historia Mexicana* (21, no. 2), "En Su Vigésimo Aniversario," features historiographic essays. Especially relevant for social history and ethnohistory are the pieces by León Portilla, González, and Borah and Cook.

2. On cultural history, particularly for colonial Mexico, see James Lockhart, "A Historian and the Disciplines," in *Of Things of the Indies: Essays Old and New in Early Latin American History* (Stanford, CA: Stanford University Press, 1999), 333–367; ibid., "Charles Gibson and the Ethnohistory of Postconquest Central Mexico," in *Nahuas and Spaniards: Postconquest Central Mexican History and Philology* (Stanford and Los Angeles: Stanford University Press and UCLA Latin American Center Publications, 1991), 159–182; ibid., "A Vein of Ethnohistory: Recent Nahuatl-based Historical Research," (Stanford and Los Angeles: Stanford University Press and UCLA Latin American Center Publications, 1991), 183–200; Janine Gasco, "Recent Trends in Ethnohistoric Research on Postclassic and Colonial Central Mexico," *Latin American Research Review* 29, no. 1(1994):132–142; John Kicza, "Recent Books on Ethnohistory and Ethnic Relations in Colonial Mexico," *Latin American Research Review* 30, no. 3 (1995):239–253; Susan Deans-Smith, "Culture, Power, and Society in Colonial Mexico," *Latin American Research Review* 33, no. 1 (1998):257–277; Cynthia Radding, "Cultural Dialogues: Recent Trends in Mesoamerican Ethnohistory, " *Latin American Research Review* 33, no. 1 (1998):193–211; Eric Van Young, "The New Cultural History Comes to Old Mexico," *Hispanic American Historical Review* 79, no. 2 (1999):211–247; Murdo J. MacLeod, "Mesoamerica since the Spanish Invasion: An Overview," in *The Cambridge History of the Native Peoples of the Americas*, vol. 2, part 2, Mesoamerica, ed. Richard E.W. Adams and Murdo J. MacLeod (New York: Cambridge University Press, 2001), 1–43; Matthew Restall, "A History of the New Philology and the New Philology in History," *Latin American Research Review* 38, no. 1 (2003): 113–134; and Susan Kellogg, "Encountering People, Creating Texts: Cultural Studies of the Encounter and Beyond," *Latin American Research Review* 38, no. 3 (2003):261–274.

3. Ranajit Guha, *Elementary Aspects of Peasant Insurgency in Colonial India* (Delhi: Oxford University Press, 1983); Edward Said, *Orientalism* (New York: Pantheon, 1978).

4. Gilbert M. Joseph, ed., *Reclaiming the Political in Latin American History: Essays from the North* (Durham, NC: Duke University Press, 2001); and Peter F. Guardino, *The Time of Liberty: Popular Political Culture in Oaxaca, 1750–1850* (Dur-

ham, NC: Duke University Press, 2005). Also see Ricardo D. Salvatore, Carlos Aguirre, and Gilbert M. Joseph, eds., *Crime and Punishment in Latin America: Law and Society since Late Colonial Times* (Durham, NC: Duke University Press, 2001).

5. While anthropologists have discussed negotiation and mediation as part of non-Western systems of dispute resolution (see, e.g., P. H. Gulliver, *Disputes and Negotiations: A Cross-Cultural Perspective* [New York: Academic Press, 1979]), a strong interest in both as part of efforts to develop alternative dispute resolution systems to lessen litigation in the U.S. legal system has developed. Goldberg and colleagues define negotiation as "communication for the purpose of persuasion" and mediation as "negotiation carried out with the assistance of a third party"; Stephen B. Goldberg, Nancy H. Rogers, Sara Rudolph Cole, and Frank E.A. Sander, *Dispute Resolution: Negotiation, Mediation, and Other Processes* (Frederick, MD: Aspen Publishers, 2007), 17, 107. Also see E. Wendy Trachte-Huber and Stephen K. Huber, eds., *Mediation and Negotiation: Reaching Agreement in Law and Business* (Cincinnati: Anderson Publishing Company, 1998). For a historically relevant discussion of mediation and arbitration by "go-betweens," see Alida Metcalf, *Go-Betweens and the Colonization of Brazil, 1500–1600* (Austin: University of Texas Press, 2005).

6. Charles R. Cutter, *The Legal Culture of Northern New Spain, 1700–1810* (Albuquerque: University of New Mexico Press, 1995), quote on 34, also see 35.

7. Representative works by Luis Reyes García, ed., include *Documentos sobre tierras y señorios en Cuauhtinchan* (México DF and Puebla: Fondo de Cultura Económica and Estado de Puebla, 1988); Luis Reyes García, ed. and trans. *¿Como te confundes? ¿Acaso no somos conquistados? Anales de Juan Bautista* (México DF: CIESAS, 2001 [1560s]); Luis Reyes García, ed., *Documentos nauas de la Ciudad de México del siglo XVI* (México DF: CIESAS and Archivo General de la Nación, 1996). Also see Paul Kirchoff, Lina Odena Güemes, and Luis Reyes García, eds., *Historia tolteca-chichimeca* (México DF: INAH, 1976 [ca. 1550]); and Francisco González-Hermosillo Adams and Luis Reyes García, eds., *El codice de Cholula: La exaltación testimonial de un linaje indio* (México DF: INAH, 2002 [late 1500s]). Important works by other Mexican scholars in the field of ethnohistory, especially of the central region, include (but are not limited to) Mercedes Olivera, *Pillis y macehuales: Las formaciones sociales y los modos de producción de Tecali del siglos XII al XVI* (México DF: CIESAS, 1978); Hildeberto Martínez, *Tepeaca en el siglo XVI: Tenencia de la tierra y organización de un señorio* (México DF: CIESAS, 1984); Hildeberto Martínez, *Codiciaban la tierra: El despojo agrario en los señores de Tecamachalco y Quecholac (Puebla, 1520–1650)* (México DF: CIESAS, 1994); Bernardo García Martínez, *Los pueblos de la sierra: El poder y el espacio entre los indios del norte de Puebla hasta 1700* (México DF: El Colegio de México, 1987); Margarita Menegas Bornemann, *Del señorío indígena a la república de indios: El caso de Toluca, 1500–1600* (México DF: Consejo Nacional para la Cultura y las Artes, 1994); and Francisco González-Hermosillo Adams, ed., *Gobierno y economía en los pueblos indios del México colonial* (México DF: INAH, 2001). For other areas, see, for example, Marcelo Carmagnani, *El regreso de los dioses: El proceso de reconstitución de la identidad étnica en Oaxaca, siglos XVII y XVIII* (México DF: Fondo de Cultura Económica, 1988); María de los Angeles Romero

Frizzi, *El sol y la cruz: Los pueblos indios de Oaxaca colonial* (México DF: CIESAS, 1996); and Pedro Bracamonte y Sosa, *La memoria enclaustrada: Historia indígena de Yucatán 1750–1915* (México DF: CIESAS, 1994). While I provide these citations so that readers see works produced by scholars on both sides of the U.S.-Mexican border (the English-language literature is discussed thoroughly in the citations in note 2), I also intend to suggest that, at least in the realm of ethnohistory, Eric Van Young's comments in an overview of English language that "one worrisome trend lies in the increasing divergence of the two national historiographies—the Mexican still committed to fairly traditional (although still compelling) questions, methods, and materialist paradigms, while at least part of the American scholarship is apparently flying off into the empyrean" are overstated. See "Two Decades of Anglophone Historical Writing on Colonial Mexico: Continuity and Change since 1980," *Mexican Studies / Estudios Mexicanos* 20, no. 2 (2004):275–326. While there are differences in approach and perspective, Mexican and North American ethnohistorians have much in common, as the essays in this collection suggest. The idea of "usable" scholarship is related to Lois Parkinson Zamora's discussion of a "usable" or "useful" past, referring to a past—or in this case, scholarship— that has value or utility (conceived of in ways that go beyond a "single-minded functionalism" in the area lying between the research and writing of scholars, on the one hand, and the readings and uses by readers). See her book, *The Usable Past: The Imagination of History in Recent Fiction of the Americas* (Cambridge: Cambridge University Press, 1997), ix; also see chap. 1.

8. Robert W. Patch's essay, "Indian Resistance to Colonialism," in the *Oxford History of Mexico*, ed. Michael C. Meyer and William H. Beezley (New York: Oxford University Press, 2000), 183–211, provides a wide-ranging overview on the subject of indigenous resistance. Also see Susan Schroeder, ed., *Native Resistance and the Pax Colonial in New Spain* (Lincoln: University of Nebraska Press, 1998). On Indian legal strategies and interactions throughout Mexican history, see Ethelia Ruiz Medrano, *Mexico's Indigenous Communities: Their Lands and Histories* (Boulder: University Press of Colorado, 2010).

9. Useful discussions of how legal systems function across a variety of societies can be found in Sally Falk Moore, *Social Facts and Fabrications: "Customary" Law on Kilimanjaro, 1880–1980* (Cambridge: Cambridge University Press, 1986); June Starr and Jane F. Collier, eds., *History and Power in the Study of Law: New Directions in Legal Anthropology* (Ithaca, NY: Cornell University Press, 1989); Sally Engle Merry, *Getting Justice and Getting Even: Legal Consciousness among Working Class Americans* (Chicago: University of Chicago Press, 1990); Sally Engle Merry, *Colonizing Hawai'i: The Cultural Power of Law* (Princeton, NJ: Princeton University Press, 2000); Mindie Lazarus-Black, *Legitimate Acts and Illegal Encounters: Law and Society in Antigua and Barbuda* (Washington, DC: Smithsonian Institution Press, 1994); Lauren A. Benton, *Law and Colonial Cultures: Legal Regimes in World History, 1400–1900* (Cambridge: Cambridge University Press, 2002); and Laura Nader, *The Life of the Law: Anthropological Projects* (Berkeley: University of California Press, 2002). Important studies of the history of law in Mexico include Toribio Esquivel Obregón's *Apuntes para la historia del derecho en Mexico* (México DF: Editorial Polis,

1937); Rafael Altamira's *Técnica de investigación en la historia del derecho indiano* (México DF: J. Porrúa e Hijos, 1939); Andres Lira González, *El ámparo colonial y el juicio de ámparo mexicano; antecedentes novohispanos del juicio de ámparo* (México DF: Fondo de Cultura Económica, 1972); Jorge Mario Magallon Ibarra, *Los sonidos y el silencio de la jurisprudencia mexicana* (México DF: UNAM, 2004); Guillermo Floris Margardant S., *Introducción a la historia del derecho mexicano* (México DF: UNAM, 1971); Javier Barrientos Grandón, *La cultura jurídica en la Nueva España* (México DF: UNAM, 1993); and Stephen Zamora, José Ramón Cossío, Leonel Pereznieto, José Roldán-Xopa, and David Lopez, *Mexican Law* (New York: Oxford University Press, 2004). On colonial law generally, see Ricardo Levene, *Introducción a la historia del derecho indiano* (Buenos Aires: V. Abelardo, 1924); Rafael Altamira, *Técnica de investigación en la historia*; Rafael Altamira, *Manual de investigación de la historia del derecho indiano* (México DF: Instituto Panamericano de Geografía e Historia, 1948); M. C. Mirow, *Latin American Law: A History of Private Law and Institutions in Spanish America* (Austin: University of Texas Press, 2004); José María Ots Capdequí, *El estado español en las Indias* (México DF: El Colegio de México, 1941); José María Ots Capdequí, *Manual de historia de derecho español en las Indias y del derecho propiamente indiano* (Buenos Aires: Talleres Gráficos de A. Baiocco, 1943); Ismael Sánchez Bella, Alberto de la Hera, and Carlos Díaz Rementeria, *Historia del derecho indiano* (Madrid: MAPFRE, 1992); and Victor Tau Anzoátegui, *Nuevos horizontes en el estudio histórico del derecho indiano* (Buenos Aires: Instituto de Investigaciones de Historia del Derecho, 1997). For social and political histories of the legal system in colonial Mexico, see William B. Taylor, *Drinking, Homicide, and Rebellion in Colonial Mexican Villages* (Stanford, CA: Stanford University Press, 1979); Colin MacLachlan, *Criminal Justice in Eighteenth-Century Mexico: A Study of the Tribunal of the Acordada* (Berkeley: University of California Press, 1974); Woodrow Borah, *Justice by Insurance: The General Indian Court of Colonial Mexico and the Legal Aides of the Half-Real* (Berkeley: University of California Press, 1983); Teresa Lozano Armendares, *La criminalidad en la ciudad de México, 1800–1821* (México DF: UNAM, 1987); Cutter, *The Legal Culture of Northern New Spain*; Susan Kellogg, *Law and the Transformation of Aztec Culture, 1500–1700* (Norman: University of Oklahoma Press, 1995); Brian P. Owensby, *Empire of Law and Indian Justice in Colonial Mexico* (Stanford, CA: Stanford University Press, 2008); and Gabriel Haslip Viera, *Crime and Punishment in Late Colonial Mexico City, 1692–1810* (Albuquerque: University of New Mexico Press, 1999).

10. Richard L. Kagan, *Lawsuits and Litigants in Castile, 1500–1700* (Chapel Hill: University of North Carolina Press, 1981), 31; Kellogg, *Law and the Transformation of Aztec Culture*, 5–6. Important compilations or commentaries on law included *Las Siete Partidas* (thirteenth century), the *Leyes de Toro* (1505), the *Recopilación de Leyes de los Reynos de las Indias* (1681), and *Política Indiana* by Juan de Solórzano Pereira (1647). Benton's term "multicentric legal order, " one "in which the state is one among many legal authorities," would seem to apply to the legal system of both Spain and New Spain; *Law and Colonial Cultures*, 11. It is important, however, to recognize that the use of the term "state" to describe the governance of Spain or New Spain, especially in the early colonial period, may, as Alejandro Cañeque

has pointed out, be problematic. See *The King's Living Image: The Culture and Politics of Viceregal Power in Colonial Mexico* (New York: Routledge, 2004) 3–11.

11. Borah, *Justice by Insurance*, 40. Also see the citations in note 8.

12. Ibid., 11–16, 80–83; MacLachlan, *Criminal Justice in Eighteenth-Century Mexico*, 13–14.

13. For a thoughtful discussion of the similarities and differences between the Hapsburg and Bourbon administration of justice, see Michael C. Scardaville, "(Hapsburg) Law and (Bourbon) Order: State Authority, Popular Unrest, and the Criminal Justice System in Bourbon Mexico City," *The Americas* 50, no. 4 (1994):501–525. On types of go-betweens, see Metcalf, *Go-betweens and the Colonization of Brazil*, 9–11. Also see Yanna P. Yannakakis, *The Art of Being In-Between: Native Intermediaries, Indian Identity, and Local Rule in Colonial Oaxaca* (Durham, NC: Duke University Press, 2008), especially chaps. 3–6. In Benton's terms, Bourbon attempts to enhance the power and efficiency of the legal system constitute an example of a "state-centered" legal order in which "the state has at least made, if not sustained, a claim to dominance over other legal authorities"; *Law and Colonial Cultures*, 11.

14. François Chevalier, *Land and Society in Colonial Mexico: The Great Hacienda*, trans. Alvin Eustis (Berkeley: University of California Press, 1963); Charles Gibson, *The Aztecs under Spanish Rule: A History of the Indians of the Valley of Mexico, 1519–1810* (Stanford, CA: Stanford University Press, 1964). Also see Frederic Hall, *The Laws of Mexico: A Compilation and Treatise Relating to Real Property, Mines, Water Rights, Personal Rights, Contracts, and Inheritances* (San Francisco: A. L. Bancroft, 1885); George McBride, *The Land Systems of Mexico* (New York: American Geographical Society, 1923); Silvio Zavala, *De encomiendas y propiedad territorial en algunas regiones de la América española* (México DF: Antigua Librería Robredo de J. Porrua e Hijos, 1940); Lesley Byrd Simpson, *The Encomienda in New Spain: The Beginning of Spanish Mexico* (Berkeley: University of California Press, 1950); Menegus Borneman, *Del señorío indígena a la república de indios*; and Martínez, *Codiciaban la tierra*.

15. See Edward Spicer, *Cycles of Conquest: The Impact of Spain, Mexico and the United States on the Indians of the Southwest, 1533–1960* (Tucson: University of Arizona Press, 1962); Elizabeth A.H. John, *Storms Brewed in Other Men's Worlds: The Confrontation of Indians, Spanish, and French in the Southwest, 1540–1795* (College Station: Texas A&M University Press, 1975).

16. The rise of social history approaches to Latin American history is chronicled in citations in note 1. On student and indigenous movements in Mexico, as well as both longer-term and more recent political changes, see Guillermo Bonfil Batalla, *México profundo: Una civilización negada* (México DF: SEP and CIESAS, 1987); Elaine Carey, *Plaza of Sacrifices: Gender, Power, and Terror in 1968 Mexico* (Albuquerque: University of New Mexico Press, 2005); Wayne A. Cornelius, *Mexican Politics in Transition: The Breakdown of a One-Party-Dominant Regime* (La Jolla, CA: The Center for U.S.-Mexican Studies, University of California, San Diego, 1996); José Antonio Crespo, *PRI: De la hegemonia a la oposición; Un estudio comparado, 1994–2001* (México DF: Centro de Estudios de Política Comparada, 2001);

Neil Harvey, *The Chiapas Rebellion: The Struggle for Land and Democracy* (Durham, NC: Duke University Press, 1998); Aída Hernández Castillo, *Histories and Stories from Chiapas: Border Identities in Southern Mexico*, trans. Martha Pou (Austin: University of Texas Press, 2001); Donald Clark Hodges, *Mexico: The End of the Revolution* (Westport, CT: Praeger, 2002); Teresa Losada, *Rebelion desde la cultura* (México DF: Editorial Joaquin Mortiz, 1988); Elena Poniatowska, *La noche de Tlatelolco: Testimonios de historia oral* (México DF: Ediciones Era, 1971); Julia Preston and Samuel Dillon, *Opening Mexico: The Making of a Democracy* (New York: Farrar, Straus and Giroux, 2004); Jorge Volpi Escalante, *La imaginación y el poder: Una historia intellectual de 1968* (México DF: Ediciones Era, 1998); Garbriel Zaid, *Adios al PRI* (México DF: Oceano, 1995); and Sergio Zermeño, *México: Una democracia utopica; El movimiento estudiantil del 68*, 2nd ed. (México DF: Siglo Veintiuno Editories, 1981). For histories of the social impact of Vietnam and 1960s social movements in the United States, see Robert Buzzanco, *Vietnam and the Transformation of American Life* (Malden, MA: Blackwell, 1999); Todd Gitlin, *The Sixties: Years of Hope, Days of Rage* (New York: Bantam Books, 1993); and Maurice Isserman and Michael Kazin, *America Divided: The Civil War of the 1960s* (New York: Oxford University Press, 2000).

17. For a brief but useful discussion of the rights of indigenous peoples from many parts of the world, including Latin America, see "The Rights of Indigenous Peoples, Fact Sheet No. 9" (Rev. 1), *Office of the High Commissioner for Human Rights*, http://www.unhchr.ch/html/menu6/2/fs9.htm. In the fall of 2007, the UN adopted the Indigenous Human Rights Declaration. The text can be found at http://www.un.org/esa/socdev/unpfii/en/drip/html. Also see Rodolfo Stavenhagen, *Derecho indígena y derechos humanos en América Latina* (México DF: El Colegio de México and Instituto Interamericano de Derechos Humanos, 1988); Rodolfo Stavenhagen and Diego Iturralde, eds., *Entre la ley y la costumbre: El derecho consuetudinario indígena en América Latina* (México DF: Instituto Interamericano de Derechos Humanos and Instituto Indigenista Interamericano, 1990); Enrique Sánchez, ed., *Derechos de los pueblos indígenas en las constituciones de América Latina* (Santa Fé de Bogotá: Disloque Editores, 1996); David Maybury-Lewis, ed., *The Politics of Ethnicity: Indigenous Peoples in Latin American States* (Cambridge, MA: The David Rockefeller Center Series on Latin American Studies, Harvard University, 2002). Histories of indigenous rights movements in various countries and regions of Latin America are beginning to be written by scholars from a variety of disciplines. General or comparative treatments include Kay B. Warren and Jean E. Jackson, *Indigenous Movements, Self-Representation, and the State in Latin America* (Austin: University of Texas Press, 2002); Erick D. Langer, ed., *Contemporary Indigenous Movements in Latin America* (Wilmington, DE: SR Books, 2003); Donna Lee Van Cott, *From Movements to Parties in Latin America: The Evolution of Ethnic Politics* (Cambridge: Cambridge University Press, 2005); and Deborah J. Yashar, *Contesting Citizenship in Latin America: The Rise of Indigenous Movements and the Postliberal Challenge* (Cambridge: Cambridge University Press, 2005).

2

R. JOVITA BABER

Empire, Indians, and the Negotiation for the Status of City in Tlaxcala, 1521–1550

In 1525, a few short years after the fall of Tenochtitlan, Pope Clemente issued a bull that designated Tlaxcala as the seat of the Bishopric of Tlaxcala.[1] By the mid-1520s, below the four *teccalli* (principal noble houses) of Tepeticpac, Quahuiztlan, Tizatlan, and Ocotelulco, along the banks of Zahuapan River, the Tlaxcalan elite designated a site for their urban center. Shortly afterward, in 1528, the nobles shared out parcels of land, and each built a house for himself in the urban center.[2] In the mid-1530s, they elected their first native governor,[3] sought the title and status of "city," and formed a *cabildo* (municipal council). Using Tlaxcala's status as a city, they litigated for boundaries to separate their community from their native and Iberian neighbors. By 1550 they had constructed a central plaza, a church, government buildings, shops, inns, and other buildings typical of a Castilian urban center, and the Indian cabildo was discussing whether it should finance the construction of a large clock for the plaza: "The City of Tlaxcala truly needs it, and it is also needed for the honor of the emperor, so that things should look attractive in Tlaxcala."[4]

In less than three decades, the Tlaxcala urban center had acquired the symbolic, territorial, and political qualities of a city—the highest-ranked municipal status in Castilian tradition. Although the status of a municipality did not guarantee particular rights and privileges (Madrid, for example, was a *villa*—the lowest-ranked category for a municipality), cities generally held jurisdiction over subject towns and villages and had boundaries that separated and protected them from being encroached on by neighboring communities. Importantly, cities also were always under the direct authority of the Crown and, therefore, tended to enjoy relative autonomy in their internal governance.[5] After Tlaxcala acquired the status of city, its nobles leveraged their symbolic capital to achieve their larger ambition of continued self-governance and relative autonomy. In essence, making a seemingly paradoxical move, the Tlaxcalan elite adopted Castilian institutions and spatial organization in order to assert their autonomy within the emerging political system.

In this chapter I first trace the Tlaxcalan elite's negotiations in the courts as they acquired the rights and privileges of a city and, second, show how they transformed their confederacy into a municipality. In examining similar phenomena, scholars have offered a number of interpretations. Investigating in the Andes, Stern asserts that native people used the colonial courts to resist colonialism. However, to his dismay, he concludes that despite the success Andeans achieved in their legal battles, their self-advocacy only served to strengthen the oppressive political and economic structures of the colonial regime. Alternatively, using a different theoretical framework to analyze law and cultural change among the Aztecs, Kellogg argues that as native people advocated for themselves in the courts, they internalized Castilian hegemony.[6] Finally, a third perspective is offered by Lockhart: he asserts that despite the adoption of Castilian institutions and norms by native people, native cultural and political forms persisted in the guise of their Castilian counterparts.[7]

Through my case study, I argue that native people consciously and strategically negotiated their interests within the empire and, in so doing, contributed to an imperial system that emerged as a fluid convergence of negotiated interests. As Castilian traditions and institutions were introduced into Mesoamerica, Tlaxcalans recognized the similarities and differences between Mesoamerican and Castilian political forms and concepts and adjusted flexibly to the changing political and legal norms. Indeed, successfully advocating within the imperial courts required an acute understanding of the Castilian legal and political system. While resistance, accommodation, and compromise were among the strategies native people used to assert their interests within the empire, their actions cannot simply be interpreted as reactions. They also pursued their own ambitions and used a variety of strategies to negotiate within the emerging social order. In the process, Tlaxcala became a model of a self-governing Indian municipality—for both the Crown and other native communities—and influenced the developing imperial system.

TLAXCALAN NOBLES AND THE STATUS OF CONQUISTADORS

Since the end of the thirteenth century, the cultural group of Tlaxcala con-sisted of at least 165,000 people and 220 settlements in an area of 1,500 square kilometers—less than half the area of the modern state of Tlaxcala.[8] No less than eight of the settlements were *teccalli* (noble houses), and approximately sixteen were *pilcalli* (minor noble houses). The rest of the settlements were villages and rural hamlets inhabited by commoners— either *mayeques* (commoners living on the noble lands) or *macehualtin* (free commoners).[9] The nobles who governed Tlaxcala were approximately 7 percent of the population. The majority of these nobles were minor nobles, or *pipiltin*. The rest were *teuctli*, or lords of a teccalli. During the fifteenth century, the Nahua noble houses and villages of Tlaxcala formed a confed-eracy in response to the increasing imperial aggressions of their neighbors and afterward allied with the Otomi communities to the north.

As the noble houses and villages united into a confederacy, each set-tlement remained physically distinct. While settlements were generally located above permanent streams and cultivated the land around them, between and around the houses and villages were extensive stretches of unclaimed and uncultivated lands. As archeologist Dean Snow describes it, Tlaxcala was "a large but dispersed rather than nucleated population."[10] For security, Tlaxcalan settlements were generally on the side of volcanoes or near the top of sedimentary hills, where they could observe the movement of outsiders. Moreover, the confederacy of Tlaxcala was buffered from the outside world by uncultivated lands called *yaotlalli*, or warring lands.[11] On these barren areas, skirmishes had often been waged and raiding armies fought in the prehispanic period. In addition, the Otomi provided mili-tary protection on the northern and western frontiers of the confederacy. Despite defending a territorial space as a unified military force against the ever-present threat of the expanding Mexica empire, Tlaxcala was neither a single political unit nor a contiguous territory.

While the communities had transformed the region into a formidable military force, they also relied on negotiation to protect their sovereignty. In addition to agreeing to participate in ritual battles—called flower wars— with the Mexica, they frequently attended state rituals in Tenochtitlan as part of their ongoing efforts of diplomacy. Through their varied strategies of negotiation—from military resistance to accommodation to concession to skillful assertion of their interests—they retained their sovereignty. Their prehispanic experience negotiating with an imperial state proved invaluable with the arrival of the Spanish.

When Cortés arrived in 1521, the Tlaxcalan warriors fought him for several days before deciding to ally with him and the other native allies to overthrow Tenochtitlan. Afterward, they (and many of the other native communities) maintained their alliances with the Spanish conquistadors in military expeditions from Florida to Guatemala. Although Tlaxcalans effectively promoted themselves as the sole or primary allies (an image that persists to today), they were one among many who participated in the conquest. What differentiated Tlaxcalans from most other native communities was their adroit and rapid use of the Spanish rhetoric of conquest to secure status in the emerging political order after the fall of Tenochtitlan.

Observing the rapidly changing political reality in the years after the fall of Tenochtitlan, the Tlaxcalan elite intended to protect their autonomy. Above all, they wanted to protect themselves from being granted as an *encomienda* (royal grant of authority over native populations awarded in remuneration for services rendered to the Crown). Although it is difficult to trace how they learned about the intricacies of the Spanish legal system (probably Cortés or other Spanish *conquistadores* [conquerors] instructed them), they clearly mastered the rhetoric and ceremony of the Castilian court rapidly. They quickly recognized that they needed to petition the Crown to secure a royal promise prohibiting the granting of themselves or their subjects to a third party as an encomienda. Indeed, rather than being ruled by a conquistador, they wanted the rights and privileges awarded *to* Spanish conquistadors.

The Tlaxcalan elite carefully crafted a petition in which they asserted that they were loyal subjects of the Crown and had served it faithfully during the pacification of New Spain. While all of their post-conquest correspondences and histories of the conquest consistently assert their service to the Crown, it is safe to conclude that they were *not* thinking about the Castilian Crown when they decided to ally with Cortés to overthrow Tenochtitlan. Rather, their long-standing animosity toward the Mexica was undoubtedly at the forefront of their thoughts. In light of their imperial ambitions and their expansive trade networks before the rise of the Mexica empire, they almost certainly perceived themselves as fulfilling a destiny as they and their Spanish allies continued to conquer the rest of Mesoamerica. Like their Spanish counterparts, they were motivated by the promise of glory, power, and wealth. Despite their personal motivations for participating in the conquest, they nonetheless understood the rhetoric of loyal service and royal privilege of the Castilian system and effectively recast their personal ambitions in language that was convincing to the Crown.

Asserting that they were loyal subjects who had fought honorably in the conquest, the Tlaxcalan nobles requested that the Crown remunerate the noble houses of Tlaxcala for their invaluable services. In addition to asking for protection against being granted as an encomienda, they wanted to remain free vassals of the Crown and to retain perpetual status as *señores naturales* (natural lords) with jurisdiction over their respective subjects and lands. Having penned the petition, they sent a delegation of nobles from the highest-ranked houses in Tlaxcala to the Iberian peninsula in 1528.[12] Presenting themselves as honorable military elite and noblemen, Don Lorenzo Tianquiztlatohuatzin, Don Valeriano Quetzalcoltzin, Don Julían Quauhpiltzintli, Don Juan Citlalihuitzin de Avalos, and Antonio Huitlalotzin sought an audience with Charles V.

Cortés also traveled with the Tlaxcalan delegation. In addition to accompanying his allies to court, Cortés had praised their military skill and invaluable assistance in his letters to the Crown. Because Cortés's letters circulated widely, Charles V and his courtiers clearly knew about the courage and hospitality of the Tlaxcalans.[13] Moreover, they would have been aware of the markets, cities, laws, and government of the Indians in New Spain. Adjusting to Castilian goals of evangelization and notions of a Christian political body, Tlaxcalans had also proven themselves to be faithful Christians. The nobles of Tlaxcala had been baptized and had welcomed the twelve mendicant friars to New Spain in 1524. They had established a monastery in Ocotelulco and had sponsored the evangelization of their Indian subjects. Without a doubt, the Tlaxcalan nobles made a much different impression on their Spanish hosts than the natives who had arrived from Hispaniola as novelties brought by Christopher Columbus. Thus, although the Tlaxcalans requested their privilege based on their military services, the strength of their argument also lay in their ability to show that they were "civilized."

Tlaxcalans were not the first or the only mainland Indians to have traveled to Iberia to petition the Crown. Two years previously, in 1526, two Mexica lords, Don Rodrigo and Don Martín, had held court with Charles V and had received an encomienda grant. In addition, coinciding with their trip, Pedro Tlacahuepantzin, a son of Motecuhzoma, and Francisco de Alvarado Matlaccohuatzin, a son of Motecuhzoma's brother, traveled to Iberia to petition the Crown for rights and privileges.[14] These "civilized" Indians, who visited the court to ask for privileges, challenged the Spaniards who continued to believe that native people conformed to the Aristotelian concept of natural slaves and were incapable of self-rule. They demonstrated that native people could rationally manage their own affairs. In 1529, during the Tlaxcalans' stay in Iberia, the Crown decided to gather the learned men of Iberia in Barcelona to discuss how to administer the natives in the Americas. After much deliberation, they reached a consensus that nonresistant Indians should not be awarded in encomiendas.[15]

Accordingly, on August 10, 1529, the Crown granted the request of the Tlaxcalans; in a royal mandate, the Crown prohibited its successors and all its officials from granting "the Tlaxcalans, their Indians and the Indians of their city" as an encomienda.[16] With this grant, the Tlaxcalans became free vassals of the Crown—a self-governing political community directly under the Crown. On the one hand, in becoming free vassals of the Crown, Tlaxcalans gained a privileged status and the relative autonomy that they sought. Similar to their Castilian counterparts, the Tlaxcalan nobles were to remain the first instance in legal cases, to administer the region on behalf of the Crown, to collect tribute for the Crown, and to evangelize the natives of Tlaxcala. Rather than owing tribute to an encomendero, they pursued and acquired another royal mandate that limited their obligation to paying a nominal tribute of 8,000 *fanegas* (bushels) of corn to the Crown. The rest of the tribute collected from their native subjects remained under the authority of the native elite. As for the Crown, it gained an unmediated relationship with its Indian subjects, which strengthened its initiative to rule the Americas through a bureaucracy rather than a military aristocracy. Indeed, the relationship demonstrated that native people did "possess such understanding as is sufficient for an ordinary citizen to conduct himself in a civilized country"—as Cortés had explained to the Crown in his second letter.[17] With these royal mandates in hand and an important alliance with the Crown, the delegation returned home in 1530. The Crown-subject relationship that was beginning to emerge was not simply imposed from above; rather, it required initiative from both sides and reflected the interests of both the Tlaxcalans and the Crown.

THE ROYAL BUREAUCRACY IN THE AMERICAS

A few years after the fall of Tenochtitlan, the Spanish monarchy had begun to develop an imperial bureaucracy to administer its newly conquered territories in the Americas. During the *reconquista* (Reconquest) of Muslim Iberia and the conquest of the Americas, the Crown negotiated with, contracted with, and rewarded private individuals who were willing to extend and secure the dominion of the Castilian Crown. During the long reconquista period, the privileges granted to those who conquered in the name of the Crown gave rise to a powerful military aristocracy. This aristocracy threatened the supremacy of the Crown. Attempting to undermine this threat, at the end of the fourteenth-century Isabel and Ferdinand took pragmatic steps to change the political relations and institutions. In an effort to expand and strengthen royal authority, Isabel and Ferdinand purposefully positioned themselves as mediators between competing groups. They nurtured their relationship with the townspeople in the northern municipalities, for example, and provided them with protection against the abuses of the aristocracy in exchange for their loyalty; they allied at the Cortes de Madrigal, in 1476, with the Crown. Together, the Crown and urban patricians limited the influence of the military aristocracy. They centralized the administration of *hermandades* (local police associations) and empowered them to punish anyone who rebelled against the Crown. The Castilian municipalities, cooperatively in most cases, also accepted royal authorities, called *corregidores*, to represent royal interests at the municipal level and to enforce royal mandates.[18]

Concurrently and correspondingly, throughout their reign, Isabel and Ferdinand reformed the royal bureaucracy in the kingdoms of Castile and Aragon. In addition to reflecting their pragmatic politics, the political transition from soldiers to bureaucrats reflected a theoretical transition from medieval contractualism to bureaucratic absolutism—as theorized by the early modern neo-Scholastics. The Crown's ability to preserve harmony, enforce justice, bring prosperity, and create balance between various semi-autonomous political communities was central to its legitimacy in both medieval contractualism and absolutism. In medieval contractualism, the Crown was considered a first among equals and therefore negotiated a relationship of service to the Crown for remuneration. In contrast, for the neo-Scholastics, kingdoms were best governed by a hierarchy of institutions administered by anonymous university-educated bureaucrats with a divinely ordained crown at the apex.[19] While the neo-Scholastics encouraged the development of a highly centralized bureaucracy, the Crown's continued dependence on subjects to provide services, finance, and fealty required that it also continue to negotiate to realize its imperial ambitions. Thus, while the reconquista and the conquests in the Americas were quite similar—both occurred as private endeavors and encouraged ambitious men (and occasionally women) to pursue their dreams of power and wealth by conquering in the name of the Crown—the conquest, significantly, occurred after the political system had begun to turn away from medieval contractualism. The Crown thus had already begun to transition royal political forms and concepts toward an absolutist bureaucracy.

Within this complex political and legal context, royal officials in the Americas aimed to undermine the emergence of a military aristocracy and to subsume it under the authority of the developing imperial bureaucracy. As we will see, they wanted to encourage the development of municipalities governed by cabildos to limit abuses and to counter the power of the encomenderos and conquistadors. Within this changing climate, the Tlaxcalans observed their status, which had been achieved as conquistadors, diminishing. In response, Tlaxcalans altered their legal and political strategies and pursued additional rights and privileges to secure a respectable position within the changing political reality. Namely, Tlaxcala became a municipality and pursued the status and title of city. Before we return to the Tlaxcalans, a further examination of the shifting political milieu in the Iberian world is necessary.

NEGOTIATION IN A SHIFTING POLITICAL LANDSCAPE

A few years after the fall of Tenochtitlan, in 1524 the Crown established the Consejo de las Indias (Council of the Indies) to administer its American territories. The Council of the Indies was modeled after the councils that had advised the Crown and administered royal affairs in the kingdoms of Castile and Aragon. All three councils held administrative and judicial authority over the royal subjects in their respective kingdoms. Reflecting Isabel and Ferdinand's reforms of the Aragonese and Castilian councils, the Council of the Indies was dominated by *letrados* (lawyers who held the highest law degree). Whereas nine of the council seats were reserved for letrados, only three seats were offered to *caballeros* (military aristocrats). Although the councils reflected the shift toward a standardized bureaucracy, they also continued to be shaped by processes of negotiations—as revealed by their composition. The councils of Castile and Aragon, for instance, reserved several seats for native representatives, as per the demands of the elite of each kingdom. The Council of Aragon, in fact, had representatives from the kingdoms under the Aragonese Crown (Valencia, Catalonia, Sicily, Naples, and Sardinia). While native people enjoyed significant success in local political and legal endeavors, the limits on their ability to influence the upper echelons of the bureaucracy was clearly reflected in their absence from the royal council that represented them to the king. They were not alone however; *criollos* (New World–born Spaniards) also lacked representation. In fact, a common late sixteenth- and early seventeenth-century critique of the council concerned its members' egregious lack of firsthand knowledge of the Americas. The concern was superficially addressed in the seventeenth century when the number of Castilian letrados who had held posts in the Americas increased.

To govern the newly conquered mainland territory, the recently formed Council of the Indies had decided to appoint five men to serve as the first *audiencia* (royal court) of New Spain. Arriving in New Spain in 1528, the president and two judges established a governing council (two of the four appointed judges died before ever serving). Shortly after their arrival, the Crown issued mandates that initiated its efforts to limit the authority of the encomenderos and conquistadors, in particular that of Hernán Cortés. While the Crown was attempting to temper the encomenderos and limit their abuses of power, the royal bureaucrats took advantage of their authority and pilfered the treasury and the local populations.[20] These early efforts to assert royal authority through a bureaucracy had been a catastrophe.

Recognizing the failure of the first audiencia, the council advised the Crown to rule New Spain as a viceroyalty—similar to the institutional structure for governing the Aragonese kingdom of Naples.[21] Further, it counseled the Crown to appoint a caballero who would be respected by the nascent military aristocracy in New Spain. After searching for a suitable candidate, the council decided to ask Antonio de Mendoza, Conde (Count) de Tendilla, to serve as viceroy. The Mendoza family was among the highest-ranked aristocratic families in Castile. As with most of the Iberian aristocracy, the Mendoza family had gained status and wealth by serving the Crown in the battlefield. Although the family had risen to power as military elite, Don Antonio de Mendoza represented a new generation of caballeros who sought to maintain their status and wealth by serving the Crown in an influential post in the royal bureaucracy. When he was approached to serve, Mendoza knew his value to the Crown and understood the rules of the game; he negotiated the compensation he was to receive in remuneration for his service to the Crown. A stubborn and confident negotiator, he drew out the negotiations for five years.

As the members of the council and Mendoza negotiated the details of his appointment, the council appointed an interim governing body, the second audiencia of New Spain, on April 5, 1530.[22] To avoid the setbacks caused by the mismanagement of the first audiencia, they endowed the second with greater legitimacy by appointing highly respected and powerful letrados: Bishop Sebastian Ramírez de Fuenleal as the president and Vasco de Quiroga, Alonso Maldonado, Francisco de Ceynos, and Juan de Salmerón as the judges.

As the new audiencia members departed for their new assignment, the Crown instructed them to investigate the condition of native people in encomiendas and to confiscate those in which local populations were treated poorly or were awarded improperly. The confiscated communities were to revert to royal dominion as free vassals of the Crown—similar to the status acquired by the Tlaxcalans with their 1528 royal decree.[23] By mandating the audiencia judges to intervene when native people were mistreated, the Crown began to strengthen its direct ties to the native population. Moreover, similar to Isabel's alliance with the municipalities to curtail the abuses of the aristocracy in late fifteenth-century Castile, Charles V reinforced his unmediated relationship with his native subjects by presenting royal authority as the protector of native people; his royal officials were to curtail the abuses and authority of the encomenderos.

The judges were pleased to have received this authority as it aligned with their own neo-Scholastic schooling on an ideal bureaucracy. Reflecting on these larger political trends and his dismay at the lack of institutional order in the early colonial state, Judge Salmerón sent a report to Charles V. Revealing his disdain for the nascent military aristocracy in New Spain, he asserted that the dismal condition of government was caused by the corrupt nature of the Castilian conquistadors:

> You cannot imagine the avarice, disorder, and laziness of the Spaniards
> in this country. Those who have *encomiendas* think only of making
> the greatest possible profit out of them, without bothering the least bit
> in the world about the welfare or religious instruction of the Indians.
> Those who have none complain imprudently to us and demand some-
> thing to live on. If told that they are young and well able to work, they
> answer saucily that they took part in such-and-such a conquest.[24]

Before they could rein in the "saucy" encomenderos, the judges needed to establish an imperial bureaucracy.

In projecting the Iberian political and legal system onto an imperial space, the Castilian Crown remained dependent on its alliances with subjects and its processes of negotiations. Wanting to counter the power of the encomiendas with an alternative political model, Judge Salmerón argued that a Spanish municipality would draw a "higher quality" settler to New Spain, and he proposed that a Spanish municipality, to be called Puebla de los Angeles, be founded.[25] He suggested that it be located within the confines of the bishopric of Tlaxcala but outside the jurisdiction of the confederacy of Tlaxcala. The site chosen was one league from Cholula and five leagues from Tlaxcala, in an area that was flat and had been depopulated with the rise of the Mexica empire because of its military vulnerability. In advertising the selected site, the founders emphasized the value of the extensive open lands for raising crops and grazing livestock. In the neighboring valley of Atlisco, a river provided sufficient water for irrigation and the cultivation of fruit trees. Moreover, there were woodlands for firewood. It seemed an ideal location for the municipality.[26]

Rather than receiving authority over native people, Judge Salmerón proposed that the settlers receive cultivable land. Nonetheless, to ensure the success of the Spanish municipality, he asked that the neighboring native communities of Tlaxcala, Cholula, and Huejotzingo contribute a labor rotation as royal tribute to assist the settlers in constructing the public buildings and residence of the town. To avoid making the settlers dependent on native labor, he suggested that the labor tribute be limited to a maximum of thirty-five days each year and to a four-year period. This stipulation, however, would not be realized; the construction of public buildings took much longer than anticipated, and the Tlaxcalan cabildo spent years petitioning the Crown to reduce or stop their labor obligation to Puebla.

Upon Puebla's founding in 1533, approximately fifty Spaniards settled in the town and began to build their houses. Shortly thereafter, Puebla was granted the status of city. Seeing the municipality flourish, encomenderos began to fear that the municipality would undermine their social position and labor resources. Indeed, as Juan de Salmerón later complained, "the encomenderos were very much opposed to it, saying that the new settlers were ruining everything by proving that the country could get along without encomiendas."[27] In addition to threatening the encomenderos, the Spanish municipality raised concern among the Tlaxcalan elite when the seat of the bishopric of Tlaxcala was transferred from the city of Tlaxcala to the city of Puebla. Responding to these changes, and ever vigilant about their status and autonomy, the Tlaxcalan nobles feared, and rightly so, that they might be placed under the jurisdiction of the Spanish municipality.

THE LOYAL AND NOBLE CITY OF TLAXCALA

To ensure continued self-government in light of the founding of Puebla, the Tlaxcalan nobles began to seek the royal entitlement of "city" for their urban center. As villages and towns were generally under the authority of a higher-ranked municipality, Tlaxcala faced the possibility of being redesignated as a village or town and placed under the authority of the nearest, higher-ranked municipality, Puebla. In addition to losing their influence over villages and minor noble houses within the province, the elite could lose the relative autonomy that they had long enjoyed.

In the early 1530s, the native nobility elected their first native governor to administer their municipality.[28] By 1536, Don Diego Maxixcatzin, the teuctli of Ocotelulco and the highest-ranked nobleman in Tlaxcala, had become the governor of Tlaxcala, and the nobles had decided that he should travel to the Iberian peninsula to represent the community before the Crown. As the governor of Tlaxcala (and, most notably, not as the lord of Ocotelulco), he was to petition for a royal mandate to secure Tlaxcala's status as a city and its direct vassalage to the Crown. For this second trip, which occurred concurrently with the Crown's growing efforts to limit the authority of the military aristocracy and to extend royal authority through a bureaucracy, the nobility decided to emphasize their status as administrators of a city. Whereas previously the petition to the Crown had been presented in the name of the nobles of Tlaxcala, Governor Don Diego Maxixcatzin presented the petition to the Crown in the name of the city.[29] Further, clearly aligning themselves with the emerging royal bureaucracy—and distancing themselves from their former ally, Hernán Cortés, who was embattled in lawsuits with the Crown to preserve his encomiendas and authority—the governor of Tlaxcala was accompanied by the audiencia judge Juan de Salmerón.[30] Finally, highlighting the Crown's obligation to reciprocate loyal service with privileges (as well as the still relevant contractual agreement that tied subjects and Crown), Maxixcatzin asserted that the Tlaxcalans were loyal subjects and, equally as important, faithful Christians. He reminded the king of the community's services to the Crown during the conquest and assured Charles V of their future services. With this strategic and well-crafted argument, Governor Maxixcatzin asked Charles V to grant Tlaxcala a coat of arms and the title La Leal Ciudad de Tlaxcala (Loyal City of Tlaxcala). To reinforce the relationship of the city to the Crown, he also requested a mandate that ensured that Tlaxcala would never be alienated from the Crown. On March 13, 1535, Charles V placed the community and its territory perpetually under its jurisdiction,[31] and on April 22, 1535, he granted the city a coat of arms and the requested title.[32]

Auspiciously, Governor Maxixcatzin's stay on the Iberian peninsula coincided with the final negotiations between the Council of the Indies and the newly appointed viceroy of New Spain, Don Antonio de Mendoza, Conde de Tendilla. When Don Diego de Maxixcatzin returned to New Spain in late 1535, the viceroy sailed on the same ship.[33] Clearly knowing the value of political networks, Don Diego Maxixcatzin made it a point to become well-acquainted with the incoming viceroy. The viceroy, in reflecting on his first meeting with the Tlaxcalan nobleman, wrote that the Tlaxcalans were "honorable people, good Christians and friends of the Spanish."[34] Unsurprisingly, while Viceroy Mendoza was in New Spain, the legal and political requests of the Tlaxcalans were often supported under the rationale that they had served the Crown faithfully during the conquest and would do so again if the occasion should arise in the future.[35]

Having acquired the title the Loyal City of Tlaxcala, the Tlaxcalans gained the privilege of continued self-rule and, in 1545, decided to form a cabildo to administer their municipality.[36] Having a centralized decision-making body was not entirely novel: as a confederacy, the nobles of each house had come together to confer on military strategy and other issues pertaining to the confederacy. Building on their pre-Hispanic experience, the elite elected minor noblemen to office: Don Diego Tlilquiyahuatzin and Don Juan de Texeda as *alcaldes* and Ximénez Leonardo Soto, Sánchez Huehuetque, Pestecoltzin, Quetzalcoltzin, Quauhuitapalcatzin, and Citlalihuitzin de Avalos as *regidores*. Similar to Castile, the elected native city councilmen collected taxes, managed communal resources, regulated markets, served as judges of the first instance in legal conflicts, and represented the community to outside authorities. While these duties were the same as those performed autonomously by each individual noble house, the city council members slowly centralized administrative decision making in the cabildo. To symbolically represent and reinforce its status, the cabildo constructed a Castilian-style city center, as noted at the beginning of this chapter.

Coinciding with the New Laws, in 1542, Tlaxcalan nobles again traveled to Castile to reaffirm their relationship with the Crown and their status as urban patricians.[37] In 1563, corresponding to a campaign against tribute increases, the Tlaxcalans again asked that they never be removed from the Crown and that they receive the title "Muy Noble y Muy Leal Ciudad de Tlaxcalan" to acknowledge their services and loyalty to the Crown.[38]

In pursuing privileges within the Spanish governing system, Tlaxcalans influenced the formal institutions that governed New Spain. Recognizing that they did not need a tutelary relationship, Charles V decreed in 1553 that his viceroys in New Spain and Peru should establish native municipalities throughout the Americas that emulated the Tlaxcalans' example.[39] Working within the system and pursuing their local interests, the Tlaxcalan nobles demonstrated that native people could govern themselves and served as a model that empowered other native communities to pursue the status of city and allowed the Crown to rein in the encomenderos in the Americas by empowering native municipalities—as Isabel had done with the municipalities in order to rein in the military orders in the peninsula.[40]

Concurrently, and also citing Tlaxcala as an example, native people throughout New Spain pursued municipal status. Although the majority of native communities became royal villages, often called *pueblos de indios*, many pursued and acquired the status of city. Tenochtitlan and Cholula acquired the title of city. Texcoco, Xochimilco, and Tacuba received the status of city in 1543, 1559, and 1564, respectively.[41] The community of Huejotzingo became a city in 1556 and Tepeaca in 1559.[42] By the end of the sixteenth century, the majority of native communities in New Spain had reverted to the Crown.[43] Those who were *realengo* (in royal domain) had a right to self-governance. Indeed, as native people pursued the status of city for their communities, they asserted their autonomy to varying degrees and enabled the Crown to strengthen the imperial bureaucracy.

LOCAL ROYAL OFFICIALS AND MUNICIPAL AUTONOMY

At the same time that Tlaxcala pursued the status of city, Bishop Ramírez de Fuenleal the president of the second audiencia of Mexico, proposed that native communities be administered by corregidores.[44] He argued that *corregimientos* (local districts) would be more humane than encomiendas and would allow the officials to reward Castilian subjects with a lucrative post in the royal bureaucracy. Moreover, the corregimientos would enable greater bureaucratic oversight by royal officials. In the 1530s, the audiencia created a single corregimiento for Tlaxcala, Cholula, and the future city of Puebla and appointed Hernando de Argueta as the first corregidor.

Similar to corregidores in Castile, corregidores in New Spain were representatives of the Crown and empowered to supersede local officials in all matters of governance and law. To ensure that the communities prospered, they were responsible for maintaining an abundance of meat, fish, and other provisions at a reasonable price and for cleaning and repairing the fences, walls, streets, highways, bridges, and other public works without harm to the Indians.[45] Likewise, they were obligated to care for and protect the weak, orphans, the poor, widows, and other destitute persons. In addition to upholding royal law and enforcing the edicts, decrees, and mandates from the Crown, the corregidor sat over the municipal council and was charged with supervising the enforcement of municipal law.[46] Additionally, those with authority over native communities were also responsible for overseeing their political and religious evangelization. Despite the extensive powers granted to the corregidores, in practice their power depended on the traditions and privileges of the municipality, the ability of the municipal elite to unite and assert its common interest, the fluctuating support they received from their superiors, and their own personal abilities.[47]

Since the corregimiento for Tlaxcala was joined to Cholula and Puebla from 1531 to 1545, the corregidor did not supervise either of the native communities closely. Rather, preferring the familiarity of a Spanish urban center, he chose to reside in and to spend his time in Puebla. Later, in 1545, coinciding with the establishment of the Tlaxcalan cabildo, Tlaxcala became an independent corregimiento. Luis Moscoso served as the first corregidor of Tlaxcala and, thereafter, the corregidores resided in Tlaxcala.[48] The second corregidor, Diego Ramírez (1546–1550) was the most active in local governance. Attending more than half of the town council meetings during his tenure, he gave advice and issued decrees on numerous aspects of local governance. After the mid-sixteenth century, once the native leaders had sufficiently demonstrated their ability to follow cabildo procedures, the corregidors generally attended only the annual elections and otherwise were absent. Most, in fact, were citizens of Mexico City and held estates outside of Tlaxcala and, therefore, often were absent from the province.

Moreover, the strong communal identity of the Tlaxcalans and their long-standing ability to act as a unified community enabled the native elite to assert its autonomy—even when the corregidor was present. For example, on October 10, 1555, corregidor Francisco Verdugo attended the cabildo meeting to request that a bridge and road be repaired. He also wanted the cabildo to assign him two watchmen and to assign his interpreter one watchman, to provide some provisions, and to direct a native woman to grind his corn. After making his case, he left the room while the cabildo members debated his requests. In the end, they decided that the bridge and road would definitely be prepared and that they would honor his requests for watchmen and provisions. However, they felt that he should hire the woman to grind his corn. Finally, they were willing to provide a watchman for the interpreter, but the watchman was not to travel far or be hired out to other people. In general, when the corregidor made procedural suggestions, the cabildo members followed his direction. However, when he infringed on their political or economic lives, the Tlaxcalans acted independently. The Tlaxcalan nobility, thus, predominately administered the region without significant interference from Spanish officials.[49] Consequently, many local traditions and institutions continued.

As several recent studies have demonstrated, the traditional elite of most native communities continued to govern and, as a result, preserved many indigenous political forms and concepts.[50] While these local political continuities could be interpreted as revealing native forms and concepts in Castilian guise, I would argue otherwise: the Crown's continued dependence on negotiation in order to govern spawned a system of compromises—a system in which political institutions accommodated and often encouraged the continuity of local customs and traditions. Indeed, on July 12, 1530, and, again, on August 5, 1555, with slightly altered language,

Charles V ordered the corregidor or *gobernador* (a different title for a similar office) to uphold the local customary laws and institutions of native people, as long as they did not contradict Natural Law or Divine Law.[51] Moreover, corregidores were mandated to inform the audiencia and viceroy about the customs, laws, and institutions of their native charges in order to preserve them. While the Crown's mandates suggest an absolute authority with the power to preserve or destroy native political forms and concepts, royal authority could not impose itself. The imperial system could not extend royal authority beyond its negotiated alliances with native elite. Although native forms and concepts were not preserved unadulterated, neither were Castilian forms implemented inflexibly.

MUNICIPAL BOUNDARIES

With Tlaxcala's status as a city and the right to govern their province in relative autonomy, Tlaxcalan nobles could establish legal boundaries to separate their community from their neighbors. Arguing that other communities were intruding on their lands, they petitioned Charles V, wrote letters to Viceroy Mendoza, and brought lawsuits to the corregidor and audiencia to resolve jurisdictional conflicts. While some of the problems arose as Spaniards settled in Puebla and solicited lands that Tlaxcalans intended to claim, many had roots in long-standing tensions with their native rivals and neighbors in Cholula, Huejotzingo, Ixtacamaxtitlan, and Zacatlan. Despite their assertions that the boundary conflicts arose from their ambitious neighbors encroaching on the pre-Hispanic lands of Tlaxcala, most of the complaints registered by Tlaxcalans, in truth, extended Tlaxcalan authority beyond their pre-conquest jurisdiction.[52] Nonetheless, I argue in this section that the Tlaxcalan elite used their relatively privileged position, influential political network, and status as a city to win court cases against their neighbors. As they leveraged their resources to realize their ambitions, they contributed to a political landscape that reflected the outcome of local tensions negotiated in the courts and the amalgamation of pre-conquest and post-conquest forms and concepts.

In 1535, the Tlaxcalans took their first jurisdictional dispute to the audiencia. They argued that after the conquest, when Cortés awarded Cholula to Don Diego de Rangel, he had accidentally assigned several villages to Don Diego that had belonged to Tlaxcala. They asked that the villages be restored to their jurisdiction.[53] The regent queen ordered that an inquiry be made and decreed that the villages be returned if the claim was valid. In 1538, Don Maxixcatzin wrote again, repeating his earlier claims. In addition, the Tlaxcalans complained that the natives of Cholula and Huejotzingo were entering their territory forcibly and damaging their crops. They asked Charles V to send someone to restore the boundary between Tlaxcala and their Indian neighbors.

Charles V ordered Viceroy Mendoza to go to Tlaxcala as soon as possible to investigate the situation and to restore the lands taken from Tlaxcala. Not knowing that most of the lands that separated Tlaxcala from their neighbors were yaotlalli and therefore considered no-man's-land, Charles V ordered the viceroy to investigate where the border had existed previously. Finally, Mendoza was to fine the natives of Huejotzingo and Cholula for any and all damages they had caused to fields in Tlaxcala.[54]

Lacking follow-up documentation, it is impossible to know whether the lands were awarded to Tlaxcala. Nonetheless, by 1559, Tlaxcalans had extended their municipal limits to the west by claiming the village of Ixtacuixtla.[55] While it is not clear whether this was the village under dispute, it is clear that the border between Tlaxcala and their Indian neighbors moved significantly further west, as Tlaxcala incorporated villages and the yaotlalli into their jurisdiction.

With their frontiers extended to the south and southwest, Tlaxcalans used the Castilian legal concept of *presura* (the right to claim uncultivated and unclaimed lands) to claim the uncultivated lands to the east of the community as *baldíos* (public lands) of the city of Tlaxcala. These lands were also yaotlalli.[56] To secure their claim to these lands, they asked Viceroy Mendoza to send a royal judge to mark and record the limits of their public lands. On May 7, 1545, Judge Gómez de Santillán from the audiencia set stone markers around the baldíos of Tlaxcala identified as Zitlaltepec, Quapiaztlan, Zihuaquillan, and Atlalhuayanca. According to the description of each baldío, they were the uncultivated lands that separated Tlaxcala from Tepeaca (southeast), Nahpaluca (southeast), and Ixtacamaxtitlan (northeast).[57] In addition to extending their pre-Hispanic boundaries further east and south, they claimed the land, which Spaniards had been settling according to presura laws, as territory of the Tlaxcalan community. The boundaries to the southeast and northeast were confirmed again in 1548.

In 1552, the Tlaxcalans had the corregidor of Tlaxcala, Hernán Darias de Saavedra, and another royal official, Fernando de Portugal, set the boundary between Tlaxcala and Ixtacamaxtitlan.[58] Although the boundary was respected quietly and passively for many years, the Tlaxcalans complained in 1557 that their neighbors were moving the markers, entering Tlaxcalan lands, and cultivating them. They asked that the viceroy send someone out to reestablish the boundary.[59] Again in 1560, they asked the viceroy to enforce the boundary between Tlaxcala and Ixtacamaxtitlan. After several years of litigation over the boundary, the viceroy directed Don Felipe de Arellano, *alcalde mayor* of Tlaxcala (the same office as corregidor but a different title), to investigate and enforce the marker placed by Hernando de Portugal between Tlaxcala and Ixtacamaxtitlan.[60] Evidently, he resolved the conflict, as no further disputes were recorded.

Simultaneous with their case against Ixtacamaxtitlan, the Tlaxcalan elite asked that the boundary separating Tlaxcala from Zacatlan be respected. Finally, in 1560, they complained, again, that the natives of the village of Zacatlan were moving the ancient boundaries that separated the two communities and were encroaching into their territory. The Indians of Zacatlan, apparently, made a counterclaim against the Tlaxcalans. The viceroy prohibited the members of both communities from entering the lands of the other and threatened them with a punishment: whoever violated the boundary line would lose his right to claim where the boundary existed.[61] The boundary line to the north, between Zacatlan and Tlaxcala, was reconfirmed. Concerned about legally clarifying their boundaries (and the other rights and privileges that they had received), Tlaxcalan leaders sent an envoy to Charles V in 1563. In their petition, they asked that the boundaries of the city of Tlaxcala be confirmed. On September 8, 1563, Charles V did so.[62]

While many of the cases were between the Tlaxcalan elite and their Indian neighbors, others arose with the arrival of Spanish settlers to Puebla. Following Castilian custom, the citizens of Puebla had begun to claim the uncultivated lands surrounding their municipality.[63] As the population grew, newcomers traveled further outside the Spanish city to find unclaimed land. Within a decade, in 1541, the Tlaxcalans complain that the citizens of Los Angles were encroaching on their lands and that their cattle were entering and trampling the cornfields of their commoners. Accordingly, they asserted that there was not sufficient land to sustain their community since it also was growing rapidly. They wanted the Crown to prohibit cattle from entering and grazing near native fields.[64]

In his response, Charles V ordered Viceroy Mendoza to prohibit cattle from grazing near native lands. He asserted that there were plenty of baldíos where the cattle could graze without harming the native population. The viceroy thus designated an alternative site for the cattle.[65] Since the first royal mandate did not solve the problem, the Tlaxcalans reasserted the need for a boundary two years later, in 1543. They asked Charles V to establish a boundary between the two communities. Engaging in the ongoing processes of negotiation, Charles V reissued the royal mandate of 1541 and instructed Viceroy Mendoza to go to Tlaxcala and mark a boundary between Puebla and Tlaxcala.[66]

Following Charles V's orders, Viceroy Mendoza traveled to Tlaxcala to facilitate a discussion between the cabildos of each city. The cabildo members of Puebla and Tlaxcala negotiated for three days before deciding where the boundary between the two cities should lie. On the final day, the viceroy, the members of the two cabildos, and a scribe met at the ravine called Xala, where the road between Tlaxcala and Tepeaca passed. Starting at this point, they walked along the Tlaxcala-Tepeaca road and up to the summit of the mountain of Matlalquiaytl (now called Malinche, as shown in a map published by Angel García Cook).[67] As they walked, they set stones along their path to mark the boundary. They divided the mountain in half; the northern half belonged to Tlaxcala and the southern half belonged to Puebla.

Having arrived at a consensus about the boundary, they had a map drawn to show the line that divided the two cities. The members of the Spanish cabildo of Puebla and the Indian cabildo of Tlaxcala each signed the document and affirmed that they agreed on the boundary. Afterward, the viceroy signed it, indicating that it was approved by his office and would be enforced. Finally, the documents were sent to Charles V.[68] The new boundary extended Tlaxcalan territory further south. With the two communities separated by stone markers, several hundred native Tlaxcalans who wanted to live on the Puebla side of the line petitioned for citizenship to the Spanish city. In 1546, the cabildo of Puebla awarded them citizenship: they each received a plot of land in the Tlaxcalan neighborhood within the city and all the rights enjoyed by the rest of the citizens of Los Angeles.[69]

Although the Tlaxcalans had defended a territorial space before the arrival of the Spaniards, the political authority of each noble house and village was exercised over its members rather than over land. Within forty years after the conquest, the Tlaxcalan nobility had established legal boundaries between their city and that of their neighbors and had asserted their authority over a territorial space twice as large as they had defended in the pre-Hispanic period. The confederation of noncontiguous noble houses had transformed the political entity of Tlaxcala into a bounded municipal territory.

As native communities accessed Castilian legal concepts and institutions to advocate, negotiate, and defend their claims, they established the limits of their community. Some, such as Tlaxcala, were more successful than others at asserting their interests in the imperial courts. Likewise, some claims were more rooted in the pre-Hispanic period, while others emerged with the arrival of new concepts and forms. This spatial reorganization of Mesoamerica reflected neither pre-Hispanic nor Castilian concepts of land and community. The geography of New Spain emerged through negotiated processes.

CONCLUSION

In becoming municipalities, native people did not necessarily internalize Castilian concepts nor did they maintain Nahua forms in a Castilian guise. Castilian municipal institutions were inherently flexible and accommodated local diversity. As native people adopted Castilian institutions strategically, they adapted them to local circumstances—as Crown subjects did throughout the Iberian world. This created a multiplicity of hybrid or composite political forms and traditions. In addition to shaping local institutions and spaces as they asserted their concerns, as we have seen, native people also influenced the networks and institutions that came to govern the empire. Even though their legal and political activities enabled the Crown to strengthen the imperial bureaucracy, the imperial structure was not necessarily oppressive to all of its native subjects. Each community's experience within the empire depended on its skill and success at negotiating its interests within the courts. New Spain, thus, emerged not as a Castilian concept but as a composite of negotiated interests.

NOTES

1. Mercedes Meade de Angulo, *Erección de Tlaxcala en Ciudad de el año de 1525 por el Papa Clemente* (Tlaxcala, Mexico: Gobierno del Estado de Tlaxcala, 1981), cites Archivo Histórico de la Biblioteca Nacional de Antropología e Historia, Colec. F. Gómez de Orozco, 21, folios 63–64.

2. "Repartimiento de las tierras y de los sitios de la ciudad de Tlaxcala," in Juan Buenaventura Zapata y Mendoza, *Historia cronológica de la noble Ciudad de Tlaxcala*, trans. Luis Ryes García and Andrea Martínez Baracs (Tlaxcala: Universidad Autónoma de Tlaxcala and CIESAS, 1995 [late 1600s]), 137.

3. Without giving a reference, Charles Gibson states, in appendix VI of his book, that Don Diego Tlilquiyahuatzin was elected as the first governor in 1534; *Tlaxcala in the Sixteenth Century* (New Haven, CT: Yale University Press, 1952; repr., Stanford, CA: Stanford University Press, 1967), 224. However, Zapata y Mendoza states that it was either in 1537, "en este año iniciaron lo del gobernador tlaxcalteca, a instancias de fray Antonio de Ciudad Rodrigo," or in 1538, "[e]ntonces el primer gobernador fue don Luis Xicotencatl." See his *Historia cronológica*, 143.

4. "[Y]uan yuh quitaque yn uel ytech monequi atl petl tlaxcallan noyui ytech monequi yn imauiztililoca yn enperador." James Lockhart, Frances Berdan, and Arthur J.O. Anderson, eds., *The Tlaxcalan Actas: A Compendium of the Records of the Cabildo of Tlaxcala, 1545–1627* (Salt Lake City: University of Utah Press, 1986), 70.

5. Helen Nader, *Liberty in Absolutist Spain: The Habsburg Sale of Towns, 1516–1700* (Baltimore: Johns Hopkins University Press, 1990); and Antonio Domínguez Ortiz, *The Golden Age of Spain, 1516–1659,* trans. James Casey (New York: Basic Books, 1971), 131.

6. Susan Kellogg, *Law and the Transformation of Aztec Culture, 1500–1700* (Norman: University of Oklahoma Press, 1995); and Steve J. Stern, *Peru's Indian Peoples and the Challenge of Spanish Conquest: Huamanga to 1640* (Madison: University of Wisconsin Press, 1982). Rather than being inspired by Marxian or Gramscian theories, my work is influenced by Anthony Giddens's ideas of "structuration," as discussed in his *The Constitution of Society: Outline of the Theory of Structuration* (Berkeley: University of California Press, 1984).

7. James Lockhart, "Some Nahua Concepts in Postconquest Guise," *History of European Ideas* 6, no. 4 (1985): 465–482. For this phenomena, he coined the term "Double Mistaken Identity" and explained that "each side of the cultural exchange presumes that a given form or concept is operating in the way familiar within its own tradition and is unaware of or unimpressed by the other side's interpretation," (477).

8. Gibson was the first to assert that prehispanic Tlaxcala was smaller than the current state of Tlaxcala; Gibson, *Tlaxcala in the Sixteenth Century,* 6. At the time of his writing, the documentation suggested a smaller size, but there was not sufficient evidence to establish the actual limits of the cultural group. Since then, however, archeological research has provided us with a fairly accurate picture of the extent of prehispanic Tlaxcala. See Angel García Cook, *Tlaxcala: Una historia compartida; Los Orígenes, Arqueología,* 16 vols. (Tlaxcala and México DF: Gobierno del Estado de Tlaxcala and Consejo Nacional para la Cultura y las Artes, 1991), 3:329, 353–354; and Dean R. Snow, "Ceramic Sequence and Settlement Location in Pre-Hispanic Tlaxcala," *American Antiquity* 34, no. 2 (1969):131–145.

9. García Cook, *Tlaxcala: Una historia compartida,* chap. 9.

10. Snow, "Ceramic Sequence and Settlement Location in Pre-Hispanic Tlaxcala," 134–142.

11. Toribio Motolinía, *Historia de los indios de la Nueva España,* ed. Claudio Esteva Fabregat (Madrid: Historia 16, 1985), 269; and Toribio Motolinía, *Memoriales o Libro de las cosas de la Nueva España y de los naturales de ella,* 2nd ed., ed. Edmundo O'Gorman (México DF: UNAM, 1971). Both were composed in the 1530s or 1540s.

12. Zapata y Mendoza, *Historia cronológica,* 137. Gibson also cites "Anales antiguos de México y sus contornos," 2 vols., comp. José Fernando Ramírez (unpublished ms., Museo Nacional, México DF), 17:728; 18:740, 767. Because Don Lorenzo Tianquiztlatohuatzin died in Castile on this trip and he was the heir to the Ocotelulco teccalli, he and the trip are mentioned in the testimonies of the litigation for the teccalli. See Archivo General de la Nación (hereafter, AGN), Tierras, vol. 20, part 1, exp. 1, fols. 43v–44r.

13. See Anthony Pagden, "Translator's Introduction," in *Hernán Cortés: Letters from Mexico,* ed. Anthony Pagden (New York: Orion Press, 1971), lx–lxvii.

14. Gibson, *Tlaxcala in the Sixteenth Century,* 164.

15. Simpson, *The Encomienda in New Spain*, 80, who cites Antonio de Herrera y Tordesillas, *Historia general de los hechos de los castellanos en las Islas y Tierra Firme del mar oceano* (Madrid: En la Emprenta Real, 1601), 2:148–151.

16. Archivo General de las Indias (hereafter, AGI), México, 1088, 1, fols. 38r–39r. Gibson (*Tlaxcala in the Sixteenth Century*, 164) states that no privilege came from this first visit to Spain; however, he did not investigate Spanish archives for his book on Tlaxcala and, therefore, would not have seen this document.

17. Pagden, *Hernán Cortés*, 279–280.

18. See, for example, John Huxtable Elliott, *Imperial Spain, 1469–1716* (repr., New York: Penguin Books, 1990), 87–88, 90–97; Stephen Haliczer, *The Comuneros of Castile: The Forging of a Revolution, 1475–1521* (Madison: University of Wisconsin Press, 1981); Marvin Lunenfeld, *Keepers of the City: The Corregidores of Isabella I of Castile, 1474–1504* (Cambridge: Cambridge University Press, 1987); and Nader, *Liberty in Absolutist Spain*.

19. Quentin Skinner, *The Foundations of Modern Political Thought*, 2 vols. (Cambridge: Cambridge University Press, 1998), 1:62; 2:118–119, 180–184.

20. Simpson, *The Encomienda in New Spain*, 73–83.

21. Ernst Schäfer, *El Consejo Real y Supremo de las Indias: La labor del Consejo de Indias en administración colonial*, 2 vols. (Madrid: Marcial Pons Historia, 2003), 2:13–16.

22. Schäfer, *El Consejo Real y Supremo de las Indias*, 2:16.

23. AGI, México, 317; Simpson, *The Encomienda in New Spain*, 84–85.

24. Simpson, *The Encomienda in New Spain*, 95.

25. AGI, México, 317; Simpson, *The Encomienda in New Spain*, 103.

26. Francisco del Paso y Troncoso, ed., *Epistolario de Nueva España 1505–1818*, 2nd ed., 16 vols., Biblioteca histórica mexicana de obras inéditas (México DF: Antigua Librería Robredo de J. Porrúa e Hijos, 1939–1942), 4:137–139.

27. Simpson, *The Encomienda in New Spain*, 103, cites Salmerón to the Queen, November 1, 1532, in Henri Ternaux-Compans, *Voyages, Relations et Mémoires Originaux pour Servir á l'histoire de la Découverte de l'amérique*, 2nd ed., 8 vols. (Paris: A. Bertrand, 1837–1841), 5:207.

28. See note 3.

29. Considering their level of political and legal sophistication, there is little doubt that the Tlaxcalan nobles authored, or at least authorized, their petitions. Moreover, their petitions were signed by the nobles; if someone else had presented the petition on their behalf, the documents would have identified their representative. Finally, native people in many parts of Spanish America were involved in similar legal activities; see Serge Gruzinski, *The Conquest of Mexico* (Cambridge: Polity Press, 1993), chap. 1. Also see "Letter by don Pedro Motecuzoma Tlacahuepantzin et al., Tacuba, 11 May 1556," in Paso y Troncoso, ed., *Epistolario de Nueva España, 1505–1818*, 16:64–66; Borah, *Justice by Insurance*; Stern, *Peru's Indian Peoples*; Taylor, *Drinking, Homicide and Rebellion in Colonial Mexican Villages*. Numerous Castilians noted, often to their chagrin, that the native population skillfully asserted their demands in Castilian courts. See, for example, "Letter to King Carlos V by encomendero Jerónimo López, 20 October 1541," in Joaquín

García Icazbalceta, ed., *Colección de documentos para la historia de México*, 2 vols. (México DF: Antigua Librería, 1866), 2:148; *Colección de documentos inéditos para la historia de Ibero-América* (Madrid: Archivo de Indias, 1927), 194.

30. On Salmerón, see Simpson, *The Encomienda in New Spain*, which cites a letter from Salmerón to the queen, dated 1 November 1532 quoted in Henri Ternaux-Compans, *Voyages, Relations et Mémoires Originaux pour Servir á l'histoire de la Découverte de l'amérique*, 2nd ed., 8 vols. (Paris: A. Bertrand, 1837–1841), 5:207. Also see Gibson, *Tlaxcala in the Sixteenth Century*, 165; Don Antonio de Mendoza, "Fragmento de la visita hecha á don Antonio de Mendoza," in Joaquin García Icazbalceta, ed., *Colección de documentos para la historia de México*, 2:87; *Colección de documentos inéditos relativos al descubrimiento, conquista y organización de las antiguas posesiones de ultramar*, 21 vols. (Madrid: Real Academia de la Historia, 1885–1932), 18:50; Mercedes Meade de Angulo, "Introducción," in *Documentos y Reales Cédulas de la Ciudad de Tlaxcala*, ed. Mercedes Meade de Angulo (Tlaxcala: Gobierno del Estado de Tlaxcala a través del Instituto Tlaxcalteca de la Cultura, 1984), which cites Archivo Histórico de la Biblioteca Nacional de Antropología e Historia, Colec. F. Gómez de Orozco, México DF, 21, fols. 63–64; and Zapata y Mendoza, *Historia cronológica de la noble Ciudad de Tlaxcala*, 141.

31. AGI, Patronato, 275, ramo 20; AGI, Contratación, 5788, 1, fols. 172v–173v; AGN, Tierras, vol. 1172, exp. 3, fol. 67; Archivo Histórico del Estado de Tlaxcala (hereafter, AHET), 1533, caja 1, exp. 6; AHET, 1535, caja 1, exp. 7; and AHET, 1530, caja 1, exp. 5, fols. 2v–9v. Also published in Antonio Peñafiel, *Ciudades coloniales y capitales de la República mexicana*, 2 vols. (México DF: Impr. y Fototipia de la Secretaría de Fomento, 1908), 2:152–153; and Francisco A. Icaza, "Miscelánea Histórica," *Biblioteca de la Revista Mexicana de Estudios Históricos de los Pueblos: Apéndice II* (1928), 21. For a detailed discussion of this cedula, see Gibson, *Tlaxcala in the Sixteenth Century*, appendix 7.

32. AHET, 1539, caja 1, exp. 10. Also published in Carlos V, *Documentos y Reales Cédulas de la Ciudad De Tlaxcala*, ed. Mercedes Meade de Angulo (Tlaxcala, Mexico: Gobierno del Estado de Tlaxcala a través del Instituto Tlaxcalteca de la Cultura, 1984); Peñafiel, *Ciudades coloniales y capitales de la República mexicana*; and Icaza, "Miscelánea Histórica," 21.

33. Gibson, *Tlaxcala in the Sixteenth Century*, 165.

34. Don Antonio de Mendoza, "Fragmento de la visita hecha á Antonio de Mendoza," 2:87n36.

35. Simpson, *The Encomienda in New Spain*, 118.

36. The Actas de Cabildo began in 1547; see the published versions by Celestino Solís et al. (1985) and by Lockhart et al. A royal cedula issued in 1585 confirms that the cabildo was established on this date; AGN, Civil, vol. 711, exp. 6, fols. 2r–3r.

37. AGN, Mercedes, vol. 2, exp. 638, fol. 257r.

38. AHET, 1551, caja 1, exp. 20, fol. 11; AGI, Contratación, 5788, book 1, fols. 172v–173v; AHET, 1539, caja 1, exp. 10, fol. 2.

39. AGI, Lima, 566, book 6, fol. 166v; AGI, Mexico, 1086, book 4, fol. 107. These are also published in Richard Konetzke, *Colección de documentos para la historia de la*

formación social de Hispanoamérica, 1493–1810, 3 vols. (Madrid: Consejo Superior de Investigaciones Científicas, 1953), 1:260–261; and Diego de Encinas and Alfonso García Gallo, *Cedulario indiano: Reproducción facsimilar de la edición única de 1596*, 4 vols. (Madrid: Cultura Hispánica, 1945–1946), 4:274. I thank Jeremy Mumford for directing me to these texts.

40. For an alternative interpretation, which examines solely Spaniards' influence on this shift, see the interpretation in Simpson, *The Encomienda in New Spain*, especially chaps. 10–11.

41. Charles Gibson, *The Aztecs under Spanish Rule: A History of the Indians of the Valley of Mexico, 1519–1810* (Stanford, CA: Stanford University Press, 1964), 32; AGN, Reales Cédulas Duplicados, vol. 1, exp. 166, fol. 150; Francisco del Paso y Troncoso, ed., *Epistolario de Nueva España 1505–1818*, 16 vols. (México DF: Biblioteca Histórica Mexicana de Obras Inéditas, 2nd ed., Antigua Librería Robredo de José Porrúa e Hijos, 1939–1942), 2:226.

42. For Huejotzingo, AGN, Reales Cédulas Duplicados, vol. 1, exp. 112, fol. 109; or Tepeaca, AGN, Reales Cédulas Duplicados, vol. 1, exp. 169, fol. 153.

43. Simpson, *The Encomienda in New Spain*, 163.

44. Lunenfeld, *Keepers of the City*, 1; and Simpson, *The Encomienda in New Spain*, 84–85.

45. Recopilación de Leyes de los Reynos de las Indias (1774), ley 12, titulo II, libro V.

46. Robert S. Chamberlain, "The *Corregidor* in Castile in the Sixteenth Century and the *Residencia* as Applied to the *Corregidor*," *Hispanic American Historical Review* 23 (1943): 234, 227; Lunenfeld, *Keepers of the City*, 3; John Lynch, *Spain under the Hapsburgs: Empire and Absolutism, 1516–1598*, 2 vols. (New York: Oxford University Press, 1981), 1:6; and Carlos E. Castañeda, "The *Corregidor* in Spanish Colonial Administration," *Hispanic American Historical Review* 9, no. 4 (1929): 457.

47. Lunenfeld, *Keepers of the City*, 2.

48. Zapata y Mendoza, *Historia cronológica de la noble Ciudad De Tlaxcala*, 149. For a more detailed discussion of the corregidores of Tlaxcala, see Gibson, *Tlaxcala in the Sixteenth Century*, 67–76; and Tlaxcala, *The Tlaxcalan Actas*.

49. James Lockhart, Frances Berden, and Arthur J.O. Anderson, "Preliminary Study: Some Themes in the Actas," in *The Tlaxcalan Actas: A Compendium of the Records of the Cabildo of Tlaxcala, 1545–1627* (Salt Lake City: University of Utah Press, 1986), 15, 95–97.

50. See the excellent studies of Robert Haskett, *Indigenous Rulers: An Ethnohistory of Town Government in Colonial Cuernavaca* (Albuquerque: University of New Mexico Press, 1991); James Lockhart, *The Nahuas after the Conquest* (Stanford, CA: Stanford University Press, 1992); and Lockhart, "Some Nahua Concepts in Postconquest Guise." I am not persuaded, however, that native culture continued because "interaction was one in which each side perceived a certain phenomenon in similar but far from identical ways, often without having any notion of the divergent perceptions of the other side"; Lockhart, *The Nahuas after the Conquest*, 467. My interpretation is also different from that of Haskett, who writes: "The ruling elite believed that they were entitled to receive significant material perquisites

and that they possessed the authority to administer their towns without recourse to or interference from Crown authorities. The combination of these factors with the basic inability or unwillingness of the colonial authorities to intervene in every aspect of indigenous municipal government allowed the cabildos to retains significant amount of local autonomy"; *Indigenous Rulers*, 85.

51. Recopilación de Leyes de los Reynos de las Indias (1774), ley 12, titulo II, libro V; and ley 4, titulo I, libro II.

52. Gibson, in *Tlaxcala in the Sixteenth Century*, 130–131, also asserted that the legal boundary extended Tlaxcalan territory significantly. However, Gibson adds that the boundary was established to protect the community from the problems caused by Spanish settlers. While this is partially true, their legal battles were not solely against Spaniards. As I show here, most were against their Indian neighbors and rivals. Thus, it appears that continued pre-Hispanic tensions also motivated the Tlaxcalans to set boundaries. As I argue throughout my dissertation, colonial society was not formed out of a conflict between Spaniards and Indians; people identified with their local community, first and foremost. Colonial society thus emerged as communities struggled against each other to define themselves and their relationship to the Crown. See R. Jovita Baber, "The Construction of Empire: Politics, Law and Community in Tlaxcala, New Spain, 1521–1640" (Ph.D. dissertation, University of Chicago, Chicago, 2005).

53. AHET, 1535, caja 1, exp. 8, fol. 8.

54. Ibid., fol. 8r.

55. Eustaquio Celestino Solís, Armando Valencia Rios, and Constantino Medina Lima, eds., *Actas de Cabildo de Tlaxcala, 1547–1567* (México DF and Tlalpan: AGN, CIESAS, and Instituto Tlaxcalteca de la Cultura, 1985), 175.

56. That they were yaotlalli is confirmed in AHET, 1723–1724, caja 63, exp. 64. See also Carlos Sempat Assadourian and Andrea Martínez Baracs, eds., *Tlaxcala, textos de su historia: Siglo XVI*, 16 vols. (Tlaxcala: Gobierno del Estado de Tlaxcala, 1991), 6:223–225.

57. AHET, 1545, caja 1, exp. 14, fol. 2.

58. Gibson, *Tlaxcala in the Sixteenth Century*, 130.

59. AHET, 1557, caja 1, exp. 28.

60. AHET, 1560, caja 1, exp. 9; AGN, Mercedes, vol. 5, fol. 112.

61. AGN, Mercedes, vol. 5, fol. 129.

62. The petition is located in the Seville, AGI, México, 94, no. 2. The cedula, according to Gibson (*Tlaxcala in the Sixteenth Century*, appendix VIII, p. 231), is located in the Bancroft Library, Mexican Manuscripts, Berkeley, California, no. 171, fol. 25r.

63. Actually, in the document, it states that the land was in the jurisdiction of Tlaxcala. It is unclear whether it was referring to the archdiocese of Tlaxcala or whether the city of Tlaxcala had claimed an even larger territory originally than what I describe in this chapter; AGI, México, 317.

64. AHET, 1535, caja 1, exp. 8, fol. 6; AGI, México, 340.

65. AHET, 1530, caja 1, exp. 5, fols. 41v–48r; Puebla Archivo Municipal (hereafter, PAM), Libro de Cédulas, fol. 36v.

66. AHET, 1543, caja 1, exp. 8, fols. 14–15.

67. See Cook, *Tlaxcala, una historia compartida,* 3:328–329.

68. AGI, México, 340. In these early documents, it was unclear whether they had always lived on land that was now defined as being within the jurisdiction of Puebla de Los Angeles or they had moved there. Nonetheless, their citizenship was indisputable. In the early seventeenth century, there was a dispute regarding the *monte* (forest) at the top of the mountain of Matlalquiaytl (Malinche), the mountain that divided the jurisdiction of the two cities. Apparently, there were violent confrontations between the citizens of Puebla and Tlaxcala. The Tlaxcalans argued that citizens of Los Angeles were coming into their territory and cutting wood. The cabildo of Puebla argued that their citizens had a right to the monte because it was on the top of the mountain. When the citizens of Puebla presented their testimonies, they stated that their ancestors had had access to this forest from time immemorial; in other words, they were descendents of Tlaxcalans who had become citizens of Puebla.

69. PAM, Actas de Cabildo, vol. 5, doc. 164, fols. 65–172v.

3

ETHELIA RUIZ MEDRANO

Translation by Michel Besson

Fighting Destiny

Nahua Nobles and Friars in the Sixteenth-Century
Revolt of the Encomenderos *against the King*

To Luis Reyes in Memoriam

*Poctli, aiahuitl: teiiotl, mahuiziotl**
[May thou rest in peace, dear friend and master.]

It is well-known that the Indians of the city of Mexico hardly ever attempted
to rebel against Spanish colonial power. In this chapter I intend to show that
the Indians of Mexico City tried to participate in the *encomenderos'* (holders of grants of tribute and labor) revolt against the king. This happened
after the Indian nobles of Mexico Tenochtitlan attempted to negotiate with
the highest Spanish authorities about the king's intention to impose a tribute policy that affected Indian interests. I believe that friars participated in
this negotiation on the indigenous side. The negotiation on the Indians'

---

* Specialists in the *Florentine Codex* tell us that this metaphor was applied to any
recently deceased public official whose vapor, a faint mist, remains, unable to
disappear, just as his honor and glory refuse to fade away.

side was carried out by the native nobility, especially by the governor of Mexico Tenochtitlan, Don Luis de Santa María Cipac. I argue that during negotiations with the Spanish authorities, the Indians of Mexico City became impatient because they believed that Spanish authorities did not understand the problems paying the new tribute would create for them. It seems likely that the Indians felt that the local Spanish authorities did not constitute a *buen gobierno*, or "good government." It thus appears that the indigenous population had a political consciousness about good and bad government, which led to their interest in participating in the encomenderos' revolt against the king of Spain. In this essay I try to bring to light the complex roles played by the Indians, encomenderos, and friars in the events of the first half of the 1560s.

This Indian political project has never been studied before. But we do know, thanks to recent research, that in colonial time, when Indians rebelled against Spanish power, they did so because of harsh economic conditions but also with a political consciousness about and against the Spanish authorities. This has been shown by Natalia Silva Prada in her study of the Indian rebellion in Mexico City in the year of 1692.[1] For her, a political critique based on the belief that authorities were not carrying out their responsibilities properly lay beneath the Indian rebellion. Indians undertook a movement to try to change this, in some instances using traditional war signals and native utopian ideas. Also, Eric Van Young shows in a recent book that while most historians believe that Indians participated in the Mexican independence movement primarily for economic reasons, they also participated because of their own ethnic political thinking, a complex and partly ancient ethnic consciousness that helped them create millenarian movements in the years between 1810 and 1821.[2] In both cases the authors have documented that the Indians had loyalty to Spanish Crown because of the protective attitude the monarchs displayed during the colonial period toward their Indian vassals.

ENCOMENDEROS CONSPIRE

On January 6, 1564, the Indians of Mexico Tenochtitlan celebrated "the feast of the three wise men." A Nahua scribe wrote enthusiastically that "all were armed. And the Mexicans fought with canoe shields, confronting those from Tlatelolco, and all were carrying their standards. Martín Xollotecatl was the impersonator of Ocelotl, and was wearing the corresponding [accoutrement] and Pedro Cuetzoc was the double of one sort of coyote, and it was done because the *alcaldes* [constables] had just started their terms." At the time, that celebration looked like nothing more than a local event. However, the anonymous scribe also notes that on the same day "the Spaniards barricaded themselves near the house of Alonso de Villanueva and they fought."[3] The latter event was connected to the unrest brewing at the time among various factions of encomenderos, some of whom were actively conspiring against Philip II, with the avowed intent to take over the audiencia as well as the most important cities of New Spain and to crown as king the second Marqués del Valle, Don Martín Cortés. This resentment was chiefly the result of the king's denying the encomenderos of New Spain and their descendants the right to perpetuate *encomienda* rights (grant of tribute and labor) to their children or others.[4]

In 1563, the only legitimate son of Hernán Cortés, the second Marqués del Valle, Martín Cortés, arrived in New Spain. In Spain he had served Philip II during the campaign of Flanders and had participated also in the military campaigns of Algeria and Germany.[5] His arrival could not have happened at a better time for the more traditional elements among the encomenderos as they were fighting for the king of Castile to grant them their encomiendas in perpetuity. The rich marqués saw himself courted by a number of these personages soon after his arrival in New Spain. Beginning in October 1565, these same people began discussing the possibility of revolt against the Spanish monarchy, keeping the territory of New Spain for themselves.[6]

That same year various encomenderos started a series of public protests, a clear indication of their rebellious intent. One Sunday in October of that year, the encomendero in Cuauhtitlan, Alonso de Ávila Alvarado, ordered the Indian potters of that village to make a large service of earthenware plates "in the old fashioned way," so that a banquet with food cooked in indigenous style could be served in honor of Martín Cortés. The dishes were brought from the closest villages; the pots and plates were decorated with a design in the shape of a crown. The encomendero and some of his guests were dressed in the manner of the Mexica nobles, and Ávila himself was disguised as Motecuhzoma. Thus dressed, they all went to the house of the marqués, who was in turn dressed as his own father, in the costume of the conquistador. During the festivities, Ávila gave the marqués and his wife a collar made of flowers and, amid the applause and shouts of the spectators, someone shouted, "Take this crown, Marquesa!" The encomenderos and the other guests dressed as Indian nobles recited poems alluding to the revolt against the king, in terms that only those involved in the upcoming revolt could understand. During the night, many of those gathered went about the town and celebrated as if there were a huge carnival.[7] Of course, all this did not go unnoticed by the Indians of Mexico Tenochtitlan.

These festivities are quite interesting in that they seem symbolically to mark the fact that the conquistadors believed themselves, as well as their descendants, to be legitimate rulers because that land had been given to them by its lord, the *huey tlatoani* (supreme ruler) Motecuhzoma. Indeed, the right of rulership by the conquistadors seems to have been seen by encomenderos as based on the "peaceful" transfer that Motecuhzoma was supposed to have made to Hernán Cortés after his entrance in Tenochtitlan. This is what was referred to by the disguises and homage rendered during the festivities offered by Ávila to Martín Cortés. The conquistadors' idea was to reign in New Spain together with the indigenous nobility in a sort of council, which would have been a way to integrate aggrieved native nobles.[8]

During the trial of Martín Cortés in August 1566, an exhibit was presented against him, a clay pot from Cuauhtitlan, from the encomienda of Alonso de Ávila, on which one could read *REIAS* (meaning "you will reign") under the image of a crown. Various Indians from Cuauhtitlan were interrogated, and it is mentioned that one of them, Pablo de los Santos, still had the mold for that pot and, when asked, declared that a mestizo called Alvarado had ordered pots to be made. The letters and the crown were done by an indigenous painter. Also on the subject of the feast in which several encomenderos had dressed as Indians, it was pointed out that they wore masks of Indians; there were more than twenty Spaniards so disguised, among them Alonso de Ávila. They also declared that they wore *suchiles*, crowns of flowers, and a "vagrant" shouted "take this crown, Marquesa" when they placed it upon the head of the wife of the Marqués Martín Cortés. Written poems were handed around, among which was one that said, "[D]o not fear the fall, if one is to climb higher."[9]

Among other sumptuous celebrations in honor of Martín Cortés, there is the mention, in the *Anales de Juan Bautista*, of the following:

> Monday, June 24, 1566 . . . the *papalocuicatl* [butterfly song] was staged, and with it the feast of Saint John was celebrated, then once the butterflies and ocelots were done with, [the feast of Saint Peter was also celebrated] on Saturday, June 29. And on the morning of that Sunday, the twin sons of the Marqués were baptized, they were taken to the temple. And all the *macehuales* [commoners] of the Marqués were there, the Lords of the Quauhnahuac came to bring decorations, and they all came with their marching bands, and their wind instrument, the great conch.[10]

This event is described in great detail in the trial of Martín Cortés. Judicial authorities considered that the baptism had been carried out as if it were a celebration in honor of the sons of a king. What is more, the canon of the Cathedral of Mexico himself, Alonso Chico de Molina, was the one who baptized the children of the marqués.[11]

In spite of that festive atmosphere, the encomenderos had been worried for quite some time. Several things clearly indicated that the Crown did not support the descendants of the conquistadors, especially if such an acknowledgment was to imply more economic loss for its already reduced revenues. Similarly, many among the encomenderos were incurring economic losses because of the progressively stronger control by royal representatives over all productive sectors, at the same time as new colonists, interested in trade and mining, encroached more everyday on their prerogatives. This evolution was especially notable among the by-then-obsolete descendants of the conquistadors, longing to have their dominion over the villages in their encomiendas confirmed by the king.[12]

With the death of Viceroy Luís de Velasco I in that same year and the departure for Spain of the *visitador general* (general inspector), Jerónimo de Valderrama, the rumor grew that the Crown opposed the right of the encomenderos to pass on their encomiendas to their descendants.[13] Under such conditions, many Spaniards started to think that the encomenderos were indeed going to revolt under the command of the Marqués del Valle.[14] That same October, the encomenderos got together in the house of Alonso de Ávila to put the last touches to their plan. Also involved in this plot were a number of soldiers, some from Peru, where encomenderos had tried several times to free themselves from the Crown of Castile.[15] Among them was a certain Pizarro, an expert in bomb making, who had quietly been experimenting with the manufacture of such artifacts in the city of Tehuantepec.[16]

The conspirators decided that on a Friday, the day of the meeting of governing bodies, they would split into groups of eight to ten men, all armed to the teeth, each group with its captain, and that one group would kill the *oidores* (judges of the Real Audiencia [Royal Court]) and the visitador. Once that was done, a signal would be given by Cristóbal de Ayala Espinosa, a clerk in the cathedral, who would ring the bells in the tower of the cathedral. That would mean it was time for another group to kill Don Luis and Don Francisco de Velasco (son and brother of the first Viceroy Velasco), as well as the royal officers and anyone who opposed the revolt. The bodies would be displayed in the square under the supervision of the marqués in order to convince the rest of the populace and the archives would be burned down "to eradicate the name of the King of Castile."[17]

One of the conspirators, Don Pedro de Arellano, would become the captain of the guard for the new king.[18] Apparently, the excuse given for the gathering of all those soldiers was a tournament to be celebrated for the Day of Santiago. Some of the encomenderos who were in on the plot, like Bernardino de Bocanegra, asked colonists and encomenderos to allow their soldiers and others to participate in the tournament in honor of Santiago and suggested that "in the manner of infantry troops, they should accompany them with their marching bands and their drums." Bocanegra sent powder for the arms, and Martín Cortés, "*mestizo* [of Indian and Spanish descent] brother of the Marqués," went to visit other aristocrats to ask them for more soldiers.[19] Alonso de Ávila said that many were in agreement and that he had confessed everything to an Augustinian friar, who in turn had absolved him, "saying he could go on and do it" in order to defend the property that others wanted to take away from him. He, however, wanted to wait until he had received news on the subject of the perpetual allotment from the king since that would constitute all the justification needed. "The friar would preach in favor of the revolt from his pulpit."[20]

In another part of the plot, a certain Francisco de Reinoso was supposed to take the city of Puebla, and other places were thus allotted among the conspirators. Don Luís Cortés was going to Veracruz to capture the port and the fleet anchored there; Don Martín Cortés was supposed to go with his men to occupy Zacatecas and its dependencies.[21] The plan was for him to take more than 500 men, capture the mines in Zacatecas, and on his way there kill the oidores of the audiencia of New Galicia. The conspirators were planning to pay their men with silver and jewels from the royal coffers; in addition they would be given clothes and lace taken forcibly from merchants' stores once the revolt was over.[22]

In the end the marqués was going to be proclaimed king and taken to his palace, and the courts would then be convened so that the judges could swear allegiance to the new monarch. Don Juan Cortés or Alonso Chico de Molina would go to Rome carrying precious gifts to ask the pope to validate the new kingdom. On the way, this representative would go through France, where he would also give presents to the French king and ask him for permanent safe passage through his lands, in exchange for which trade would be promoted and entrance guaranteed to all nations into the country. A certain Espinosa would go to San Lucar, and from there to Sevilla, to discreetly fetch the oldest son of the marqués and then sail to the Canary Islands with an empty caravel that would go back filled with wine for New Spain. The new king would allot all the land, naming counts and marqueses, and would "place all around his throne a class of noble Indians, closely bound to the Mexican monarchy."[23] The friars would support the new king. These talks went on until the end of 1565. At the beginning of

1566, between growing doubts and the illness that struck Ávila, the plot fell apart.[24]

In 1566, arguing that a possible plot existed against the rights of the Crown, the oidores of Mexico, together with the son of the first Viceroy Velasco, Luís de Velasco II, decided to suppress the potential uprising. The audiencia acted swiftly and arrested the conspirators one after the other in order to keep the news as quiet as possible. They also summoned the marqués under the pretense that a ship that had recently arrived from Spain was carrying a letter from the king, a letter that was supposed to deal with the perpetual renewal of the encomiendas.[25]

Trustingly, the marqués went to the audiencia, but once he stepped inside, he was arrested on the spot by the authorities. Events then accelerated rather quickly. Most of the conspirators were decapitated and their heads remained exposed for the education of all future potential rebels. Undoubtedly, the spectacular end of the sons of those who at one time held sway over the land must have deeply impressed the spectators, especially the Indians, who may have associated that scene with their ancient war rituals and sacrifices.

Some colonial codices, like the one from Tepechpan, clearly show the image of those decapitated nobles.[26] The warlike interpretation that the Indians may have made of those events can be seen in the *Anales de Juan Bautista*. The entry for July 16, 1566, says that "Martín Cortés, Don Luís Cortés, Don Luis de Castilla, Bernardino Bocanegra, Alonso [and Gil] Davila were arrested because they were talking of taking arms and they were remitted to the Court."[27] Further on, the same source specifies that

> [o]n this day, Tuesday November 18 of the year 1567 . . . they took
> down the coats of arms of the Marqués, which were in all locations
> where his macehuales lived, Coyohuacan, Atlacuihuayan, etc. This is
> the time when they became macehuales of the tlatoani, emperor of the
> whole world. And in all parts it was done thus, his arms were destroyed
> and from then on the Marqués left his macehuales, etc.[28]

The execution of the conspirators followed closely upon the confiscation of all their possessions. In a number of cases, the destruction of their houses was ordered and salt was spread all over the grounds as a sign that the original owner had died in a state of damnation for having tried to rebel against the king. The other sons of Cortés were also condemned: the mestizo Don Martín Cortés, son of the Indian interpreter Doña Marina and the conquistador, was expelled from his lands and tortured; his half-brother Luís Cortés, son of a Spanish woman named Ana de Hermosillo, was sentenced to give up all of his possessions and banished for ten years to Oran (Africa). The Marqués Martín Cortés was forever banished from New Spain.[29] Others were sentenced to house arrest under threat of death. They included Don Luis de Castilla, Don Pedro Lorenzo de Castilla, Hernán Gutiérrez Altamirano, Lope de Sosa, Alonso de Estrada, Juan de Guzmán, Bernardino Pacheco de Bocanegra, Fernando Córdova, Luis Ponce de León, Juan de Valdivieso, and many others.[30]

Reading through the trial documents relating to Martín Cortés, it becomes clear that members of the indigenous nobility were expected to participate in the government of this "new kingdom." Another aspect of the conspiracy that emerges is that during long planning sessions, the marqués sought the advice of some theologians, Franciscans for the most part, and above all the canon, Chico de Molina, who seems to have spent a lot of time trying to convince Cortés of the theological basis that allowed for the takeover of a kingdom if a king was deemed unfair.[31]

THE INVOLVEMENT OF THE FRIARS

In spite of the fear among the Spanish population of being accused of involvement in the plot, a number of friars gave testimony in favor of the accused, especially the marqués, maintaining he had remained faithful to the Crown and that no conspiracy had ever existed against Castile's sovereign. For instance, among the witnesses in that trial, one can find the *comisario general* (commissary general) of the Order of San Francisco, Fray Diego de Olarte; as well as Fray Antonio de Guete; Fray Francisco Cimbrón; Fray Domingo de la Anunciación, prior of Santo Domingo; Fray Cristóbal de la Cruz; Fray Vicente de las Casas; friars of Santo Domingo; Fray Salazar, a Dominican; and Fray Miguel de Alvarado, guardian of the Augustinian order and relative of the brothers Ávila.[32] Let us consider for a moment one of the witnesses, defender of the accused, Fray Diego de Olarte, connoisseur of all things indigenous.

Fray Diego de Olarte, together with the better known Motolinía, wrote a letter to the Crown, in 1554, giving detailed information on the characteristics of the pre-Hispanic Indian nobility and the way in which indigenous people had brought tribute to their lords.[33] Furthermore, Olarte had been a soldier under Hernán Cortés throughout the conquest, having taken the Franciscan habit after that. That detail, as well as the fact that other members of his order had in fact been involved, earned Olarte the suspicion of himself having participated in the revolt. He was even called to Spain, where he had to justify his conduct. A sworn enemy of the secular clergy, he was fighting for a Church without bishops and, we may suppose, for total "spiritual" jurisdiction over the Indian people of New Spain, just what Hernán Cortés would have liked and just what the conspirators probably desired too.[34] As for the canon Chico de Molina, he was also a great friend of the Franciscans and the enemy of Archbishop Montúfar. The canon played a vital role in the conspiracy, as he was supposed to be the envoy sent to Rome to obtain the pope's blessing for Martín Cortés's dominion over New Spain.

As a reward, the canon was to have been made archbishop of the new kingdom.[35] The plan was for him to travel with "ships to Rome, carrying rich gifts," worth approximately 800,000 ducats, to remit to the pope in return for his anointment of the marqués as king. Passing through France, he was also to bring gifts "to forge an alliance with that kingdom" and the rebels. The half-brother of the marqués, Luís Cortés, and Alonso de Ávila had asked the canon to try to convince the marqués to "stop delaying" the launching of the revolt. At the same time, Fray Luis Cal and the very same Chico were to preach from their pulpits in support of the revolt once it was launched. One witness, Gonzalo Sánchez de Aguilar, even declared that, as he was riding through the main square, he met the canon who asked him if he knew anyone expert in the art of war, to which Sánchez asked if it was to wage war against the Indians or against the Spaniards, which was not the same proposition. The canon gave him the example of someone who would be able to repel an invasion by French troops.[36]

In the end, however, instead of the bishop's miter, all Chico managed to obtain was a rather dramatic end. Shortly after the revolt was crushed, he was sent as prisoner to Madrid, where he was tortured so much that he was left seriously disabled for the rest of his life.[37] The participation of the canon should not come as a surprise, especially in light of his arguments against the validity of the rights of the king over New Spain, all the more if the latter was unable to manage the land and treated his vassals badly. In that context, it is clear that, at the time, general ill will existed toward the monarch not only among the encomenderos but also within the religious orders and among the Indian nobility.

This unhappiness had its roots just a few years before in 1560, when a young and erudite Alonso Chico de Molina, who was not even thirty-five years old, was named canon of the cathedral by King Philip II.[38] Right away, almost from the very day he arrived in New Spain, he started having problems with Archbishop Alonso de Montúfar, just like the friars. In fact, starting with a theological discussion that took place during a conversation one night in September of that year, Montúfar and his assistant, Bartolomé de Ledesma, accused Chico of having Protestant ideas, and shortly thereafter he was denounced by Montúfar to the Inquisition. After several discussions with various theologians, the canon was forbidden to preach or to ever discuss theology publicly, but in spite of those charges, the Supreme Council of the Inquisition in Madrid soon forgave the polemical canon and in 1561 declared him absolved of any heresy.[39]

It is interesting to note that in the conflict with Montúfar, the canon received support from several Franciscans and Augustinians, especially from Fray Alonso de la Veracruz, who in turn was denounced by Archbishop Montúfar because of his tendentious writings against taxation of the Indians.[40] Other influential religious personages who publicly supported Chico de Molina included the Franciscan guardian Fray Diego de Olarte, the important Franciscan theologian Fray Juan de Focher (discussed below), as well as the prior of the Augustinian order in the city of Mexico, Fray Antonio Isidro.[41]

The time when the Dominican Montúfar was named archbishop and when he arrived in New Spain (1551–1554) came shortly before the great persecution on the Iberian peninsula of the movement initially launched by Erasmus, a persecution led by the inquisitor Fernando Valdés. Thus, the nomination of Montúfar may have been tied to that persecution. We might note that the first archbishop of Mexico had been, as a youngster, a protégé of Fray Diego de Deza, demoted in 1507 from his post of general inquisitor because of his harsh repression of the converted Jews.[42]

From the beginning of his time in New Spain, and in spite of his Dominican origins, the archbishop declared a merciless war against the members of the three religious orders present there.[43] Aside from those purely religious affairs, he also had personal interests to protect as, through his brother, he was the owner of rich mines in the area of Temascaltepec. He maintained those with alms received from pious merchants and miners, which should have been used to refurbish the small chapel dedicated to the Virgin of Guadalupe.[44] Indeed, this servant of God was quite a financial expert. The idea of augmenting the revenues of the royal domain through the taxation of the Indians was one of the reasons, in fact, that Philip II had pushed for his being made archbishop. The idea of taxing the Indians and saving money for the Crown must have caused a fierce polemic between the prelate and the friars from the three orders present in New Spain, especially the Franciscans, who staunchly opposed imposing new tributes on the Indians.[45] Many letters from friars accused the king in veiled terms of wishing to stop supporting the process of evangelization, some of them going so far as to remind Philip II that the titles and sovereign rights he had over the Indies were based on the work of Christian conversion of the original inhabitants of his colonies.[46] One can see the outcome of that discussion in the *Anales de Juan Bautista*, especially when the scribe mentions that there were days when Montúfar prohibited the opening of the church of the Franciscan convent while the friars still manifested their resentment against him.[47]

It is important to note also that the Crown itself imposed jurisdictional limits upon the friars through the power granted by royal patronage and also through the *fiscal* (prosecutor) of the audiencia of Mexico. One can clearly see that, just from 1560 to 1562, a great number of inquests and royal decrees were promulgated, as well as suits brought by the fiscal before the audiencia of Mexico, all of those proceedings directed against the friars, especially the Franciscans. For example, the Franciscan Fray Juan de Focher, one of the staunchest supporters of the canon Chico de Molina in his controversial dispute with the archbishop, not only spoke Nahuatl and wrote a grammar of it but was also often consulted to pass judgment on matters related to sacraments and other issues. Members of the three orders came to him regularly to clarify obscure theological points. Focher also wrote the *Tratado de Calimaya*, following which the archbishop named a secular priest in Calimaya and expelled the Franciscans, leading to destabilization among the Indians of that village. In that text Focher accused the archbishop of having violated the privileges of the regular orders as well as the decrees of the king and treated Montúfar "with great harshness and went as far as considering him as excommunicated, pending the Pope's confirmation."[48]

Similarly, in 1560 the Crown authorized an investigation into the public expenses incurred by the indigenous governor of Tepeaca. One of the accusations leveled against the governor was that he had placed a vast amount of native manpower at the disposal of the Franciscans for the construction of their monastery in that town.[49] That same year, an order came from Castile to punish the Augustinians of Ocuytuco, in the bishopric of Michoacán, for having used the Indians there to build a mill and for keeping a vast number of them working on treadle looms, all for the profit of the friars.[50] In 1561 the Augustinians were again brought before a tribunal, this time as a consequence of a claim they had made themselves: they asserted that some clerics had set fire to the convent in Tazazalca, in the bishopric of Michoacán, while the friars were inside.[51] Coincidentally, their claim was supported by none other than Álvaro Ruiz, who would later be the lawyer for Martín Cortés during his trial together with the encomenderos for the failed rebellion against the king.[52]

In 1562, the order of San Francisco also met with problems with the Crown, as in that year Archbishop Montúfar supported the request placed before the Council of the Indies by the encomendero of San Juan Teotihuacan against the friars of that province. They alleged that the friars were protecting the local *cacique* (ruler) and pressuring the Indians to abstain from paying their tribute. Some witnesses also declared that the friars had gone so far as to explain to the Indians during a mass that they did not have to keep paying tribute to any Spaniard or even to the king.[53]

The very same year of 1562, the inspector of the Franciscan order in New Spain, Fray Francisco de Bustamante, had to beg the Crown not to carry out an order of expulsion of various members of his order from the colony. The motive behind the decree was an accusation that those Franciscans had burned down the church in Cuitzeo in the bishopric of Michoacán. Bustamante alleged that they had done so only because the Indians of that locality had been ordered by the viceroy to congregate in the village of Aran and that they refused to obey in order to better pursue their idolatry.[54] Last, still in 1562, it was the Dominicans' turn. They were accused by the fiscal of the audiencia of not having followed the orders of the proper authorities, such as Archbishop Montúfar, and of having severely punished various idol worshippers from Titiquipaque, in the bishopric of Oaxaca.[55]

All those quarrels involving the religious orders of New Spain no doubt caused them severe political damage, and they are proof of the interest of the Crown in limiting the role of the friars among the Indian people. Those measures were strictly followed by the fiscal, and we need only point out that, before 1550, it is difficult to imagine that friars could have been summoned to appear before the audiencia because of their personal activities within their village posts or even for having prosecuted the cases of idolatry. Naturally, the friars deeply resented that change. It is thus not surprising that they allied themselves with the canon Chico de Molina against Archbishop Montúfar, in spite of the many threats of excommunication by the latter if they kept giving Chico their support, thereby causing upheaval among the population of Mexico City.[56] It was in this difficult context that some of the friars became radicalized, moving closer to the encomenderos in their intent to rebel against the Crown, as we shall see later. The hopes of the "party of the Indians," made up mostly of friars and some royal civil servants, were seriously impaired and we can still hear today echoes of their claims in the denunciation made by Fray Gerónimo de Mendieta in his *Historia Eclesiástica* and in various letters from the friars in which they criticized those royal policies that tended toward rejection of protection for Indian vassals. It is within this context that Alonso de Zorita wrote his *Historia de la Nueva España*.[57]

From the middle of the sixteenth century on, starting with the crowning of Philip II, several important political changes occurred in the capital, basically centered on the king's financial needs and in the interest he took in royal properties.[58] As a consequence of those needs, the Crown kept increasing taxes and tributes, which affected the finances and perceptions of the king by his subjects negatively throughout his various possessions. In some of those regions, people reached the stage of questioning royal authority, but not only in the American colonies. Between 1559 and 1577, the Crown kept raising the taxes levied against the cities in Spain itself. Delegates in the Spanish legislature refused to pay for the costs of running the royal house. Around the mid-1560s, the courts of Castile managed to oblige Philip II to consult them before raising taxes. This difficult situation was further exacerbated by urban riots, and in 1575 Philip II had to declare bankruptcy.[59]

The state of his patrimony drove Philip II to go so far as to promote the idea that the encomenderos and the Indians, in particular the indigenous nobles from New Spain and Peru, should offer a financial "service" to the king, buying in perpetuity the rights inherent in encomienda. The king himself proposed in 1563 that the indigenous nobility be able to present a bid to acquire those rights and thus free themselves from the encomendero authority. The proposal reached the Council of State via the bishop of Verapaz, the Dominican Pedro de la Peña, and consisted of requiring the Indians of New Spain to pay Philip II 2 million pesos over a period of five years in exchange for which the king would place all the indigenous towns under the direct authority of the royal Crown.[60] That proposal marked the highest point of the negotiations between the Indian nobles, in the name of their own people, and the Crown, even if between the two, acting as go-betweens, we find the friars.

As a consequence of the proposal, the Indian nobles computed the tribute they could afford to pay once their people were all under the royal umbrella. They also estimated the cost of the 2 million pesos divided among all the villages and individuals. Their agent in the matter was the aforementioned Dominican Pedro de la Peña. The negotiation was undoubtedly complex and lengthy.[61] We should not be surprised that a friar was actively promoting the project. It is more than probable that, in those times of political strife aimed at the religious orders, their members would have worked to push the offer of the Indian nobles. We even find in part of the report taken to Spain by the bishop of Verapaz that as far as the supervision of the execution of a number of points of the "contract" between the King and the people and Indians of New Spain was concerned, it was recommended that the supervisors would be a friar and the oidor Alonso de Zorita. However, the project seemed to imply that the Indians were going to be granted a certain degree of supervisory power over the villages, and that is probably the reason why the project ended up being rejected by the Crown. According to a number of authors, King Philip II was not thinking in terms of a sort of republic but rather of a patrimonial, hierarchical, and sacred structure.[62]

Within that context of political participation by the friars, it is not surprising that a number of them would come to be accused of involvement in the rebellion of the encomenderos and the Marqués del Valle. Thus, once the conspirators had been arrested in July 1566—during the trial of the marqués in front of the oidor Doctor Ceynos and the scribe Gordian Casasano—the cleric Ayala de Espinosa, one of those implicated in the conspiracy, presented a letter sent to him and signed by Fray Luis Cal, Franciscan guardian of the monastery of Texcoco, in an apparent gesture of repentance. On July 22, 1566, the audiencia sent an order to the provincial of the Franciscans, Fray Diego de Olarte, to arrest Cal. Apparently, the Franciscans were not the only ones involved in the great conspiracy, as on August 8, 1566, the prior of the Augustinians was informed that a friar from that order, Fray Josepe de Herrera, was also guilty of conspiring with the Marqués del Valle.[63]

Among the accusations levied against Cal, confessor of the Marqués del Valle, was that he had talked to Fray Diego Cornejo about the fact that there were people determined to rebel and that the inhabitants of New Spain thought badly of the king.[64] The Indians were angry because the king had raised the tributes imposed on them, and the Spaniards were angry because he was taking property and rights away from them, when in fact it was they who had conquered the land. Cal went into detail about how the friars and encomenderos would split New Spain among themselves and would send the pope sums of money to obtain recognition from him of whomever the encomenderos would choose as their new king. Cal also asserted that among the conspirators there were a number of "lettered gentlemen" who were imparting their advice on the legitimacy of expressing doubts about the rightful title of the Castilian Crown over America, since King Philip II did not govern New Spain "as a king but as a tyrant."[65]

In this context, the accountant and administrator of the cathedral, Cristóbal de Ayala de Espinosa, who was, as indicated earlier, one of the original members of the conspiracy, singled out the friars as being the main actors in the rebellion. Espinosa also declared that the marqués was the head of the conspiracy and that he wanted to keep New Spain and become its king, and that he, Espinosa, knew this from having seen the marqués and heard about him not only from his allies, friends, and parents but also "from his own confessor, Fray Luis Cal, as it is amply shown from what has been written about the rebellion." The same cleric affirmed that the Ávila brothers, perhaps owing to their delicate situation as prisoners because of the conspiracy, had denounced several friars as members of the cabal during their questioning.[66] The loquacious cleric also added that the priors of the orders had not taken enough care to punish the friars involved in the conspiracy, while Archbishop Montúfar had indeed punished the clerics caught up in the failed rebellion. And he ended his declaration by saying that even Fray Joseph de Herrera had "shamed himself from the pulpit" and pronounced sermons against the oidores.[67] In fact, he pointed out that the prelates of the orders had left the friars at liberty so they could keep on preaching against the oidores. Espinosa ended his testimony by declaring that the canon himself, Alonso Chico de Molina, had on several occasions called the royal general judges "heretics," his anger echoing that of the friars and the encomenderos against the highest representatives of the king.[68]

The fact that the same unhappy feelings held by vast segments of New Spain's population against the Castilian Crown were very much in existence at the same time in Peru provides important evidence about the politics of this period. Just as in New Spain, the origin of the discontent toward the king was a consequence of the policies limiting the power of the encomenderos over the Indians. In the case of some friars, the resentment centered on the catastrophic loss of population suffered by the Andean people and the excessive levels of exploitation imposed on them. However, it is clear that, both in New Spain and in Peru, encomenderos and Indians shared similar motives to distrust Philip II, and that in the case of New Spain one can even find common interest between friars and colonists against the king. But until recently, it was not as clear that part of the Indian nobility, especially in Mexico Tenochtitlan, might have been interested in participating in this rebellion.

HIGH-LEVEL INDIGENOUS POLITICS

Thanks to work of Luis Reyes, as editor and translator from the Nahuatl of the *Anales de Juan Bautista*, we can now try to explore that avenue. These annals long remained unpublished, with only an unpublished translation by the scholar Ángel María Garibay, as well as a short article on the subject by the same author, in existence.[69] The *Anales* provide the information that allows us to establish a probable link between the Indians of New Spain and the rebellious movement of the encomenderos. I should point out that this source covers especially the events occurring in the years 1560 to 1567. In the text we can find many references to the conspiracy and clues to the contacts that must have existed between some parts of the indigenous nobility and the conspirators.

For instance, the *Anales* mention the participation of the Indians in various religious and civil feasts together with the marqués, and they point to the military character of Martín Cortés as well as to his characteristics as lord. "Then on Tuesday the twenty-fifth of July of the year 64, the feast of Santiago was celebrated and the Spaniards went there. And Don Martín Cortés was carrying the blue cloth flag with the image of Santiago; Don Martín was wearing his armor. And also on that occasion they had bull-fights."[70] Similarly, the *Anales* mention that on January 14, 1565, the feast of the infant Jesus was celebrated and that there was a procession in the convent of San Agustín, in which the Indians danced. The scribe adds that there was a fiesta where again there were bullfights in the courtyard of the palace "with which they amused the Marquesa." They also say that on March 4 of that year, the Spaniards and the Indians went to greet the marquesa in Santa Fe, as she was returning from a stay in Toluca. They point out that "to receive her, they did as they usually do for the greeting of a king."[71]

Two days later the Indians of the four quarters of Tenochtitlan gathered together with their coats of arms in order to "receive the Marquesa." However, to prevent anybody from being hurt during the war and carnival games, it was decided that those games would be held in the marketplace. "The *ocelotl* [jaguar] and the *cuitlachtli* [wolf] were paraded in front of the Indians, Pedro Tzopilotl and his son José Clement were shooting firearms in the air. And where people were playing, a cleric came out [to playact] in front of the audience and he was parodying the bishop with his mitre. And when he started his satire in front of the people, all those who were playing walked away."[72]

But the *Anales* also points to difficult moments in the political life of New Spain directly related to the conspiracy. Thus it relates how, on July 16, 1566, the Marqués del Valle was arrested for his attempted rebellion, together with his half-brother Don Luís Cortés, Don Luis de Castilla, Bernardino de Bocanegra, Alonso Dávila, and Gil Dávila, and that "they were taken prisoners for having talked of war, and they were sent to the court." Once the conspirators had been arrested, the authorities gathered many weapons inside the government palace in the courtyard where they placed "Spanish military guards, and all armed themselves." The authorities also immediately called all the *alcaldes mayores* (chief executive and judicial officials of local communities) of New Spain to come before them to be interrogated about the rebellion.

> And they went to bring the Spaniards from Zacatlan, Michoacán,
> Pánuco, and Huaxyacac, to see if they knew anything, and they also

arrested the priests. And they placed a military watch to protect the archbishop as well as the lords [*tlatoque*] royal general judges, all were protected. And nobody could enter the palace and nobody could bring demands as the Real Audiencia was closed.[73]

The *Anales* also relates the executions of a number of the insurgents, saying that on August 3, 1566, "they decapitated Alonso Dávila, and his younger brother Gil González Dávila, and at the exact time of the Ave Maria they were put to death." It is also specified that the heads of the encomenderos remained on top of lances for six days "and on Friday night they took them down," the conspirators were buried in San Agustín, "and on the following day was the feast of San Lorenzo."[74] It is interesting to note that in the margin of the passage about the execution of the encomenderos the Indian scribe wrote "close the *tapanco* [*sic*]." The *tlapanco* was the upper part of a building, and the scribe may have been referring, in an obscure way, to something hidden or closed within the upper part of a construction.[75] We will come back to this passage at the end of this chapter.

The writer of the *Anales* at times seems to manifest a certain empathy with the conspirators. He mentions, for instance, that on November 6, 1567, the oidores arrested more conquistadors and "many *honorable Spanish persons*." The writer notes that "it was just an incarceration," implying, perhaps approvingly, that these had not been executed like the first ones.[76] This same source mentions the exile of the marqués, who was sentenced by three judges from Castile. "[T]hree of them arrived . . . one was the judge of the Marqués . . . and it was because Alonso Dávila had been executed for having talked about going to war."[77]

Finally, we should mention that in paragraph 418 of the *Anales*, we find the names "Juan Ponce de León[,] Don Ángel de Villafaña[,] Pedro de Ciruelo." Luis Reyes says that "the mention of those three sixteenth-century personages remains a mystery."[78] We may be able to shed some light on that enigma, mentioning that while Juan Ponce de León was one of the first conquistadors, contemporaneous with Hernán Cortés, a certain Luis Ponce de León was one of the conspirators accused of belonging to the cabal of the Marqués del Valle, so maybe that paragraph refers to that Luis rather than to Juan. On the other hand, Ángel de Villafaña, apparently a wealthy Spaniard, was keeping one of the participants in the rebellion imprisoned in his house, a certain Francisco de Reynosa, whose supposed mission would have been to take the city of Puebla.[79] Of Pedro de Ciruelo we know nothing.

The difficulties incurred by the Indian population because of the tax reforms of Philip II were undoubtedly one of the major reasons for the interest the Indian nobility had in participating in the proposed rebellion. At that time, the Crown refused any possible reduction in the taxes paid by the indigenous population, exemptions were greatly limited, and the number of potential contributors to the tribute paid to the Crown was increased. The tribute was to be individualized and standardized, eight *reales* [one peso] and half a measure of maize per taxable individual.[80] As was to be expected, the reforms to the tax system that the visitador Jerónimo de Valderrama tried to implement were opposed by the Indians and, as we have seen, also by the friars. The nickname that Valderrama earned for pushing those reforms was "afflicter of the Indians." The visitador, however, managed very quickly, in 1563 and 1564, to have all the Indian villages inspected and accounted for. In the case of Mexico Tenochtitlan, the Indians who before that paid neither goods nor monetary tribute had, starting with his visit, to pay 20,178 pesos and 10,589 measures of maize. Such an increment made the average Indian unable to pay any tribute whatsoever to the Nahua lords or the native nobility.[81]

At first the local authorities of Tenochtitlan tried to negotiate with the royal envoys and to avoid the implementation of the tax reform. Mostly their advisors in the matter were the friars at large, and not only the Franciscans. A number of Franciscans from the local convent discussed rebellion against the Crown's decision to increase the tributes to their noble followers and to prevent the possibility that the macehuales should stop tilling the ancestral lands of the Indian lords. From their pulpits, the friars encouraged the Indians to pray to be saved from the imposition of tribute until negotiations with the audiencia took place. In this context, the *Anales* mentions that Pedro de Gante in 1564 accompanied a number of Indian authorities when they went to plead in favor of the Indians of Mexico Tenochtitlan before the audiencia, arguing that they already contributed with their participation in public works as well as by providing grass and fodder. The petition presented to all the auditors asked to exempt the Indians from paying any tribute, whether goods or money.[82]

Some of the discussions the friars had with Valderrama were explained in detail to the Indians in church. For instance, the *Anales* mentions that the guardian of the convent in Mexico, Fray Melchor de Benavente, explained that he mentioned to Valderrama that the Indians from Mexico Tenochtitlan could not pay the required tribute since they did not own land for agriculture and that they were instead contributing with their labor in public works as well as by providing hay and fodder. On top of that, they also helped the friars in the convent. But, as the guardian told the engrossed Indians, the inspector affirmed that they only would have to pay the tribute and not the rest.[83]

The native authorities, tired of not receiving any answer to their demands about the tribute and in spite of their negotiations with the Crown's representatives, ended up choosing not to answer the order from Valderrama to come together so he could tell them about the new taxes. As shown in the *Anales*, Valderrama called Fray Melchor de Benavente one Saturday in July and asked him, seeing as how he was well informed about the *altepetl* (city-state), to notify the Indians about what they were to contribute. He also asked him about the governor, the alcaldes, and *regidores* (another kind of cabildo member), accusing them of not obeying him and of turning a deaf ear to his repeated calls to order.[84] The negotiations were more and more centered on that subject, as the Crown had indeed decided to apply the new tax policy. For instance, this was the only subject of discussion in one of the Franciscans chapters held in Xochimilco. In order to better draw up a plan of action, Fray Miguel de Navarro asked the Indian authorities in Mexico on August 18, 1564, to take a petition to the Franciscan chapter in Xochimilco, where it would be mentioned that the Indians could only pay four *tomines* (a *tomin* equaled one-third of a peso). They were to give the petition to the provincial of the order so that the friars would be able to defend that position in front of the Spanish authorities, especially the archbishop Montúfar. Navarro also told them that if those authorities did not make a decision, the friars would appeal to the king and talk about the matter with Philip II himself.[85] The provincial, apparently in favor of reducing the tribute, declared at the end of the meeting and in clear reference to the inspector Valderrama that

> whoever mocks the people, let him not be given any charge. Be him viceroy or visitador, if he does not assume his charge in truth, if he afflicts anyone with anything, he is very close to hell, he belongs in hell. He will then be sent to hell, there to be locked forever and remain prisoner. He will never get out unless he repays for the suffering he has caused the people, etc. Let us pray the Lord with a Pater Noster and an Ave Maria so He will listen to me.[86]

Shortly thereafter, toward the end of September 1564, Fray Alonso de Molina, famed author of the *Vocabulario en lengua castellana y mexicana*, told the indigenous authorities of Mexico that they should not worry: a committee of friars had gone to Castile "to discuss with your lord, the emperor" about the tribute problem, assuring them that if the king would not listen, they would go to see the pope in Rome, and urging them in the meanwhile to have patience.[87]

Aside from these problems, the friars seem to have been negotiating with the Indian craftsmen of Mexico, such as the tailors, to prevent them from manipulating the elections of the Indian authorities and thus seriously damaging the political influence of the nobility.[88] In all of these dealings, we see that the friars met with the rebelling groups, one after the other, in order to advocate for the Indian nobles. This group of craftsmen was ready to put their demands before the noble authorities of the community, and they also tried to get the friars to be their mediators. "The tailors, who had quarreled about the altepetl . . . later went to talk to the priest of Santo Domingo, named Diego de Toral, and they told him that in what referred to their community they had not seen justice done as they wished in their hearts."[89] For the Indian nobles of Mexico Tenochtitlan, the craftsmen were in large part responsible for the tribute increases, partly because they earned good salaries for their work:

> Today January 21, 1564, the oidores came to the palace, sent by the inspector and the viceroy. They were sent so that we would pay tribute to the emperor. Thus it was said that each person was going to pay a tribute of one peso and one measure [on quahuacalli] of maize. And they impose a tribute on us in this manner because of those who caused problems, thus it was said to the lord [tlatohuani], the tailors, the carpenters, the quarry workers that every week they were earning four pesos, they all said the same. And for that reason we all got taxed and each one of us has to pay a peso and a measure of maize every year.[90]

The indigenous nobility resented both the imposition of tribute and the way their authority was being limited. We find support for this in the way craftsmen tried to garner the posts of authority within the community. In the midst of all this, the nobility and the friars severely reproached the royal authorities. We know this happened especially when the friars preached to the Indians. Furthermore, on other occasions, the friars had already been accused of talking only of politics from their pulpits to the Indians, going so far as telling them when the king suffered a defeat in one of his war campaigns.[91] This exchange of information between friars and Indians is important, and in order to better understand its impact, we must look at the fundamental importance that oral discourse had for Indians, in this case for the Nahuas, before the conquest.

For the Nahuas, and in general for Mesoamerican populations, the word had a vital and symbolic force. A key to Mesoamerican thought processes resides, according to Gary Gossen, in the extraordinary power of spoken and written language as a symbolic entity in itself, beyond its neutral role as medium for routine communication."[92] We know that the friars not only preached traditional sermons from their pulpits but they discussed political actions, events were commented on, and plans were made to better the delicate situation in which the Indians found themselves, in this case because of the proposed increase in tribute.

Most of the attacks of the friars were directed against Jerónimo de Valderrama, who, as mentioned earlier, was the royal authority designated to implement the new tax structure. He had a very negative opinion of the friars, as well as of the native lords. His correspondence with the king shows a clear will to limit both the privileges and political role of both groups.[93] The death of the viceroy Luís de Velasco in 1564, who clearly mediated between the royal interests and those of the indigenous nobility and who was an authority who was close to the friars, left all groups without any clear political support. And this opened the door to the protests both of the friars and of the natural indigenous leaders.

The Dominican Fray Thomas Chavez, for example, compared Valderrama during one of his sermons to the devil inspiring kings to increase their fiscal domain.[94] This was a clear reference to the policy that would render the tribute payable by individuals and impose the tribute on those Indians attached to the lands of the Indian nobles, who until then had been exempted. Indeed, that policy aimed at making tribute payers of the nobles themselves. Other friars, in a more discrete manner, mentioned Philip II in reference to the abrupt decrease in the Indian population throughout the land. Fray Jacinto de San Francisco, for example, wrote to the king, saying that "he was crying tears of blood" at seeing how the Indians "have perished from such hard labors," many of them without any teaching of the faith, all because of the increase of the royal taxes. As Carlos Sempat Assadourian has written, the fiscal pressure on the Indians had serious consequences because it eroded the economic basis for the power of local chiefdoms.[95]

There is much evidence in the *Anales de Juan Bautista* of the desperate fight by the nobles of Mexico to prevent the application of the tribute increase. As explained earlier, the urban population paid only through service in public works. The authorities of Mexico Tenochtitlan, also as seen earlier, tried to defend themselves against the tribute in the viceregal court. However, during the negotiations held with the audiencia, the Indians could clearly see that this was a lost cause. The oidor Ceynos, for instance, told them to pay the tribute. He remarked that perhaps they did not remember they used to pay tribute to Motecuhzoma, giving up their own sons for the sacrifices to the ancient gods.[96]

Another time, the nobles of Mexico Tenochtitlan reproached Ceynos, saying that justice was "seeing" only one side, not taking into account the "sufferings" endured by the Indians because of the tribute they had to pay. Ceynos answered abruptly, telling them to bring their tribute, which, in fact, "was not very much, just one peso and three tomines." He also mentioned that the nobility and governor would also have to pay. Unfortunately, and in spite of the efforts exerted against it, the tax policy was slowly hardening. On May 13, 1566, it was decided that young men and women should also pay tribute. That position became official on March 15, 1567, through a proclamation given in the marketplace. Upon hearing that, the Indians from the four quarters wrote a petition to the authorities trying to prevent that sector of the population, until then exempted, from having to contribute.[97]

But without any doubt, the person most affected by the proposed changes to the tribute policy was the governor of Mexico Tenochtitlan, Don Luis de Santa María Cipac, the last of the lineage of indigenous rulers of Mexico. It is clear from the *Anales* that his successor, also coming from the lineage of the lords of Mexico, never managed to become governor of Tenochtitlan, because he fell victim in 1566 (the year of Martín Cortés's conspiracy) to a political ploy of other Indians, who denounced him to the audiencia. They accused him of having committed incest, which the authorities seized as a pretext to invalidate his quest for the governorship. That action prevented the original nobility from keeping power.[98] Shortly before that, in 1564, the governor Santa María Cipac had contracted a matrimonial alliance with the daughter of the descendants of the royal house of Tlatelolco. The wedding is mentioned in the *Anales*, which describes various dances and songs done to celebrate that occasion.

> On that Sunday of June 4, 1564, there was a procession . . . [i]n the atrium of Santo Domingo. Thus the governor Don Luis de Santa María got married there, the one he married was Doña Magdalena Chichimecaçihuatl, daughter of the late Don Diego; preaching was done for them and they were blessed twice, top and bottom. As they were bringing the lady [*cihuapilli*] they played wind instruments in the temple and on the way over, as they were arriving they also were playing wind instruments. Arriving at the palace, at the foot of the stairs, the people from the church [*teopantlaca*] and the singers stood there and sang to her. And once she was inside, then they started to dance, first they interpreted the *chichimecayotl* [about the Chicimecs] and then they started the *atequilizcuicatl* [about water pouring] and the lord [*tlatohuani*] in person danced. And then they painted his drum [*ihuehueuh*], they gilded it. Lords [*tlaloque*] and nobles [*pipiltin*] had come from all the villages. And in the huts outside of the palace, there were the ancient soldiers [*quahuehuetque*] and in their homes, the Otomis danced during two nights.[99]

It is interesting to note that several songs mentioned in the *Anales*, such as the ones quoted earlier, also appear in the *Cantares Mexicanos*, for example, the song of chichimecayotl as well as the atequilizcuicatl. Some of these songs refer to bellicose themes, for instance, the name *quahuehuetque* was given to the ancient soldiers and the term "Otomis" refers to an "order of horsemen."[100]

The singing of those songs during the wedding of Santa María Cipac, member of the lineage of Tenochtitlan and last lord of royal blood to govern, was not done just to entertain the audience. The songs had an important symbolic content for the Indians who listened to them, and they transmitted a message specifically centered on the greatness of the native kings and lords as well as the ritual importance of war. Those elements carried a traditional meaning, one of resistance, just at the time when the Tenochca were threatened by strong fiscal pressures and when their governor was seeing his power of negotiation with the colonial authorities on this subject seriously diminished.

I should also mention that the *Cantares* was written around 1585, but that the songs were collected among native informers between 1550 and 1570.[101] In that sense, the *Cantares* and the *Anales* are contemporaneous, but this is not the only coincidence, as the contents of the *Anales* deal at length with various feasts and songs that the Indians celebrated and sung on distinct religious and civil occasions. These were still linked to the idea of power, in this case colonial power, but also with clear reference to the authority of the ancient *tlatoque* (rulers) of Mexico. "Today, Sunday fourteenth of April of 1566, they painted all the Mexican tlatoque, all those who ruled during the time that the empire [*tlatocayotl*] lasted. On a cloth, they painted them, together with the arms of the emperor. Any and all of the governors were standing on top of a nopal." As for the *Cantares*, its inspiration, according to Bierhorst, was the indigenous tlatoque.[102] In spite of the fact that the songs of both sources contain obscure metaphors, in both we find echoes of native kings and of war songs. Such echoes seem to transmit messages of resistance and of desire for a return to the old and traditional indigenous order.

We should also consider the messianic movement led by a "macehual" named Juan Teton around 1560. Of that movement we know only what is alluded to in the *Anales*: it seems that Teton lived in Michmaloyan and convinced several Indian inhabitants from Atlapolco (Atlapulco in the state of Hidalgo) and from Cohuatepec (which I have not been able to identify) that the end of days was fast approaching when "the count of the days will be tied, darkness would fall and the *tzitzimime* would come and eat us and then a transformation of the people would happen."[103] The tzitzimime were terrifying creatures who killed men and devoured them.[104]

Juan Teton was warning people that all baptized Indians would suffer a terrible transformation: for example, those who would eat the meat of a cow, a pig, or a sheep would turn into a cow, a pig, or a sheep, respectively, and even those who used *ayates* (a kind of blanket) made of wool would become sheep themselves. Those threats had to do with the end of a cycle of fifty-two years, when the normal order would be thrown into disarray. Juan Teton's threat was directed specifically at those among the Indians who had accepted the European customs, including the food, clothing, and any other form of material culture alien to traditional indigenous practices. As a way of preventing that from happening, Teton offered to wash the head of the Indians, which would erase the sign of baptism, and advised them to jealously guard maize and the paper from the earth, *amate*, among other natural products.

One thing that should be stressed, in the context of all these events, is that the marriage of the governor Santa María constituted the last occasion when the government of Mexico Tenochtitlan and Tlatelolco was in the hands of descendants of the ruling dynasty. In Azcapotzalco, the governor, Don Antonio Cortés Totoquihuaztli, was also directly linked to the nobility of Tlatelolco and was the descendant of the lords of his *altepetl* (city-state), who also were the subjects of laudatory songs in the *Cantares*.[105] The fact that the descendants of the legitimate nobility of Mexico, Tlatelolco, and Azcapotzalco were governing during the time of the attempted rebellion of Martín Cortés helps explain the interest manifested by Santa María in abetting a new king, the marqués Martín Cortés, to govern with the support of the legitimate rulers. But in spite of his lineage, the governor Santa María Cipac was in a difficult political situation vis-à-vis his subjects. On various occasions, he had gone to see members of the audiencia to appeal the new tribute policy but without any success.[106] When, finally, he refused to pay the tribute, Valderrama ordered on September 27 that he be thrown in jail, together with the alcaldes, regidores, and other native authorities.[107]

The situation was dire for Don Luis de Santa María Cipac. On July 13, 1564, Don Luis Santa María, accompanied by all the local authorities, had to announce the amount of the tribute to his people in the *tecpan* (palace) of Mexico Tenochtitlan. The *Anales* underlines the indignation of the people and shows them starting a revolt for that reason. The tecpan was deluged with stones, and the people tried to attack their governor, calling him a coward and shouting that his attempts at negotiating an agreement with the oidores and Valderrama had brought only misfortune and humiliation. They reminded Santa María Cipac that they, the people of Mexico, did not own any land, and asked from where they were going to produce the money necessary to pay the new tribute, which was set at one peso and four tomines annually.

> Where will we take it from? And all the ancient women started to cry and to get very angry. And a man, a neighbor from Amanalco called Huixtopolcatl, said: Who is talking? Is it Tlilancalqui? Or maybe it is Quauhnochtli? Or maybe Ezhuahuacatl? What is happening to that little vassal? Who does he think he is? And the people were shouting every time more. They were saying: Is it that the lords, the governors who came to take care of the people asked for something that now they want to impose on us, that tribute? What would those men, the lords, have said, when the altepetl was vanquished, when we were conquered? Did Quauhtemoc ever go out and beg? Did he say anything? They said many words.[108]

Trouble was only averted because several encomenderos arrived on horses, but mostly because Don Martín Cortés, the mestizo son of Doña Marina and Hernán Cortés, managed to appease the crowd. Here we have to wonder what Don Martín was doing so close to the tecpan of Mexico Tenochtitlan, and especially at that most opportune moment. We must remember that Don Martín Cortés, the mestizo, was one of the most faithful followers of his half-brother in the conspiracy. Can it be that he had arrived to observe the reaction of the people of Mexico when told they were going to have to make the new tribute payments to the king? Whatever may be the case, it is interesting that this mestizo son of Cortés and Marina should make himself so well respected by the Indians and thus help control the revolt against the governor Don Luis de Santa María.[109] Shortly thereafter, the friars suggested to the nobles and the authorities of Mexico Tenochtitlan that they should send a few friars to negotiate the annulment of the new tax policy. They also suggested that they could even reach the pope himself to prevent the enactment of the tax policy of Philip II.

The idea of communicating with the pope related to the role of the celebrated friar Bartolomé de las Casas, as defender of the Indians, who tried to prevent the tax policy by all means, even going as far as presenting his case to the Council of the Indies. We should also remember that it was he who, at the same time, supported the attempt by the *kurakas* (native rulers) of the Andes to buy the rights to the encomiendas from Philip II. In New Spain that role was taken up by his great friend and collaborator, Fray Pedro de la Peña. Las Casas forcefully developed the idea of restitution: how giving back lands and domains to the Indian nobles would help the king to avoid suffering punishment in the next world as his power over the Indies had no legitimate basis.[110]

CONCLUSION

Let us return to what was happening to the governor of Mexico, Don Luis de Santa María Cipac. He was caught between a rock and a hard place, as he had no way of convincing the authorities to ease up on the payments, while his own people had tried to stone him and rebelled at the news of the new tribute. The Spanish authorities did not have any respect for his status and all his attempts at negotiating with them to prevent the application of the tribute had been in vain. To make matters worse, the friars who had been negotiating together with the Indians to avoid paying the tribute were everyday becoming weaker politically within the immediate circle in the court of Philip II. Furthermore, the possible rebellion of Martín Cortés was on the verge of being discovered.

The *Anales* mentions that in May 1565, a few months before the arrest and jailing of the rebellious encomenderos, Don Luis Santa María Cipac went up to the roof of his house, armed with his sword and shield, fought all night long against invisible enemies, shouting what sounded like war cries "like he was possessed." In the end, exhausted, he let himself fall from the roof. "In the morning, the land was silent, so preoccupied by what had just happened," and shortly thereafter, he died.[111] It is worth remembering that when the *Anales* mentions the execution of the brothers Ávila, active participants in the marqués's conspiracy, there is a note in the margin: "close the *tlapanco*." It was on the high part of the house, from the terraced roof, a tlapanco perhaps, that Don Luis Santa María fought his last battle. One cannot help comparing the scene in which Don Luis was fighting with the death of the emperor Motecuhzoma, stoned and falling from the terrace where he was standing, dead perhaps at the hands of his rebellious people, themselves rendered desperate by their surrender to the Spaniards.[112] Don Luis Santa María Cipac also decided to die from a terrace, but he died fighting. Yet in the end, just like Motecuhzoma, he dropped from a roof. Thus, the last lord of Mexico, descendant of the legitimate lords of that land, who had ultimately become mere vassals, left the ground free for the victorious king, Philip II, to do as he pleased.

The stories collected in the *Anales* show that any intention to wage war against the monarch remained at the stage of mere omens:

> A tornado rose from the heap of earth at the foot of the largest church, there was a great flash of lightning and it was as if a weapon had been discharged. Thus the people saw how the earth was opening its jaws. And when the tornado was ebbing, the Spaniards were saying that Motecuhzoma was emerging. And, following his own path, he arrived at the place where the market was held, and a black man tore off his clothes and threw them into the water. And, coming back, he went to

where the excavation was made in the earth, and there, the wind dissipated over the mound of earth.[113]

This passage is interesting because there are numerous stories in contemporary Mexico that mention the disappearance and return of the *tlatoani* (Nahua supreme ruler), Motecuhzoma. There are ethnographic accounts from all over Mesoamerica about this. In most of them the central personage is a king, known as Moctezuma or Montezuma, who has supernatural powers, and he is the patron of humanity. This king possesses the universality of the civilized, he knows all languages, and he gives name to all things. He gives the land, he can link to an Indian group or to a single community by creating his geographical surroundings, and he gives rain to his people, assuring the harvest, protecting his sons from illness, or punishing them for wrongdoing. He is the son of an unknown father and is borne under miraculous conditions. He hides from this world vanquished by unnatural means, and in order to save himself, he penetrates the earth with his army. When needed by his people he will reappear.[114] In that last passage from the *Anales*, the author says that the Spanish were afraid that Motecuhzoma "was emerging," that is, reappearing. Maybe as the prophecy that the contemporary Indians mention, the anonymous scribe of the *Annals* was thinking that the moment of war had come, the moment for rebellion against the king of Spain was about to begin.

Through these pages I have tried to explain that important groups of Indians and Spaniards felt deep discontent over the king's policies in this epoch. In this particular case I have described how the Indians of Mexico City tried to avoid the imposition of tribute. I proposed the hypothesis, based especially on the *Anales of Juan Bautista*, that perhaps the Indians of Mexico Tenochtitlan, specifically the indigenous nobles, were interested in the project of some encomenderos to make New Spain an independent kingdom ruled by the son of the conqueror Hernán Cortés, Martín Cortés. It is important to note that in this new kingdom the Indian nobility was to have played an important role. In this context this Indian nobility may have been motivated to look with special interest on the plan to rebel against Philip II of Castile.

NOTES

1. Natalia Silva Prada, *La política de una rebelión, los indígenas frente al tumulto de 1692 en la Ciudad de México* (México DF: El Colegio de México, 2007).

2. Eric Van Young, *The Other Rebellion: Popular Violence, Ideology, and the Mexican Struggle for Independence, 1810–1821* (Stanford, CA: Stanford University Press, 2001).

3. Juan Bautista, *¿Cómo te confundes? ¿Acaso no somos conquistados? Anales de Juan Bautista*, ed. and trans. Luis Reyes García (México DF: CIESAS and Biblioteca Lorenzo Boturini y Nacional Basílica de Guadalupe, 2001), 184. This chronicle, probably composed in the 1560s, was attributed to a Juan Bautista, but the true author remains unknown.

4. Discussions about encomienda can be found in Silvio Zavala, *La encomienda indiana* (México DF: Editorial Porrúa, 1973); Simpson, *The Encomienda in New Spain*; José Miranda, *El tributo indígena en la Nueva España durante el siglo XVI* (México DF: El Colegio de Mexico, 1980); and Ethelia Ruiz Medrano, *Reshaping New Spain: Government and Private Interests in the Colonial Bureaucracy, 1531–1550* (Boulder: University Press of Colorado, 2006).

5. Manuel Orozco y Berra, *Noticia histórica de la conjuración del Marqués del Valle: Años de 1565–1568; Formada de nuevos documentos originales y seguida de un estracto de los mismos documentos* (México DF: Edición del Universal, Tipografía de R.Rafael, 1853), 22.

6. Ibid., 37.

7. Ibid., 37–39.

8. Orozco y Berra, *Noticia histórica* (see the introduction). For months, Orozco y Berra pored over all the material dealing with the acquittal of the conspirers through their trial, documents that are today in the Harkness Collection, at the Library of Congress in Washington, DC, but at the time he consulted that abundant source in the nineteenth century, they were held in a private collection.

9. A large part of the information regarding this event can be found in the Archivo General de Indias (hereafter, AGI) Patronato 203, no. 6, "Proceso general contra Martín Cortés." The trial is made up of nearly 2,185 folios (or 4,370 pages) in the Library of Congress's Harkness Collection, Washington, DC. It is also narrated in part in the chronicle of Suárez de Peralta in Juan Suárez de Peralta, *Tratado del descubrimiento de las Indias: Noticias históricas de la Nueva España*, preliminary note by Federico Gómez de Orozco (México DF: Secretaría de Educación Pública, 1941 [1588]), chaps. 29–39. Also see Orozco y Berra, *Noticia histórica*, and Luis G. Obregón, *Rebeliones indígenas y precursores de la independencia Mexicana: En los siglos XVI, XVII y XVIII*, 2nd ed. (México DF: Ediciones Fuente Cultural, 1952), 127–204.

10. Bautista, *¿Cómo te confundes?* 149

11. AGI Patronato 203, no. 6.

12. Zavala, *La encomienda indiana*; Simpson, *The Encomienda in New Spain*; James Lockhart, "Encomienda and Hacienda: The Evolution of the Great Estate in the Spanish Indies," *Hispanic American Historical Review* 49 (1969): 411–429; Francois Chevalier, *La formación de los latifundios en Mexico* (México DF: Fondo de Cultura Económica, 1982); Ethelia Ruiz Medrano, "Las primeras instituciones del poder colonial," in *Gran historia de Mexico ilustrada*, coord. Bernardo García Martínez, 4 vols. (México DF: Planeta DeAgostini-CONACULTA-INAH, 2002), 2:41–60; and Ruiz Medrano, *Reshaping New Spain*.

13. María Justina Viejo Sarabia, *Don Luis de Velasco, virrey de Nueva España, 1550–1564* (Sevilla: Escuela de Estudios Hispano Americanos, 1978).

14. A number of the Dominicans swore during their questioning that they had been the confessors of the Ávila brothers before they had been executed and that, in the instant just before his death, Alonso de Ávila had acknowledged the existence of a plot. Other friars, also under oath, mentioned they had seen a letter from the Marqués del Valle in which he gave detailed instructions for the uprising. Most of them also involved some Franciscans in the revolt, but it is strange that all the Dominicans who were interrogated seem to have been aware of the conspiracy headed by the marqués, but none of them before their questioning thought of denouncing the plot. See Obregón, *Rebeliones indígenas*, "Como apéndice: Información practicada en noviembre de 1567 por los jueces pesquisidores D. Alonso Muñoz y D. Luis Carrillo," 194–204.

15. AGI Patronato 203, no. 6, which gives the testimony of Francisco Morales, a scribe, who relates that for the rebellion they will be supported by people who would come from Peru, "[p]eople who had rebelled in that kingdom."

16. There is talk of the manufacture of "bombs" by a certain Pizarro, a man from Peru, who was supporting the revolt of Cortés in Obregón, *Rebeliones indígenas*, "Como apéndice," 203–204.

17. Library of Congress, Harkness Collection, Mexico; Document XV: July 1566, April 1567, "Proceso general contra Martín Cortés," in Orozco y Berra, *Noticia histórica*, 39–41.

18. AGI Patronato 203, no. 6, testimony of Alonso de Aguilar.

19. Ibid., testimony of Cristóbal de León.

20. Ibid., testimony of Alonso de Aguilar.

21. Library of Congress, Harkness Collection, Mexico, Document XV, July 1566, April 1567, "Proceso general contra Martín Cortés"; Orozco y Berra, *Noticia histórica*, 39–41.

22. AGI Patronato 203, no. 6.

23. Library of Congress, Harkness Collection, Mexico, Document XV, July 1566, April 1567, "Proceso general contra Martín Cortés"; Orozco y Berra, *Noticia histórica*, 39–41.

24. Orozco y Berra, *Noticia histórica*, 42–43.

25. Ibid., 45–52.

26. *Tira de Tepechpan: Códice colonial procedente del Valle de Mexico*, ed. Xavier Noguez, 2 vols. (México DF: Instituto Mexiquense de Cultura, 1996 [1500s]), 2: illus. 18.

27. Bautista, *¿Cómo te confundes?* 149.

28. Ibid., 163.

29. Orozco y Berra, *Noticia histórica*, 45–52, 59–61.

30. Ibid., 45–52.

31. Orozco y Berra, *Noticia histórica*, 57; AGI Patronato 212, no. 1, "Proceso contra Alonso Chico de Molina."

32. AGI Patronato 203, no. 6.

33. Georges Baudot, *Utopia and History in Mexico: The First Chroniclers of Mexican Civilization (1521–1569)* (Boulder: University Press of Colorado, 1995), 54.

34. Ibid., 303.

35. Ibid., 62, 67, 304–305.

36. AGI Patronato 212, no. 1, testimony of Gonzalo Sánchez de Aguilar.

37. Obregón, *Rebeliones indígenas y precursors de la independencia Mexicana*, 188; Magnus Lundberg, *Unification and Conflict: The Church Politics of Alonso de Montúfar OP, Archbishop of Mexico, 1554–1572* (Sweden: Lund University, 2002), 191.

38. AGI Patronato 212, no. 1, confession of Chico de Molina.

39. Richard E. Greenleaf, *La Inquisición en Nueva España siglo XVI*, 3rd ed. (México DF: Fondo de Cultura Económica, 1995), 161.

40. Ibid., 136–137; regarding the support he gave to Alonso Chico de Molina, 160.

41. Ibid., 157–158.

42. Ethelia Ruiz Medrano, "Los negocios de un arzobispo: El caso de Fray Alonso de Montúfar," *Estudios de Historia Novohispana* 12 (1992): 63–83.

43. Robert Ricard, *La conquista espiritual de Mexico*, 4th ed., trans. Angel Maria Garibay (México DF: Editorial Jus, 1947); Georges Baudot, *Utopia and History in Mexico*; ibid., *La pugna franciscana por Mexico* (México DF: Alianza Editorial-Conaculta, 1990).

44. Ruiz Medrano, "Los negocios de un arzobispo."

45. AGI Justicia 158; in 1556, a royal query about the subject concerning whether Indians must pay tithe, 444 fols. Montúfar's project is clearly expressed in several letters. See Archivo de la Real Academia de la Historia, Madrid, Colección de Don Juan Bautista Muñoz, ms. vol. 70, A-115: 1556 letter from Montúfar and the other bishops to the king, about taxation of the Indians, fols.12–33v, as well as another letter dated November 25, 1556, from the bishop of Tlaxcala, in which he denounced the fact that the three orders were getting ready to write against the prelates because of their desire to tax the Indians, a subject about which they "are not in the right." Also see Archive of the Real Academia de la Historia, Madrid, Colección de Don Juan Bautista Muñoz, ms. vol. 70, A-115: 1556 letter from Montúfar to the council, about the taxation of the Indians. In that letter the archbishop affirms that, via an order of 1543, taxation of the Indians was authorized, to be done in wheat, silk, and cattle. Also see AGI Indiferente General 2978, in which there are a great number of letters and court orders dealing with the question of the taxation of Indians. Most of these were sent to the Crown by friars of New Spain, and some treat the same subject regarding the viceroyalty of Peru. Some have been published and analyzed by Georges Baudot in *La pugna franciscana por Mexico* (México DF: Alianza Editorial-Conaculta, 1990).

46. Some of these letters can be found in *Códice Franciscano*, ed. Joaquín García Icazbalceta (México DF: Editorial Chavez Hayhoe, 1941 [1500s]); AGI, February 16, 1564, information about a sermon preached against the King; Greenleaf, *La Inquisición en Nueva España siglos XVI*, 142–143.

47. Bautista, *¿Cómo te confundes?* 189–191.

48. *Códice Franciscano*, siglo 16, 24–25, and 31.

49. AGI Justicia 205, no. 1.

50. Ibid., no. 3.

51. AGI Justicia 161, no. 1.

52. Orozco y Berra, *Noticia histórica*, 322.

53. AGI Justicia 1029.

54. AGI Justicia 206.

55. AGI Justicia 279.

56. Greenleaf, *La Inquisición*, 56.

57. Fray Gerónimo de Mendieta, *Historia eclesiástica indiana*, 3rd ed. (México DF: Editorial Porrúa, 1980 [1596]); Alonso de Zorita, *Relación de la Nueva España*, ed. Ethelia Ruiz Medrano, 2 vols. (México DF: CONACULTA, 1999 [1585]).

58. Modesto Ulloa, *La hacienda real de Castilla en el reinado de Felipe II*, 3rd ed. (Madrid: Fundación Universitaria Española Seminario "Cisneros," 1986), especially chaps. 24 and 25.

59. Charles Fago, "Philip II and the Cortes of Castile: The Case of the Cortes of 1576," *Past and Present* 109 (1985): 25–43.

60. Archivo de Simancas, Valladolid, Spain, Estado, exp. 114, nos. 267–269.

61. Ibid.

62. Jaime Contreras, "Dios, casa y reynos: Felipe II; Católico pero no romano," unpublished ms.

63. AGI Patronato 203, no. 6, "Proceso general contra Martín Cortés."

64. Orozco y Berra, *Noticia histórica*, 151

65. AGI Patronato 203, no. 6, "Proceso general contra Martín Cortés."

66. Orozco y Berra, *Noticia histórica*, 151–152.

67. Ibid.

68. Ibid.

69. Ángel María Garibay K., "Un cuadro real de la infiltración del hispanismo en la alma india en el llamado 'Códice de Juan Baustista'; Dos Conferencias sobre Transculturación," *Filosofía y Letras* 9 (1945): 213–241.

70. Bautista, *¿Cómo te confundes?* 202

71. Ibid., 299, 307.

72. Ibid., 309.

73. Ibid., 149.

74. Ibid., 151.

75. Ibid. In the right margin written horizontally is the text *"celar el tlapanco."* See also note 32 of that text, in which it is explained that *celar* ("to close") in Spanish also means *esconder* ("to hide") and *guarder* "to keep."

76. Ibid., 163, emphasis added.

77. Ibid., 165, 167.

78. Ibid., 331n172.

79. Orozco y Berra, *Noticia histórica*, 45–52; Obregón, *Rebeliones indígenas*, 201.

80. Ulloa, *La hacienda real de Castilla*, 704; also see note 86 below.

81. Miranda, *El tributo indígena*, 133–139.

82. Bautista, *¿Como te confundes?* 283, 289–290.

83. Ibid., 201, 203.

84. Ibid., 201.

85. Ibid., 201, 203.

86. Ibid., 237.

87. Ibid., 255, 257.

88. One can find parts of that quarrel referred to in a publication by Luis Chávez de Orozco, *Códice Osuna* (México DF: Ediciones del Instituto Indigenista Interamericano, 1947 [1565]). We should note, however, that this subject is actually extraneous to the *Códice Osuna*, since the latter primarily deals with pictographic denunciations made by the Indians against various royal offices during the visit of Jerónimo de Valderrama.

89. Ibid., 139.

90. Ibid., 185–187.

91. Ruiz Medrano, "Los negocios de un arzobispo"; Letter from Jerónimo López to the emperor Charles V in Francisco del Paso y Troncoso, *Epistolario de Nueva España*, 16 vols. (México DF: Biblioteca Histórica Mexicana de Obras Inéditas, 2nd ed., Antigua Librería Robredo de José Porrúa e Hijos, 1939–1942), 4:166–167.

92. Quoted in Louise M. Burkhart, *The Slippery Earth: Nahua-Christian Moral Dialogue in Sixteenth-Century Mexico* (Tucson: University of Arizona Press, 1989), 12.

93. France V. Scholes and Eleanor B. Adams, *Documentos para la historia colonial de México (Cartas del Licenciado Jerónimo de Valderrama y otros documentos sobre su visita al gobierno de Nueva España, 1563–1565)*, vol. 7 (México DF: José Porrúa e Hijos, 1961). Also see AGI México 92, letters for his Majesty from the Licenciado Valderrama, inspector of the audiencia of Mexico and of the commissioners who took care of the rebellion (the latter refers to the conspiracy or rebellion of the Marqués del Valle) from 1563 to 1568.

94. AGI México 281, report on a sermon against the king, February 16, 1564.

95. *Códice franciscano: Siglo XVI*, 221; Carlos Sempat Assadourian, "La despoblación indígena en Perú y Nueva España durante el siglo XVI y la formación de la economía colonial," *Historia Mexicana* 38, no. 3 (1989): 425–426.

96. Bautista, *¿Como te confundes?* 239, 241.

97. Ibid., 267–268, 147, 169.

98. Ibid., 155: "And again there was dancing outside of the palace and there was a *palo volador* [flying pole]. And when he was going to be installed as governor and he was going to start his term as public servant with the palo used by the voladores, but they caused his ruin, Don Pedro de la Cruz, Don Martín Ezamallin, Don Luis Huehueçaca, Don Lucas Tenamaz and Don Antonio Momexicaitohua, thus they went and said in the superior [court] that Don Pedro Dionisio, who wanted to be governor, had lain with Tlaco, his stepmother, and also he had had a son from his younger sister and for that reason he was prevented, it could not be done."

99. María Castañeda de la Paz, "El plano parcial de la Ciudad de México: Nuevas aportaciones en base al estudio de su lista de *tlatoques*," in *Símbolos de poder en Mesoamérica*, ed. Guilhem Olivier (México DF: Instituto de Investigaciones Antropológicas, Instituto de Investigaciones Históricas, UNAM, 2008), 393–426; Bautista, *¿Cómo te confundes?* 197, para. 156.

100. John Bierhorst, *Cantares Mexicanos: Songs of the Aztecs* (Stanford, CA: Stanford University Press, 1985); Bautista, *¿Cómo te confundes?* 197nn84–87.

101. Bierhost, *Cantares Mexicanos*, 9.

102. Ibid., 22.

103. Bautista, *¿Cómo te confundes?* 157, para. 43.

104. The tzitzimime are nocturnal demons that arrive at the end of a cycle of fifty-two years to devour mankind. "Tenth Chapter, wherein is described the disposition of those who kept watch when the new fire appeared"; "Nevermore would the sun come forth. Night would prevail forever, and the demons of darkness would descend, to eat men"; Fray Bernardino de Sahagún, *Florentine Codex*, trans. Arthur J.O. Anderson and Charles E. Dibble (Santa Fe, NM: School of American Research and University of Utah Press, 1977 [1569]), 7:27.

105. Castañeda de la Paz, "El plano parcial de la Ciudad de Mexico"; Bierhost, *Cantares Mexicanos*, 22 and Canto 36, 207.

106. Bautista, *¿Cómo te confundes?* 211–213.

107. Ibid., 253.

108. Ibid., 215, 217. The Nahuatl terms refer to the names of the first authorities of the Aztec government.

109. Ibid., 219.

110. Henry Raup Wagner, *The Life and Writings of Bartolomé de las Casas* (Albuquerque: University of New Mexico Press, 1967), 209–240.

111. Bautista, *¿Cómo te confundes?* 318.

112. This passage about the conquest is to be found in various sources. I cite Zorita, *Relación de la Nueva España*, 1:581–582. I thank Prof. Guilhem Olivier for pointing out the similarity between these two passages.

113. Bautista, *¿Cómo te confundes?* 316.

114. Alfredo López Austin, "Los reyes subterráneos," II Congreso Internacional de Cultura Maya, manuscript, 12–13, n.d.

EDWARD W. OSOWSKI

Indigenous Centurions and Triumphal Arches

Negotiation in Eighteenth-Century Mexico City

Annual Catholic festivals marked cycles of time during the history of the viceroyalty of New Spain. For the indigenous residents of the valleys of Mexico and Toluca, the season beginning with Semana Santa, Easter Holy Week, and ending with the festival of Corpus Christi was a sustained period of holiday, feasting, celebration, and, as this essay will explain, political negotiation with Spanish rulers in Mexico City. In eighteenth-century documents one encounters the strange image of people of Nahua ethnicity, as well as those of African heritage, dressing in the costumes of Roman soldiers during Holy Week processions and all-night vigils. The symbolism of these masqueraders, who were called *armados* (soldiers) or centurions, had deep historical origins in post-conquest sixteenth-century New Spain and in the mythology of Catholic conversion.

In the worldview of many living during the colonial era, indigenous people dressing in breastplates and plumed helmets, with spears in hand were not donning an ironic disguise. Instead, the outfit was a sign of the universal triumph of Christianity, which was annually celebrated from Holy

Week to Corpus Christi. Like the ancient Romans, who had been pagans, albeit empire-building heathens, the Nahuas too were once nonbelievers with an impressive civilization. And like the Roman soldier who stood at the foot of the Christ's cross on Good Friday, the Nahuas also converted to the "true" faith. In the eighteenth century, *cabildos* (indigenous municipal governments) stationed armados at representations of Santo Entierro (the Tomb of Christ), hoping that the vigilant soldiers would signal to the rest of New Spain that the native elite made a good-faith effort to be patrons of Catholicism. The native elite also had an interest in coordinating aspects of the annual Corpus Christi celebration in Mexico City in order to ideologically justify their existence within the Spanish colonial order.

Juan Pedro Viqueira Albán writes that the most important and largest public festival in eighteenth-century Mexico City was Corpus Christi. Papal bull and royal decree required the presence of every class, ethnic group, guild, *cofradía* (lay religious organization), and government and ecclesiastical official. The festival represented the ultimate triumph of Christ over death, Satan, and non-belief through the miracle of the transubstantiation of the Eucharist.[1] Celebrations lasted eight days and culminated in a massive procession with the communion host. Starting from the side door of the cathedral, a giant procession of people marched through the streets of Mexico City, eventually returning to the cathedral through the front entrance.[2]

Officials from rural indigenous town councils brought contingents of people who walked from their homes in the Toluca Valley, the Valley of Mexico, Tula, and Cuernavaca, and on the day before the procession, they built triumphal arches or covered the streets with branches and flowers. In 1615, Juan de Torquemada claimed that there were "more than a thousand" elaborate "triumphal arches" under which the procession marched.[3] From 1777 to 1780 there was an average of 297 decoration spaces, many of them with arches in the street. Each space represented a *cabecera*, a head town where the municipal council met, and its *pueblos sujetos*, subject towns.[4] The order of appearance of the native towns as marked by the arches was a public display of municipal status. The arches covered the streets of Mexico City's wealthiest commercial and residential districts located in the *traza*—the Renaissance grid of streets legally, but not in reality, reserved for Spaniards.[5] The traditionally Nahua communities of Texcoco and Xochimilco, which had been officially designated as cities, occupied the highest-status positions in front of each of the two cathedral doors. Communities with the less-important categorization of *pueblo* were further away. The two most important indigenous city councils, however—San Juan Mexico City and Santiago Tlatelolco—were conspicuously absent. Rather than building the arches, their city council members and the indigenous *interprete general*, the salaried interpreter general of the Juzgado General de Indios (General Indian Court), coordinated the construction and enjoyed the privilege of marching in the procession.

In this essay, I focus on the impressive resourcefulness of indigenous leaders who benefited from symbols of Hispanic Catholic triumph when they bargained with the ruling institutions of late colonial New Spain. Mexico City was the heart of Hispanic hegemony in the viceroyalty of New Spain, but from within it, the two indigenous city councils were not powerless. I argue that throughout the eighteenth century, native leaders forced officials in Spanish governmental institutions to negotiate with them on how they would draw sufficient numbers of indigenous participants to the festivals. The indigenous leaders who organized their people to take part in the two urban festivals thus exercised considerable local power despite the imperial symbolism of the celebrations. Although the law obligated native people to attend these celebrations, they, in reality, wanted to participate because it empowered them. The state did not have to coerce them to be there.

This essay about religious rituals involves the issue of political negotiation because the people of eighteenth-century New Spain held that politics and religion could not possibly be separated. Only Christians had rights and protection under Iberian law. The Spanish world considered the possession of the "true" faith the fundamental requirement for the political legitimacy of the indigenous leaders who were known to have descended from pre-conquest nonbelievers.[6] Ambiguity about the indigenous people's proper place in the religious and political life of New Spain meant that residents would always have room to negotiate. There were two contradictory visions of social order grounded in religious legitimacy at work. On the one hand, all Christians were in harmony when they lived under the rule of the universal Catholic monarchs, spiritually equal in the Body of Christ. On the other, the legal institution of the two legal republics, the *república de indios* and the *república de españoles*, required Christians to have separate legal duties and oppositional privileges.

Representatives of the two republics thus struck bargains when they organized the urban festivals together. Imagine the two parties making a contract to accomplish this shared goal. Both sides desired indigenous participation but each party needed it for different reasons. Indigenous communities made public that they were making a good-faith effort to be loyal Christians when they constructed Corpus Christi arches and staged costumed reenactments of the burial of Christ during Holy Week. Indigenous people wanted to publicly assert their Christianity because their legal rights literally depended on it. Spanish society was often skeptical about the strength of the faith of native people, and so the indigenous people often loudly proclaimed it through ostentatious festivals as proof of their faith. Native governments had legal rights as the separate legal sphere of the república de indios, and when members of the institutions of the república de españoles violated these rights, the indigenous people aggressively appealed to the Juzgado General de Indios. República de indios was synonymous with the indigenous municipal council. Essentially, when indigenous municipal governments defended their organization of Catholic rituals, they protected their political autonomy and authority over their people.

The people of the república de españoles needed indigenous participation in Catholic rituals and so were willing to negotiate with them. If the triumphal arches and centurions were to successfully represent the universal victory of Catholicism in the world, then the native people of the Americas needed to be represented in the street theater of Easter week and Corpus Christi festivals. Thus, European rulers were dependent on indigenous leaders to deliver the community participants so necessary for the symbols to work because of historical circumstances revealed in the eighteenth-century history of the organization of Corpus Christi arches and Holy Week masquerades.

THE PROCESS OF NEGOTIATION OVER INDIGENOUS BUILDERS OF TRIUMPHAL ARCHES

The historical circumstances of three time periods during the eighteenth century required indigenous organizers of Corpus Christi celebrations to do their best to respond to colonial demands, legally enforced religious obligations, and urban epidemics. The result was that the indigenous city councils of San Juan Mexico City and Santiago Tlatelolco, along with the interpreter general, treated Corpus Christi as a festival of revenue, social status, and town-council authority. Ironically, Spanish officials had been partially responsible for encouraging indigenous councils to make demands of native labor, which, as a result, reinforced local indigenous municipal authority. During the first period, between 1731 and 1748, the Church and Spanish officials challenged the councils to make the arches fit new standards of decorum. The second period began in 1776, when, acting through the Juzgado General de Indios and Spanish *ayuntamiento* (the Spanish city council), Viceroy Antonío María de Bucareli y Ursúa (1771–1779) criticized the native leaders' pattern of organization as corrupt, but, in fact, the urban councilmen had coordinated builders of the Corpus

Christi arches to meet Spanish demands. In the third period of the 1790s, the councilmembers of San Juan and Santiago managed to maintain their power via the organization of people and resources for Corpus Christi; however, the more aggressive viceroys of the time challenged native corporate power over festival labor to an even greater degree.

During urban epidemics and famine-producing droughts of the early 1730s, San Juan and Santiago closely guarded their duty to shade the Body of Christ from the intense sun, with San Juan acting as the most important patron city council. They were objectively the main authorities that could mobilize the indigenous population, and the Spanish ayuntamiento depended on them to deliver. During a *matlazahuatl* (probably typhus) epidemic in 1731, the Spanish city council appealed to the leadership of San Juan to convince their people to attend Corpus Christi. The ayuntamiento ordered San Juan to enlist the help of municipal council officials from subject pueblos who helped collect royal tribute and the alms for saints: alcaldes, *merinos*, and *padrotes* (community officials). The Spanish ayuntamiento communicated to San Juan its awareness of how the epidemic had completely taxed the native population of the region. Realizing that the procession would be a failure without the arches, it requested the presence of the people of San Juan, despite the great sacrifice. The epidemic made two things clear to the Spanish and Indian city governments. First, arch construction depended on significant numbers of native participants that the population within the confines of the city could not fully supply. Second, the already-existing power structure of the council of San Juan had to be utilized and allowed free reign to mobilize the indigenous population.[7] San Juan reinforced its status as the only native council strong enough, in dire times, to come through for one of the most important religious events of the Christian calendar.

Although during the plague year the Spanish and indigenous municipal councils banded together out of necessity, rivalries between the two councils erupted two years later. On June 3, 1733, the day before the Corpus Christi procession, solicitor of the Indians in the Juzgado General de Indios, Don Juan del Campo de Velarde, appeared before Don Joseph de Padilla y Estrada, the *corregidor* (district magistrate) of the Spanish ayuntamiento. Campo represented the urban indigenous leaders who complained that the palace guard had interfered with their exclusive privilege to build arches along San Francisco Street. He reminded the Spanish city council that this violated the king's decree that stated that only the Indians could shade the host, a copy of which Don Joseph had personally dispatched to his clients. During the day of construction, a group of soldiers had taken over the work, directly violating the rights of the Indians. Apparently, it caused quite a scandal because at this late hour, on the eve of the great procession, the solicitor of the Indians had assembled twelve leaders as witnesses to testify to this violation.[8]

Don Joseph used the opportunity to lecture the twelve that they were not following their obligations diligently. He accused the indignant men of being ignorant of their duties and lazy in fulfilling them, and, hence, the interdiction of the soldiers was likely a planned tactic to force the issue of poor coverage of the streets by the Indians. Padilla reminded them that the arches were supposed to stretch from the doors of the cathedral near the altar that open out onto the great cobblestones of Tacuba Street, following along Santa Clara and then over San Francisco Street, leading into the principal door of the church. The magistrate complained that during the previous year the arches had barely covered the street. He lectured them that the shade roofs must be tightly woven with flowers, and not just be made of old *petates* (woven mats) and a few tree branches disgracefully thrown together. Padilla emphasized that the *indio principales* (prominent Indians eligible for municipal councils) of each cabecera must know exactly what part of the street that they were supposed to cover. The twelve leaders all responded emphatically that they did not need to be reminded of their obligation to decorate, but many of them also admitted that they did not know that each subject town belonging to their cabeceras was supposed to build its own arch.[9]

Several years later, the Provisorato de Indios y Chinos, the ecclesiastical tribunal and regulatory agency separate from the regular Inquisition, also complained about what it viewed as disgraceful coverage. The ecclesiastical tribunal held the municipal councils of San Juan and Santiago directly responsible for the poor quality of the arches. In 1748, the unnamed *provisor* (ecclesiastical magistrate) used the Spanish ayuntamiento to lodge a complaint against San Juan and Santiago. The Spanish ayuntamiento in turn presented the provisor's complaint to the "deputies of the festival," who were specifically named as the *gobernadores* of San Juan and Santiago and the interpreter general Don Patricio Antonio López.[10] The high church official was offended by the arches' shoddy construction and held the two top municipal officials of San Juan and Santiago personally responsible. He complained that the Indians constructed coverage that was so poor that sunlight was pouring onto the route of the communion host. The structures looked less like austere and triumphant arches than the crude curtains that could be seen on country houses.[11]

In another conflict in 1751, the councils of San Juan and Santiago acted jointly to assert their rights over jurisdiction, each claiming extensive authority as two *parcialidades* (large districts of confederated urban and suburban Indian communities). San Juan aggressively fought against the Real Colegiata de Guadalupe (the College of Canons of the Sanctuary of Guadalupe), which wanted to take charge of nearby indigenous labor for its own arches. In 1733, the cabildo of Santiago Tlatelolco had lost its jurisdiction over the indigenous people who lived in the settlement around the Guadalupe shrine.[12] This loss of jurisdiction to the Villa de Guadalupe contributed to the altercation between San Juan and the Real Colegiata. Prior to the upcoming festival in 1751, the members of the Real Colegiata petitioned the Spanish ayuntamiento to be given the right to enlist people to build arches. Their reasoning was that they did not have the numbers of native parishioners required to construct them for their own church of the Colegiata. They proposed to enlist the help of the native parishioners of the Villa de Guadalupe, San Cristóbal Ecatepec, Santa María Magdalena, Tlapaltitlan, San Bartholomé, San Andrés, Cuautepec, and San Miguel Chalmita. The Spanish municipal government responded by sending a representative to deliver the request to a meeting of the gobernadores of the parcialidades of San Juan and Santiago.

The interpreter general and gobernadores of Santiago and San Juan admonished the Spanish ayuntamiento and Colegiata for their pretensions and sternly instructed them on the festival jurisdictions of the parcialidades. They claimed that any native people in the area of the Villa of Guadalupe were under the jurisdiction of the gobernador of Santiago Tlatelolco. Tlatelolco also had authority over San Cristóbal Ecatepec and its thirteen subject pueblos. Six of the communities that the Colegiata requested directly belonged to San Cristóbal Ecatepec. San Juan claimed jurisdiction over Santa María Magdalena and all its surrounding barrios. The interpreter general claimed that each of the communities had its own gobernador (meaning they were no longer legally bound to Tlatelolco's cabildo) but that each owed a *pension* (payment) of six to eight pesos to San Juan and six pesos to Santiago. The interpreter also had the right to collect fees from Ecatepec in the amount of twelve pesos. Technically, the gobernadores of San Juan and Santiago were to use the money from these fees to pay for the arches and flowers that they spread along the pavement of the street. The native leaders reported that the remaining pueblos requested by the Colegiata de Guadalupe were under the jurisdiction of the interpreter general. The interpreter stated that he was not likely to release them because he had to cover more than 1,500 *varas* (1,252.5 meters) along the procession route in Mexico City's traza.[13] The interpreter then claimed that it would be impossible to comply with their obligation without the six pueblos attached to Ecatepec that had been requested by the Colegiata de Guadalupe.[14] In the end, they conceded the rest of the pueblos to the

Colegiata, but the interpreter warned that withdrawing festival labor from Ecatepec would harm the authority of the cabildos of San Juan, Santiago, and the subordinate one in Ecatepec. He even went so far as to dramatically predict that it would be impossible for the municipal government of Ecatepec to function without the subject pueblos.[15] From the perspective of the native elite, control over the people and resources of Ecatepec was more than just a matter of festival organization; it was a matter of saving face as municipal authorities in the urban councils.

The councils of San Juan and Santiago further expressed how important the privilege was to their authority in their response to the obligation of Corpus Christi during the period of great epidemics from 1784 to 1787. In April 1786, San Juan and Santiago were the only communities to commit scarce resources and precious labor during a time of terrible drought. This was a considerable sacrifice for the two communities and the city as a whole. The interpreter general wrote to the Spanish ayuntamiento that the state of emergency required that every native work on growing food crops for relief. Because of dwindling food reserves, the natives of the pueblos could not afford to come to the city for Corpus Christi. The interpreter general reported that the two governments would fulfill the Indians' obligation by building the arches from the principal door of the church to the mouth of San Francisco Street.[16]

The Corpus Christi records of the proceedings of the Spanish ayuntamiento of Mexico City clearly demonstrate that the city councils of San Juan Mexico City and Santiago Tlatelolco were the main organizers of indigenous participants from the city and surrounding towns. But the documents are also evidence that the festival preserved more ancient indigenous political organization. Following a precedent that the Nahuas most likely established in the mid-sixteenth century, the city council of San Juan was ranked higher than its partner council of Santiago. This may have originated in the pre-conquest Mexica municipal pattern of hierarchically arranging the rotation of tribute and political authority. This ranking is apparent in eighteenth-century petitions from the two Nahua communities delivered through their lawyers to the Spanish ayuntamiento. Spanish officials always listed, according to order of importance, the two communities as the "Parcialidades de San Juan y Santiago."[17] The superior status of San Juan over Santiago was annually reinforced through their joint organization of Corpus Christi arches and their authority over the rural town councils that they enlisted.

Spanish demand for indigenous participation in the festival from the 1730s to the 1780s ensured that urban native rulers exercised independent political authority over indigenous residents, but by the 1770s, reformist

Spaniards thought this power was unacceptable. The numbers of indigenous participants may have increased during the century. In 1733, Corregidor Padilla of Mexico City admonished San Juan and Santiago for not sufficiently covering San Francisco Street. Therefore, we can assume that his admonition signifies low attendance or lack of enthusiasm. From 1777 to 1780, officials of the Spanish ayuntamiento and audiencia no longer scolded the indigenous cabildos for poor coverage but, instead, complained of too much participation. Information collected from 1777 to 1780 was compiled during the ayuntamiento's investigation of the public disturbance caused by the large numbers of rural natives in the capital. Because of incomplete records of attendance, it is impossible to determine conclusively if there was an increase in the number of rural participants during the eighteenth century. The data from this period indicates an average of 1,000 indigenous builders of the arches. This is roughly the same figure that Torquemada reported in *Monarchia Indiana* (1615).[18] One can speculate that the actual numbers of builders was low in 1731 compared to 1615 but then returned to the seventeenth-century level by the 1770s. Other evidence indicates that the actual number of indigenous people from surrounding areas in attendance was greater than 1,000. For example, a 1776 report places 2,000 *macehuales* (Spanish for Nahuatl *macehualtin*, commoner Indians) at a banquet celebration, in addition to an estimated 100 honored guests from rural and urban indigenous councils. Finally, Viceroy Bucareli complained that San Juan and Santiago were demanding participation of towns far beyond the legally established distance from the city. These distant towns most likely increased the numbers.

On May 31, 1776, six days before the large procession, the corregidor of the Spanish ayuntamiento reported the disruption caused by the great multitude of indigenous people who came to the capital to build arches. He complained that, after building the arches, participants had sullied the decorum of the city with their grave immorality. He also thought that their participation caused needlessly suffering because their poverty was exacerbated by the money that they spent at the festival. These poor people came walking unreasonably long distances to the capital at great expense to themselves and their families. Another city council member, Don José Gonzales Casteñeda, proposed bold measures to prevent this from happening during that year's upcoming event. As Don José saw it, the most pressing problem was the fact that the governors of San Juan and Santiago were abusing their positions by requiring people to come even when they could not afford it. More significantly, he accused the governors of exacting *derramas* (involuntary contributions) from anyone in attendance.[19]

The Spanish city council had commissioned San Juan to supply the participants from the rural areas with materials free of charge once they arrived. Customarily, the Spanish council gave San Juan and Santiago 180 pesos to pay for the building materials and flowers, but the gobernadores of San Juan and Santiago pocketed the money and then charged derramas for building materials. A representative of Viceroy Bucareli accused the Nahua councilmen of full-scale corruption. He exclaimed, "We can be sure that the Indians that work on the decoration of the arches do not see one real of the 180 pesos that [the Spanish ayuntamiento] gives to the gobernadores of the two parcialidades and to the interpreter general."[20]

When the rural participants instead brought along their own materials, it created a great mess in the streets. One can imagine up to 1,000 people assembling arches with thatch and branches, which they carried through the already notoriously congested streets of Mexico City. Each town brought along chickens and lambs as payment to the interpreter general, which created further pandemonium. More often, rather than bringing their own cumbersome material, participants were forced to buy the materials from San Juan, Santiago, and the interpreter general. An official from the regular Inquisition calculated that during the 1777 processions, poor participants had paid a total of 600 pesos for wood and *petates* (mats) for the arches. Also, delegations from surrounding rural towns paid the interpreter general and the cabildos an additional amount of 666 pesos for the rights to cover the streets and build shades (*pies derechos y cielos*) that would span 1,882 varas (1,571.5 meters) of street and use 1,880 wooden beams (*morillos*).[21] San Juan and Santiago exacted other kinds of specialized derramas in order to harass certain communities that wanted to participate. As evidence, the authorities pointed to how the governors of Santiago Tlatelolco would not allow their own parish of Santa Ana to participate unless they paid a flower tribute. Other gobernadores demanded that towns furnish derramas of the building materials themselves, and they did not pay for these materials with cabildo funds.[22]

In the opinions of the viceroy's officer and the Spanish ayuntamiento, the most conspicuous sign of the gobernadores' abusing the macehuales was the great banquets that the native leaders enjoyed during Corpus Christi. A memorandum from the 1776 celebration gives us a vivid depiction of the Nahua banquet scene that was divided along class lines. That year San Juan and Santiago each took 60 pesos out of a Spanish ayuntamiento fund of 182 and the builders never received the remaining 62 pesos, which disappeared. The councils held an expensive breakfast and lunch on the day of the major procession, but not everyone ate the same quality and portions of food. In the minds of the Spanish officials, this was an example of the despotism of the indigenous gobernadores. While the indigenous notables ate soup, meat, fine bread, and sweets two times that day, the 2,000 macehuales each received only one tamale, a little piece of peasant bread (*pan baso*), and a small portion of honey. The interpreter general's behavior was viewed as being particularly offensive. On the day of the banquet all of the participants brought tribute of chickens, a few turkeys, and money to the house of the interpreter general. During the banquet of 1776, the interpreter general received 150 to 200 hens and 100 pesos from the participants. Not all of the goods were consumed on that day. The memorandum states that the "ancient interpreters" also generally made a profit from the fowl, many of which were roosters that could be used for breeding. Finally, the interpreters had been raising the numbers of participants to a level that was higher than acceptable because recently they had been requiring that even more towns participate. The 1776 report states that they were requiring the attendance of towns that were between sixteen and twenty leagues away, such as Tulancingo, Pachuca, and Cuautla de Amilpas, which violated the legal limit of fourteen leagues.[23] In 1777, an official from the Juzgado General de Indios reported that even more cabeceras outside of the official fourteen-league mark were included in the interpreter general's call to attend. The official discovered Cuernavaca, Cempoala, Ixtlahuaca, and Guazcasaloya on the list but could not prevent them from coming that year because of time constraints.[24]

Viceroy Bucareli's agent recognized in the 1728 Real Ordenanza that the interpreter general cited in the dispatches encouraged poor natives to participate. According to the viceroy, this was the first step toward their great personal hardship. He stated that it was not the lowly natives who were the source of the problem: "All this is done in the name of the decorum of our city and is not caused by the vulgarity of the Indians." He did, however, accuse the indigenous leadership of taking advantage of this royally sanctioned obligation. Under the "guise of honor" of complying with the king's commands, the governors were abusing their own sad people.[25] The two most powerful indigenous cabildos of Mexico City were exacting obligations from native communities. Bucareli condemned the rulers from the surrounding native communities for draining their community chests of resources in order to pay for the privilege of having their towns participate in the festival.[26] On April 16, 1777, Bucareli issued an edict to the gobernadores of San Juan and Santiago that asserted that the Spanish ayuntamiento of Mexico should be the only patron and mayordomo of the decoration. His main strategy for controlling the monetary abuses of the cabildos was to assert royal patronage through the authority of the Spanish ayuntamiento of Mexico.

The revelations of corruption set in motion a period of attempts at reform between 1777 and 1790. The interpreters general were increasingly criticized by the viceroys as having too much independence from the Spanish ayuntamiento. Bucareli and Revillagigedo attempted to reduce the interpreters' power by ordering the Spanish ayuntamiento to keep better watch over their activities.[27] The year 1787 marks a change in the policy of utilizing the interpreter general to organize the indigenous communities. In that year the Spanish ayuntamiento deprived the interpreter general of his privileges to send the dispatch to surrounding native towns. They defied custom when the Spanish corregidor issued the summons personally.[28]

Bucareli intended to set a new precedent for the regulation of arch construction. However, the details of the reform plan speak of the difficulties of putting the domination of the Spanish ayuntamiento into practice. The Spanish council was now to be in charge of electing the deputies of the festivals, but only upon approval of the Nahua city councils. Also, he proposed that the Spanish council would take over measuring the decoration spaces and keep track of compliance with the fourteen-league rule. The Spanish ayuntamiento was charged with preventing the towns outside of the jurisdiction from coming to the capital. But it appears that Bucareli's plan was not wholly effective. In 1780, the dispatch decreeing strict adherence to the fourteen-league rule was still being sent out, but the attendance request list contradictorily included Cuernavaca and Yautepec, which the previous viceroy had complained were outside the limit.[29]

Even though Viceroy Bucareli tried to stop Nahua municipal officials from directing the organization of Corpus Christi, in the end, Bucareli had to compromise over the issue of indigenous leadership. Instituting these changes would still require retaining the interpreter general, whose monetary interests and political loyalty remained with the indigenous municipal councils. The viceroy needed the interpreter to measure the decoration spaces, mediate negotiations among arriving rural delegations who jockeyed for high-status positions in the streets, and coordinate lesser native officials to oversee the construction of the arches.

Bucareli and the Spanish city council soon realized that they had to compromise their reform plans in the interest of maximum coverage of the street and maintaining order among the towns. Bucareli halfheartedly asserted that the precise measurement of the street would lead to equality instead of corruption among the pueblos. In principle, San Juan and Santiago would be forced to comply with the wishes of the Spanish town council, which was formally in charge of the measurement. Once again, the reality was different. Bucareli did not completely abolish the *repar-*

timiento (forced purchase) of food and materials exacted by San Juan and Santiago on the surrounding pueblos.[30] Instead, the Spanish town council was to fix the repartimiento so that it was an equal rate for all pueblos. This was intended to diminish the status of San Juan and Santiago as the greatest beneficiaries of the sales because they had charged variable rates, with higher prices for higher-status decoration spaces. Bucareli encouraged the Spanish town council to monitor who the two parcialidades selected as alcaldes and merinos in order to prevent them from spending festival funds on orgiastic pulque parties.[31]

Regarding the interpreter general's power, Bucareli merely "suggested" that the Spanish town council abolish his collection of food tribute during Corpus Christi. He called this tax "extortion" because it prevented poorer towns from participating when they could not afford the payment.[32] On the other hand, his reservations about completely abolishing the system indicate that he understood the necessary but implicit relation between large-scale indigenous participation and the power of the interpreter. The Crown desired maximum participation by native people and the most decorous coverage possible, but this depended on how energetic the interpreter general was in organizing. Bucareli ultimately realized that the interpreter general's power lay in having extensive control of the festival labor.

What is more, indigenous leaders bargained for maintaining the status quo by playing on the viceroy's fears of the breakdown of civil order. Before the great procession in May 1777, Don Laureano de Aguila and Don Lazaro de la Peña, gobernadores of San Juan and Santiago, respectively, along with their alcaldes and merinos, who acted as deputies of the procession, urgently responded to Bucareli's call for reform. San Juan, Santiago, and the interpreter general issued a combative joint petition in Spanish that demonstrated the solidarity between the two indigenous councils. The indigenous officials asserted that maintaining customary patterns of organization was vital to the political stability in their urban communities as well as in native towns in the rural areas. They insisted that they could not fulfill their duty of decoration for the glory of the capital without the help of the *pueblos foráneos* ("foreign" rural towns). The indigenous city councils claimed that the only way they could manage the construction was to require that each pueblo and barrio pay for the privilege. Most importantly, San Juan and Santiago insisted that the political union of the two depended on their customary collection of the payment. They warned the Spanish ayuntamiento and viceroy that it would be "impossible" to withdraw this custom, because without it, "they will not honor their ancient obligation that they see as the hereditary privilege of their ancestors and the two parcialidades might never come together as one."[33]

They further stated that they did not need the Spanish ayuntamiento to tell them how many people were needed to decorate. In fact, they claimed that no one could limit the numbers of indigenous people who came because they could never dampen the immense enthusiasm for the honor that they would gain through attendance. Therefore, the gobernadores explicitly stated that there was a connection between the political stability of the rural communities and procession attendance.

The city council officials of San Juan and Santiago believed that they needed to negotiate to preserve their coordination of indigenous labor during Corpus Christi because they believed it was essential to their political authority. The arches communicated to two audiences the message that the men in the city councils were legitimate leaders, either Spanish authorities in the Juzgado General de Indios, Real Audiencia, and Provisorato de Indios or indigenous council members from rural towns around Mexico City.

Regarding the Spanish audience, the city councils of San Juan and Santiago capitalized on the fact that they had the legal duty to mobilize municipalities under their jurisdiction and rural towns with independent cabildos. By royal decree, only people of the legal category of "indio" were permitted to decorate the streets with arches of flowers and branches for the Corpus Christi celebration. Both the Spanish and the indigenous city councils took the obligation seriously, but for different reasons. The Spanish ayuntamiento and viceroys understood the primary importance of the Indians' compliance as submission to their authority, whereas the native elite treated the duty as an opportunity to exercise independent authority. Submitting, as good Catholic rulers must, indigenous leaders gained legitimacy with European colonial rulers, which aided them in maintaining authority as local representatives of the king.

The arches were intended for an indigenous audience as well. San Juan and Santiago reinforced the political traditions of the participating rural town councils by giving them the opportunity to send officials to the high-status festival in the capital. As Table 4.1 indicates, the fact that rural town councils did not send their lowest-ranking officers indicates that the religious festival was politically significant. Most rural towns in attendance, indeed, dispatched one of four of the highest-status town council officials to lead pilgrimages of community members to Mexico City: gobernador, alcalde, *regidor mayor*, or *regidor*. Alcaldes and regidores (aldermen) were the most numerous of town council officials who led their community members to the procession in the capital. From 1777 to 1780, almost 60 percent of the participant leaders held the title of alcalde (including alcalde ordinario) or regidor, each of which were represented in equal numbers (29 percent). The rolls of participation in arch building demonstrate that,

Table 4.1. Numerical occurrences of Cabildo officers in attendance at Corpus Christi, Mexico City, 1777–1780

Cabildo Position	1777	1778	1779	1780	Total 1777–1780	Percentage of Four-Year Total
Alcalde	2	20	23	12	57	23.36
Alcalde Mayor	1	0	0	0	1	0.41
Alcalde Ordinario	15	0	0	0	15	6.15
Alcalde Pasado	1	0	0	0	1	0.41
Alguacil Mayor	3	1	0	0	4	1.64
Capitán	1	5	0	6	12	4.92
Gobernador	2	6	2	15	25	10.25
Juez	0	1	1	0	2	0.82
Juez Alcalde	0	0	0	2	2	0.82
Mandón	0	1	3	1	5	2.05
Merino	0	2	3	0	5	2.05
Regidor	13	14	26	17	70	28.69
Regidor Mayor	22	8	0	11	41	16.80
Teniente de Gobernador	1	0	0	0	1	0.41
Unspecified	1	2	0	0	3	1.23
Total	62	60	58	64	244	

Source: AHCM Proc., vol. 3712.

in general, the same person was not named as alcalde or regidor each year from a given town. One can interpret this as meaning that local leaders of Corpus Christi contingents from each municipal subdivision (*barrio* or pueblo sujeto) were picked on a rotational basis. Alcaldes and regidores were the most frequent officials to attend the procession because this allowed each municipal subdivision of each town to be represented by an arch or decoration space in the streets of the capital on a rotational basis. This reduced the financial burden of the obligation and distributed political status evenly throughout the rural community back home.[34]

The high number of representatives from these two offices ensured distribution of status and financial stress, and it also gave them an opportunity to gain the status useful for ascending to the higher offices of gobernador, regidor mayor, and alcalde ordinario in local town councils. In the hierarchy of status of the eighteenth-century town council, the alcaldes and regidores were in the middle of the social scale and both were lower than gobernador and regidor mayor.[35]

INDIGENOUS CENTURIONS MAKE HOLY WEEK COMMERCIAL CONNECTION

Indigenous governments did not simply take an adversarial position against non-Indians in order to preserve their festival authority. Sometimes economic connections with non-Indians gave indigenous people power. The many carnival features of Corpus Christi and Holy Week processions, especially costumes and food, formed bonds of economic interest that linked indigenous governments with non-native groups. During the eighteenth and early nineteenth centuries, Spanish city governments, viceroys, and independence period constitutional magistrates issued bans on consumption and entertainment. In the 1790s, Viceroy Revillagigedo attempted to ban people from dressing as Roman centurions during Semana Santa, and indigenous municipal governments resisted. In fact, indigenous councils in surrounding rural towns were able to preserve the popular practice because they signed yearly contracts for the rental of costumes with Mexico City clothing renters who had socially important non-Indian investors. Indigenous leaders had the power to bargain for the maintenance of the religious ritual, which was important to them as a symbol of community pride, because they had economic bonds with Spanish merchants.

Great urban festivals such as Corpus Christi and Holy Week were short periods of intense commercial activity for the residents of Mexico City. Ecclesiastical law obliged all "indios" to cease working and observe the feast days of Corpus Christi and Holy Week, as was required of people of all ethnic groups. The Mexican provincial church councils and a papal bull required indigenous people to comply with this cessation of work as a matter of faith.[36] Officials often complained that indigenous people spent too much money on large quantities of *pulque* (maguey-based alcoholic drink), meals, and sweets during the festivals; in short, faithful festival participants spent money. Because the religious calendar dictated when commercial activity would boom, petty merchants of various ethnic groups could annually count on religious festival times, plan for them, and invest in them.

Indigenous governments maintained municipal status and gained economic opportunities from Mexico City's festival cycles, but non-elite indigenous people stood to benefit as well. During the week of Corpus Christi, council officials extracted indigenous labor in order to build arches and compelled them to pay for their feasts. At the same time, their efforts to bring rural natives to the city increased business for urban venders. Town council officials from the rural pueblos gained status in the eyes of their urban counterparts as those who brought people to decorate and buy food in the city. The indigenous officials in Mexico City claimed that the rural families who walked to the capital believed that the hardship was worth it because they were compensated with the honor of attending.[37]

During Corpus Christi celebrations ambling market vendors of various ethnic identities, including indigenous peoples, sold great amounts of food and sweets, causing traffic congestion as they traversed the procession routes. As in contemporary popular events in Mexico City today, these strolling merchants could be heard yelling over what were supposed to be solemn and quiet occasions. Spanish city council officials also complained that the altars set up by cofradías and individuals along the way caused further disruption. On the day of the Corpus Christi procession of 1765, for example, the Spanish town council issued an order to the militia to prevent people from setting up food stalls along the procession route.[38]

The 1771 *visita* of José de Gálvez, his inspection tour of New Spain, marks the beginning of a period of more aggressive attempts to reform the festival economy and use of public space that lasted until 1822. Beginning in 1765, Gálvez worked to increase revenues for the royal treasury through various measures such as creating the royal tobacco monopoly and streamlining silver mining in New Spain.[39] In order to reduce royal expenditures, Gálvez significantly decreased the amount of money that the treasury disbursed to the Spanish ayuntamiento of Mexico to pay for urban processions. The festivals that received reductions were those that had fallen out of favor with the top levels of colonial government. While the festivals of Corpus Christi, Our Lady of Guadalupe, and Saint Joseph maintained their funding, the various processions of Easter week would receive either significantly reduced financing or none at all after 1771.[40]

Then, in 1791, city councilmen and viceroys began a more concerted effort to ban market activities during Holy Week and Corpus Christi. However, the fact that officials repeated the same prohibitions for the next thirty-one years is evidence that these activities were never regulated out of existence. In April 1791, Viceroy Revillagigedo banned all stalls that sold fruit, sweets, *chia* (a flowering plant called *salva hispanica*), pastries, and rattles in an attempt to strike order along the Holy Week procession routes and church plazas. People were feasting all week when they were supposed to be fasting. Also, congested streets made it difficult for processions to travel their routes. Revillagigedo attempted to mandate order in the processions by making it illegal for people to build small stages or platforms where episodes of the Passion of Christ were depicted.[41] Over the coming years, Revillagigedo's ban was published and delivered to offenders, apparently without much effectiveness. In 1801 and 1803, one finds the corregidores of the city council issuing copies of Revillagigedo's ban but augmenting it by making the punishments harsher for transgressions.[42] The city council was still issuing the same prohibitions after independence. The only difference was that in 1822 the city council officials were calling on their authority as post-independence *alcaldes constitucionales* (constitutional aldermen) in order issue the bans.[43]

Although mobile venders and stalls along streets caused worry over traffic disorder, viceroyal officials were also concerned with collecting rents and licensing fees as part of the reform of the royal treasury. Petty merchants in the streets were not confined to the plazas, which made it more difficult to collect rents from them because treasury officials and the magistrate of the plaza only monitored established plazas and market areas. In 1771, Gálvez instructed public officials that they should collect the rents and licensing fees owed by the market-stall owners in the Plaza Mayor as well as the merchants along the street. Gálvez remarked that owners of small stalls and simple tables were the most remiss in their payments.[44]

Commerce and the theatrics of Catholicism went hand in hand in Mexico City. The urban festivals of Corpus Christi and Holy Week were dramatic events that involved religious plays, masquerades, and coordinated dances in the streets. Merchants, guilds, and shopkeepers enthusiastically participated in religious spectacles, supplying the necessary props, costumes, and financial backing. Many of the tradesmen involved worked as producers of apparel. During the seventeenth and early eighteenth centuries, guild masters of various trades bonded prominent residents of Mexico City so they could contribute money to Corpus Christi dances and fireworks. One can find many master tailors, hat makers, shoemakers, and weavers among the records of these financial backers.[45] Many of their customers were the indigenous residents of Mexico City and rural communities.

The Indians enjoyed wearing costumes during Corpus Christi and Holy Week processions, which upset reform-minded ecclesiastical and civil officials throughout the eighteenth century. A major complaint of the viceroy was that the native people spent too much money on the costumes when they were already poor. Such expenditures by indigenous people increased the chance that they would not be able to pay royal tribute. One of the most popular masquerades happened during Holy Week when people dressed as armados. Mexico City's indigenous people and *castas* (people of mixed race) dressed as Roman centurions and soldiers, wearing coats of mail, breastplates, and helmets and carried weapons. In Mexico City and many rural towns, Nahua armados played their most important role on Good Friday. Marching in afternoon processions, the soldiers surrounded effigies of the deceased Christ or images of his tomb. Burial images were then deposited on altars in parish churches where the soldiers held all-night vigils, guarding his body until dawn.[46] These figures also had key parts in passion plays performed on Palm Sunday and Good Friday. As the plots progressed, the soldiers were transformed from pagan Romans who menaced the twelve apostles to Roman Catholics who, by the end of the plays, declared their faith in the Resurrection.[47]

Although this was most often a solemn occasion for indigenous people, audiencia officials attempted to extinguish what they viewed as an expensive, ridiculous, and sometimes threatening military masquerade. During the 1790s, the viceroys Revillagigedo and Bucareli worked through the Spanish ayuntamiento of Mexico City in order to issue ordinances against wearing armado costumes within the city. Revillagigedo first banned the practice in 1790, but the practice continued. In 1794, the viceroy's subordinates were still reporting to Revillagigedo that the native residents of Tlatelolco were dressing as soldiers and marching and even riding horses in total disarray.[48] Authorities singled out Santiago Tlatelolco as the main source of residents dressing as armados because of their conspicuous presence on Holy Wednesday and Good Friday. On Holy Wednesday, armados from Santiago Tlatelolco led the city's procession that began in San Francisco Tepito. During the afternoon and evening climax of the Friday memorial of Christ's death, the city's mourners removed an image of the Santo Entierro from the church of Santiago Tlatelolco. Until nightfall, the armados hosted the procession and traveled to deposit the remains on the altar of the church of Santo Domingo.[49]

In 1794, shortly before Easter, Revillagigedo renewed a campaign to put an end to the armados and those that rented the costumes to them. His main concerns about the soldiers in the city were the lack of decorum and order that they brought to the processions and the financial burdens on those filled the role.[50] As part of the week's processions, armados participated in scenes that reenacted Christ's suffering (*pasos*). These Stations of the Cross in the street congested the thoroughfares and impeded the movement of the processions, especially when armados, who were allegedly inebriated, accompanied the pasos. Armados paid for their costumes out of personal funds or special confraternities elected and financed someone to don the outfit. The viceroy believed that individuals were spending so much money on the office that "they leave their poor wives and children naked; others lose their houses." More importantly, Revillagigedo felt that the expenditures ultimately prevented people from paying tribute.[51]

Initially, Revillagigedo planned to ban the practice not only inside the city but also in the entire viceroyalty of New Spain. From 1794 to 1804, officials were concerned with the disorder that armados were supposedly causing in towns and provinces outside Mexico City. There were wild rumors in the capital that in rural areas, drunken, mixed-race armados were raping women in churches and forcing indigenous officials to relinquish their ceremonial staffs of office (*varas*). In April 1794, Revillagigedo required that priests report on the state of indigenous parishes where

armados were popular. The most renowned vigils, which indigenous centurions attended, occurred in San Angel, Xochimilco, Tacuba, and two
towns in the district of Tacuba, Tlalnepantla and Azcapotzalco. An anonymous letter written "in the name of the poor" moved Revillagigedo to
investigate because the authors accused the priests in these towns of forcing indigenous people to rent costumes.[52] Despite the alarmist hearsay,
Revillagigedo and, later, Bracinforte generally received news from rural
curas that their armados were orderly and pious and not under onerous
financial burden to carry out the function.

In fact, some ministers, such as the ones from Xochimilco and Azcapotzalco, reported that the armados were Spanish and casta and not Nahua
residents. The priest from Xochimilco commented that Holy Thursday and
Friday were the only days of the year that the natives were not drunk; "on
these two days their honor returned."[53] In contrast to these two places, the
parish priest of Corpus Christi Tlalnepantla reported that both "Indians
and residents" were very protective of this "ancient custom" in the town.
Even though both groups shared the custom, the ceremonial office exercised a strong influence over yearly elections in the indigenous town council. Commenting on the selection of the armados, the exasperated priest
stated, "The choice that the gobernadores and indios principales make of
the participants and officials of the soldiers causes me more than a little
embarrassment." Later, a faction of "malcontents" lobbied the priest to
remove from office the armados that the indios principales had elected.[54]

Continual reports of how the contentious selection and riotous behavior of the armados caused disorder made viceroys wary of the practice in
the provinces and Mexico City. But banning the armados could also create problems. For example, in 1797 the priest of San Angel complained to
Viceroy Branciforte that all his parishioners had gone to neighboring jurisdictions when the corregidor of Coyoacan banned armados. He regretted
that he was "left with a town without people" and that no one was available
to carry out the ceremonies of the Good Friday vigil.[55] The most striking
episode occurred in Santa María Amealco in Queretaro. On Good Friday
in 1799, several indigenous armados began using the props they carried as
real weapons in a riot aimed at the local priest and Spanish residents of the
town. Men dressed for the procession attacked the priest during mass with
their lances and swords. The Spanish residents in attendance at the church
attempted to protect the priest but one of the armados threw his lance into
the crowd surrounding the father, striking the cleric in the head.[56] Shaken
by what had happened in 1794, officials of the audiencia carefully watched
for possible violence that might arise in other places, such as Cuautla de
Amilpas, for the next ten years.[57]

Money was just as much an issue as public disorder when it came to the campaign to ban the armados. In order to address the issue of what he viewed as excessive expenditures on costumes, Revillagigedo specifically targeted Mexico City's clothes' renters (*alquiladores de ropas*). In March 1794, the corregidor of Mexico City delivered orders to eight clothes' renters whose shops were located in the traza near Tacuba Street. He ordered that under no circumstances were they to show or rent armados costumes to anyone regardless of class or ethnicity. The same order was delivered to the indigenous gobernadores of San Juan and Santiago, Don José Gerardo Diaz and Don Lázaro de la Peña, respectively.[58] The various clothes rental houses annually signed contracts in January with the indigenous city governments, delivering to them armados costumes and lances on credit.

The owners of the rental houses, as well as tailors working for them, responded to the viceroy through the umbrella organization of the tailor's guild and its partner confraternity of Homo Bono. The confraternity of Homo Bono had male, female, Spanish, and Indian tailors and apparel workers as members.[59] One of the petitioners who testified to the viceroy in 1794 was a young indigenous tailor and cacique from San Juan.[60] During Holy Week, the confraternity was a visible presence in the processions. They appeared on Holy Thursday wearing red tunics (*túnicas encarnadas*).[61] Their more important function was that they organized the formation of the armados from Santiago Tlatelolco on Good Friday and Easter Sunday. The confraternity outfitted a contingent from Tlatelolco with costumes free of charge. Individual clothes renters signed contracts with the indigenous city governments for numerous additional armados in addition to the contingent organized by Homo Bono.[62]

In several complaints to the viceroy in 1794 and 1795, the renters, dealers, and tailors argued that the viceroy's ban would destroy their businesses. They made the majority of their yearly profits on the Holy Week rentals. The capital that they made during Lent was always reinvested in the following year's season. Eight people presented their financial records in an attempt to prove that they would all default on their debts to their landlords if costume rentals were cancelled. It was a powerful argument because their creditors were undoubtedly the wealthiest merchants in the city.[63] In two cases, powerful clergy members testified to their support of the businesses. Don Matheo Mariano Millan de Figueroa, Inquisition official and tithe collector of Tenancingo, was landlord to business owner Doña María Josepha de Campos. The Inquisition official rented the house in order to generate funds as the executor of a prominent deceased woman's *capellanía*, a trust that funded masses for the benefit of her soul. Another clergy member worried that he would no longer be able to respect the capellanía of the Duque de Terranova, whose last will and testament stipulated monetary support of armados in perpetuity.[64] Finally, the tailor guild's confraternity claimed that it was also suffering adverse affects in 1795 because the revenue from costume rentals helped finance their pension fund as well as support new apprentice apparel workers who had to now be released from work.[65]

In the end, the viceroy was not swayed by their arguments to allow the armados within the city. Nevertheless, Revillagigedo was forced to compromise when it came to the renters doing business with towns outside of the city limits. He believed that they did the majority of their business with these exterior locales. Because each town rented the costumes on credit, rental houses would be left with a large amount of unpaid debt. The information provided by the guild demonstrates how indigenous people and Spaniards in small towns supported local processions and vigils by making commercial connections in Mexico City. Credit tied urban shopkeepers to the rural towns of Tepoztlan (district of Cuernavaca), San Juan Teotihuacan, Cuautitlan (district of Tacuba), the city of Texcoco, and Tepepan (district of Xochimilco). Many of these towns had contracts with several different Mexico City rental houses for each season.[66] In sum, the guild's combative response to the viceroy's ban, combined with curas' reports of peaceful armados in surrounding rural native parishes, convinced Revillagigedo not to ban the practice outside of Mexico City.[67]

CONCLUSION

Spanish institutions such as the Juzgado General de Indios, the Spanish ayuntamiento of Mexico City, and the Inquisition did not simply coerce indigenous leaders to organize their communities to participate in Holy Week and Corpus Christi festivals, nor were the native rulers simply exploiting and profiting from their communities. The festival economy afforded economic benefits for non-elite participants who were from the Indian and non-Indian communities. When indigenous town councils made economic alliances with non-indigenous people, they participated in a multi-ethnic Catholic culture, strengthening their negotiating power but also making the religion unique to New Spain.

Indigenous city and town councils had the power to negotiate the way that they organized their residents' participation in Corpus Christi and Holy Week because colonial demands and legal theories about civil order were contradictory. The Spanish ayuntamiento, Real Audiencia, Catholic Church, and important urban businesses depended on the república de indios to deliver builders, customers, and spiritual communicants in the

Body of Christ. Negotiation was possible only because European and indigenous parties agreed that their contract produced benefits for their shared religion, but each disagreed on what those benefits were. Triumphal arches and Roman soldiers were explicitly imperial Catholic images that seemingly would nullify indigenous claims to local municipal power. By organizing people and resources for the construction of Corpus Christi arches, however, the indigenous governments of San Juan Mexico City and Santiago Tlatelolco performed a symbolic sleight of hand. The arches stood as yearly reminders to the residents of Mexico City that the Spanish ayuntamiento and the audiencia did not have enough authority over indigenous people to draw them to the festival that celebrated the universal triumph of Catholicism.

On the other hand, the power to negotiate was more than just a testament to the internal continuity of indigenous forms of social organization. As participants in the great urban festivals of Corpus Christi and Holy Week, indigenous people maintained connections with people of other ethnic groups through credit, commerce, and guild membership. The native governments of Mexico City, Santiago Tlatelolco, and those in the provinces secured contracts with merchants in order to organize contingents of armados for Holy Week. Indigenous centurions were a striking—and, in some authorities' view, threatening—presence in processions and all-night vigils; they faithfully guarded the tomb of Christ, and yet brazenly marched through the streets of Mexico City. These Roman soldiers of Christ challenged the new Bourbon political and economic order that the viceroys were attempting to establish during the 1770s to the 1790s. At this time, activist diocesan priests also worked to instill their own vision of order in people's religious practice, which they thought should be more rational and less emotional and sensory than the religiosity that they believed their parishioners displayed. One aspect of religion that they found incompatible with this vision was the popular religious theater and the apparent excesses of Holy Week penitential rites.[68] Undoubtedly, the reformist viceroys Bucareli and Revillagigedo attempted to extinguish the popular theatrical elements of the Holy Week–Corpus Christi festival cycle. However, as the era of the viceroyalty of New Spain neared its end, these men were not concerned primarily with proper decorum. In their drive to increase monarchical centralization, the Bourbon viceroys worked to dismantle the political order that originated with the establishment of the colony in the sixteenth century. The late eighteenth-century viceroys viewed the arches, centurions, and negotiations, which brought indigenous actors to the streets, as symbols of an antiquated style of governance employing local accommodation that had allowed indigenous styles of municipal organization to survive. From the point of view of the indigenous town and city councilmen of the valleys of Mexico and Toluca, their arches were triumphs of their vision of an indigenous Catholic social order.

NOTES

1. Juan Pedro Viqueira Albán, *Propriety and Permissiveness in Bourbon Mexico*, trans. Sonya Lipsett-Rivera and Sergio Rivera Ayala (Wilmington, DE: Scholarly Resources, 1999), 83–84.

2. Clara García Ayluardo, "Confraternity, Cult, and Crown in Colonial Mexico City, 1700–1810" (Ph.D. dissertation, Cambridge University, Cambridge, 1989), 30–31.

3. Fray Juan de Torquemada, *Veinte i un libros rituales i monarquia indiana* (Madrid: Nicoás Rodríguez Franco Impresor, 1724 [1615]), vol. III, book 17, chap. 7, p. 224.

4. Archivo Histórico de la Ciudad de México (hereafter, AHCM), Procesiones (hereafter, Proc.), vol. 3712, exps. 9–12.

5. Ibid., exp. 3.

6. *Recopilación de leyes de los Reynos de las Indias*, 3rd ed., 4 vols. (Madrid: Mandadas imprimir y publicar por la Magestad Catolica del Rey Don Carlos II, 1774), libro 6, titulo 7, ley 1; Juan de Solórzano Pereira, *Politica indiana* (Amberes: H. y C. Verdussen, 1703), vol. 2, chap. 29, pp. 115–116.

7. AHCM Proc., vol. 3712, exp. 2, fol. 2r.

8. Ibid., exp. 3, fols. 1r–3v.

9. Ibid., fols. 4r–7v.

10. Ibid., exp. 4, fol. 2r.

11. Ibid.

12. William B. Taylor, "The Virgin of Guadalupe in New Spain: An Inquiry into the Social History of Marian Devotion," *American Ethnologist* 14 (1987): 12.

13. One *vara* was equal to roughly one meter (0.835 meters).

14. AHCM Proc., vol. 3712, exp. 5, fols. 3r–3v.

15. Ibid., fol. 4r.

16. Ibid., exp. 16, fols. 1r–1v.

17. Ibid., exps. 2, 4, 5, 7, 12.

18. Torquemada, *Veinte i un libros rituales i monarquia indiana*, 224.

19. AHCM Proc., vol. 3712, exp. 7, fols. 1r–1v.

20. Ibid., fol. 2r.

21. Ibid., fol. 12r.

22. Ibid., fol. 3r.

23. Ibid., fols. 7v–9v.

24. Ibid., fol. 26r.

25. Ibid., fol. 3v.

26. Ibid., fols. 14v–15r.

27. Ibid., fols. 10r–15v; exp. 19, fol. 1r.

28. Ibid., exp. 17, fol. 1r.

29. Ibid., exp. 18, fols. 1r–1v.

30. Repartimiento was used here in the sense that San Juan and Santiago forced the attending pueblos to purchase the materials when they arrived.

31. AHCM Proc., vol. 3712, exp. 18, fols. 15r–16r.

32. Ibid., fols. 15r–15v.

33. Ibid., fol. 24r. The original Spanish text is "porque no compliran con aquella antigua obligación que miran como privilegio heredado de sus passados y que jamás juntarian las dos Parcialidades por si solas."

34. AHCM Proc., vol. 3712, exp. 7, fol. 28v.

35. For more information on the debate over whether there was a system of advancement in the cabildos directed by service in a ladder of religious offices, see John Chance and William B. Taylor, "Cofradías and Cargos: An Historical Perspective on the Mesoamerican Civil-Religious Hierarchy," *American Ethnologist* 12 (1985): 1–26.

36. Archivo General de la Nación (hereafter, AGN) Indios, vol. 58, exp. 152, fol. 237; *Concilios Provinciales Primero y Segundo, Celebrados en muy Noble y Muy Leal Ciudad de Mexico, Presidiendo el Illmo. y Rmo. Señor D. Fr. Alonso de Montufar, en los años de 1555 y 1565: Dalos a Luz el Ill.mo Sr. D. Francisco Antonio Lorenzana, Arzobispo de esta Santa Metropolitana Iglesia* (México DF: En la Imprenta de el Superior Gobierno, 1769), council 1, chap. 18, p. 69. Serving viceroys cited the papal bull in the dispatch that they sent to request that rural natives come and decorate.

37. AHCM Proc., vol. 3712, exp. 18, fol. 28.

38. Ibid., exp. 6, fols. 2r–3r.

39. D. A. Brading, *Miners and Merchants in Bourbon Mexico, 1763–1810* (Cambridge: Cambridge University Press, 1971), 27–28; John Lynch, *Bourbon Spain: 1700–1808* (Cambridge: Basil Blackwell, 1989), 172–173, 344–346.

40. Condumex 351.71.571 CRO, Visita de Gálvez, "Plan de las funciones votivas annuales que celebra la Nobilisima Ciudad . . .," fols. 21–23.

41. AGN Historia, vol. 437, exp. 3, fol. 1v.

42. AHCM Proc., vol. 3712, exps. 25, 26.

43. Ibid., exp. 35.

44. Condumex 351.71.351 CRO, "Visita de Don Joseph Gálvez," fols. 5–7.

45. AHCM Fiestas, vol. 1066, exp. 1, fols. 1–77. The records cover the Corpus Christi celebrations from 1694 to 1728. The files also record the selection of an indigenous *pregonero* (crier) who had to meet the requirement of being an *indio ladino* (Indian who spoke Spanish).

46. AGN Historia, vol. 437, exps. 3, 6, 7, 8, 12; AHCM Proc., vol. 3712, exp. 23.

47. Three passion plays from the Amecameca region, with parts for centurions, are contained in AGN Inquisición, vol. 1072. One of these is published in "Las Representaciones Teatrales de la Pasión," *Boletín del Archivo General de la Nación* 5, no. 3 (May–June 1934). Also see Fernando Horcasitas, *El Teatro Náhuatl: Épocas Novohispana y Moderna* (México DF: UNAM, 1974), 1:97.

48. AGN Historia, vol. 437, exp. 6, fol. 1v. Regarding the procession on Good Friday, an internal report states, "En la tarde sale otra de Santiago, la constean la Parcialidad vestidos de Armados, a pie y a cavallo, sin orden forma."

49. AGN Historia, vol. 437, exp. 8, fols. 3r–v.

50. Ibid., vol. 476, exp. 3, fols. 1–3. In earlier times, audiencia officials were concerned with Nahua drunkenness and debt caused by theatrical festivals. For example, in 1784, officials responded negatively to the "hijos del pueblo" of Santa Cruz in Xochimilco, which requested a license to perform the "danza de plumas" at their titular saint fiesta.

51. AGN Historia, vol. 437, exp. 8, fol. 1.

52. AGN Cofradías, vol. 14, exp. 3, fols. 135r–140v; AGN Historia, vol. 437, exp. 7, fols. 1–39.

53. AGN Historia, vol. 437, exp. 7., fol. 6.

54. "Causandome esto no pocas mortificasiones, que resultan de la Eleción que los Governadores è Indios principales hasen de sugetos y cargos de la Soldadesca pues siendo ellos quienes la practican de este objeto que me repugna." Ibid., fol. 11. Funding of Holy Week activities was politically contentious in other places. In 1797, the merino of the town of San Dionicio Yauquemecan, near the city of Tlaxcala, complained that other member towns were no longer contributing alms to pay for the candles for the customary vigil; AGN Historia, vol. 437, exp. 11, fols. 1–9. Indigenous rulers also sometimes forced people in their communities to fund Holy Week centurions; AGN Historia vol. 88, exp. 20, fols. 1–4, 13v. In 1775, Francisco Diego of Ixquimilpan petitioned the Juzgado General de Indios to stop the "gobernadores" of his region from forcing him to use resources he had reserved for a miraculous image in his town.

55. AGN Historia, vol. 437, exp. 12, fols. 1–5.

56. AGN Bienes Nacionales, vol. 1112, exp. 46, fols. 1–13r.

57. AGN Cofradías, vol. 14, exp. 3, fols. 134–148. The rumors that Viceroy Yturrigaray articulated about acts of violence committed by mixed-race men in disguise in Cuautla de Amilpas seem to have been completely unfounded.

58. AHCM Proc., vol. 3712, exp. 23; AGN Historia 437, exp. 8, fols. 2r–2v.

59. AGN Bienes Nacionales, vol. 117, exp. 1. The papers and membership forms included in this file cover the years 1690 to 1811. The saint is described as "San Homo Bono natural de Cremona, Profesor y Patrón del Arte de Sastreria." There were no restrictions in terms of race for membership and many women were members.

60. AGN Historia, vol. 437, exp. 8, fol. 25v.

61. Ibid., exp. 6, fol. 1v.

62. Ibid., exp. 8, fol. 24r.

63. Brading, *Miners and Merchants*.

64. AGN Historia, vol. 437, exp. 9, fols. 10–20.

65. Ibid., fols. 2–3.

66. Ibid., fols 26r–33r. The other towns that rented costumes were Tacubaya, Tacuba, Tlanepantla, San Angel, Misquaque, Coyoacan, San Augustín de las Cuevas, Estayuca, Atlapulco (Xochimilco), Acapuzalco, and Gualguagan. Also listed

are pueblos named only by titular saints: La Magdalena, La Piedad, San Juacito, San Mateo, and San Simón.

67. AGN Historia, vol. 437, exp. 5, fols. 6–7. Spanish commercial interests in distant provincial cities also helped convince Revillagigedo not to ban Holy Week armados and festivals. For example, the vecinos of Patzcuaro, Valladolid, who were mine, sugar mill, and hacienda owners promised to control the excesses of the many indigenous people who came to the fairs held during Holy Week.

68. D. A. Brading, *Church and State in Bourbon Mexico: The Diocese of Michoacan, 1749–1810* (Cambridge: Cambridge University Press, 1994), 11–34.

5

MARÍA DE LOS ÁNGELES ROMERO FRIZZI

The Power of the Law

The Construction of Colonial Power in an Indigenous Region

> The differences that matter between *pueblos* and over which they fall
> out pertain to land, water, and mountains. This forms the most clam-
> orous problem for the *audiencia*, leads the Indians into expenditures
> they cannot afford, and sets in motion legal disputes which after ten or
> twenty years have yet to be clarified or resolved.
>
> —*Carta de Fray Jerónimo de Mendieta, 1562*

Over the course of a little more than three centuries—from the end of
the fifteenth to the first decades of the nineteenth century—the Spanish
Crown managed to conquer and subjugate a vast, far-flung territory.[1]
Its success in this enterprise depended in great measure on its ability to
impose a set of laws and juridical norms over people of different cultural
traditions.[2] Furthermore, the Spanish state managed not simply to bring
those it conquered under control but to regulate and reshape their lives—
as specific subjects of the Crown—through the instrumentality of laws
and judicial practice. Tangible evidence of this power is found in the count-
less documents, still reposing in the archives, that have survived from that

period. Yet, despite the reams of evidence, little is actually known about the concrete mechanisms through which these laws and judicial regimens of Spanish origin were imposed over both individuals and discrete groups. The power that the law carried, and the ability of the Crown and its agents to impose it, cannot be explained in purely linear fashion, as the inexorable outcome of the wars of conquest. Rather, behind the seemingly obvious history is a more nuanced reality and—so far as this study is concerned—a deeper question: how were the structures of colonial power, both visible and invisible, formed and elaborated?

To answer that question, one must reflect on problems that resulted from the application of Spanish laws and a Spanish legal system within entirely different cultural contexts.[3] My approach—a micro-historical one—entails the detailed analysis of a single case within a limited physical area. Utilizing this approach and focusing on the particular case under study, enables us to reenter and grasp the day-to-day world in which Spanish legal principles and procedures had a direct impact on the life of indigenous communities in the southern region of New Spain. More concretely, such focused analysis gives us, first, an idea of the way the laws of the Indies came to be imposed in regions containing large majorities of indigenous people; second, it allows us to reflect on the problems that sprang from the application of a legal code within a society lacking such a tradition; and, third, it will help to expose the roots of the agrarian problems that afflict present-day society in Mexico's indigenous regions.[4] The case to be examined occurred around the end of the seventeenth century and the beginning of the eighteenth. It concerns a conflict, over the issue of land, that took place in the Sierra Zapoteca, which sits to the north of the present-day city of Oaxaca, in the southern part of Mexico.

THE REGION

Although Mexico's mountain ranges are not comparable to the Andean chain, they still managed to form, during the colonial period, a formidable barrier to the penetration of Spanish interests.[5] The steep incline of their slopes helped check the Spanish hunger for land, and only in those areas where other attractions existed, such as silver deposits, did the mountains cease to be an obstacle for miners, settlers, and others.[6] Bereft as they were of silver and other precious metals, the mountainous areas had little draw; consequently, their Spanish settler population constituted a small island encircled by a sea of indigenous communities.

Over the three centuries of colonial rule, the Spanish town of San Ildefonso de la Villa Alta—tucked away in the Sierra Norte of Oaxaca—

never managed, even during the best of times, to reach 200 inhabitants (approximately forty families). In contrast, the population of the 110 Indian communities surrounding it fluctuated between 20,000 persons in 1622 and more than 40,000 at the end of the eighteenth century. Moreover, virtually every indigenous community in the district contained a larger population than San Ildefonso; the average number of inhabitants in each community, at the beginning of the eighteenth century, was in the vicinity of 330. Near the end of the century (1789), this figure had reached 420, although some communities, such as Santo Domingo Choapan and San Juan Yalalag had populations in the eighteenth century that exceeded 1,000.[7]

The region held such little attraction for the Spanish that, when preparing documents during the eighteenth century, the serving *alcalde mayor* (chief judicial and administrative official of a district) could not count on having the services of a Crown-appointed notary or scribe (*escribano*).[8] This beleaguered situation differed from that in some other Spanish settlements. For example, in the community of San Pedro and San Pablo Teposcolula, located in the Mixteca Alta section of the present-day state of Oaxaca, a royal notary of recognized standing was permanently on call.[9]

Although the region of the Sierra Zapoteca was relatively isolated from the main centers of Spanish settlement, the leaders of its indigenous communities constantly called upon San Ildefonso's alcalde mayor to help them resolve grievances and conflicts, particularly when two or more communities were involved.[10] In none of the cases studied did the alcalde mayor take the initiative to intervene in an attempt to ease tensions, craft a peaceful resolution, or administer justice by meting out punishment to the guilty parties.[11] On the contrary, in all of the conflicts that arose between two or more communities, Spanish law was applied at the express request of the indigenous authorities themselves. When a conflict broke out, the members of the Indians' *cabildo* (community council) would set off across the mountains, arriving—after a journey of one, two, or perhaps three days on foot—in the town of San Ildefonso, in order to explain themselves to the alcalde mayor and request his intercession to resolve the problem. It might well be thought that the disposition of the indigenous leaders to approach the alcalde mayor and request his intervention in their conflicts was a reflex conditioned by the conquest, an expression of servility, and a natural outgrowth of years of warfare and imperial rule. The reality, however, was not so simple.

My purpose in this study, as I have stated, is to demonstrate that the recourse to Spanish law in these disputes was made at the behest of the Indians themselves and resulted from a complex process in which a multiplicity of factors came into play. Clearly, the precipitating factor was the conquest, which brought the unleashing of arms and the stark realities of war. These events played an important role for two reasons; first, they helped the Spanish conquerors to impose their own law, and second, the experience of the conquest shaped Indians' impressions of and beliefs about the Spanish. Of all the factors that persuaded the indigenous authorities to accept Spanish law and its officers, the most influential were the ideas that the Indians formed about the people who subdued and ruled them.[12]

The central questions, present since the sixteenth century, with which they grappled—who were the Spanish, from where had they arrived, and what was the basis of their power—continued to hold sway in the centuries that followed and underlay, to a considerable extent, the reasons that the Indians adduced to obey their Spanish overlords, pay them tribute, and request that they intercede and serve as judges in settling their disputes. The notion of Spanish power that the Indians elaborated sprang from their sacralized vision of not just nature and the cosmos but power itself and led to such questions as, What was the relationship between the power wielded by the Spaniards and that possessed by their gods? What was the power of the indigenous rulers and of their own gods in comparison to that of the Spaniards?

Conflicts between and among indigenous communities of the sierra evolved in such a way as to suggest that even years after the conquest, the Indians continued interpreting Spanish power in fundamentally sacred terms. Over the course of the sixteenth century, wise men and spiritual leaders within the indigenous communities had tried to make sense of the foreign presence, of the Spaniards' sudden, mysterious arrival, and the resultant epidemics that swept the countryside. In their search for explanations, they had no other option but to fall back on their own system of thought, their own way of comprehending the world. Thus, they interpreted those who so abruptly materialized before them as embodying and representing a new era of power, a new sun, a new cosmic cycle similar to that which had given birth to their civilization.[13] Pointedly, documents composed by the Zapotec at the end of the conquest period and during the first years of the century that followed invoke Spanish law and its symbols of power in the same sacred terms that had underlain the basis of power of the pre-Hispanic indigenous rulers. During pre-colonial times, native rulers had received the emblems of their gods by means of a journey to the heavens; after 1521, they received them by the grace of the Spanish emperor, following a voyage to Spain.[14] Although the trend was not universal, by the end of the seventeenth century there were indigenous leaders who, through contact with the Spanish, had developed a more Western idea of laws and courts, an idea more in line with that held by the Spaniards.[15]

Furthermore, in coming before the alcalde mayor to request his intervention, the Indians were acting upon more than a set of supernatural
beliefs; they were motivated by self-interest as well. The conflicts that
erupted between Indian communities propelled them to seek the intervention of the Spanish magistrate.[16] Such conflicts, arising out of rivalries
for power or from the need or the ambition to control more land, predate
Spanish conquest and colonization. Indeed, armed encounters between
indigenous communities had been an integral part of prehispanic society; documents from the early sixteenth century make reference to long-
existing rivalries between native kingdoms and to violent confrontations.[17]
Documents from the colonial period leave the impression that a substantial
number of conflicts between Indian settlements originated when one community attempted to take possession of lands belonging to another.[18] In a
peasant society whose very existence depends on the ability of its people to
wrest a living from the land, periodic struggles to control the land might
be viewed as natural, if not inevitable. Nevertheless, the nature of these
conflicts, the way in which they evolved, and the fact that they endured
for decades, in some cases even continuing to the present day, imply that
their causes were more complicated than a community's perceived need to
acquire more land. The analysis of these conflicts will provide insight into
the structural dynamics of native society and involve factors such as the
linkages among its members, their relationship to the land, their ideas of
power and hierarchy, and the nature of the connections among indigenous
communities, on the one hand, and between these communities and the
exercise of Spanish power, on the other.

METHOD OF ANALYSIS

Understanding the nature and development of conflict among the indigenous communities of the sierra requires that one first reflect on a suitable
methodology. Yet the attempt to uncover and describe the motivations
and thought patterns of the indigenous population through the analysis
of colonial legal documents and other writings from New Spain presents
serious challenges. The difficulty stems from a classic problem, or limita-
tion: namely, despite all that has been written about the inherent traps of
textual interpretation, historians continually confuse and mistake what
they read in the documents with the reality that they seek, unconsciously
assuming that the content of a document, or at least part of that content,
corresponds in some way with what they wish to find. Such, however, is
not always the case. At times, in certain instances, there is a significant
gap or difference between what a particular document expresses about

something and what the broader society has to say about it.[19] At bottom, a document constitutes a dialogue between figures from the past, a dialogue between these figures and the reality of which they are a part; and is thus the fruit of quite diverse circumstances. Moreover, when the dialogue is cross-cultural in nature, when the individuals represented in it are from different cultures, it can take on added complexity, or—in some cases—become all but incomprehensible.[20] This explains the intrinsic difficulty that we find in relying on the written record of the viceregal period in attempting to penetrate and grasp the Indians' point of view.

To cloud the picture even more, the majority of the documents in question are legal in character, encumbered by arcane judicial terminology and short on simple, straightforward description. In theory, Spanish law established a series of procedures, or safeguards, that would permit all of the central parties in a dispute to be heard and have their day in court. These procedures included the opportunity to state one's case fully, to present witnesses on one's own behalf, and to employ the services of interpreters and legal counsel. Yet, in the end, the densely legalistic nature of the process worked to obfuscate a person's arguments, burying them under a blanket of incomprehensible legal terms and references, while simultaneously ignoring the fact that anyone who was involved in a judicial process could lie, present false evidence, and call dishonest witnesses.

In the judicial proceedings that were the basis for the documents dealt with here, situations arose that had the effect of distorting or concealing the Indians' motives and reasoning.[21] Certain of these situations should be apparent to any historian, but others are more difficult to intuit. I will attempt here to elucidate some of them and thereby promote a clearer understanding of the documents. One of the first problems was that of language, since in many indigenous areas few people were bilingual. Although no census exists that would have recorded the rate of bilingualism within the mountainous areas of Oaxaca for the colonial period, it can be said, based on the documents under study, that some 98 percent of people in the sierra who authored a complaint or gave testimony as witnesses required the services of an interpreter.[22] An equally high number were unfamiliar with the written language and could not read what the escribano was recording during the trial or legal proceeding. Moreover, a good many of the Indians who served on a cabildo were incapable of even writing their own name. Generally, each indigenous *pueblo* (indigenous settlement or community) had only one or two persons who knew how to read and write, these being the scribes of the self-same council. As such, they served as intermediaries between their own leaders and the alcalde mayor. At the same time, their command of Spanish was sometimes so limited that they, too, needed to use interpreters. Furthermore, even those who spoke and wrote Spanish did not always clearly grasp nor use with sufficient fluency the legal terminology employed in the documents.[23] The latter were replete with unfamiliar words, unfamiliar even to many Spaniards themselves. Indeed, great numbers of individuals involved in disputes and lawsuits had no clear idea of the technical terms in which their case was being recorded and described.[24]

Beyond the difficulties associated with the use of language and the written word, however, still more complicated problems haunted the documents; namely, those that sprang from the different mental outlooks particular to the two societies and from the different concepts of law and justice that each held.[25] When the indigenous authorities came before the alcalde mayor to request his intervention, it was not simply the individuals involved in the dispute who confronted each other in his quarters but, rather, two distinct cultures and two separate legal codes: that of the Spanish magistrate, with his ideas and image of the world, and that of the Indians, the two interlinked in a complicated, ever-changing relationship. Even today, in some of Mexico's indigenous zones, the same conflict between two cultures and two legal codes persists; for example, a Tzotzil Indian of Chiapas might find when appearing before a judge that the latter has little or no understanding of his arguments or reasoning. The degree of understanding brought by the judge will hinge on how much knowledge he has of indigenous culture. Furthermore, the law and legal procedure as applied by Indian judges differed sharply from their counterparts as applied by non-Indian judges. On occasion, the procedures followed by the former may strike us as devoid of logic and good sense.[26] Moreover, this condition still obtains today, but how much more serious and prevalent must it have been during colonial times?

On the other hand, documents emanating from the Oaxacan sierra, or from any indigenous region, were drawn up in the offices of the alcalde mayor, and those staffing its tribunal would have been more concerned with following existing procedure and the strict letter of the law than with trying to divine the murky roots of the Indians' problems. The legalistic tone and language of the documents and the prescribed views and interests of the alcaldes mayores and their factotums together suppressed the Indians' perspective to such an extent that a simple reading of the documents is bound to miss it. On top of this problem are the difficulties that exist in trying to translate the concepts of one culture into the language of another.[27]

Although Spanish documents of a legal cast and spirit clearly conceal part of the life of the Indian pueblos, they are not completely alien to the reality that produced them. As emphasized above, they are the fruit of a dialogue, a dialogue marked at times by confusion and plagued by incorrect readings and invalid translations but capable nonetheless of being deciphered, if only partially.[28] Every document that finds its way into our hands is unique, as unique as were the individuals who participated in its creation. Thus, only a minute analysis of each document will bring us what we wish to know, or bring us close enough to apprehend it: the world of the Indian and the life, ideas, and problems that it contained.[29] Furthermore, in this effort to comprehend the Indians, the legal records themselves provide us with a vital key, as a considerable number of them incorporate material authored by Indian scribes in their own languages. These writings, which include wills, letters, and—of greatest value—the so-called *títulos primordiales* (primordial titles),[30] give us a clearer picture of native society; for example, how its lands were organized, how its internal conflicts played out, and how its people interpreted their past. Without the insight—incomplete as it may be—that these documents afford us into how indigenous society construed such concepts as power and hierarchy and how it viewed its rights in relation to land and territory, it would not be possible to understand why the Indians turned to the use of Spanish law or what impact this development had on their lives.

Moreover, to bring ourselves closer to the indigenous world we must employ a subtle methodology, weaving carefully back and forth from one type of document and modality to another, from Zapotec writing to writing in Spanish, from the present to the past, from the Zapotec language and its concepts to our own language and its ideas. For example, if we wish to understand the role played by authorities on the Indian cabildo, we need to know how the Indians themselves explained it, in their own language, as set down by their own scribe, as opposed to simply reading a translation of their account made by the Spanish scribe. To be truly aware of the totality of the role they played in mediating matters both sacred and profane, we must know the nature of their actions in religious ceremonies as well as in civil affairs; furthermore, we need to know the content of their activity in today's world in order to have an idea—remote though it may be—of what their conduct and actions were in centuries past and to enlighten ourselves about the various tasks and duties that they fulfilled, which go unmentioned in the documents.[31] In aspiring to understand the past history of the indigenous population, we must begin with its present reality, for if we lack an understanding of contemporary indigenous society, how can we think that we will come to know its earlier incarnation through documents written by Spanish magistrates and infused with Spanish ideas and legal terminology?

Only by continually weaving between past and present, reflecting on the subject of our interest, are we able to delineate and gain insight into the complexities of indigenous history. Only in this movement from one document to another, from our own ideas to those of native society, can we continue, by degrees, to reconstruct this history.

THE VILLAGES OF THE SIERRA

After many years, by sifting through numerous documents, undertaking visits to the sierra, conversing with friends, and reading extensively about the past and present, I have tried to reconstruct the shape and texture of life in a Zapotecan village during the colonial period. What I present here is a model that future research will either confirm or modify, a somewhat atemporal model to be sure, but without which there is no way to understand the history of the Zapotec, the changes that they experienced, and the linkages and rivalries that existed both among the Zapotec themselves and between Zapotec and Spanish society.[32]

It is common to think of the Indian pueblos as Indian republics, or—put another way—as having constituted rural communities possessing a cabildo, a particular hierarchy of designated posts, and communal lands. This definition, however, is inadequate, as it fails to yield an understanding of the dynamic of conflict internal to the pueblos, either individually or between and among them. More specifically, an understanding is needed of Zapotecan community organization similar to that found in the studies done on Nahuatl communities by Pedro Carrasco, James Lockhart, Mercedes Olivera, and Luis Reyes.[33] In our case, by analyzing documents written in Zapotec and by using a particular methodology, it becomes possible to discern—behind the dominant discourse of the legal record—other points of view and other interests and to reconstruct the internal organization of a mountain pueblo. In this approach, moreover, I also endeavor to understand the relationships among the people of an indigenous community in terms of kinship and evolving positions of power and prestige.[34]

The heart of Zapotecan social organization was the pueblo, or *yetze*, as it was known in the form of Zapotec spoken in the mountains.[35] To judge from documents written in this language, a pueblo was no more than a rudimentary human settlement, but within this nucleus, what mattered above all else were the relationships that tied people together, real or symbolic kinship relationships as well as relationships of power and prestige.[36] A yetze was the union of several lineages or family lines, as a rule three or four, characterized by a powerful sense of common identity.[37] The notion that the people who made up a yetze embodied the prestige of their community was a central element in their identity and in their daily lives. Insofar as conflicts between one settlement and another created, and still create, difficulties in the sierra, this situation derives in part from the idea that a hierarchy exists among them. As a concept, the prestige of a pueblo is invisible, but its members struggle constantly to endow the concept with visible, material support; in the past this support took the form of a sacred power made manifest in the temple and its objects, in the person of the pueblo's leaders and power holders, and in the land. Even today, the prestige held by a community continues to be based on these three factors.[38]

As noted above, a pueblo comprised several lineages, among which there also existed highly elaborate hierarchical relationships. Moreover, out of all the lineages, one was deemed the most powerful and prestigious, and its leader served as the head of the full group of family lines.[39] The prestige that an individual enjoyed in his pueblo was determined by the position that he held within his lineal group. His proximity to the sacred founders of the lineage, the capacity to trace his own descent from them in a direct line, how well he knew his own genealogy—these factors controlled whether he belonged to what the Spaniards defined as the indigenous nobility, or *principales*, and the Zapotec termed *xohuanas*. The serfs in this system were those who could not establish a clear line connecting themselves to the ancient founders of the group. They therefore were consigned to performing menial tasks, such as carrying firewood, cutting grass to feed domestic animals, and retrieving and conveying messages. In addition, they were subject to taxation.[40] Given the importance that lineages had in the structure and internal functioning of the pueblo, it is necessary to have a detailed picture of them. Unfortunately, however, very little is actually known about the lineages. The títulos primordiales—the sacred texts that relate the migration of family lines, the founding of their pueblo, and the act by which they took possession of their land— make reference to these lineages only through the names of their leaders, and these in turn, at least for those cases that are known, are males only. This fact leads us to think that the lineages were patrilineal, that leadership positions were occupied by men, and that the ownership of land passed down to male heirs. At the beginning of the eighteenth century, the Zapotec used the term *tronco* (branch) to refer to what we call lineage.[41] In such instances, everyone belonging to a tronco had the same surname, save the serfs, who were not included in these select groups.[42]

A pueblo or yetze viewed itself, symbolically, as a great family, and the terms that the Zapotec employed when referring to each other reflected both this ideal construct and the genuine ties of reciprocity and assistance that they had developed among themselves. Yet to see the settlement as constituting a great family does only partial justice to the vigorous networks of solidarity and mutual aid that existed among its members, networks that, in remote times, must have been similar to those that continue today to be active ingredients in the life of Mexico's indigenous communities. All the same, the close relationships that obtained between family groups could fragment for any number of reasons. The most frequent cause of such ruptures, though, was the struggle waged by leaders of secondary lineages to accede to the position of highest prestige and power in the pueblo. There were other causes behind the fragmentation of lineages, such as population growth and demographic change and the need to augment landholdings in order to feed a greater number of family members. The splitting up of lineages could also occur on the basis of peaceful arrangements.[43]

The conflicts that broke out within a pueblo did not take place simply between one man and another; rather, they involved one or another group or groups of families. The conflicts took place, then, between different lineages. A man never stood alone in his difficulties; if someone encountered a problem with the members of another lineage or group of families, his own lineage lined up to support him. This element of group loyalty heightened the intensity of conflict. When lineages broke apart, the bitterness and pain of separation could be every bit as powerful as the ties that had previously united them. Indeed, in such grave situations, problems were only resolved by the expulsion of the alienated group or by the voluntary separation of the leader and his people, who then found themselves obliged to scour the land in search of a place where they could establish a new pueblo.[44]

Such splitting off or expulsion of a group was a principal cause of the migrations so frequently mentioned throughout Mesoamerican literature from pre-Columbian times to the present.[45] These migrations might involve traveling only a short distance from the pueblo that was abandoned, or they might entail lengthy journeys, covering considerable distances. The latter occurred especially in times of great political upheaval, such as those wrought by the fall of Monte Albán or Tula, or—predictably—by the Spanish conquest and the devastating epidemics that followed it.[46] In the post-conquest period, some mountain pueblos were obliged to move and resettle themselves as many as three times.[47] Numerous maps and *lienzos* (canvases) from the colonial era, written in Zapotec and using the Spanish alphabet, refer time and again to a pilgrimage, to the act of taking possession of certain lands either peacefully or by force, and to the founding of a new pueblo.[48]

The migration of a pueblo and the physical journey that its members made across mountains, rivers, and unknown places until coming to found a new pueblo was the most important event in their history. In pre-Hispanic times, the experience was recorded in lienzos and screenfolds and evoked in songs and other forms of expression. During the colonial period, it was again represented in lienzos and maps and—for the first time—was given formal written expression in the complex texts that have come to be known as the títulos primordiales.[49] It is difficult to overstate the significance of these texts. The títulos primordiales are the written version of the origin stories, stories that served as the key legal foundation of the identity of a new pueblo. As such, they were nothing less than its birth certificate, its Bible, its Koran, its own sacred book: they were the ultimate proof of its existence as an autonomous community.

The leaders of family lines held on to these documents as the most compelling evidence to sustain and validate their claims over particular lands.[50] It is not known how, before the arrival of the Spanish, the indigenous rulers resolved their differences, outside of resorting to war; yet some process—nonbelligerent in nature—must have existed, and it is possible that these sacred titles played a purposeful role within it. Indeed, it was for this very reason that pueblo authorities placed the sacred documents at the disposal of Spanish magistrates. From an early point in the development of New Spain, moreover, it is clear that the courts accepted codices and other pictorial renderings as proof of what the pueblos declared about their history and matters related thereto. At the same time, the Indians undoubtedly had their own reasons for introducing these documents, and it behooves us to understand them. To the extent that uncertainty may have surrounded the titles, how did it arise? How did Spanish magistrates interpret and make sense of the indigenous documents? What benefit did it bring to the Indians to preserve their written history and use it to prove the legitimacy of the claims they made before the courts of New Spain?

THE OBSCURE MANTLE OF THE LAW: A CASE STUDY

What follows is the detailed study of a particular case, in which, in 1715, a Zapotecan pueblo, San Juan Juquila Rincono,[51] made the text of its sacred history available to the alcalde mayor of Villa Alta in order to prove its right to hold certain lands in a dispute with the neighboring community of San Juan Tanetze.[52] I endeavor to reconstruct the arguments made by each of the parties involved and the procedures that they used to make them: these included the traditional arguments, based on custom and the appeal to an ancient right, and the attempts that they made to apply the laws of the Indies in their own favor, as well as the use of other elements that they had appropriated from Hispanic culture. I further attempt to understand how the interests of Indian pueblos were reinterpreted by the Spanish *procuradores* (untitled lawyers) to whom the Indians had to turn as a condition of having their case presented before the colonial judicial authorities. Finally, I analyze the legal process and its impact on the evolution of the conflict, how it affected intra-pueblo relationships, and how it served to help construct networks of power in New Spain.

The conflict between Tanetze and Juquila apparently began in October 1715, when both pueblos contested control over some lands that had remained unoccupied as the result of the depopulating of Totolinga, another Zapotecan pueblo. The dispute, however, had important antecedents, which can be traced back at least sixty-five years, to 1650. Traditionally, Totolinga enjoyed lower status and rank as a settlement than Juquila;[53] furthermore, as the result of an epidemic it had become depopulated and its lands left vacant. Totolinga's survivors—three or four *caciques* (leaders or prominent members of the community) plus a handful of families—had resettled themselves in Juquila, where they were accepted after an agreement was worked out between both pueblos. In the words of the document, the residents of Juquila declared, that they accepted them because "they are our forbearers as our old ways record."[54]

The band of Totolingans agreed to cede their lands to Juquila, in return for which the residents of Juquila would construct a bridge so that the priest who had served the parish would be able to make his way. In 1674, the authorities of Juquila and the Totolinga survivors gave testimony to the alcalde mayor of the agreement that had been established between them, through which, "in peace and by consent," the lands belonging to Totolinga could be "at the service" of the people of Juquila.[55] At the same time as this occurrence, the neighboring pueblo of San Juan Tanetze had begun making use of the same vacant lands. To guarantee its right to these lands, Tanetze had allocated them to its *cofradía* (religious brotherhood) of San Juan Bautista and also rented them out to some residents of Juquila. It then used the rent money to fund its celebration of the festival of San Juan.

The dispute between the two pueblos, however, involved more than just the conflict over land. In 1715, when the difficulties between Tanetze and Juquila were heating up, it became evident that they were embroiled in a complicated rivalry concerning power and prestige. Thus, while their struggle over land was important, their conflict was not limited to this issue. During the sixteenth century, Tanetze had been larger than Juquila. Moreover, its population had been quite sizeable, enabling it—since that time—to have as its priest a member of the secular clergy.[56] At the end of the seventeenth century, however, the relationship between

Table 5.1. Evolution of the population

Year	1548	1568	1622	1703	1742
Tanetze	3,297	1,694	1,312	235	349
Juquila	919	338	299	313	466
Totolinga	683	155	88	—	—

Source: John Chance, *Conquest of the Sierra: Spaniards and Indians in Colonial Oaxaca* (Norman: University of Oklahoma Press, 1989), 50–51.

the two communities reversed itself; the population of Juquila had grown, which apparently fueled the development of certain rivalries between it and Tanetze (see Table 5.1). The conflict that developed in 1715 needs to be understood against this backdrop.

In that year, on a day in October, four authorities from Juquila—a *regidor* (councilman) and three *alcaldes* (council members who also had judicial responsibilities)—came before the alcalde mayor of San Ildefonso de la Villa Alta to present a complaint against the alcalde and several other residents of Tanetze for having treated them with gross disrespect. In their declaration, made through the services of the interpreter for the district court, they stated that the Tanetze authorities had been so bold as to detain their alcalde and regidor over a debt of forty pesos. The latter, so the complaint alleged, had been tied up and bustled off to jail and, were it not for the timely intervention of a Tanetze resident, would have been subjected to a whipping. In addition, the Juquilans accused their Tanetzean neighbors of having placed a series of nine crosses and stone markers on the Totolinga lands.

For their part, the Tanetzeans explained that between the two pueblos there existed a very old custom, called *guelaguetza*, which entailed the proffering of mutual assistance. In accordance with this custom, they—the Tanetzeans—had gone to Juquila to help the pueblo put a roof on its church. In return, Tanetze had requested that the Juquilans reciprocate by lending the same type of assistance. On the surface, all seemed equitable, but the judicial records detail certain demands that had been made by Tanetze that upset the equilibrium. Specifically, Juquila declared that when Tanetze helped in constructing the new roof on its church, the material that had been used was straw. And in return for the assistance received, Juquila had not only fed the Tanetzeans but had presented each of them with a roast chicken when they returned to their pueblo. Some months later, Tanetze requested that the favor be returned. Juquila thus prepared to fulfill its obligation of guelaguetza, except that Tanetze upset the balance by requiring that Juquila roof the Tanetze church not with straw but with tile. When Juquila rejected this requirement, Tanetze responded by demanding that Juquila at least pay the cost of the tiles, which came to the exact sum of forty pesos.

Moreover, to prove their legal right to the land on which the nine stone markers had recently been placed, the authorities of Juquila presented the alcalde mayor with the signed agreement of 1674, along with some documents written in their own language that they believed would also prove their right to hold the lands that had once been part of the ancient community of Totolinga. These latter documents (*memorias* or chronicles), written in Zapotec, were of the utmost importance. The first document, and also the longest and most complex, contained the story of the founding of Juquila; this was Juquila's sacred history, the so-called *La Memoria de Juquila*. The second document, much shorter and less involved, was *La Memoria de Totolinga*.[57] The Spanish magistrate hearing the case requested that his court interpreter translate the Zapotecan documents into Spanish, and once the translations were completed, he had them attached to the record. Apparently, however, the magistrate never bothered to read the translated versions, nor did he make any attempt to familiarize himself with their contents.[58] In truth, both histories would have been difficult to understand, even if the magistrate had been motivated to do so. For that, he would have had to possess a mastery not of the Zapotec language but of elements of Zapotecan and Mesoamerican philosophy, such as what it expounded about the intricate nature of relationships of power and about connections between the realms of religion and politics and between sacred history and the act of taking possession of particular lands. Perhaps the sole person qualified to understand the document and to explain it to the alcalde mayor was the court interpreter, a Zapotec Indian by the name of Gabriel Manzano. This individual, however, did no such thing; he confined himself to translating the Zapotecan writings into Spanish and to attaching the translation to the record. After that, he kept silent. No reference exists in the record suggesting that any attempt was made to understand the memorias.

It is indeed interesting that the authorities of Juquila preserved the two memorias, their own and that of Totolinga, in the pueblo's archive. When they are scrutinized closely and carefully, it is possible to note the superior power that Juquila commanded in relation to Totolinga. That Juquila enjoyed greater prestige is evident, first, in the simple fact that its memoria was considerably longer and more complex. Yet the principal distinguishing factor was that the authorities of Juquila had gone overseas, to Spain, to receive the emblems of power and governance, whereas their counterparts from Totolinga had traveled no further than the Valley of Oaxaca, where these emblems were presented to them by ancestral authorities of Juquila.[59]

Returning to the conflict between the two communities, a critical question arises: why did the Juquila authorities hand over these sacred documents to the alcalde mayor? They must have done so because, to their way of thinking, the documents constituted the main proof of their right to the lands that Tanetze now also claimed. Juquila felt justified in keeping these lands because they had been part of a community subordinated to its power, a condition that was ratified in its memorias as well as in the agreement signed in 1674 with the Totolinga survivors, which had been recorded in the presence of the alcalde mayor at that time.

Since the Tanetze authorities did not possess such written evidence of their community's right to the lands, they skillfully resorted to other arguments that carried more weight in the Spanish legal system. They asserted that the lands belonged to their cofradía, and that with the funds obtained from renting them out, the pueblo was able to celebrate the festival of the Santísima Imagen de la Virgen. This argument was supported by the pueblo's priest, who went further and called upon the Juquilans to see the light of reason and pay the forty pesos, and thereby put an end to the conflict. When the authorities of Tanetze were summoned to make a declaration in front of the alcalde mayor, they stated that they had detained Juquila's alcalde only because he owed the forty pesos and, further, that it was not at all certain that they had encroached upon the disputed lands. On the contrary, they asserted that a person from Juquila had trespassed, occupying lands that were not his, and that they had only restored some stone markers that were cracked and broken.

The problems between Juquila and Tanetze take on greater meaning when they are understood as integral parts of a wider situation that involved intra-pueblo rivalry and hierarchy. Clearly, subjecting the alcaldes and regidor of Juquila to detention and physical mistreatment was a serious affront to their prestige and authority. What is more, if Tanetze had lost almost 80 percent of its population, the pueblo would have had no driving need to add to its lands. In point of fact, what it had done was to rent the lands under dispute to residents of Juquila, whose population was growing, using the funds to pay for the festival honoring its patron saint. It was a matter of status. A sumptuous celebration would elevate the prestige of Tanetze, despite its diminished population. The struggle over land needs to be seen in this context.

The conflict was a battle fought not with arms but with legal cunning. The party that won would be the party best able to manipulate the arguments in its favor and also cultivate useful connections with the local representatives of Spanish power and authority. In this type of struggle, the community more steeped in tradition, more tied to its own notions and system of justice—holding to the idea that its ancient documents were the most convincing form of proof—stood less chance of victory than the community that knew better how to handle the procedures and dictates governing the laws of the Indies. Fatefully, it appears in this case as though Juquila believed that its sacred writings, both its own memoria and that of its long-ago subordinate community, Totolinga, were arguments in its favor. Juquilan representatives also tried to explain the reasons underlying their position by delivering these documents in Spanish, for which purpose it asked a resident of San Ildefonso to translate them, so that they could be presented to the alcalde mayor: "With all due solemnity [we present to you] all of our records, the first being from the year 1521; in which you will find a lengthy exposition of all that pertained to our original founding and of all the rewards of land that we earned through our gentility and good offices."[60]

These efforts notwithstanding, from the outset of the conflict Tanetze seemed to be more artful in finding ways to impress and convince the alcalde mayor, as, for example, when its authorities presented themselves to the alcalde in the company of the schoolmaster, who could perform the valuable task of translating what was said and written down. They also managed to gain the support of their parish priest, a witness of unquestioned authority, and their lawyers were more skillful. Ultimately, however, Tanetze's greatest advantage appears to have been its success in managing to bring onto its legal team, in 1716—one year after the litigation began—a citizen of Villa Alta who was expert in legal terminology and knew how to compose and present a legal case. This individual, who used a variety of tactics to contradict and deflate Juquila's claims, asserted that his clients were ready to present their own records, that is to say, their own long-held titles. Yet the promised documents were never produced, because some days later it was reported that they had been destroyed in a fire. Tanetze's residents nonetheless held to the claim that the lands had been theirs from time immemorial and, furthermore, that they could bring witnesses from neighboring communities to testify that Juquila's titles were of "no merit," were in fact "false and of evil motive"; that the parish priest himself had tried to "point [the residents of Juquila] in the direction of law and reason"; and, finally, that if all of the foregoing were not sufficient, they would bring the priest with them so that he could corroborate the facts.[61]

Juquila was apparently much less skilled in knowing how to present its argument. The pueblo relied on a single individual, in all likelihood a

Zapotec Indian, who made a not only fruitless but also counterproductive attempt to research and understand the laws of the Indies. In 1716, this person argued, on the basis of reasons grounded in Zapotecan tradition, that the lands under litigation had belonged to his forbears, as set down in the records of old, and that they had concluded an agreement with three or four caciques of Totolinga. He further wrote:

> We submit before your grace these lands as royal lands pertaining to and being of the King our Lord, who was the absolute owner of said pueblo of Totolinga, which ceased to exist . . . and to avoid disagreements and expenses we beseech that this submission be admitted and the lands be declared, as such, royal lands, which belong to His Majesty, may God preserve him for many years, and may he likewise come personally to give witness to these lands and to mark out for us the six hundred *varas* that His Majesty holds and has under his protection.[62]

Behind this appeal, which gave the impression of being based on knowledge of the Spanish system of power and of the rights of the monarchy over the lands, there clearly seeped through elements of a Zapotecan way of thinking, which confused rights possessed by its ancient founders with those adhering to the Spanish monarch. The illogic and ignorance of the argument advanced by Juquila's advocate became evident when he expressed the expectation that the king himself would appear in person to distribute—in each direction—the 600 *varas* (units of land) that belonged to the pueblo. He further confused the matter by adding—later in the document—that the king would proceed to distribute Tanetze's lands in the same manner. Obviously, the king had not parceled out and distributed the lands in person, nor would he; the notion, however, that he had, and would again do so, corresponded to Zapotecan belief, according to which the land had been given over to the founders of the ancient pueblos by the sacred authorities themselves. The muddled reasoning was seized upon by Tanetze's lawyer, who argued that, in accordance with Spanish law, Juquila had no right to seek 600 varas for another community, adding that it employed this tactic only because it lacked the needed titles and, furthermore, had always intended to meddle in outside matters, when in fact the record itself enumerated Juquila's titles.

For more than a year, from September 1715 to the end of 1716, authorities from the two pueblos made various trips to the Spanish town, bringing witnesses with them from neighboring settlements as well as from their own communities. Around November 1716, both Tanetze and Juquila found it necessary to engage the services of Spanish representatives from Villa Alta, who would presumably present their legal arguments more effectively. From this point forward, however, the case took on a somewhat different coloration; as arguments—on the part of both parties—began to drag out unnecessarily. Each side simply denied the claims of its adversary, without marshalling any evidence, and by calling upon the testimony of supportive witnesses. The case steadily dissolved into a jumble of claims and counterclaims, each party accusing the other of pursuing its interests out of malice and base motives, of spreading falsehoods and committing perjury, and of acting with scant fear of the Almighty—all the while protesting that its claimants held legitimate title to the lands. The case got bogged down for days and then months inside the office of the alcalde mayor. The legal documentation became thicker and thicker, making it progressively more difficult to follow the trail of the arguments. As the accusations flew back and forth, insults were tacked on and the Zapotec tradition of titles was itself depreciated. At one point, the Tanetze representative stated that Juquila's titles were false, because they were no more than simple scribblings that lacked any real authority. At another point, he asserted that they belonged not to Juquila but to the pueblo of Yalina, which had loaned them to Juquila, an argument that could have easily been refuted if the alcalde mayor had simply read the translation inserted at the beginning of the documentation.[63] On yet another occasion the Tanetze representative brazenly claimed that Juquila lacked any titles whatsoever.

At last, after nearly a year and a half had transpired since the litigation began, the alcalde mayor of Villa Alta—without clarifying the reason for his actions—proceeded to hand down a definitive ruling: he declared that the lands under dispute belonged to Tanetze. Nevertheless, the case went on; the definitive ruling lacked finality, as Juquila appealed the judgment and managed after some time to secure half of the disputed lands. In its appeal, Juquila claimed that when Tanetze rented out the lands, it had done so using force, and asserted again that it was the rightful owner of the lands. The key factor, however, that caused the alcalde to set aside his initial ruling was the engineered ambiguity of the case. The arguments made by the attorney for one pueblo were discredited by the attorney for the other, and vice versa, and each in turn bottled up his adversary's arguments in arcane legal terminology and technical points of law. Each party made whatever assertions it found convenient, and the mountain of paperwork kept on growing—this in a society in which very few were literate and even fewer still were conversant with legal reasoning and terminology. The case devolved into a string of writs and pleadings, followed by their subsequent annulment; of appeals brought and appeals denied; of judicial procedures that lurched in one direction and then another; and of the summoning of witnesses who spoke no Spanish and had even less ability to read what had been recorded in writing. Over the course of four years—from 1715 to the middle of 1719—the case went on being heard exclusively within the office of the alcalde mayor, save for a single exception, when a notice concerning it was sent to the procurador of the Real Audiencia in the city of Antequera.

It is impossible not to draw the impression that the attorneys for both pueblos deceived their clients, deliberately adding to the paperwork in order to pad their earnings. This situation became clear when the case reached the chambers of the Real Audiencia in Mexico City, whose judges made the following observation about it: "[E]verything set out thus far lacks clarity and justification."[64] At the end of 1719, Juquila's alcalde and scribe decided to travel to Mexico City to represent the interests of the pueblo and, once there, handed over authority to an attorney of the high court as a condition of his taking the case. Some days later, the Juquila plaintiffs succeeded in getting the court to validate the ruling that the alcalde mayor had made in favor of Juquila, the ruling, made on appeal, that had divided the lands into equal parts shared between the two pueblos. The legal travail, however, had yet to run its course. Tanetze—through its own lawyer—challenged the ruling, requesting that it be nullified, stating again that it was the rightful owner of the lands and that it had been given a half-share that was actually smaller than Juquila's, and summoning such other farfetched arguments as the claim that "its witnesses were better and more suitable" and had been selected by the authority of His Majesty, the king.[65]

The case was reopened, but henceforth its claimants had to travel all the way to Mexico City, and the lawyers who argued before the audiencia charged more dearly, to be sure, than the wily types who flocked around the alcalde in Villa Alta. Around 1721, apropos of the higher outlays, the Juquilans stated that if the case were carried to the bitter end, "its cost will be greater than what the lands are worth."[66] All the same, the case stretched out until the end of 1725, and over the course of these last four years, the pueblos' legal representatives continued their incessant wrangling, until the audiencia at last confirmed that the lands should be divided in half, thus circling back to the very solution that had been arrived at some ten years earlier.

It had become clear during the many years of the case that the conflict between Tanetze and Juquila was not confined to the struggle over land but concerned deeper competition and rivalry between the two pueblos. In antiquity, indigenous diplomacy, as manifested in the custom of guelaguetza and in the recourse to Zapotecan titles, had in all likelihood regulated relationships between communities, anchoring them within a framework of exchange and equilibrium. The native inhabitants, of course, did not live in a world of complete harmony; the wars that periodically broke out between them attest to that. Nonetheless, I have the impression that the aforementioned equilibrium became even more fragile when Indian pueblos tried to dominate neighboring communities by manipulating Spanish power and institutions to their advantage. In their eagerness for standing and prestige, the pueblos themselves helped to bolster the Spanish legal system—a corrupt system ridden with complications and red tape—and collaborate simultaneously in undermining both their ancient custom of guelaguetza and the system of Zapotecan titles.

CONCLUSION

The great volume of judicial records that exists today in state and national archives is tangible evidence that Spanish power managed to reach into the most remote areas of southern New Spain. To grasp just how this was accomplished is complicated and involves identifying and understanding overlapping relationships of power, relationships between the metropolitan center of New Spain and the more peripheral indigenous regions, on the one hand, and among the Indian communities themselves on the other. The two sets of relationships became intertwined, thus the application of Spanish colonial law must be studied in relation to the internal organization of the Indian pueblos and their own conflicts and rivalries.

In the majority of cases, such application of Spanish law cannot be understood as an attempt to secure justice. Rather, it should be seen as part of a system or network of alliances whose objective was the exercise of power. The Indian pueblos supported the heavy outlay of resources and human energy exacted by the colonial judicial system and its workings for the sole purpose of weakening their enemy—the rival pueblo. Yet as part of this process, the ancient system of indigenous law that by all rights had existed to stabilize relationships between one community and another, aided possibly by recourse to the títulos primordiales, was losing its own meaning and force. Although translated into Spanish, the Zapotecan titles were cast aside, the content of their sacred histories was ignored and, still worse, devalued and made the object of derision. Even the final agreement signed between Juquila's authorities and the Spanish magistrate was brushed aside; once concluded, it should have obviated any need for the case to continue for another ten years, but terminating the case at that point would have undercut the bureaucratic power of the Spanish legal system and its representatives to manage the affairs of the indigenous population. The alcalde mayor, the local attorneys, the Mexico

City attorneys, on up to the judges of the audiencia all would have seen their power curtailed. To extend the process indefinitely, tying it up in a legalistic and esoteric discourse, formed part of their structure of domination. The conflict could also have been shortened if, in all the legal arguments surrounding the guelaguetza, impartial witnesses had been called who could have explained the nature and practice of this Zapotecan custom, but such interest patently did not exist.

Nowadays, what is called indigenous law is purely internal to Indian communities, and the time-honored custom of resorting to outside laws and authorities as an element of power and force continues—the appeal now, of course, being not to colonial but to national authorities. Nevertheless, the foundations for manipulating the laws and for dragging out their enforcement indefinitely were put in place in those long-ago times. The practice of manipulation was and continues to be a central component of structures of power.

NOTES

1. This work forms part of a research project dealing with conflicts over land in the indigenous communities of the state of Oaxaca, Mexico. The project was begun as part of a larger study, concerning the Sierra Zapoteca, in collaboration with Nancy M. Farriss and Arthur G. Millar, funded by the National Endowment for the Humanities and the Paul Getty Foundation.

2. From the outset of colonization, the Spanish Crown attempted to impose order on the machinery of conquest and bring the recently conquered lands under a system of control. To this end, between 1492 and 1550, some 100,000 regulations and administrative orders were issued, collected, and reproduced in 200 volumes of *cédulas* (decrees) kept in the Council of the Indies. See Alonso de Zorita, *Leyes y ordenanzas reales de las Indias del Mar océano* (México DF: Miguel Ángel Porrúa, 1985 [1574]), especially articles by Alfonso García Gallo, 15–26, and Beatriz Bernal, 31–142.

3. Stuart Hampshire offers an important perspective on this issue—the consideration of legal systems as elements of the philosophical system characteristic of a society—in his book, *Justice Is Conflict* (Princeton, NJ: Princeton University Press, 2000). Hampshire's central focus is the study of conflict and its regulation in multicultural situations.

4. On agrarian conflicts during the nineteenth century, see Manuel Esparza, *Conflictos por límites de tierras, Oaxaca* (Oaxaca: Archivo General del Estado de Oaxaca, 1991). On similar conflicts in the twentieth century, see Sergio Sarmiento, *Conflictos agrarios y perspectivas del campo oaxaqueño* (Oaxaca: CIESAS, Instituto de Investigaciones Sociológicas, UABJO, INI, 1999).

5. Eulogio Gillow, archbishop of Oaxaca, referred in 1889 to the region's isolation, describing its inhabitants as living between ravines and mountain crests;

Apuntes históricos sobre la idolatría e introducción del cristianismo en Oaxaca (México DF: Ediciones Toledo, 1990 [1889]), 89.

6. On the matter of the mountains and their influence in the sixteenth century, see John K. Chance, *Conquest of the Sierra: Spaniards and Indians in Colonial Oaxaca* (Norman: University of Oklahoma Press, 1989), 17, 29, 89. Near the end of the eighteenth century (1794), there were 83 haciendas (large landed estates) in the Intendency of Oaxaca, compared to 824, 478, and 139 in the Intendencies of Mexico, Puebla, and Tlaxcala, respectively. The mines in Oaxaca were few in number and of little value; only those of Villa Alta enjoyed a certain degree of fame, but their economic worth was negligible. Data taken from José Miranda, "Evolución cuantitativa y desplazamientos de la población indígena de Oaxaca en la época colonial," in *Estudios de historia novohispana*, 2 vols. (México DF: UNAM, 1968), 2:139; Miranda bases these claims on information provided by Alexander von Humboldt.

7. Population statistics furnished by Chance, *Conquest of the Sierra*, 35–48, 63.

8. In 1674, the alcalde mayor commented on the "lack of a person in this town to administer justice," explaining that a particular document was "signed by me, since there is neither a public nor a royal notary, either in this town or for 20 leagues around." Archivo General de la Nación (herafter AGN) Tierras, vol. 335, exp. 5, Autos de San Juan Tanetze sobre sus tierras, 1715.

9. Documents for the year 1580 from the Archivo Histórico del Poder Judicial de Oaxaca (hereafter, AHPJO), Sección Teposcolula, Oaxaca.

10. At this time, the research focuses on studying disputes over land that occurred between villages. At a later stage, we will analyze how such conflict played out within individual villages, elaborating a typology of the same. Findings are based on documents in the AGN, Ramo Tierras, and on documents in the AHPJO, Sección de Villa Alta, Oaxaca.

11. As based on documents in the AGN, Ramo Tierras, and on documents in the AHPJO, Sección de Villa Alta, Oaxaca, dating to the sixteenth to the eighteenth centuries.

12. The explanation of the conquest as bringing a new era of power, as heralding the dawn of a new cosmic period, has been given detailed treatment in María de los Ángeles Romero Frizzi's *El sol y la cruz: Los pueblos indios de Oaxaca colonial* (México DF: CIESAS, INI, 1996), 107–117, and "Los cantos de los linajes en el mundo colonial," *Memorias de la Academia Mexicana de la Historia* 43 (2000): 46–47. On the Mesoamerican concept of cycles of creation and destruction associated with changes in society, see Miguel León Portilla, *La filosofía náhuatl*, (México DF: UNAM, 1993), 402–408, and Maarten Jansen, "La serpiente emplumada y el amanecer de la historia," in *Códices, caciques y comunidades: Cuadernos de Historia Lantinoamericana* 5 (1997): 11–64.

13. From the best-known cosmic myth, called "El quinto sol," as narrated by Fray Bernadino de Sahagún, in Chapter 1, Book 3, and Chapter 2, Book Seven, of his *Historia general de las cosas de la Nueva España*, 2 vols. (México DF: Consejo Nacional para la Cultura y las Artes and Alianza Editorial Mexicana, 1989 [1570s]).

14. See note 12.

15. For example, Don Felipe de Santiago, the *cacique* (indigenous leader or powerholder) of Yazona (a Zapotecan mountain village) knew how to write and had a keen understanding of the laws of New Spain. Capitalizing on this knowledge, he tried in 1698 to take possession of certain lands not belonging to him. AGN Tierras, vol. 167, 2nd part, exp. 2. In the Mesoamerican mind, power was highly sacralized. Such belief had also existed in Europe, given that monarchs were viewed as God's representatives on earth and as possessing curative powers. See Marc Bloch, *Los reyes taumaturgos* (México DF: Fondo de Cultura Económica, 1988). A more secular, rationalist idea of power began to gain importance during the Renaissance and came to full fruition during the French Revolution.

16. It is typically thought that such disputes over land were provoked by the Spanish authorities in order to keep the Indian villages divided against each other, and thus more readily under imperial control. The reasons for these disputes, however, were more complicated, although they did lead to this result. Reports exist about disputes over land between two villages in the Sierra Zapoteca that predate the arrival of the Spanish. See Archivo General de las Indias (AGI) Justicia 205, no. 5. (The document is dated 1558 but refers to skirmishes prior to 1521.)

17. AGI Justicia, vol. 205, no. 5.

18. It is also common to think that the conflicts over land had one cause— the ill-defined boundaries separating adjacent villages; yet a reading of the documents in the AGN, Ramo Tierras, and an analysis of contemporary problems demonstrate that such conflicts arose for a number of reasons, all of which require elucidation.

19. Among the examples that afford the best understanding of the difference between the Spanish and the indigenous ways of seeing things are the títulos primordiales, which contain the Indians' ideas of history and their right to the land. As Miguel León Portilla observed, "[c]onsiderable time would have to pass for the awareness to dawn that native testimonies existed which were worthy of careful consideration." See *La filosofía náhuatl* (México DF: UNAM, 1993), 456.

20. I have drawn generally upon works by such authors as Mikhail Bakhtin, Isaiah Berlin, Jacques Derrida, Clifford Geertz, Jack Goody, Emilio Lledó, and Tzevetan Todorov.

21. See the work of Juan Carlos Martínez Martínez, "El expediente judicial desde una perspectiva dialógica: ¿Heteroglosia o monoglosia," *Cuadernos del Sur* 9, no. 19 (2003): 43–50.

22. This state of affairs, however, cannot be generalized to New Spain as a whole, or even to all of Oaxaca. Laura Waterbury, for example, in her study on the Valley of Tlacolula, Oaxaca, found that a significant number of Indians did not need to use an interpreter during the course of judicial proceeding; "In a Land with Two Laws: Spanish and Indigenous Justice in Eighteenth Century Oaxaca, Mexico" (Ph.D. dissertation, University of Illinois at Chicago, Chicago, 2004). On the state of bilingualism in the Sierra Zapoteca, see Chance, *Conquest of the Sierra*, 124.

23. Some members of the Indian nobility of both Oaxaca and of other regions of New Spain studied in Mexico City's university, but they were few in number

(Margarita Menegus Bornemann and Rodolfo Aguirre, *Los indios, el sacerdocio y la Universidad en Nueva España, siglos XVI–XVIII* [México DF: Centro de Estudios Sobre la Universidad, UNAM, and Plaza y Valdés, 2006]). The archives do contain documents written in Spanish by Indians, for example, Archivo General del Poder Ejecutivo de Oaxaca (hereafter, AGEPEO), Ramo de alcaldías mayores, testamentos en español, vol. 21, exp. 1, 1708; from the same archive and section is Carta del alcalde de Teotlaxco, vol. 14, exp. 28, 1708; Quejas vs. la Cabecera de Teotalzingo, AGN Tierras vol. 282, exp. 4, 1763, and so forth.

24. Stuart Hampshire *Justice Is Conflict* views such court proceedings as a central problem in legal and judicial processes.

25. Isaiah Berlin, *El sentido de la realidad. Sobre las ideas y su historia* (Madrid: Taurus, 2000), 14–15. It is precisely this difference in mental outlook that makes the work of translation from one language to another so difficult.

26. Excellent examples of these problems will be found in Witold Jacorzynski's *Estudios sobre la violencia: Teoría y práctica* (México DF: CIESAS and Miguel Angel Porrúa, 2002), see in particular the chapter by Jane F. Collier, 123–139.

27. As the Dominican monk Juan de Córdova wrote in 1577, "the various meanings of their language and words do not coincide with ours." See Fray Juan de Córdova, *Vocabulario en lengua çapoteca*, edicion facsimilar (Oaxaca, México DF: Ediciones Toledo, INAH, 1987 [1587]), 12. In fact, many of the entries in Córdova's *Vocabulario* contain long explanations of Zapotecan terms rather than their translation into Spanish; Juana Vásquez Vásquez, personal communication, 1966. 28. Jacques Derrida's notion of a "double reading," as expressed in his book *Writing and Difference* (Chicago: University of Chicago Press, 1978), is the method of documentary interpretation to which I refer here.

29. For example, we have assumed that the Indians agreed to organize their government in conformity with the town councils of Castile because the Spaniards decreed it so in their laws. Yet if we focus on what the Indians say in their writings, in their títulos primordiales they relate how the pueblo's founders received their staff of office not in fidelity to the Castilian model but amid the ceremony that established the pueblo and, in concert, accorded recognition to the new power of the Spanish. See María de los Angeles Romero Frizzi and Juana Vásquez, "Memoria y escritura: La Memoria de Juquila," in *Escritura zapoteca, 2500 años de historia*, by María de los Angeles (México DF: CIESAS, INAH, 2003), 393–448.

30. The títulos primordiales contain the Indians' own version of their history; they are documents of a sacred character that relate the origins and founding of Indian communities. For more on them in a broad context, see Enrique Florescano, *Historia de las historias de la nación mexicana* (México DF: Taurus, 2002), 183–229; and also see ibid., "El canon memorioso forjado por los Títulos Primordiales," *Colonial Latin American Review* 11 (2002): 183–230.

31. The presentation by Ubaldo López García at the III Mesa Redonda de Monte Albán, INAH, Oaxaca, summer 2002, invoked numerous examples from the municipality of Apoala, in the Mixteca Alta of Oaxaca, to illustrate the symbolism still present today when one group of officials is replaced by another. It is

difficult to find references in the judicial documents to the symbolic and ceremonial aspects of such transference of authority within indigenous pueblos.

32. The documents demonstrate that the organization of Zapotecan society changed notably between the time of the early colonial world and the eighteenth century, owing to the tension and interrelationship between processes internal to the Indian pueblos and the wider society of New Spain.

33. In addition to works on the Nahua, there is the study on Mixtec society by Kevin Terraciano, *The Mixtecs of Colonial Oaxaca* (Stanford, CA: Stanford University Press, 2001), chap 4; and likewise Gerardo Gutiérrez's study of the Tlapa, in the state of Guerrero, presented as a paper at the IV Mesa Redonda de Monte Albán, Oaxaca, 2004. In my own estimation, one of the best-realized studies is that by Nathan Wachtel, *El regreso de los antepasados: Los indios urus de Bolivia, del siglo XX al XVI* (México DF: El Colegio de México, Fondo de Cultura Económica), 2001.

34. Power and prestige among the Zapotec also implied certain economic differences. John Chance, *Conquest of the Sierra*, 125–132, advances the idea that economic distinctions among the Zapotec became more pronounced in the eighteenth century because they were tied to the monopoly trading privileges held by the alcaldes mayores.

35. In the Valley of Oaxaca, the pueblo was called *quèche*, of which there were different types: pueblos with a small outlying settlement and population, pueblos of considerable size and a large resident population, and small pueblos. See Fray Juan de Córdova, *Vocabulario en lengua Çapoteca*, 332v.

36. To reconstruct the internal organization of a Zapotecan pueblo, I have used a method that combines several approaches: reading documents written in Zapotec, principally as found in the AGN, Tierras, 335, exp. 5; reading works by specialists in anthropological theory, for example, George Murdock; consulting theoretical works in the field of interpretive anthropology, with special reference to Clifford Geertz; and undertaking visits to some of the Zapotecan mountain communities, particularly to Villa Hidalgo Yalalag, where I was fortunate to experience the unexcelled hospitality of my friend Juana Vásquez and her family.

37. I define the term "lineage" to mean a group of people who are related to each other through a line of descent and who can trace their common relationship through a series of genealogical ties as set down in the prevailing line of descent. It is difficult to study the kinship system in the Indian pueblos through colonial documents. At present, this study is barely in its initial stages and is being carried out through the analysis of Zapotecan wills contained in the AGN, Tierras, and in the AHPJO.

38. Concerning the rivalries that existed between pueblos, see the document pertaining to Tepanzacualco, 1761, AGN Tierras, vol. 852, exp. 1. In 1898, Monseñor Guillow wrote, "They ardently wish to have the administrative seat and allege rights for themselves because they once came to the rescue of their parish priest"; Diario de Monseñor Guillow, Archive of Don Luis Castañeda Guzmán, Oaxaca. A schoolteacher from the Ayuuk Indians (Mixes) told me, on a past occasion, about

the tensions and rivalries over prestige that exist between communities and the importance that priestly vestments and religious objects in the churches hold for them.

39. These statements are based on an analysis of *La Memoria de Juquila*, AGN Tierras, 335, exp. 5. On the problems associated with understanding the kinship system in the sierra, see Chance, *Conquest of the Sierra*, 130. The study of the sierra kinship system needs to be based principally on a careful analysis of documents written by the Zapotec, since material authored by the Spanish is filtered through their own cultural lens.

40. Request presented to the alcalde mayor by the principales of the village of Yagayo, 1706, AHPJO, Villa Alta, caja 2, exp. 91, fol. 1.

41. See Chance, *Conquest of the Sierra*, 129. In the document AGN Civil, 120, exp. 6, fol. 69, the term "tronco" is used to refer to what we call lineage. In this case, everyone belonging to a tronco has the same surname.

42. AGN Civil, 120, exp. 6, fol. 69v; AGN Tierras, vol. 167, 2nd part, exp. 2.

43. Written records attesting to such peaceful partings within and between pueblos are very few. One exception is found in the account books of San Baltasar Yatzache el Alto, 1732. In 1732, Yatzache el Bajo broke off from the pueblo of Yatzache el Alto, and for this reason, the members of the two communities elected to divide their goods, a decision they recorded in the account book of the latter community; Archivo Parroquial de Zoochila, district of Villa Alta, Oaxaca.

44. The primordial titles are the richest source of information about the founding of new pueblos. See, for example, Título Primordial de Santo Domingo Yojovi, held in the Archivo Municipal of Yoxovi, cited by Michel R. Oudijk, "La toma de posesión: Un tema mesoamericano para la legitimación del poder, *Relaciones [El Coligio de Michoacan]* 91 (2002): 104. See also La Memoria de Juquila and La Memoria de Yacuini, in AGN Tierras, 335, exp. 5, and the glosses to the *lienzo* (sheet of woven cloth that contains information about the history of families, communities, etc.) of Tabaá in Michel Oudijk, "Espacio y escritura: El Lienzo de Tabaá," in *Escritura zapoteca*, by María de los Angeles Romero Frizzi (México DF: CIESAS and INAH, 2003), 377–390.

45. Records of these movements of people are contained in the ancient lienzos as described by Michel R. Oudijk, *Historiography of the Benizáa: The Postclassic and Early Colonial Period* (Leiden, The Netherlands: Research School of Asian, African and Amerindian Studies, 2000), 224. Reference to the migration of pueblos has also been carried down in the oral traditions maintained by various contemporary Zapotecan communities. See Deborah Cruz Hernández, Lo que dicen los viejos (unpublished ms. in author's possession, 1998). One such example is the following: the elders in the pueblo of Lachatao recall that their ancestors had left the community of Zaachila in ancient (pre-Hispanic) times and, as part of this tale, they still know the names of all of the places through which the members of the group passed during their travels. On the oral tradition that records these ancient and contemporary movements of people, see the second volume of the Instituto Nacional Indigenista's *Sierra Juárez: Trabajo comunitario; Identidad y memoria histórica de los pueblos*, 2 vols. (México DF: INI, CEHCAM, 1994).

46. The documents relating to grants of land and the resettlement of pueblos can be read from a dual perspective, that of the Spanish and that of the indigenous. The Spanish ordered these movements of populations and conceded new titles, whereas the Indians saw in these concessions and decrees a way to obtain legal title and sanction for the founding of a new settlement. For a case in point, see AGN Mercedes, vol. 7, fol. 159, whereby in the resettlement of the pueblo of Ixtlán (in the Sierra Zapoteca), a smaller, associated community takes the opportunity to obtain autonomous pueblo status. This case and others like it, however, do not negate the fact that on various occasions the formation of new settlements took place under duress and involved violence.

47. Witnesses confirmed the same of the settlement of Juquila. See AGN Tierras, vol. 335, exp. 5. Furthermore, tradition passed down to the present day in some of the pueblos of the Sierra Zapoteca and the Sierra Mixteca recounts how the pueblos were founded after their members had crossed great distances or, in other cases, traveled only a short distance.

48. During the colonial period, the founding of a new pueblo and the status it gained as an autonomous administrative entity were symbolized by breaking ground on the construction of its church. See Oudijk, "Espacio y escritura," 385; Lockhart, *The Nahuas after the Conquest*, 16; Romero Frizzi and Vásquez, "Memoria y escritura," 403.

49. The explanation of the títulos primordiales as a Mesoamerican tradition has been covered in Florescano, *Historia de las historias*.

50. In its last section, the *Memoria de Juquila* provides the place-names that indicate where, exactly, it was founded as a pueblo. See AGN Tierras, vol. 355, exp. 5; Romero Frizzi and Vásquez, "Memoria y escritura," 430–446. The sacred text of Chilam Balam de Chumayel contains the origin myth of the Yucatecan Maya and mentions, in addition to the migration, "to the surveyor, he who is going to prepare the measurements of land to be placed under cultivation." It later says, "[H]e came . . . to mark off the measurements"; see the edition edited by Mercedes de la Garza (México DF: SEP, 1985 [1700s]), 41.

51. The community today is known as San Juan Bautista, and it sits in the Sierra Zapoteca, to the north of the city of Oaxaca, in the area known as that of the Zapotecos del Rincón.

52. Everything argued in this part of the chapter is based on the analysis of the document Juquila contra Tanetze, 1715–1726, AGN Tierras, vol. 335, exp. 5. In this case study, it is the page numbers of the document, not its *fojas* (folios), that are cited, because I made use of photocopies that were numbered sequentially. On the other hand, the numbering of the document is not consecutive, it starts over in several places, and there are fojas without a number.

53. I found no evidence in the documents that Totolinga was subject to the authority of Juquila or paid it tribute. The assertion that Juquila considered the other pueblo to be of lower rank in the hierarchy of power is based on a comparative analysis of the memorias of Juquila and Totolinga, both of which are contained in the AGN Tierras, vol. 335, exp. 5.

54. Ibid., 19.

55. Ibid., 3.

56. Chance, *Conquest of the Sierra*, 22n27, 77, 156. Over the last eighty years of the seventeenth century, Tanetze lost some 80 percent of its population, while Juquila experienced a modest increase in its population.

57. A detailed analysis of the *Memoria de Juquila* is contained in Romero Frizzi and Vásquez, "Memoria y escritura." The pueblo of Juquila had originally been founded around the time of the conquest. Its members subsequently moved and reconstructed the pueblo in a new location.

58. Nowhere in the record is there any reference that would lead one to think that the alcalde mayor read any part of the memorias.

59. *Memoria de Totolingua* (or Yacuini), found at the beginning of the record, AGN Tierras, vol. 355, exp. 5.

60. Ibid., 4.

61. Ibid., 17.

62. Ibid., 21.

63. Ibid., 115.

64. Ibid., 211.

65. Ibid., 248, 264.

66. Ibid., 287

YANNA P. YANNAKAKIS

Costumbre

A Language of Negotiation in Eighteenth-Century Oaxaca

On September 15, 1700, a seismic shift in the balance of political forces shook the district of Villa Alta, Oaxaca, a rugged, mountainous region far removed from colonial power centers. The residents of the Zapotec pueblo of San Francisco Cajonos and eighteen surrounding pueblos rose up in a violent rebellion that shocked and unsettled the small Spanish population of roughly 150 people who lived in the administrative seat of Villa Alta. More than a century and a half after the conquest of the Sierra Norte, it appeared that Spanish colonial rule was not a fait accompli. Neither the economic exploitation of the region's 30,000 to 40,000 indigenous residents through the *repartimiento* (forced production) of cochineal dye nor the "spiritual conquest" of the region by the Dominican order had made the district's native peoples into docile colonial subjects. The events of 1700 unleashed a period of Spanish repression, administrative reform, and native resistance. The rebellion had other political effects as well: it intensified jurisdictional disputes between ecclesiastical and civil authorities as well as between the secular Catholic hierarchy and the Dominican order and marked a decades-long renegotiation of the terms of local rule among *pueblos de indios* (Indian municipalities), the Church, and the state. Much of this negotiation took place within the colonial legal system and was articulated in terms of the opposition between state power and *costumbre* (local custom).

Historians have widely acknowledged that the legal system played a primary role in making Spanish colonialism work at a political and economic level and in producing a political-cultural hegemony. Susan Kellogg's landmark study argues that Nahua use of the Spanish legal system produced a hybrid legal culture rather than a wholesale transformation of Nahua legal-political custom. Although it often served locally defined native interests, legal culture ultimately tied Nahua elites and communities to Spanish systems of authority and undercut native autonomy.[1] Kellogg's case study of central Mexico points to the strong historical connection between legal and cultural pluralism and colonial state formation.

More recently, the close relationship between plural legal systems and state formation has come to the attention of scholars of world history. Lauren Benton's ambitious comparative work on legal regimes posits that colonialism as a global phenomenon concerned itself largely with the construction of legal institutions that emerged as a negotiation between local legal orders (what colonizers recognized and labeled as custom) and state legal orders. Benton cautions us against accepting "states' claims to legal sovereignty at face value."[2] If we fall into this trap, "early colonial authorities then appear as comprehensive political powers rather than internally fragmented entities that tended to insert themselves within local power structures."[3]

Both Benton and Kellogg articulate a close relationship between flexible, pluralist systems of law and the growth of state power and legitimacy in colonial settings, made possible through a process of cultural and legal negotiation between native peoples and colonial authorities. Their work demonstrates that analysis of negotiation as colonial process must consider the reciprocal effects of negotiation on both native peoples and the state. Colonial states and legal institutions did not exist as static monoliths but rather emerged over time in dialectic with native litigation and political-legal culture.

This chapter addresses the renegotiation of local rule in the district of Villa Alta following the Cajonos rebellion through an examination of a sixty-year-long *cabecera-sujeto* dispute (a dispute between a pueblo that served as a religious/administrative center and the surrounding pueblos subject to its authority) in the parish of San Juan Tanetze–San Juan Yae. The analytical focus centers on the use of costumbre by Zapotec litigants as a rhetorical strategy and language of negotiation with the Crown and Catholic Church. The recognition and valorization of costumbre in medieval Castilian legal tradition allowed the Spanish state over time to incorporate significant territory in the multi-ethnic and religiously diverse Iberian peninsula and, then later, to patch together the cultural and political incoherence of its Spanish American holdings. As a language of negotiation, costumbre provided an ideal tool of empire.

But in the hands of indigenous litigants in the Americas, costumbre as legal discourse also provided a weapon with which to challenge state authority. The deployment of costumbre by Spanish lawyers, indigenous legal agents, and indigenous witnesses produced centrifugal effects in the colonial order, defying the imperial impulse toward centralization and homogenization by asserting the preeminence of the local and the particular. By claiming the validity of costumbre, indigenous people not only resisted but also shaped colonial law. In the cabecera-sujeto dispute under study, through their deployment of costumbre as legal rhetorical strategy, Zapotec litigants wittingly or unwittingly inserted themselves into an eighteenth-century debate about the validity of costumbre in relationship to an increasingly rationalist and centralized concept of state law.

PRELUDE TO NEGOTIATION: REBELLION, REPRESSION, AND REFORM

Our story begins on the evening of September 14, 1700, when Jacinto de los Angeles and Juan Bautista, the Zapotec *fiscales* (priest's assistants) of San Francisco Cajonos, Villa Alta, reported to the pueblo's Dominican priest that the *mayordomo* (steward) of one of the pueblo's *cofradías* (Catholic brotherhoods) was hosting a feast and leading his guests in idolatrous rites. Two Dominican friars and several Spaniards accompanied the fiscales to the house, burst in, and startled and dispersed the crowd gathered at the celebration. The three men investigated the remains of the feast and confiscated evidence of idolatry: beheaded turkeys, a bleeding doe, and other ritual implements. They reported their findings to the ecclesiastical authorities and local officials in the administrative center of Villa Alta.

The next day, violence erupted when a furious crowd from San Francisco and some of the nearby pueblos surrounded the Dominican convent with the priest, fiscales, Dominican friars, and a handful of Spaniards inside. The crowd demanded that the priest turn the fiscales over to them. The Spaniards, terrified for their lives, complied, and the crowd left with the two men, whom they whipped, tortured, and put to death for their betrayal and intervention in the pueblo's affairs. The repression that followed was horrific. A criminal investigation of the entire municipal government of San Francisco and other leaders of and participants in the rebellion ensued, involving torture on the rack and forced confessions. Almost two years later, in January 1702, fifteen men from San Francisco were garroted, and their bodies were drawn and quartered. Spanish officials displayed their remains around the pueblo and on the Camino Real as a warning to would-be idolaters and rebels.[4]

The Cajonos rebellion was not a sudden rupture but rather represented the culmination of decades of increasing tensions between the sierra's pueblos de indios and colonial authorities over the question of indigenous semiautonomy. David Tavárez has demonstrated that for approximately forty years prior to the rebellion, the church hierarchy and the *alcalde mayor* (Spanish magistrate) had begun to undermine the foundations of the region's Pax Hispanica through a policy of confrontation with Zapotec pueblos over what the Catholic Church defined as idolatry and, more pointedly, through more frequent prosecution of cases of idolatry. This policy of confrontation impinged upon the relative autonomy of the region's pueblos and produced serious tensions and cleavages between pueblo elites who aligned themselves more closely with the friars and those who maintained a degree of distance.[5] This edgy atmosphere provided a context—a tinderbox—for the events of 1700.

The Cajonos rebellion marked a turning point in the power relationships of the district of Villa Alta. Perhaps most importantly, the events of 1700 allowed the alcalde mayor and secular church authorities to make common cause against Dominican hegemony in the region. The new bishop of Oaxaca, Fray Angel Maldonado (1702–1728), was the key figure in the assault against the Dominicans. Eager to change what he argued was the misadministration of the sierra, Maldonado launched a bold policy of administrative reform and a wide-ranging and systematic extirpation effort.[6]

First, Maldonado sought to purge the pueblos of the district of Villa Alta—notoriously some of the most "idolatrous" in Oaxaca—of non-Christian practices. As an immediate response to the Cajonos uprising, he conducted a parish inspection in the jurisdiction of Villa Alta and enlisted the help of Licenciado Joseph de Aragón y Alcántara, curate of Ejutla (an administrative center in the valley) and a renowned extirpator. During this first visit, Maldonado implemented an "innovative and unorthodox" strategy of extirpation.[7] He offered a general absolution and legal amnesty for any pueblo that turned over its *maestros de idolatría* (the culturally loaded term used by Spaniards to refer to native ritual specialists) and ritual implements. Upon return to the sierra in 1704, the bishop reaped the benefits of this strategy. From 1704 to 1705, Licenciado Aragón y Alcántara recorded verbal and written confessions concerning "idolatrous" practices from all of the district's pueblos, with the exception of the Chinantec region, and confiscated ninety-nine ritual calendars and other sacred objects. The calendars were sent to Spain and the sacred objects burned in the plaza of Villa Alta to the horror and dismay of the region's population.[8]

Maldonado coupled the extirpation campaign with a dramatic reform of the loose, understaffed, and geographically diffuse administration of the Dominican order in the district of Villa Alta. A long-standing power struggle between the Dominican order in Oaxaca and the bishops, who in theory presided over the evangelization of the region, helps to explain the ambition with which Maldonado designed his program of parish reform. Maldonado's designs represented part of a larger struggle throughout New Spain among the mendicant orders, the secular Church hierarchy, and the Spanish Crown. In the remote regions of New Spain where an absence of formal state structures tended to be the rule, the missionary orders had considerable economic and political power and ran remote areas as small fiefdoms. Their interests often clashed with those of the Crown and the Church hierarchy, and as a result, these two arms of the Spanish empire periodically attempted to curtail their power. The accession of the Bourbon dynasty to the throne in 1700 marked a watershed in this process as the Bourbons centralized power in the hands of the secular Church hierarchy, which answered to the king. This process occurred at the expense of the missionary orders over the course of the eighteenth century.

Since the conquest, with the exception of the Rincón region in which secular priests (clergy who did not belong to a religious order) ran the parishes of Tanetze and Yae, the Dominicans had staked their claim to the Sierra Norte. During the early colonial period, despite occasional flare-ups between the jurisdiction of the Dominicans and civil authority, the Crown and the bishops of Oaxaca were content to allow the Dominicans to serve as colonial overlords in the sierra. However, beginning in the early seventeenth century, there were sporadic attempts on the part of the bishops of Oaxaca to rein in Dominican power. With the support of the Crown, Bishop Juan Bartolomé de Bohórquez e Hinojosa (1617–1633) and Bishop Bartolomé de la Cerda Benavente y Benavides (1639–1652) attempted to subject the Dominican *doctrinas* (districts) to the direct authority of the bishops, but the Dominicans mounted a vigorous and largely successful resistance.[9]

The Cajonos rebellion provided an opening for the renewal of this power struggle and an opportunity for the Church hierarchy to wrest power from the Dominicans. Bishop Maldonado framed the incident as proof of the insufficiency of the Dominican presence in the sierra. As a remedy, he replaced Dominican curates with secular clergy and increased the number of parish priests in the district from twelve prior to 1702 to twenty-one by 1705. As he increased the number of parish priests, he increased the number of cabeceras. From 1705 to 1707, the six Dominican doctrinas of the sierra (Villa Alta, San Francisco Cajonos, Choapan, Totontepec, Juquila Mixes, and Quetzaltepec) and three secular doctrinas (Tanetze, Yae, Yagavila) were expanded to eighteen secular parishes. By the mid-eighteenth century, there were twenty parishes.[10]

Maldonado's parish reform constituted a serious threat to the native political order of the district of Villa Alta. One of the most important changes introduced was the enforcement of the cabecera-sujeto parish structure. Throughout New Spain, the Spanish model of spatial organization relied on the centralized and hierarchical cabecera-sujeto structure as a means of organizing tribute collection and evangelization. Cabeceras tended to be the power and population centers of a particular region or jurisdiction and, as such, governed their smaller neighbors and collected tribute for the Crown from the settlements that surrounded them. In addition to their political and administrative roles, cabeceras also served as the parish seats of the Catholic Church. Given their position, they had the right to demand financial contributions and labor from their sujetos for the maintenance of the parish church and the celebration of religious festivals, obligations often resented by the subject pueblos.

Chance has noted that the cabecera-sujeto structure of the district of Villa Alta was largely undeveloped in comparison with other regions of New Spain.[11] As a result, the native pueblos of the sierra were not accustomed to the rigid hierarchy that defined cabecera-sujeto relations. A reinvigorated cabecera-sujeto structure thus led to a reordering of relationships of power among sierra pueblos, and the enforcement of the cabecera-sujeto model engendered long-term conflict between the parish seats and their neighbors.

Maldonado attempted to institute a program of nucleation (*congregación*) as a complement to administrative centralization. With the support of the alcalde mayor of Villa Alta, Diego de Rivera y Cotes, Maldonado recommended to the viceroy that the district's pueblos should be congregated into settlements of at least 400 heads of household each; that each pueblo have a Spanish teacher; and that the alcalde mayor should have the right to place lieutenants in pueblos where he deemed it necessary. The viceroy approved the proposal in 1706 to a flurry of protest from Villa Alta cabildo officers.[12] The protestations of sierra cabildos may have had some effect, since it appears that, of these proposals, only the one concerning the stationing of schoolmasters was implemented.[13]

In sum, Maldonado's parish reform effected a political centralization of the district's native pueblos under the control of the secular hierarchy of the Catholic Church. In this regard, the decade that followed the Cajonos rebellion resembled a second conquest of the Sierra Norte. Maldonado believed that a tighter administrative ship—more priests, more parish seats, more densely populated settlements (in a word, centralization)—would establish greater social control, leading in turn to the eradication of idolatry. The establishment and enforcement of a more rigid hierarchy among indigenous pueblos, in which cabeceras would serve as command centers and their superior position with regard to their subject pueblos would be clearly demarcated and maintained, would further bolster efforts at social and political control. This program of centralization chafed against the long-standing political autonomy of the pueblos of Villa Alta and displaced the decentralized administrative structure that had been the rule in the region prior to the tumultuous events of 1700.

COSTUMBRE IN THE PARISH OF
SAN JUAN TANETZE–SAN JUAN YAE

From the start of the Catholic evangelical enterprise, the establishment of parishes in the Rincón region of the district of Villa Alta—in which the parish of San Juan Tanetze–San Juan Yae was located—created political tensions among the region's pueblos de indios. When the first Spanish missionaries arrived in the Zapotec Rincón in the 1530s, they established two parishes, both secular, in the pueblos of Tanetze and Yagavila. In doing so, the Church administration followed what they determined to be the pre-Hispanic pattern of regional power relations, Tanetze and Yagavila having been the most populous communities in the region at the time of the conquest. At a certain point, Church authorities split the parish of Tanetze in two and installed a secular priest in the pueblo of Lalopa. Within a few years, however, they moved the parish seat to San Juan Yae, another pre-Hispanic population center, and designated it as a second cabecera (in addition to Tanetze) on the eastern side of the Cajonos River.[14] By dividing the parish of Tanetze, the Church hoped to facilitate the evangelistic enterprise by allowing two resident priests to share the large expanse of territory that made up the eastern Rincón. For the local residents, however, this meant double the burden; they had to provide the livelihood for two curates and pay for their services, a substantial economic expense and drain of local resources.

The extent of the burden of the maintenance of two priests on the surrounding pueblos became clear in 1617 when the *cabildos* (municipal councils) of the pueblos of Yae, Lalopa, and Lahoya (Xaca) petitioned the Real Audiencia to rejoin the parishes of Yae and Tanetze under the cabecera of Tanetze. Their request was demographically and economically driven. During the previous decade, a congregación had taken place, resulting in the deaths of many inhabitants of the Rincón, particularly in the region around Yae. As a result, Yae's residents could no longer pay the tribute required to maintain a parish priest. The aggregation of the parishes that ensued rearranged the region's relationships of power. By demoting Yae to a subject pueblo of Tanetze, the Church reinforced loose horizontal political relationships between Yae and its neighbors; as of 1617, they were all subject to the authority of Tanetze.[15]

Eighty years later, the situation could not have looked more different. The population of the region had recovered, and the material conditions in the region's pueblos de indios had improved. Bolstered by these developments, in 1695, Yae's cabildo petitioned Bishop of Oaxaca Isidro Sariñana and the Real Audiencia for recognition as cabecera. The colonial Church and state concurred, thereby resurrecting Yae as a hub of colonial ecclesiastical and political administration.[16] But this recognition of Yae as cabecera was de jure and not de facto, as none of the surrounding pueblos recognized it as such.

The surrounding pueblos justified their refusal to recognize Yae as cabecera through claims to a local tradition of community autonomy and egalitarianism. In lieu of a hierarchical cabecera-sujeto model, a variety of local arrangements provided a degree of political, commercial, and religious integration among Rincón pueblos and shared power among its elites. A multi-pueblo religious brotherhood—the cofradía of the Virgin of Yabee—provides one manifestation of this horizontal form of inter-pueblo integration. The region's elites formed the cofradía to serve as custodian of the hermitage constructed at the site and to maintain and adorn the Virgin's image. The leadership of the cofradía, represented by the governors of six Rincón pueblos, also oversaw the *tianguis* (local market) held in Yae.[17]

The phenomenon of multiple cabeceras in the Rincón region of the sierra provides another manifestation of the district of Villa Alta's decentralized political system. Part of what defined the region's political relationships was the unusually peripatetic nature of its parish priest and the claim that the priest had no fixed residence.[18] In remote, rural regions of New Spain, priests often traveled extensively in order to serve the far-flung pueblos of their parishes, but most had a permanent residence in the cabecera. According to both Spanish officials and Rincón Zapotecs, however, the parish priest of San Juan Tanetze–San Juan Yae moved from pueblo to pueblo, every few days or so, such that in the thirty years that he had served the parish, he had never spent more than a month in one pueblo. Since he was always on the move, the priest celebrated major religious festivals in the pueblo that he happened to be in on the appointed day of the festival, rather than celebrating them in the cabecera. In his testimony to the Real Audiencia during initial investigations into the case, the alcalde mayor made clear that he found the peculiarities of the Rincón custom to be an administrative nightmare. He characterized the region as a "monster with four heads" (*un monstruo con cuatro cabeceras*) in which at least four pueblos felt that they had the "rights of a cabecera" (*fueros de cabecera*).[19]

The priest's constant movement must have had significant symbolic value for the region's residents, demarcating multiple loci of sacred power and reinforcing the horizontal nature of political relationships in the region. Upon closer scrutiny, the "monster with four heads" appears to have been what Marcello Carmagnani has called an "ethnic district"—native territory governed according to native concepts of space and power—whose composition and political organization eluded the understanding of Spanish officials.[20]

After the Cajonos rebellion, San Juan Yae's efforts to reestablish and reinforce its status as cabecera coincided with Maldonado's efforts to regularize the diffuse cabecera-sujeto structure of the district and thus reconfigure the "ethnic district" along the lines of a Spanish blueprint. In a petition presented to Maldonado dated December 7, 1702, the officials of San Juan Yae requested that the parish priest observe all major religious feast days in San Juan Yae, the cabecera. A second petition presented to Maldonado by the officials of San Juan Yae in April 1703 requested that Maldonado uphold Sariñana's provision of 1695, which recognized San Juan Yae as cabecera. Eager to tame the "monster with four heads," Maldonado insisted on the recognition of three cabeceras (Tanetze, Yagavila, and Yae) in the Rincón region, and that Yae's de jure status as cabecera should be de facto.[21] In response, the pueblo of Santiago Lalopa and then later the pueblo of Santiago Yagallo, both of which under Maldonado's plan were designated as subject pueblos of San Juan Yae, led a legal rebellion against the bishop's order.

COSTUMBRE AS LEGAL RHETORICAL STRATEGY

The history of parish formation, the Cajonos rebellion, and Maldonado's reforms served as a prelude to the renegotiation of power relationships in the parish of San Juan Tanetze–San Juan Yae during the eighteenth century.

These events, which focused the centralizing and reformist eye of the state and Church hierarchy on the district of Villa Alta, pushed Zapotec elites to reassert the political autonomy of their pueblos. As for so much of the colonial history of New Spain, the legal system provided the arena for the enactment of political struggle and negotiation between the colonial state and pueblos de indios, and Spanish law and legal discourse provided the rhetorical tools.

A close reading of the rhetoric of the case requires equally close attention to the historical actors who did the writing and the talking that moved legal cases along. Until recently, historical and anthropological literature on pueblos de indios and indigenous communities has tended to consider the pueblo or the indigenous community as an undifferentiated whole, particularly when they engaged outside forces or ethnic others. More recent scholarship, particularly of the colonial period, has made much of the divisions within pueblos de indios created by status, wealth, and kinship, as well as political factionalism.[22] In light of this historical deconstruction of "pueblo," we should be careful not to position the pueblo as historical actor but rather specify who within the pueblo was utilizing the legal system and who was constructing and deploying the legal strategies to pursue an objective. Generally speaking, cabildo officers, caciques, and principales directed legal ventures, although not as a united front or in lockstep. Often, legal disputes masked factional struggles among pueblo elites, some of whom pursued a legal case to enhance their own power, and others of whom opposed legal action.

If pueblo elites were at times divided on the question of legal action, the structure of native society left *macehuales* (commoners) little choice as to their participation in legal cases. Macehuales participated in litigation through their contributions to the *caja de comunidad* (pueblo treasury), which often provided resources for lengthy litigation.[23] *Derramas* and other forms of illicit taxation also provided funds for costly and lengthy legal cases (we must remember that the legal insurance of the General Indian Court was available only for individual Indian commoners, not for legal cases involving an entire pueblo or a member of the Indian nobility).[24] Commoner discontent over derramas could fuel pueblo factionalism through manipulation by one elite faction or another. Elites often deployed public discontentment over head taxes as a weapon against a native governor or *alcalde* (magistrate) who pursued a legal case too aggressively.[25]

Spanish law prescribed the identity of the historical actors involved in legal conflicts: according to the law, indigenous people could not represent themselves in court. Questions of cross-cultural competence also limited the direct participation of indigenous people in the legal system. Many pueblo elites, particularly in peripheral regions of New Spain, did not have the technical skills—bilingualism, literacy, and familiarity with legal protocols—to effectively pursue legal cases. Intermediary figures, both Spanish and indigenous, remedied these obstacles to indigenous litigation and often profited significantly from their roles. Municipal councils hired *apoderados* or *agentes* (individuals given power of attorney by the municipal government) to facilitate a case through the first stage of litigation. This most often involved the drafting and presentation of a petition to the alcalde mayor in the district court. In the district of Villa Alta, apoderados and legal agents were often *caciques* or *principales* (indigenous nobility) from the pueblo engaged in the litigation or, if the pueblo was small, from the cabecera of the district. Spanish and mestizo residents from Villa Alta also served frequently as apoderados and agentes, although less so over the course of the eighteenth century, most likely as a result of a general increase in the number of indigenous elites who possessed the necessary skills to perform the intermediary role. If the litigation progressed beyond the district court, municipal councils hired a lawyer, usually a Spaniard from Villa Alta or Antequera. If the case went to appeal in the Real Audiencia, they generally hired a lawyer in Mexico City to represent them in the royal court.[26]

The role of legal intermediary suggests that indigenous litigation was not necessarily a pretext for Spaniards to manipulate native grievances for their own profit, as some historians have suggested, although Spanish judges often assumed this was the case in large part because of their prejudices toward Indians as highly suggestible and incapable of independent thought or action. In the case of Villa Alta, indigenous apoderados and governors often traveled to the district seat of Villa Alta or to Antequera to consult with Spanish lawyers. If the case went to appeal, indigenous apoderados migrated to Mexico City and resided there for months or even years in order to keep tabs on the case that they had been hired to follow. This does not mean that litigation was not an exploitative affair; indigenous apoderados could take advantage of their role for their own profit as easily as did the Spaniards. Rather, the presence of intermediaries, who by definition of their role were accountable to the people who hired them and were required to mediate between their clients and Spanish lawyers and officials, indicates that native litigation was a collective, interethnic affair, mitigated by bonds of debt and obligation. The technicalities of litigation—legal strategy, rhetorical strategy, presentation of witnesses, composition of petitions—were more often the product of collective strategizing on the part of pueblo elites, municipal officers, apoderados, and lawyers than they were the full creation of a powerful Spaniard. As shall be demonstrated below, the consistent and skillful deployment of costumbre as a legal rhetorical strategy in the cabecera-sujeto dispute of San Juan Yae and its neighbors over almost four decades was attributable to a collective process in which an interethnic legal team participated.

Documents signed by the municipal officers of Yagallo, Yae, and other pueblos involved in the litigation authorized local indigenous notables from Yae and Tanetze with power of attorney and eventually authorized lawyers in Mexico City to take over the case. For example, on July 29, 1744, the cabildo of San Juan Yae gave power of attorney to Don Juan de Mendoza, a cacique of Yae, "so that he can find the titles, *reales provisiones* [royal decrees], papers, books, and other documents in the archives of the ecclesiastical courts that contain information verifying that San Juan Yae has been and continues to be the cabecera."[27] A day later, the cabildo of Yae issued a second power of attorney to Don Joseph Sanchez Pizarro for the express purpose of representing them in the Real Audiencia in the case against the allied pueblos over the matter of cabecera status.[28] On the same day, the cabildos of the allied plaintiff pueblos gave power of attorney to Don Antonio de Aldas, a cacique from San Juan Tanetze.[29] The interethnic legal teams appointed by the cabildos of the plaintiffs and defendants, in concert with pueblo elites and witnesses, produced the rhetoric of the case with reference to a rich repertoire of Spanish legal discourse.

Costumbre as a Spanish legal concept and as it was deployed by the legal teams of both the plaintiff pueblos and San Juan Yae embodied the principle of local autonomy in the face of an increasingly state-centered legal system. As such, it constituted both a metaphor for local autonomy and a rhetorical tool for its defense. Costumbre as it was applied in the Americas by Spanish jurists and indigenous litigants had its roots in the medieval period of the Iberian peninsula, a pluralistic society of Catholic, Muslim, and Jewish municipalities held together in a loose and uneasy coexistence through the recognition of local cultural and political auton- omy. As Woodrow Borah has pointed out, on the eve of the conquest of America, the Iberian peninsula was a patchwork of laws, customs, and competing jurisdictions.[30] As the *reconquista* (Reconquest) brought more towns and settlements under Christian rule, each community adopted its own *fuero* (body of customary law), which codified laws and procedures related to local governance, including punishment of crime and sexual mis- conduct, and the criteria and process for selection of officers of municipal cabildos.[31] Whether Christian, Muslim, or Jewish, the fueros drew heavily from the tradition of Roman law, such that despite the local particulari- ties, they were remarkably consistent.[32] The coexistence of royal law and local custom combined with jurisdictional plurality (secular and religious) lent a significant degree of elasticity and complexity to the Iberian legal framework.

Despite the general elasticity and decentralization of this legal system, from the thirteenth century forward, costumbre existed in increasing tension with royal authority. During this period, the Crown attempted to shift the balance away from the fueros in favor of royal authority by issuing the Fuero Royal and the Siete Partidas and by asserting its role as the court of appeal. The Crown increased its judicial power further in 1348 with the Ordenamiento de Alcalá, which established an order of precedence for sources of law, the most important of which was the superiority of royal law to fueros. In practice, however, local custom continued to inform most judicial decisions. Where the Crown exercised its greatest legal influence in local matters, then, was through its role as a court of appeal, a role that it would continue to play in the Americas through the institution of the Real Audiencia (Royal Court).[33]

One article in particular from the Siete Partidas had a substantial effect on the legal framework that the Crown applied to its American holdings. The Crown insisted that it have jurisdiction over cases involving widows, orphans, the elderly, crippled, infirm, poor, or generally wretched since royal courts could provide quick judgment and thereby avoid the substantial costs of litigation. In keeping with this model, the Crown placed native inhabitants of the Americas under this umbrella of minors or the generally wretched and classified them as wards of the state, entitled to summary judgment in a general Indian court and exemption from legal fees through a system of legal insurance.[34] Native litigants worked this paternalist arrangement in their favor by taking advantage of their right to summary judgment, which produced a remarkable backlog of litigation in colonial courts, and through what Lauren Benton has called "jurisdictional jockeying," that is, by playing local and ecclesiastical courts off of the Real Audiencia and by playing civil and ecclesiastical courts off of one another.[35]

The coexistence of a preeminent royal legal authority with an officially prescribed respect for native custom created a legal system during the first quarter century of Spanish colonial rule characterized by "strong legal pluralism," a clearly established hierarchy among sources of law.[36] In the abstract, the Spanish Crown reproduced the relationship between the fueros of medieval Castile and royal authority: in the realm of self-government, native custom under the supervision of the administration of the Indies could be preserved as long as it did not challenge Christianization. The relationship between native custom and Spanish law was codified in the New Laws of 1542 and again in the *Recopilación de las Leyes de las Indias* in 1680:

> That the laws and good customs [*buenas costumbres*] that the Indians had in the past, and those that they have made since they were Christians, and any new laws that they make if these laws do not conflict with Christianity, nor with the laws of this book be respected.[37]

> That in lawsuits among Indians, there should be swift and summary determination of the case, maintaining their customs [*usos y costumbres*] as long as they are not clearly unjust.[38]

> That with particular attention, the Spanish governors and judges make note of the order and manner of living of the Indians, their government and form of maintenance, and inform the Viceroys or Courts, and respect their good customs [*usos y costumbres*] that are not contradictory to our sacred faith.[39]

By the time of the publication of the *Recopilación*, however, much had changed since the promulgation of the New Laws. The formal and legal respect for native custom expressed in the *Recopilación* was mitigated by all of the transformations wrought by evangelization and colonialism itself. Native relationships of power, supra-pueblo alliances and rivalries, commerce, and social relations at all levels were changed by the attack on native political-religious hierarchies at the time of the conquest. In short, colonialism severely curtailed the autonomy of native custom in relationship to Spanish law. By the seventeenth century, recourse to native custom by Spanish jurists had been confined primarily to procedures for local elections and disputes over cabecera-sujeto relationships.[40]

The continued valorization of costumbre in theory despite its erosion in practice can be attributed to the influence of seventeenth-century Spanish jurist Juan de Solórzano Pereira. Solórzano's *Política Indiana* (1647), republished three times during the eighteenth century, was considered by jurists and legal practitioners of the time to be one of the most important sources on the laws of the Indies other than the *Recopilación*. Solórzano can be considered the last great Spanish jurist to champion costumbre. Trained in the Humanist and Renaissance traditions and espousing a conservative approach to the law, Solórzano sought continuity with what he perceived to be the great tradition of the Siete Partidas in his effort to strike a balance between the primacy of royal authority and respect for local custom. Throughout the eighteenth century in Spanish America, Solórzano's theories provided inspiration and rhetorical tools to legal agents and lawyers who sought to assert the authority of native custom in the face of increasingly centralized royal political and legal power.[41]

The diminution of native custom throughout the colonial period (in practice, if not in theory) produced a shift in the legal framework of the audiencia of Mexico from one of "strong legal pluralism" to a "state-centered legal order," in which "the state has at least made if not sustained a claim to dominance over other legal authorities."[42] But this increasingly state-centered legal order maintained some of the flexibility and loopholes that had characterized the strong legal pluralism of medieval Iberia and the early colony, largely through a decentralized legal structure. The decisions of individual local magistrates rather than judicial precedent and previous case decisions determined the enactment of justice in the local jurisdictions of New Spain. Each decision was in effect autonomous from what had gone before and judges rendered their decisions based on specific enactment or codified clause. If there were none available, the Crown, audiencia, or viceroy could issue an edict or ordinance of good government.[43]

The practice of specific enactment combined with the power of both local and royal jurists to interpret Indian custom made jurisdictional jockeying an effective legal strategy on the part of indigenous litigants. Costumbre could be interpreted differently by judges in different jurisdictions or stages on the ladder of appeals. The decentralized nature of the legal system made for a cycle of endless litigation. It also made costumbre potentially unstable, subject to the interpretation of a range of legal opinion. In the case of Santiago Yagallo and associates against San Juan Yae over the question of cabecera status, both the plaintiffs and the defendants utilized jurisdictional jockeying and deployed their own version of costumbre with a degree of success in the district court, ecclesiastical court, and the Real Audiencia. Their procedural and rhetorical strategies help to explain the long duration of the case, as judges across legal jurisdictions interpreted and reinterpreted the custom governing cabecera-sujeto relationships in the district.

The deployment of costumbre as legal rhetorical strategy by the plaintiff pueblos (Santiago Yagallo and associates) and the defendant pueblo (San Juan Yae) and its interpretation and application by Spanish judges during this decades-long cabecera-sujeto case produced a struggle over the meaning of costumbre. In petitions and court testimony, the legal agents, lawyers, and witnesses of the plaintiff pueblos rendered costumbre in its romantic and primordial connotations. In its romantic connotation, costumbre emerged spontaneously from the will and practices of the people.[44] The primordial connotation located costumbre in a distant past. Together, the romantic and primordial connotations presented a picture of long-established consensual and popular practices that emanated from everyday life since time immemorial. After establishing the romantic-primordial nature of costumbre, the plaintiff pueblos deployed a number of rhetorical oppositions to render costumbre as it defined power relations among pueblos in the region as flexible, contingent, and reciprocal—as a set of horizontal relations.

Not surprisingly, the legal case of San Juan Yae rested on the same romantic-primordial definition of costumbre. But rather than present "very ancient custom" in terms of horizontal relationships among the pueblos of the district, the legal team of San Juan Yae presented a vertical model that squared with the model of pueblo relations intended by the Spaniards: one parish and administrative seat to which the surrounding pueblos contributed labor and material resources during major fiestas or times of need, such as the repair or reconstruction of the parish church or priest's residence.

From 1695 to 1769, Spanish jurists found in favor of both interpretations. But over time, the balance tilted in favor of San Juan Yae. In the audiencia's 1743 decision in the case, from which it did not waver despite the appeals of Santiago Yagallo and its allies, the judges of the audiencia applied their own definition of costumbre, which had little to do with the romantic-primordial claims of either Yagallo or Yae. The audiencia narrowly interpreted costumbre in matters concerning cabecera-sujeto relations as the "obligations" owed by subject pueblos to the cabecera, without reference to antiquity or local practice. The audiencia's interpretation represented a universal principle to be applied to all regions of New Spain regardless of local conditions or temporal considerations. As my analysis will elucidate, this struggle over the meaning of costumbre had significant repercussions for power relationships in the district of Villa Alta and the relationship between costumbre and royal legal authority.

Resistance to the demands on the part of San Juan Yae that its subject pueblos respect their "obligations" to Yae as cabecera and that they attend and provide the labor required of them as subject pueblos during the major fiestas of the Catholic ritual calendar began in 1709. On August 9 of that year, the cabildo officers and legal agent of Santiago Lalopa, a neighboring pueblo of San Juan Yae, presented a petition to the alcalde mayor of Villa Alta capitán Antonio de Miranda y Corona in which they situated Yae as an arriviste or modern cabecera and their own pueblo as an old (and, by extension, venerated) cabecera.[45]

The petition provides an example of the deployment of a romantically and primordially defined costumbre and of the legal strategy of jurisdictional jockeying on the part of the legal agent and municipal officials of Santiago Lalopa. The petition makes a clear opposition between the "modern cabecera" (cabecera moderna) of San Juan Yae, which because of its recently recognized status did not bear the weight of ancient custom to legitimize its position, and the antiquity of Lalopa's cabecera status based on ancient custom and obligation (*por costumbre y obligación anti-gua; desde antiguos tiempos por costumbre de celebrar; como que hemos sido de cabecera primero y antigua*). In effect, the petition produces a hierarchy of sources of political legitimacy: romantic-primordial costumbre first (the source of Lalopa's cabecera status) and then more recent royal or ecclesiastical fiat (the source of Yae's cabecera status). This hierarchical positioning fell within the framework of legal pluralism established by the New Laws and reconfirmed by the *Recopilación* in 1680: Indian custom should be maintained if not contradictory to Christianity. Despite the clarity in the law, however, the political context of the post-Cajonos rebellion and Maldonado's reforms muddied this hierarchy in the eyes of the alcalde mayor who had to decide the case: should Indian custom be respected in a region whose recent history included violent rebellion and a fruitful extirpation campaign?

As the alcalde mayor weighed the merits of the case, he turned to the decrees issued by both civil and ecclesiastical authorities on the matter. The plethora of decrees in favor of the cabecera status of both Lalopa and Yae reveal a strategy of jurisdictional jockeying on the part of both legal teams, who appealed their cases repeatedly in both civil and ecclesiastical courts. The petition presented by Lalopa referred to a Real Provisión dated March 17, 1696, and three decrees on the part of the Bishop of Oaxaca, whose dates were unspecified. The legal team of San Juan Yae presented three bishop's *actas* (acts), which specified that Santiago Lalopa and its subject pueblos Lahoya and Yatoni should attend the major religious celebrations in Yae and comply with the obligations required of subject pueblos. The first act, dated March 4, 1695, was clearly overridden by the decree of March 17, 1696, in favor of Lalopa. But the other two, issued during the tenure of Bishop Maldonado, likely came out of Maldonado's centralizing vision whose cornerstone was the enforcement of the cabecera-sujeto structure. The legal team of San Juan Yae also presented a Real Provisión, dated June 15, 1709, in favor of their position, which no doubt sparked the dispute in question.[46]

As he made his decision, then, the alcalde mayor had to weigh the merits of local custom against the orders of Maldonado's administration. In addition, he had to think about the delicate political balance of the district. After all, a breach of pueblo autonomy had produced a dangerous uprising in San Francisco Cajonos nine years earlier. The bishop may have felt that political-administrative reform was the key to social control, but the alcalde mayor who had to live within and rule the district may have felt that a more pragmatic and accommodating approach would better maintain the district's political equilibrium. In the end, the alcalde mayor found in favor of Santiago Lalopa. He justified his decision with reference to the actions of his predecessor, the dean and cabildo, and the *cura adjustor* (assistant curate)—all of whom had traditionally recognized Santiago Lalopa as a cabecera—and a *real decreto* (royal decree) dated March 13, 1704.⁴⁷ It appears that local custom—romantic-primordial custom and the political arrangements of the district—in combination with a conservative political approach on the part of the alcalde mayor outweighed the bishop's mandate, at least at this particular moment in time.

After the 1709 legal dispute between San Juan Yae and Santiago Lalopa, legal activity concerning the cabecera status of San Juan Yae went dormant. This may have been a result of the tense post-Cajonos atmosphere or perhaps a reading on the part of the officials of San Juan Yae that assertion of its cabecera status in the courts would meet with an unfavorable response. The situation changed in 1734 when the alcalde mayor of Villa Alta began an investigation as to why the pueblos of Santiago Yagallo, Santa María Yaviche, and Santa María Lachichina did not attend major religious fiestas in San Juan Yae or meet the obligations that accompanied the status of subject pueblos. On September 18, 1734, the legal teams of Yagallo, Yaviche, and Lachichina presented four Zapotec witnesses who provided testimony on the matter. The identity of the speakers reveals an effort on the part of the legal team of the plaintiff pueblos to present credible witnesses. All of the men who testified were principales of pueblos that were not directly involved in the dispute but close enough in proximity to have significant knowledge of the conflict and the customary relations of the region. The court identified three out of four as *indios ladinos* (Hispanicized Indians) who testified in Spanish and wore Spanish clothing. This presentation of self as Hispanicized, acculturated Indians might have gone some way to mitigate Spanish prejudices that Indians were natural liars, prone to perjury, and incapable of giving credible testimony. Furthermore, three out of four of the witnesses hailed from long-standing cabeceras, three from San Juan Tanetze and one from Santa Cruz Yagavila.⁴⁸ Cabeceras were often commercial as well as administrative centers. From the perspective of Spaniards, the indigenous elites of these centers tended to be more cultivated and "civilized" than the natives of smaller subject pueblos.

The testimonies of the four witnesses presented by the legal team of the plaintiff pueblos evince a conflict between two competing interpretations of costumbre: the romantic-primordial connotation (the position taken by the plaintiff pueblos and their witnesses) versus the instrumental, legal connotation—*obligaciones* and *asistencias* (service and labor) owed by subject pueblos to their cabeceras—imposed from the outside by institutions alien to the region. Don Francisco de Aldas, a sixty-two-year-old principal from San Juan Tanetze, whom the court scribe described as "very skilled in the language of Castile, and dressed as a Spaniard" (*bastantamente ladino en la lengua castellana y vestir traje de español*) juxtaposed these two versions of costumbre to produce a powerful rhetorical effect:

> The parish of San Juan Tanetze is made up of twelve pueblos but because of very ancient custom, the parish priest does not reside in any of them. . . . And this witness, having seen so, knows that in 1731, they gathered in the pueblo of Yae for the fiesta of Corpus and the municipal officials of the pueblos of Yagallo, Lachichina, and Yaviche brought the common folk from their pueblos so that they could help those of Yae build the arch made of branches for the procession. But they did this because the parish priest, who celebrated the fiesta of Corpus there, asked them to do so, and not because of obligation to them or custom. Although they have attended this fiesta and others sometimes when they were celebrated in the pueblo of Yae, it has been voluntarily.[49]

Aldas's first use of costumbre establishes the legitimacy of local custom through antiquity and achieves a second rhetorical objective: the association of local practices with a lack of fixity or structure ("the parish priest lives in none of them"). Aldas goes on to juxtapose the flexibility and contingency of the primordial custom of the region with the fixity and obligation associated with cabecera-sujeto relationships in general: Yae's neighboring pueblos attended the celebration of Corpus in Yae in 1731 because their priest asked them to, "not because of obligation or custom" (*no por obligación ni costumbre*). In the closing line of this excerpt, Aldas reinforces this juxtaposition between the flexibility and contingency of the region's romantic-primordial custom with the fixity and hierarchy of custom cum obligation. He asserts that Yae and its neighboring pueblos had traditionally enjoyed horizontal, reciprocal relationships: they attended fiestas in one another's pueblos out of courtesy and reciprocity and "voluntarily, in keeping with what the residents of Yae have done" (*voluntariamente en correspondencia de que lo han echo en la misma forma los de Yae*).

Don Pedro de Yllescas, a sixty-one-year-old principal and *indio ladino* from San Juan Tanetze, reinforced the juxtaposition presented by Aldas. His testimony echoes the rhetorical strategy articulated in the 1709 case brought by Lalopa. If costumbre was "primordial" (*antigua*), then "modern" claims to political authority had little legitimacy. And more pointedly, if costumbre was old, it could not be invented anew, and if it emanated from the practices and will of the people, it could not be imposed from above or from the outside:

> The residents of Yae want to force custom where it had been enacted freely because even though it is true that on other occasions, the

municipal officials of the three pueblos attended the celebrations in
Yae, it was because of reciprocity, because the officials of Yae had also
attended celebrations in their pueblos, and not because of custom or
obligation.[50]

Yllescas's elegant juxtaposition of Yae's (and the bishop's) attempt to "force
custom" (*hacer costumbre fuerza*) with "that which had been done freely"
(*lo que entonces se hizo de gracia*) posits an autonomous space for romantic-
primordial custom. Like Aldas, he also juxtaposes romantic-primordial
custom with costumbre as "obligation" (*obligación*).

The last two witnesses, Juan Pasqual Martín, a sixty-four-year-old
principal and indio ladino from Santa Cruz de Yagavila, and Don Marcial
Vargas y Velasco, a seventy-five-year-old principal from the pueblo of
Reagui, reinforced the rhetorical opposition between the contingency of
romantic-primordial custom and the fixity of custom as legislated from
the outside. Like the witnesses who came before him, Martín describes the
contingent celebration of major fiestas in the pueblo where the peripatetic
parish priest "happens to be" (*en el pueblo que le coge*), "without making it
custom or a fixed thing because it is the will of the pueblos" (*sin que en esto
haga costumbre ni cosa fija por que es la voluntad de los pueblos*).[51] For his part,
Vargas laments the efforts of Yae to impose a custom where there had not
been one and where the will of the pueblos did not consent to such an
imposition: "the parish priest ordered the officials of the pueblos to attend
the fiesta and bring people to help build the arches for the procession, and
because of this help, the officials of Yae want it to be customary" (*lo mandó
dicho padre cura y los oficiales de república de dichos pueblos asisiteron y llevaron
gente que ayudara a poner los arcos para la procesión y que por esta asistencia
quieren los dichos de Yae que sea costumbre*).[52]

The alcalde mayor's investigation of Yae's complaints that the pueblos of Yagallo, Yaviche, and Lachichina did not attend the major religious
fiestas in Yae or comply with their obligations as subject pueblos continued through the year 1735. As part of the investigation, the alcalde mayor
required the officials of Yaviche to appear in front of him to answer his
questions. When asked why they refused to attend the fiestas, the officials
responded as follows:

> They [the officials] said together in a unified voice that the people of
> Yae are very haughty, and that they want to subjugate them and order
> them, and that their community [*común*] does not want to comply . . .
> and that they feel the imperiousness with which those of Yae want to
> dominate them, and they add that it was a great hardship for them to
> attend Semana Santa in Yae, and that they did it only in order to obey

the bishop's decree, insisting all the while that it should not become custom, and that they repeat and insist that no one had counseled or advised them.[53]

The answer of the officials of Yaviche reveals the resentment they felt toward Yae for its pretensions to cabecera status and the perception on their part that Yae was an upstart pueblo seeking to dominate the pueblos around it. They also insisted that they acted independently and not as pawns in some larger political struggle fomented by their priest or anyone else. It is likely that either the legal team of Yae suggested that the plaintiff pueblos were being manipulated from the outside or that the alcalde mayor himself jumped to this conclusion. In either case, as discussed above, the officials of Yaviche had to address Spanish prejudices that Indians were easily manipulated and dependent upon Spaniards for any coordinated or organized action.

As with the testimony taken a year earlier, the officials of Yaviche expressed their resistance to the notion that costumbre could be made anew or imposed from outside. The legal team of Santiago Yagallo echoed this sentiment in a March 1743 petition to the audiencia presented in their appeal to the audiencia's decision earlier that year in favor of Yae. In the petition, they claimed that the only reason that they attended the celebration of Corpus in Yae in 1731 was because their parish priest had asked them to, not because of any "obligation, contrary to what has been said, nor can they introduce custom because of this one act, because to do so requires much unanimity" (*obligación como de contrario se dice ni pudiera por ese unico acto introducirse costumbre por que se requieren mucho unanimo de introducirla*).[54] According to this formulation, costumbre could not be imposed because its legitimacy rested in the unanimity, consensus, or will of the pueblos.

In 1741, six years after the alcalde mayor's investigation, the legal teams of Santiago Yagallo and other neighboring pueblos brought a civil suit against San Juan Yae over the question of its cabecera status. As the case makes clear, in the intervening years between the investigation and the civil suit, Yae had continued to insist that its neighbors comply with the obligations required of them as subject pueblos. Romantic-primordial costumbre provided the cornerstone of the case presented by the plaintiffs. The themes of contingency, reciprocity, and flexibility that had characterized local practice in the testimony of the witnesses during the investigation came to dominate the petitions, witness examinations, and testimonies produced by the lawyer, legal agent, municipal officials, and witnesses for Yagallo and its allies.

In June 1741, the Spanish lawyer for Santiago Yagallo and associates, with the likely cooperation of the legal agent and high-ranking officials of Yagallo and the other plaintiff pueblos, presented to the court a list of questions intended to structure the testimony of the witnesses who testified on their behalf. Two questions, asked in succession, addressed the customary relations between pueblos of the region. The first question asked whether the festivals of Corpus Christi, Christmas, Holy Week, and others are celebrated in the pueblo in which the "padre cura happens to be since he has no fixed residence in any of the pueblos of the parish (with the exception of the titular saint's day, which is celebrated in the pueblo of the patron saint)." The second question asked whether the service (*asistencias*) provided during these Church events is or has been given "freely because of the good relations obtaining among the pueblos of my clients and San Juan Yae and because of the style [*estilo*], practice [*práctica*], and custom [*costumbre*] that when there is an event in one of these pueblos, the residents of Yae attend, and when there is one in Yae, the residents of the other pueblos attend."[55]

The language of the questions is reminiscent of that of the 1734 testimony of Don Francisco de Aldas. Contingency ("they celebrate in the pueblo where the priest happens to be") as opposed to fixity ("he has no fixed residence") represents one of the major thematic oppositions and rhetorical tools of the questions. Free will as motive for attendance of the fiestas in Yae ("the help has been given freely") and reciprocity ("good relations") represent a second set of rhetorical tools. In these questions, costumbre is not a "fixed thing" (*cosa fija*) imposed from above but the "estilo, práctica" of the people, emanating from below.

The lawyer and legal team of the plaintiff pueblos deployed a discourse of costumbre that embedded its purportedly local characteristics—contingency, flexibility, and free will—in a standardized legal discourse about costumbre. Solórzano's legal theory informed the rhetoric of their questions and the responses of the witnesses. In *Política Indiana*, Juan de Solórzano Pereira, the Spanish jurist and champion of costumbre, elaborated a specific vocabulary that accompanied the use of costumbre in colonial era legal cases in Castile and Spanish America. Drawing from Solórzano's vocabulary, lawyers and legal agents routinely utilized the words "práctica," "estilo," and "uso" interchangeably with "costumbre," reinforcing its roots in local practice. Legal agents and lawyers also used "modo" (style), "manera" (manner), and "orden" (order) interchangeably with "costumbre," but with less frequency. In addition to this catalogue of synonyms around which the meaning of "costumbre" was constructed, Solórzano identified a number of verbs—"introducir" (introduce), "guardar" (maintain), and "observar" (observe)—used to express a range of relationships between costumbre and royal authority. A legal conservative and proponent of tradition, Solórzano favored "guardar" over "introducir" in matters concerning costumbre.[56] If he had rendered the decision in this case, he would likely have found in favor of Santiago Yagallo and the other plaintiff pueblos.

Given the wide circulation of *Política Indiana*, the lawyer for Santiago Yagallo may well have read Solórzano or relied on the *Recopilación*'s codification of costumbre, replete with some of the vocabulary elaborated by Solórzano. In his study of costumbre, Victor Tau Anzoátegui claims that the *Recopilación* was often the only legal text to be found in most cabildos in the viceroyalty of the Rio de la Plata from the last decade of the seventeenth century until the Crown issued the Real Ordenanza de Intendentes in 1784.[57] The *Recopilación* enjoyed a wide circulation in the viceroyalty of New Spain as well. Nearly every territorial jurisdiction had "at its disposal" a copy of the *Recopilación*.[58] In the 1734 petition presented on behalf of Santiago Yagallo, the legal team contested the right of outsiders to impose custom from above by claiming that "much unanimity" was needed to "introduce" costumbre. Here, the legal team deployed "introducir" negatively as a rhetorical device for legitimizing the popular roots of costumbre. Furthermore, by utilizing the vocabulary most frequently associated with the legal concept of costumbre, the legal teams of both sides of the dispute strengthened their legal claims through a demonstration of legal competence and familiarity with the language of the law.

The thematic oppositions embedded in the questions served to structure the testimony of the witnesses, who in their responses expressed the particularities of local custom within the parameters of Solórzano's standardized rhetoric of costumbre.[59] If we consider the relationship between the questions posed to witnesses and witness testimony in musical terminology, the questions provided simple themes upon which witnesses could improvise. The sum of witness testimony, then, served to rehearse the same themes while preserving the individuality of each witness's improvisation. Repetition of major themes balanced by a diversity of details provided the building blocks of a strong legal case. Ideally, by the end of the testimony, the Spanish judge would be able to recite the particularities of local custom from the perspective of the plaintiff pueblos and would consider the violation thereof as an injustice.

The witnesses presented by San Juan Yae replicated the romantic-primordial interpretation of costumbre deployed by the legal team of the plaintiff pueblos but changed the relevant content. They attempted to persuade the court of the antiquity of Yae's cabecera status by refuting the picture of reciprocity and contingency painted by the witnesses presented by the plaintiff pueblos and replacing it with a picture of a romantic-primordial custom of hierarchy and obligation.[60] To complicate matters, Juan Bartolomé, a principal from Yatoni and witness for Yae, stated that the reason that the pueblos of Lachichina, Yagallo, and Yaviche did not attend the major religious fiestas was because of a dispute between Don Antonio de Saavedra, the parish priest, and Don Juan de Mendoza, the governor of Yae. Out of hatred for Mendoza, Saavedra asked the subject pueblos not to provide the customary labor and materials for the fiestas.[61] Another witness for Yae, Francisco Javier de Medina, a Spaniard and resident of Antequera (the city of Oaxaca) who had been living in the parish of San Juan Yae for eight years, testified that during the celebration of Corpus Christi in 1733, the alcalde of Yae asked the parish priest to send an order to Yagallo, Lachichina, and Yaviche that required them to comply with their obligations to Yae. Saavedra refused, arguing that he did not want the pueblos to provide help since Yae "was not the cabecera, nor had it ever been."[62]

If the testimonies of Bartolomé and Medina were true, by turning a blind eye to or even encouraging the resistance of Yagallo, Lachichina, and Yaviche to compliance with their obligations as subject pueblos, the parish priest may have been a primary player in the conflict. The invocation of the priest as puppeteer who encouraged the pueblos of Yagallo, Yaviche, and Lachichina to ignore their obligations as sujetos undercut earlier claims of Yaviche's cabildo to independence in their motives for bringing the case against Yae. This scenario would indeed be in keeping with Spanish prejudices about Indian disputes, some of which have been adopted by modern historians: wherever there was an Indian dispute, a Spaniard was most likely pulling the strings. But ethnohistorical research has shown that more often, long-standing political rivalries and disputes, sometimes centuries long, simmered beneath the surface structure of colonial administrative and political organization, often without the full knowledge or understanding of Spanish judges and officials. In this particular case, given the long-standing tensions over Yae's cabecera status, dating at least to 1617, it seems more likely that if the priest was indeed involved, his meddling provided a spark for the long fuse of power struggles in the district and opened a space for a renewal of resistance to Yae's claims to cabecera status on the part of its neighbors.

THE AUDIENCIA'S DECISION: A
RATIONALIZATION OF COSTUMBRE

In December 1743, the audiencia rendered its decision, ruling in favor of San Juan Yae's claims to cabecera status. The audiencia justified its ruling through recourse to an interpretation of costumbre that eschewed contingency and reciprocity in favor of a hierarchical set of relations defined by "obligaciones" and "asistencias" owed to cabeceras on the part of their subject pueblos.[63] But despite its decision in favor of Yae, the audiencia made clear that it still awaited a title that the legal team of Yae had promised to produce that would prove their cabecera status and detail the obligaciones and asistencias owed them by their subject pueblos. The very notion that costumbre could be ascertained from a legal document reveals the gulf between the concepts of costumbre deployed by the legal team of Yagallo and the audiencia, respectively. From the perspective of the plaintiff pueblos, romantic-primordial custom was legitimized by social practice over time, not by legal fiat.

The audiencia's definition of costumbre as "obligaciones y asistencias" reveals the limits of romantic-primordial costumbre as rhetorical strategy on the part of native litigants. In the eyes of the audiencia, for the case of cabecera-sujeto relations, costumbre could only be interpreted in one way: the hierarchical cabecera-sujeto model imposed by the Spaniards themselves. This use of costumbre makes clear that costumbre as a legal concept served the needs of empire more than it reflected the practices of indigenous groups or protected their autonomy. By the eighteenth century, in the hands of the audiencia, costumbre had been rendered neutral as its meaning had come to eschew the inconveniences and subtleties of local practice and to reflect the imperial imperatives of standardization, centralization, and universality.

The lawyer for Yagallo and its allies recognized this tension in his own use of costumbre and that of the audiencia. In a 1744 petition to the audiencia appealing the 1743 decision, he protested the homogenization and universality of the concept as applied by the audiencia:

> What is this custom and what are the *asistencias y obligaciones* that have constituted custom? Because according to its nature and as delineated in royal law, judges must not and cannot impose custom. Rather, habitual acts and deeds repeated over the long term constitute custom, which is why Indians do not observe the same custom. Rather, the customs that they observe are as numerous and diverse as are the pueblos themselves.[64]

The struggle over the meaning of costumbre captured so pointedly by the lawyer for the plaintiff pueblos may be traced again to Solórzano and a tension in his elaboration of the concept of costumbre. Solórzano defined costumbre as both a juridical norm and as a habit acquired by doing something continuously over time. As royal legal authority became increasingly centralized, it appears that the audiencia interpreted costumbre as juridical norm rather than as long-standing local practice. In an effort to combat the audiencia's interpretation, the petition penned by the lawyer of the plaintiff pueblos echoes Solórzano's articulation in *Política Indiana* of costumbre as practice and as regionally variable: "No less different are the customs of each region than the winds that bathe them and the municipalities that divide them."[65] Solórzano's favorable reading of romantic-primordial costumbre marked the end of an era. A rationalist trend in legal theory launched a significant assault on romantic-primordial costumbre that coincided with the case of Santiago Yagallo and associates versus San Juan Yae.

The trend toward the centralization of legal power in the hands of the king (*la potestad legislativa*) and away from local custom that had begun in medieval Castile accelerated substantially during the eighteenth century. Bourbon devotion to enlightened absolutism and the rationalization of imperial rule may in part explain the divergent legal interpretations of costumbre apparent in the case of Santiago Yagallo and allies versus San Juan Yae. A proclamation dated December 13, 1721, and issued to the audiencia of Mexico emphasized the primacy of royal law and the importance of its literal interpretation and application.[66] Twenty-one years later, in 1742, the Council of the Indies warned the viceroy of New Spain "to observe without exception the laws of the Kingdom, no matter the custom [*práctica, uso o costumbre*] introduced or intended by the Viceroys and Ministers."[67]

In tandem with the centralization of legal power in the hands of the king, during the second half of the eighteenth century, royal jurists increasingly abandoned or disregarded local custom as a legitimate source for legal decisions in favor of an instrumentalist application of costumbre that served the enlightened absolutist policies of the Bourbon kings. From 1747 to 1774, four royal jurists—Tomás Manuel Fernández, Manuel Silvestre Martínez, Juan Francisco de Castro, and Juan Antonio Mujál y de Gibert—launched an attack on costumbre that embodied the rationalist spirit of the period.[68] In particular, Castro's treatise, *Discursos críticos sobre las leyes y sus intérpretes*, reflects the legal trend:

> We do not need to go far in order to demonstrate the dim uncertainty in matters of custom. Far from finding solace in custom, litigants frequently experience major frustration. It is more useful for the republic to adorn itself with the laws that are the fruit of the sleepless nights of our wise legislators than to vacillate due to a system of law that is so uncertain and rife with variations, as is the case with custom. . . . [I]t would therefore serve the public peace to banish all custom since it is derogatory to the law.[69]

In the last two decades of the century as the Bourbon Reforms rationalized the administration of the Indies through the system of intendencies, Spanish jurists such as José Pérez y López and El Conde de la Cañada continued their attacks on costumbre in favor of la potestad legislativa. By the turn of the century, the consensus of Spanish jurists centered on the absolute power of royal authority in legal matters and left little room for recourse to local custom.[70]

The shift toward rationalist legal theory in the metropole may have had some effect on the audiencia's decision in the case of Santiago Yagallo and associates versus San Juan Yae. The chronology of the shift appears to coincide to some degree with the chronology of the case, although it is difficult to be sure since the timing of the appeals remains somewhat shadowy. The plaintiff pueblos appealed the audiencia's 1743 decision in 1744.[71] The documentation of the case, however, ends in 1745, at which point the audiencia rejected the appeal of the plaintiff pueblos.[72]

Legal cases from 1750 and 1769 suggest, however, that the dispute continued after the audiencia's 1744 decision. In 1750, Don Cristóbal Flores, governor of Yae, and a number of Yae's officials and principales brought a case of abuse of authority against their legal agent Don Francisco de Mendoza (the same man who had served as governor in the 1730s and had quarreled with the priest, Don Antonio de Saavedra). Armed with the pueblo's power of attorney from 1733 until 1750, Mendoza had played a central role in the case against Santiago Yagallo and associates. Flores and his allies complained that Mendoza had asked them to authorize legal business—and therefore further expenses—without explaining the exact content of said business. It is possible that Mendoza had continued to conduct legal business related to the cabecera-sujeto dispute in response to the plaintiff pueblos' continued appeals.[73]

A legal document from 1769 further suggests that the appeals may have continued until that date. The last of the 104 pages of the document records the request by the lawyer for Yae for the return by the audiencia of the provisions and decrees that Yae's legal team had submitted in support of their claims to cabecera status. The first 103 pages contained copies of petitions, testimony, and appeals on the part of the litigants from 1731 to 1744, as well as a copy of the Real Provisión from 1743. This amalgam of the case may have represented what the judges reviewed for final appeal sometime between 1744 and 1769.[74]

If not directly influenced by the 1764 and 1765 treatises of Martínez and Castro, the decision of the audiencia may have reflected ideas that were in the air or brewing during this period. Even if there were no direct connection between legal theory in Spain and the audiencia's decision in the case (which would be difficult to believe), it is interesting to note that the political conditions obtaining on the ground in the district of Villa Alta from 1700 forward spoke directly to the political debates in Spain concerning the validity of local custom and native autonomy versus royal legal authority and the centralization of political power. This is not surprising when one considers that the centralizing and authoritarian policies of Bishop Maldonado (Oaxaca's first Bourbon bishop) and their deleterious effects on native autonomy brought the spirit if not the letter of the Bourbon Reforms to the district of Villa Alta earlier than to other parts of New Spain. Bourbon efforts during the 1740s and 1750s to secularize and centralize parish administration throughout its American holdings mirrored Maldonado's attacks on Dominican hegemony in Villa Alta.[75] The case of Santiago Yagallo and allies versus San Juan Yae represented a response on the part of the litigants of both sides of the case to these new conditions and an impulse to negotiate a favorable outcome for themselves.

CONCLUSION

The narrative of the tumultuous eighteenth century in the district of Villa Alta raises some important questions concerning negotiation between pueblos de indios and the state as colonial process. As the events of the eighteenth century—the Cajonos rebellion, the repressive state response, Bishop Maldonado's reforms, and the legal rebellion of Yagallo and its allies—make clear, negotiation was not a given, a priori mode of post-conquest colonial politics but occurred in response to specific historical conditions. If Spanish military conquest, coercion, and indigenous accommodation had produced a tentative Pax Hispanica in Villa Alta, then the violence of the Cajonos rebellion undid it temporarily. Repression and reform rearranged relationships of power to the detriment of indigenous autonomy, and from this point of departure, a renegotiation of power relationships through the legal system arguably became the most viable mode of political struggle.

The historicization of negotiation is critical to our understanding of colonialism in New Spain. Of late, the historical literature has emphasized hegemonic processes such as the contested nature of evangelization of the native population, the incorporation of indigenous elites into the colonial bureaucracy through the system of native cabildos, and the channeling of indigenous grievances through the legal system.[76] This emphasis on cultural and political negotiation in the literature has both contributed significantly to our understanding of Spanish colonialism and yielded its own set of problems. Most importantly, the causes and effects of episodic native violence and Spanish coercion, particularly in the more remote regions of Mesoamerica, have tended to be ignored or de-emphasized (especially in comparison to the scholarship on the Andes), with a few notable exceptions. The case of eighteenth-century Villa Alta, like that of the Tzeltal region of Chiapas studied by Kevin Gosner and Robert Patch, suggests a pattern of eighteenth-century colonial relations in peripheral regions characterized by breaches of indigenous semiautonomy on the part of the state or Church, violent native response, state repression, accommodation, and the renegotiation of local rule.[77] These eighteenth-century examples should encourage historians to consider negotiation as a mode of colonial politics that required certain historical conditions in order to flourish. As the term "renegotiation" implies, negotiation was not a permanent process but occurred in fits and starts in dialectic with native violence and state coercion, which could either close or open the space for negotiation anew.

The long and varied life of costumbre in pueblo-state litigation sheds light on aspects of negotiation that deserve more scrutiny: specifically, the idioms or languages produced, struggled over, and shared by the brokers of state and pueblo interests. The deployment of costumbre by the legal teams of the plaintiffs and defendants in the case of Santiago Yagallo and associates versus San Juan Yae represented part of a longue durée process of political struggle and concomitant negotiation and renegotiation with colonial authorities, both within the legal system and outside of it. As the events of eighteenth-century Villa Alta reveal, local history conditioned the salience of costumbre as a language of negotiation. Rebellion, repression, and reform at the local level worked in combination with political and legal centralization and rationalization in the metropole and the colony to reshape the meaning and constrain the power of costumbre as rhetorical strategy in the hands of interethnic legal teams. The reshaping of costumbre by native extralegal collective action and legal strategizing had a reflexive effect: the audiencia's narrow interpretation of costumbre shaped local arrangements of power through legal decisions.

The decline in the legitimacy of romantic-primordial costumbre in colonial courts over the eighteenth century mirrored the diminution of native autonomy and the breakdown of colonial understandings between pueblos de indios and the state during the same period. In this regard, in addition to providing scholars with both a tool and an object for analysis of negotiation as colonial process, the recognition in Spanish courts of romantic-primordial costumbre as a legitimate source of law also serves as a barometer of pueblo-state relations over the course of the colonial period. The transition in New Spain from a colonial regime characterized by "strong legal pluralism" during the first two centuries of colonial rule to a "state-centered legal system" during the last century of the colony undercut the political and legal space for negotiation between pueblos de indios and the state and rendered the state and its legal institutions more rigid and monolithic. The legal flexibility and jurisdictional complexity of New Spain's colonial institutions had allowed for extensive negotiation between local people and colonial authorities. Ultimately, this flexibility and complexity had underwritten the process of colonial state formation, native autonomy, and the success of the Spanish imperial project. The Bourbon attack on this system in the name of greater political control produced the opposite effect in the long term. By diminishing space for negotiation, the Bourbons shattered the colonial system that was a product of two centuries of political struggle as well as the possibility for renegotiation. Perhaps the recourse to rebellion, violence, and extralegal forms of expressing discontent on the part of pueblos de indios during the last decades of the eighteenth century may have resulted in part from the apparent futility of negotiation. In this regard, the decline of romantic-primordial costumbre during the last decades of the colony may have augured the end of the colonial order.

NOTES

Please note that from 2001 to 2003, the Archivo del Poder Judicial de Oaxaca (APJO) recatalogued the Archivo del Juzgado de Villa Alta (AVA) and imposed a new system of *legajos* (files) and *expedientes* (case files). My citations reflect the pre-2001 system. In all cases, I refer to the title of the document so that it can be more easily found.

1. Susan Kellogg, *Law and the Transformation of Aztec Culture, 1500–1700* (Norman: University of Oklahoma Press, 1995).

2. Lauren Benton, *Law and Colonial Cultures: Legal Regimes in World History, 1400–1900* (Cambridge: Cambridge University Press, 2002), 9.

3. Ibid., 9.

4. Archivo del Juzgado de Villa Alta (Oaxaca, Mexico) (hereafter, AVA) Criminal (uncatalogued) (1701), "Contra los naturales del pueblo de San Francisco Cajonos por sedición, sublevación e idolatría." See also Eulogio Gillow, *Apuntes históricos sobre la idolatría e introducción del cristianismo en Oaxaca* (México DF: Ediciones Toledo, 1990 [1889]).

5. David Tavárez, "Idolatry as Ontological Question: Native Consciousness and Juridical Proof in Colonial Mexico" *Journal of Early Modern History* 6, no. 2 (2002): 120–121. Tavárez argues that from 1665 to 1736, the alcaldes mayores and tenientes de alcalde of Villa Alta presided over at least a dozen idolatry trials.

6. The voluminous documentation generated by Maldonado's wide-ranging investigation of Dominican administration of the indigenous pueblos of Oaxaca

and the "idolatrous" practices of the pueblos of the district of Villa Alta can be found in the following legajos in the Archivo General de las Indias (Seville, Spain) (hereafter, AGI): AGI México 879 (investigation of Dominican administration of indigenous pueblos in Oaxaca), AGI México 880 (legal conflict between Maldonado and the Dominican order regarding Maldonado's plan to overhaul Dominican administration by dividing Dominican doctrinas and appointing secular clergy), AGI México 881 (testimony concerning Dominican administration of the doctrinas of Villa Alta and plans to divide the doctrinas and put them under secular administration), and AGI México 882 (more documentation on reform of church administration in Villa Alta and the testimony of the cabildos of the district of Villa Alta regarding the "idolatrous" practices of their communities; this legajo also includes the ritual calendars confiscated from the pueblos of Villa Alta by Maldonado's chief extirpator Licenciado Joseph de Aragón y Alcántara). Much of the information in this documentation has been synthesized by Chance, Alcina Franch, and Tavárez. See John K. Chance, *Conquest of the Sierra: Spaniards and Indians in Colonial Oaxaca* (Norman: University of Oklahoma Press, 1989), 151–175; José Alcina Franch, *Calendario y Religión Entre los Zapotecos* (México DF: Universidad Nacional Autónoma México, 1993); David Tavárez, "Invisible Wars: Idolatry Extirpation Projects and Native Responses in Nahua and Zapotec Communities, 1536–1728" (Ph.D. dissertation, University of Chicago, Chicago, 2000).

7. Tavárez, "Invisible Wars," 397.

8. Ibid., 397–405.

9. Ibid., 239–244; Alcina Franch, *Calendario y Religión*, 17–18.

10. Chance, *Conquest of the Sierra*, 156.

11. Ibid., 13.

12. Alcina Franch, *Calendario y Religión*, 19–25; Chance, *Conquest of the Sierra*, 156, 165–167.

13. Chance, *Conquest of the Sierra*, 167.

14. For a history of the parish structure of the Sierra Norte, see Chance, *Conquest of the Sierra*, 77–78, and Peter Gerhard, *A Guide to the Historical Geography of New Spain*, rev. ed. (Norman: University of Oklahoma Press, 1993), 369.

15. Archivo General de la Nación (Mexico City, Mexico) (hereafter, AGN) Tierras, vol. 2775, exp. 9 (1617), fols. 1–18v. Chance also discusses the history of Yae's parish status as well; see Chance, *Conquest of the Sierra*, 77–78.

16. In a case brought to the alcalde mayor of Villa Alta by the cabildo of Santiago Lalopa in which the pueblo claimed its own cabecera status independent of San Juan Yae, the cabildo of Yae offered three Reales Provisiones dated 1695, 1702, and 1703 in which the audiencia affirmed Yae's cabecera status. AVA Civil, exp. 102 (1709), "Los naturales del pueblo y común de Santiago Lalopa se oponen de ser subordinados del pueblo de San Juan Yae." See also Rosenbach Museum and Library, Philadelphia, New Spain Collection, 462/25, pt. 22, no. 6, 1736–1769, 48v, for an inventory of the Reales Provisiones and "instrumentos" submitted in the case, dated from 1695 to 1742.

17. The Virgin of Yabee (the Virgin of the "Monte de las Mariposas") represented a local deity whose veneration became integrated with that of the Catholic

Virgin Mary over the course of the colonial period. Rincón communities designated a hilltop above Yae as the site for her veneration. Each of the pueblos represented by the cofradía bought and contributed expensive decorations and ornaments (*alhajas*) for the cult of Yabee. Once the cofradía of Yabee was dissolved, the pueblos fought over the division of the alhajas. For details about the cofradía and the fight over the alhajas and ornamentos, see Rosenbach Museum and Library, Philadelphia, New Spain Collection, 462/25, pt. 21, no. 2 (1735–1744); 462/25, pt. 21, no. 3 (1744); 462/25, pt. 25, no. 1 (1736–1741).

18. It appears that the priest without fixed residence was not unique to the northeastern Rincón; the parish of Yagavila (also part of the Rincón) on the western side of the Cajonos River shared a similar tradition. In 1691, Yagavila's officials complained to the Real Audiencia that the major religious celebrations surrounding Easter should be held in Yagavila, the cabecera, since carrying the paraphernalia for these celebrations to subject pueblos posed a hardship. See AGN Indios, vol. 30 exp. 448 (1691), fols. 418v–420.

19. Testimony given to the Real Audiencia on June 11, 1735, by alcalde mayor of Villa Alta Don Joachin de Padilla y Estrada in a case concerning parish relationships in the partido of San Juan Yae–San Juan Tanetze. Rosenbach Museum and Library, Philadelphia, New Spain Collection 462/25, pt. 21, no. 2 (1735–1744), fols. 6v–8.

20. Marcello Carmagnani, "Local Governments and Ethnic Governments in Oaxaca," in *Essays in the Political, Economic, and Social History of Colonial Latin America*, ed. Karen Spalding, 107–124 (Newark: University of Delaware, 1982), 107–108, 111.

21. Refer to note 16 above. See the Reales Provisiones dated 1695, 1702, and 1703 in which the audiencia affirmed Yae's cabecera status. See also AVA Civil, exp. 102 (1709), "Los naturales del pueblo y común de Santiago Lalopa se oponen de ser subordinados del pueblo de San Juan Yaée"; Rosenbach Museum and Library, Philadelphia, New Spain Collection, 462/25, pt. 22, no. 6 (1736–1769), 48v.

22. See John Chance's work on the Sierra of Puebla. John K. Chance, "The *Barrios* of Tecali: Patronage, Kinship, and Territorial Relations in a Central Mexican Community," *Ethnology* 35, no. 2 (1996): 107–140; ibid., "The *Caciques* of Tecali: Class and Ethnic Identity in Late Colonial Mexico," *Hispanic American Historical Review* 76, no. 3 (1996): 475–502; ibid., "The Noble House in Colonial Puebla, Mexico: Descent, Inheritance, and the Nahua Tradition," *American Anthropologist* 102, no. 3 (2000): 485–502.

23. Dorothy Tanck de Estrada, *Pueblos de indios y educación en el México colonial, 1750–1821* (Mexico City: El Colegio de México, 1999), 490–530.

24. For a discussion of the General Indian Court and the legal insurance of the Half Real, see Woodrow Borah, *Justice by Insurance: The General Indian Court of Mexico and the Legal Aides of the Half-Real* (Berkeley: University of California Press, 1983).

25. For a discussion of the internal dynamics and politics of legal cases in native pueblos of the district of Villa Alta, see Yanna P. Yannakakis, "Indios Ladinos: Indigenous Intermediaries and the Negotiation of Local Rule in Colonial

Oaxaca, 1660–1769" (Ph.D. dissertation, University of Pennsylvania, Philadelphia, 2003); ibid., *The Art of Being In-Between: Native Intermediaries, Indian Identity, and Local Rule in Colonial Oaxaca* (Durham, NC: Duke University Press, 2008).

26. See Yannakakis, "Indios Ladinos" and *The Art of Being In-Between*, for a discussion of legal intermediaries, legal teams, and legal strategies.

27. AVA Civil, 11, exp. 26 (1744), "Protocolos de Instrumentos Públicos," doc. 26.04.

28. Ibid., doc. 26.05.

29. Ibid., doc. 26.08.

30. Borah, *Justice by Insurance*, 8.

31. Benton, *Law and Colonial Cultures*, 43.

32. Borah, *Justice by Insurance*, 8.

33. Ibid., 8–9.

34. Ibid., 11–14.

35. Benton, *Law and Colonial Cultures*, 80–126. Lauren Benton coins the term "jurisdictional jockeying" in her discussion of jurisdictional tensions in Catholic and Islamic imperial legal traditions.

36. Benton has elaborated a series of heuristic terms for analysis of imperial legal regimes: multicentric legal orders, state-centered legal orders, and strong and weak legal pluralism; Benton, *Law and Colonial Cultures*, 11. Recopilación de Leyes de los Reynos de las Indias. 1998. *Recopilación de Leyes de los Reynos de las Indias*, 3 tomos [1681]. Madrid: Imprenta Nacional el Boletín Oficial del Estado.

37. *Recopilación de Leyes de los Reynos de las Indias*, vols. 1–3, Edición facsímil coeditada por el Centro de Estudios Políticos y Constitucionales y el Boletín Oficial del Estado (Madrid: Imprenta Nacional del Boletín Oficial del Estado, 1998 [1681]), 1:218; libro 2, titulo 1, ley 4: "Que se guarden las leyes que los Indios tenían antiguamente para su gobierno, y las que se hicieren de Nuevo," El emperador D. Cárlos y la Princesa Doña Juana Gobernadora en Valladolid, August 6, 1555.

38. *Recopilación*, 1:346, libro 2, titulo 15, ley 83: "Que las Audiencias tengan cuidado del buen tratamiento de los Indios y brevedad de sus pleytos," El Emperador D. Cárlos en la ley 20 de 1542, La Reyna de Bohemia Gobernadora en Valladolid, March 11, 1550; D. Felipe II en la Ordenanza 70 de Audiencias de 1563; Y en Madrid, July 3, 1571; Y en la Ordenanza 79 de Audiencias, en Toledo, May 25, 1596.

39. *Recopilación*, 2:120–121, libro 5, titulo 2, ley 22: "Que los Gobernadores reconozcan la policía que los Indios tuvieren, y guarden sus usos en lo que no fueren contrarios a nuestra Sagrada Religion, y hagan que cada uno exerza bien su oficio, y la tierra esté abastecida y limpia, y las obras públicas reparadas," El Emperador D. Cárlos, y la Emperatriz Gobernadora en Madrid, July 12, 1530.

40. Borah, *Justice by Insurance*, 35–45.

41. Victor Tau Anzoátegui, *El poder de la costumbre: estudios sobre el derecho consuetudinario en América hispana hasta la Emancipación* (Buenos Aires: Instituto de Investigaciones de Historia del Derecho, 2001), 309–340.

42. Benton, *Law and Colonial Cultures*, 11.

43. Borah, *Justice by Insurance*, 254.

44. Paola Miceli, "El derecho consuetudinario en castilla: Una crítica a la matriz romántica de las interpretaciones sobre la costumbre," *Hispania* 63/1, no. 213 (2002): 9–28. Miceli urges us not to take the romantic connotation of "costumbre" at face value. She argues that contrary to scholarly and popular assumptions, costumbre did not originate in the popular will and practices of the people of medieval Castile but rather had its origins in Castilian legal institutions and was used as a juridical tool for controlling diverse peoples.

45. AVA Civil, exp. 102 (1709): "Los naturales y común del pueblo de Santiago Lalopa se oponen de ser subordinados del pueblo de San Juan Yaée."

46. Ibid.

47. Ibid.

48. Rosenbach Museum and Library, New Spain, 462/25, pt. 21, no. 3 (1734–1744), fols. 34–42v.

49. Ibid., fols. 34–34v.

50. Ibid., fols. 36–36v.

51. Ibid., fols. 38–38v.

52. Ibid., fols. 42–42v.

53. AVA Civil, exp. 148 (1735), "Averiguación del porque no asisten a las fiestas de Semana Santa y otras los naturales de los pueblos de Yagallo, Lachichina y Yaviche."

54. Rosenbach Museum and Library, New Spain, 462/25, pt. 21, no. 3 (1735–1744), fols. 21v–22.

55. Ibid., fol. 1.

56. Anzoátegui, *El poder de la costumbre*, 318–336.

57. Ibid., 245.

58. Charles R. Cutter, *The Legal Culture of Northern New Spain, 1700–1810* (Albuquerque: University of New Mexico Press, 1995), 37.

59. Rosenbach Museum and Library, New Spain, 462/25, pt. 21, no. 3 (1735–1744), fols. 26–28.

60. Ibid., pt. 25, no. 1, fols. 22–24v.

61. Ibid., fols. 26v–27.

62. Ibid., fols. 21v–22v.

63. Ibid., "Real Provisión," December 1743.

64. Ibid., pt. 21, no. 2, fol. 67v.

65. Anzoátegui, *El poder de la costumbre*, 328, citing Solórzano, *Política Indiana*, 2(25):9.

66. Anzoátegui, *El poder de la costumbre*, 257 citing Archivo General de la Nación, *Acuerdos del extinguido cabildo de Buenos Aires*, series 3, 4:606–609, Buenos Aires, 1907–1933.

67. Anzoátegui, *El poder de la costumbre*, 257, citing libro 2, titulo 1, ley 1: de la RI, de José Lebrón y Cuervo, publicado por Concepción García Gallo, "José Lebrón y Cuervo: Notas a la Recopilación de Leyes de Indias; Estudio, edición e indices," *Anuario de Historia del Derecho Español* 40 (1970): 408.

68. Anzoátegui, *El poder de la costumbre*, 249–252.

69. Ibid., citing Juan Francisco de Castro, *Discursos críticos sobre las leyes y sus intérpretes en que se demuestra la necesidad de un nuevo y metódico cuerpo de Derecho para la recta administración de justicia* (Madrid: J. Ibarra, 1765; 2nd ed., 1829), 1:118–199.

70. Anzoátegui, *El poder de la costumbre*, 252–253.

71. AGN Tierras, vol. 2771, exp. 10 (1744); Rosenbach Museum and Library, New Spain, 462/25, pt. 21, no. 3 (1744); pt. 21, no. 2 (1735–1744); pt. 29, no. 3 (1741–1744).

72. AVA Civil, exp. 188 (1745), "El pueblo de San Juan Yae contra Santiago Yagallo y consortes sobre punto de cabecera"; AVA Civil, exp. 189 (1745), "El pueblo de San Juan Yae contra Santiago Yagallo sobre punto de cabecera."

73. AVA Civil, exp. 207 (1750), "Las justicias del pueblo de San Juan Yae se quejan de las malas acciones que viene efectuando Francisco Mendoza contra la administración actual."

74. Rosenbach Museum and Library, New Spain, 462/25, pt. 22, no. 6 (1736–1769).

75. William B. Taylor, *Magistrates of the Sacred: Priests and Parishioners in Eighteenth-Century Mexico* (Stanford, CA: Stanford University Press, 1996), 13.

76. For the case of evangelization as cultural dialogue, negotiation, and contestation in New Spain, see Louise Burkhart, *The Slippery Earth: Nahua-Christian Moral Dialogue in Sixteenth-Century Mexico* (Tucson: University of Arizona Press, 1989); ibid., *Holy Wednesday: A Nahua Drama from Early Colonial Mexico* (Philadelphia: University of Pennsylvania Press, 1996); and for a case study of the Andes, see Kenneth Mills, *Idolatry and Its Enemies: Colonial Andean Religion and Extirpation, 1640–1750* (Princeton, NJ: Princeton University Press, 1997). For analysis of the legal system as a hegemonic institution, see Kellogg, *Law and the Transformation of Aztec Culture*, and Cutter, *The Legal Culture of Northern New Spain*. For examination of the incorporation of Andean elites into the Spanish political order in the Andes, see Karen Spalding, *Huarochirí: An Andean Society under Inca and Spanish Rule* (Stanford, CA: Stanford University Press, 1984), and Steve J. Stern, *Peru's Indian Peoples and the Challenge of Spanish Conquest: Huamanga to 1640* (Madison: University of Wisconsin Press, 1982).

77. Kevin Gosner, *Soldiers of the Virgin: The Moral Economy of a Colonial Maya Rebellion* (Tucson: University of Arizona Press, 1992), and Robert W. Patch, *Maya Revolt and Revolution in the Eighteenth Century* (Armonk, NY: M. E. Sharpe, 2002).

7 CUAUHTÉMOC VELASCO ÁVILA

Translation by Michel Besson

Peace Agreements and War Signals

Negotiations with the Apaches and Comanches in
the Interior Provinces of New Spain, 1784–1788

Negotiation becomes necessary whenever two forces find themselves in relative equilibrium and realize that political agreement is better than the continuation of open conflict. In a paradoxical way, in the last decades of the eighteenth century, just as the Spanish state seemed to be strengthening in America and consolidating its borders, it was developing a policy centered on the search for new alliances and a greater stability. At the same time, the various nomadic peoples in northern New Spain were going through a phase of transformation: some were becoming extinct; others were confronting serious difficulties; while still others were strengthening and feeling more able everyday to stop the Spanish progression onto lands and natural resources they rightfully considered their own.

In this chapter, I discuss the contacts and the negotiations led by the Comanches and the Mescalero Apaches with royal authorities in the region that today encompasses the Mexican–New Mexican–Texas border as they tried to reach some form of peace in the decade of the 1780s, a crucial moment as royal policy was being defined about the peoples living on the borders. I will examine what forms the negotiations took, who the actors were who took part in them, and what those negotiations entailed in terms of political dealings and cultural exchange. We will see the interests and relations that were part and parcel of those negotiations. The contradictions and conflicts that existed between the native peoples coming from varied ethnic and societal backgrounds, as well as the tensions with which they had to deal, will become apparent.[1]

TIMES OF REFORM AND DEFINITION

The so-called epoch of the Bourbon reforms was a period of modernization for the political machinery of New Spain, a time when a series of mechanisms were set up to make the relation of dependence vis-à-vis the Spanish Crown more efficient, and an age of change in the mentality of politicians and royal administrators. However, as I progressed in my research, I found that the ideal model pursued by the Crown was becoming more short-lived as more and more incoherence appeared between the announced purposes of the king, the attitudes and proposals of the top civil servants in the American possessions, and the activities of lower-level officials in charge of implementing the measures.

At the time, a generally rationalist frame of mind dominated, and I think that the feeling of success possessed by the reformers toward the end of the eighteenth century was in large part the result of the triumph of some of the fundamental ideas behind the Enlightenment. Thus, rather than try to identify what the correspondence may have been between the plans of the various ministries and the actual actions of the government, it may be better to seek an understanding of how a few fundamental ideas came to form part of the arguments used by bureaucrats and elites of New Spain.

Among those ideas, and for the purpose of the present study, a new concept about territorial expansion and the management of the frontiers seems particularly important. Anthony Pagden shows how, starting with the last years of the seventeenth century, European dominating groups started realizing what great dangers lay in out-of-control territorial expansion. According to him, one of the greatest challenges faced by the European empires in this period was knowing how to harness their own agents in their desire to conquer new territories. Those empires had been built on the basis of a certain vision of military virtue. To change that concept meant thinking anew about the very bases of the empire, since many civil and military servants believed fervently that the best way to serve their kings was to augment their possessions, to open new provinces, or to show themselves capable of great military feats.[2] For that reason, one of the arguments repeated in many documents of the time was the need to contain what was called "the spirit of the conquest," which blinded most men to the "new" thinking.

The Spanish Crown, the main promoter of the reforms, especially in the time of Charles III, was preoccupied by the defense of its territories in the face of threats from other European powers. However, in Spain's American possessions, the progress of settlement was slowed in those regions where the exploitation of natural and human resources no longer justified the investment needed in the pacification or evangelization of the local people. Thus, in the most remote settlements, the threat caused by the Indian populations was greater, as those were not subject to the king, being nomadic or semi-nomadic in nature. During the eighteenth century, great efforts were expended to build a stable border in northern New Spain in order to safeguard the systematic exploitation of local resources and guarantee the safety of the settlers. That task involved many men and numerous resources, implied defining specific strategies, and put to the test the abilities and will of those on the front lines.

Minister Joseph de Campillo y Cossío in his *Nuevo sistema de gobierno económico para la América* (1743) proposed to give special attention to the control of the frontier territories and to modify the relations existing with the "heathen" Indians as well as with "the nearby nations." His idea was to establish "trade relations with the wild Indians," just as other powers had done in America, taking advantage of their "passions" and "taming their tastes."[3] As we shall see later on, those ideas coincided with the treatment the Crown intended for the northern Indians more broadly. Obviously, as Pagden affirms, the defense and consolidation of the empire required political virtues that were distinct from those of the conquerors and demanded a different type of government: prudence was needed over courage, wisdom over strength.[4] We shall see also how the treatment of hostile Indians remained a matter of discussion, especially how best to achieve their pacification, a discussion that had its origins in the deeper debate among colonial officials about how to serve the king's interests without abandoning one's own.

THE COMANCHES: THE MOST FEARED OF ALL THE NATIONS

Captain Hugo de O'Conor was *comandante inspector* (commandant inspector) of the northern border between 1771 and 1776. That post gave him ample opportunity to accumulate experience and deep knowledge of the ways of living and character of local Indians.[5] He considered the Comanche nation, composed of "such proud and well-developed people," to be "the most feared among them, because of the firearms they had acquired from the English and which they used in a most expert way, as well as because of their courage and audacity, and because they never were given to fleeing, but would have rather chosen dying or conquering." He also pointed out that this nation had more than once given evidence of "being more civil and politically savvy than the other barbarians, their neighbors."[6] At the same time as he was consolidating the territorial defenses and exalting the Spanish military forces facing the unpredictable and fast-moving nomads of the north, this soldier also thought about the necessity of establishing alliances and pacts with a number of Indian groups in order to build a system of regional counterbalances that would guarantee the safety of settlers, ranches, *haciendas* (large landed estates), and mining centers.

Civil servants and those in charge of dealing with the border Indians realized that, practically speaking, a generalized conflict with all rebellious peoples was impractical. Military efforts would have to be carefully thought out in advance. In 1777, Teodoro de Croix took over as *comandante general* (general commander) of the Provincias Internas (Interior Provinces). He was a career soldier, without any experience of the frontier in New Spain. Initially, he believed that peace would be achieved through a considerable increase in the troops and a general campaign against all Indians.[7] However, before launching into action, he had the good sense to consult those among his men who had "the highest ranks, and had accumulated the longest experience and knowledge" on the border during three meetings held between December 1777 and July 1778, and they agreed that it was necessary to wage a campaign against the Apaches, who remained the most feared and dangerous Indians of that province. They insisted that it was of the utmost importance to cultivate the friendship of the Comanches, giving them gifts, to keep them disposed to help in a campaign against the Apaches.[8]

To bring about rapprochement with the Comanches, Atanasio de Mézières, an administrator, Indian agent, and diplomat in Louisiana and Texas, was commissioned to try to promote friendship, so that trade routes could be opened from Louisiana all the way to the source of the Missouri. He thought that by entering into an alliance with the Comanches as well as the Wichitas, it would then be relatively easy to lead a campaign to defeat the Lipanes. In the spring of 1778, Mézières managed to start talks with the Tahuacanos and succeeded in entering the village of the Tahuayaces (two Witchita groups), but he could not enter in direct contact with the Comanche chiefs nor could he consolidate even the beginning of an alliance.[9]

The general campaign planned against the Lipanes did not materialize because it was never approved by the Crown, nor did it get the necessary reinforcement in troops and resources needed to make it viable. Thus, Commandant Croix had to maintain a policy of control, confrontation, and conciliation with the various Indian groups, according to the specific circumstances of each region.[10]

In February 1779, José de Gálvez, Minister of the Indies, sent Croix an instruction summing up the interest of the Crown in a new policy as regarded the hostile groups of the north, noting that the circumstances as well as the way the natives waged war seemed to render impossible the pacification of the northern frontier via an offensive war. The commandant was thus instructed to limit his actions to the defense of the villages, haciendas, ranches, and other Spanish settlements. He was to organize expeditions with the goal of pushing the Indians far from the frontier or forcing them to sign a peace treaty and start a lasting friendship. He was not to try and oblige them to live in fixed settlements nor to force them to serve the Spaniards. They were supposed to be attracted to a more civilized life through the presentation of gifts and trade of Spanish goods, including firearms, the idea being that they would end up dependent on that market. As the last phase of their pacification they were to be evangelized.[11]

But seen from a local point of view, things looked very different. The departure of Ripperdá from the governorship of Texas in November 1778 and the death of Mézières seemed to foreclose the possibility of a solid alliance with the Indians of the north. Domingo Cabello, who succeeded Ripperdá, had no interest whatsoever in promoting the French trade coming from Louisiana and had a totally different idea of the relations existing between the Spaniards and the native warriors. In a word, Cabello did not trust any possible alliance in any form.[12]

His experience with the Indians who came down to Béxar to trade and beg for gifts convinced him of "their ever changing and voluble character, and of their inability to stay true to any of their treaties or agreements."[13] He thought that the Lipanes had to be confronted head on, without the support of the Comanches or other northern groups. Such a plan would require troops and resources, which he never managed to get, thereby obliging him to discuss and negotiate with the Indians, in spite of the poor opinion he had of them.

In 1783, Felipe de Neve, who succeeded Teodoro de Croix, decided on an aggressive policy to put an end to the feigned amity of the Lipanes and to wage war on them until they had no choice but to perish or give up. For that campaign, he counted on the coordinated action of the regional troops of Coahuila, Texas, and Nueva Vizcaya, which he was thinking of using as a two-pronged attack, together with the support he was expecting from the Comanches and the Wichitas.[14] However, he never had time to flesh out the campaign or his alliances, as death caught up with him in August 1784. The status of the Interior Provinces then changed, as they once again passed under the authority of the viceroy of New Spain. With the royal order of 1784, the situation did not look promising. Paradoxically, the way things turned out in 1785 in both Texas and New Mexico forced a rapprochement with the so-called Indians of the North.[15]

THE TREATY WITH THE COMANCHES IN TEXAS

Cabello had to abandon his considerable prejudices when, in February 1785, delegations from the Tahuayaces and the Huecos, two of the Wichita groups, came to Béxar to negotiate for peace.[16] The governor was obliged to treat them as distinguished guests, and he signed a document in which he acknowledged the courage of Chief Guersec and his loyalty to the Spaniards and Cabello's own authority. The Indian representatives agreed to live as vassals of the king and to fight against the enemies of the Spaniards, the understanding being that they would wage war against the Comanches. They were given a standard to be placed in the village of Chief Guersec, as well as a medal of merit, an officer's staff, and the hat and jacket of a captain for him to wear. On May 16 of the same year, other representatives of Guersec arrived in Béxar. Cabello received them cordially, and after the ritual smoking of the peace pipe, the delegates told him of their wish to be helped in their war against the Panishmahas. Cabello excused himself, telling them the Comanches had caused a lot of damage in San Antonio and Nacogdoches. In passing he reminded them of their promise to wage war against the Comanches. The negotiation remained inconclusive that day.

The following day, six Vidais Indians appeared unexpectedly to present their respects to the governor. Seeing their enemies in the *presidio* (fort) caused much resentment, but Cabello managed to convince them that nobody would attack them. Showing a great deal of diplomacy, he gave them the same friendly treatment as he had given the Wichitas, asked them what kind of relations they had with the Lipanes, and, during long and delicate negotiations in which tobacco and food apparently played a major role, managed to convince all of them that organizing a campaign against the Lipanes was of utmost importance. Finally, he avoided having to give support to the Tahuayaces and contented himself with asking for help from the chief of the Tahuacanos. Cabello was soon in a position where he could envision building up a large coalition against the Lipanes. However, even though the peace he had attained with the Wichita groups prevented them from forming a dangerous alliance with the Comanches, the latter were still a threat because they were known to form the nation that was both the largest and most experienced in war. When Bernardo de Gálvez became viceroy in 1785, the immediate aim of the Crown was to form a greater alliance that would guarantee, once and for all, peace in the province.[17]

The desire to form an alliance with the Comanches was expressed in several ways. In July of that year, Juan Bautista de Anza, governor of New Mexico, sent out the information that close to 400 Comanches, together with their families, had arrived in the village of Taos to carry on some trade there. They entered the village without showing any mistrust, carried on their own "fair" in an orderly fashion, and left "many pelts, uncured leather, meat and over sixty horses, in exchange for other goods." The Indian chiefs were of the opinion that the Comanches wanted peace with the Spaniards. Anza commented in his report that "at all times during his governorship, he had never experienced such proofs of their good faith."[18] Domingo Cabello, preoccupied by the need he felt to promote a peace agreement with the Comanches, sent Pedro Vial and Francisco Xavier Chávez to start talks with the eastern Comanches via the Tahuayaces' chiefs. Vial had lived as a trader among the Tahuayaces and knew their language and was on friendly terms with their chiefs. Chávez had been a captive of the Comanches, who later sold him to the Tahuayaces, so that he knew the customs and the languages of both peoples.[19] The envoys left on June 17 for Nacogdoches, where they settled. There they met with the Chief Guersec, of the Tahuayaces, and Chief Eschas, of the Huecos, who received news of the upcoming negotiation with pleasure and offered to accompany the two Spaniards. On their way, they sent a letter to Chief Siscat Gainon, of the Tahuacanos, to prevent him from sending his own men to fight the Comanches.

When they arrived in the Tahuayace village, they were greeted with an "exceedingly magnificent entrance." Unfurling a Spanish flag and shooting guns to salute them, Guersec hosted them in his own house. The following day, many men got together for a "parliament" in which Guersec gave a thoughtful speech explaining the reason for the envoys' arrival and affirming that all should consider the great captain of San Antonio as more than a father, since he had decided that all Indians were to be "as friends and deal one with another as such, forgetting the deaths and the thefts of horses which had previously taken place." All present manifested their approval and began to shout so loudly that "it was as if the sky was coming crashing down or as if all the land around was sinking."[20]

The Wichita captains sent a reconnaissance party to look for the Comanches. They soon found a chief and his men. The Comanche captain immediately went to the village, where he received the news with apparent satisfaction and said that he thought all of his nation ought to accept peace. Together with the envoys and the Wichita captains, they left on August 29 to go to Comanche territory. The Spaniards described their arrival on the following day. The visitors were received by a large crowd and taken to a large tent made of cured buffalo skins, where they were housed. Their equipment was unloaded, their horses and mules taken care of, and they were fed a large quantity of buffalo and deer meat, as well as fruit and potatoes.[21]

The first day and those that followed saw other chiefs, captains, ancients, and "young ones" come from various settlements. The Spanish envoys, as well as Guersec and Eschas, tried to convince the Comanches of the need to form a lasting peace agreement, also giving the principals tobacco, knives, and other "trinkets." Several Indian captains asked whether the Spaniards were suffering from any illnesses, as the Comanches had had the experience of French settlers who contaminated them with smallpox, from which two thirds of the nation's population had died. The Spaniards answered, "[T]hey just had to look around and since we had arrived in that settlement, no cloud had passed across the sun, everything was very clear and resplendent, which showed that we had come in good health, and that satisfied them."[22] This is but one example of the Spanish diplomats' use of Comanche symbolic language.

The general meeting was held on September 10. It was a large group in which all the men participated in their finest regalia and to which Vial came, carrying the Spanish flag, on a very tall pole, which he erected in the center. Vial noted that there were around 700 men seated in four concentric circles, with a multitude of women and children remaining standing. The main chiefs, Camisa de Hierro (Iron Shirt) and Cabeza Rapada (Shaved Head), invited the Spaniards and the Wichita chiefs to sit with them in the innermost circle. Immediately, the guests brought out a large pipe that they proceeded to light before passing it around. When the tobacco was finished, the Comanche chiefs asked the envoys to speak, and Pedro Vial stood up to explain how they had personally convinced the "great captain" of San Antonio, as the Indians called the governor, to make peace with the Comanches and to have them included among those peoples who received gifts. He told them that the governor was inviting the captains to visit him so he could tell them directly of his interest for peace with them and his desire to wage war against the Apaches.

Chief Guersec repeated Vial's words and expressed how the other Wichita, Iscani, and Flechero chiefs very much desired them to be friends with the "great captain" in San Antonio and the Spaniards, because the other option was to turn their backs and wage war. After that intervention, a loud murmur rose among the audience. The Comanche chiefs later decided that they would meet again the following day and that they would then give their answer. Through the rest of that day and night, the groups held meetings and discussions, with "all the streets staying illuminated in such a way that we believe that none of them could sleep at all." Guersec and Eschas were present in the parliament of the chiefs, and they later they told the envoys that the Comanches had decided to make peace. The following day, the circle was again convened, they again smoked the pipe, and Chief Iron Shirt spoke. He noted, "[E]very time you have talked to us you have done so without any trouble, and the sun has not been obscured by clouds," and stated that the Comanches would wage war on the Apaches and Lipanes and they would name three *captaincillos* (lesser captains) to visit Cabello.[23]

The only condition Iron Shirt put on the agreement was to be given free passage in order to wage war on the Lipanes. He also offered to visit Cabello as often as possible and promised to pass on the news to his "comrades and brothers," the Yamparicas, so that they too would accept the peace with the Spaniards from San Antonio. Finished with his speech, he arranged the *naquisa* (see note 24) that had been given to him and let fly a long shrieking shout to show everyone that all were in agreement about the peace.[24]

The envoys and designated Comanche captains arrived in San Antonio on September 29. Cabello heard about the friendly reception his envoys had been given and of the will of the chiefs to conclude a pact, so he sent his troops to greet them and take them to his own house. Along the way a crowd gathered to catch a sight of the Indian chiefs, who were sporting a Spanish flag and appeared happy with the way they were treated. In a letter dated November 25, Cabello detailed his conditions for a peace treaty, which included ending all hostilities in Texas and beyond, the freeing of "Christian" captives, trading with Spanish traders but not with those of other European nations, waging war on the Apaches and Lipanes (and allying themselves with all other allies of the Spanish), and getting permission to wage war against the Apaches and Mescaleros in Coahuila. In return for faith and "constancy" in the alliance with the Spanish, a gift would be given to the Comanche captains and other important leaders of that nation.[25]

The chiefs said they gladly accepted those conditions and that they did not doubt the same would occur throughout their nation. They planned to come back to San Antonio with an answer as soon as possible, but, afraid he would not be able to greet and treat such a large delegation of Comanches as they deserved, Cabello asked them to come back in "six moons," in order to prepare. Meanwhile, news arrived that a large contingent of Lipanes was camping sixteen leagues away from San Antonio, ready to pounce on the Comanches when they left. Cabello asked for reinforcements from the presidio of the Bay of Espíritu Santo. As the captains and their wives were leaving, he gave each a complete set of clothing as well as other "trinkets." Later he commented that "the Comanche captains remained in awe when they saw what he had given them and because of his respectfulness in having clothed them, which is what they most admired." The Lipanes, on the other hand, manifested their discontent and frustration by uttering some threats and by killing some calves.[26]

THE TREATY WITH THE COMANCHES IN NEW MEXICO

At the same time that the Texas contingent was negotiating, Governor Juan Bautista de Anza in New Mexico had the opportunity to launch a formal process of negotiation with the Comanches and was able to include the *rancherías* (hamlets) of the Yupes and the Yamparicas, while also achieving reconciliation between the Comanches and Utes, about which I will discuss some of the more relevant elements.[27]

As a result of the good treatment that had been given to the Comanches when they came to Taos to do some trading in 1785, and because they knew that they would achieve peace if all the Comanche groups were asking for it, an important meeting was held on the banks of the Nepestle River that included the largest and most powerful of the Cuchutica, Yupe, and Yamparica chiefs. Most of the Comanche settlements were represented in that gathering, and they elected Chief Ecueracapa as their envoy to negotiate a new peace agreement as well as the opening of trade in New Mexico. To witness those agreements, Ecueracapa called upon an Indian originally from New Mexico, Joseph Chiquito, who spoke some Comanche. In December, he called several meetings in which representatives from various settlements discussed the terms of the proposed peace. Once Chiquito had been thoroughly briefed, he was sent to Pecos with three captains to give news of the naming of Ecueracapa as the "plenipotentiary" envoy and to ask the Comanches for cessation of all thefts by the Jicarillas. The emissaries were well received in Santa Fe. Four days later, the captains decided to return home and asked Joseph Chiquito to accompany them, to which the governor agreed, sending with them a few other neighbors from Pecos and a Spaniard, who brought a horse and a red hat to Ecueracapa as a sign of Spanish trust.

News of the projected peace spread rapidly in the region, causing some worry to the Utes, who had been loyal to the Spaniards for quite some time and who were the sworn enemies of the Comanches. They sent the captains Moara and Pinto to the governor, to whom they "declared themselves with force against the proposed peace," protesting against his preference for the rebels over the faithful and obedient allies. Anza realized that to avoid war the only alternative was to sign treaties with both nations at the same time, and so he proposed to wait for the Comanches to arrive so they could negotiate an agreement with him serving as the go-between.

Seeing how friendly the relations were with Ecueracapa, it occurred to Anza that it would be possible "to subdue little by little the whole nation and place it under the King's authority without ever using violent methods." He said so in private to the Indian chief, and Anza told him that, should the latter accept, he could count on his support and that he would be granted a medal from the king. Apparently Ecueracapa did not quite understand the intention of the governor and answered that, naturally, he would work to maintain the fidelity due the king and that he would thus "accept the proposed medal, in order to have the opportunity to better serve and acknowledge the sovereign."

This last point is important as the whole process reveals the emergence of a new kind of leadership with a new sort of power that transcended that of the captains or the chiefs of each settlement, a new power associated with the process of the negotiation itself. Anza was trying to consolidate this new form of institution, seeing it as a conduit for royal power. Ecueracapa perhaps understood, however, that his own power rested on his ability to convince the other Comanche captains and that he could not really claim to exercise or represent any compulsory centralized power.

It is obvious that those agreements contributed greatly to the modification of the regional balance, that they allowed a greater stability for productive activities, and that they gave a modicum of tranquility to the Indian peoples who signed them. Obviously, too, they were little appreciated by the Apaches, who saw themselves partially surrounded and subjected to great pressures.

FIRST NEGOTIATIONS WITH THE APACHES: THE MOST AGGRESSIVE NATION, 1779–1782

Viceroy Bernardo de Gálvez was one of the most influential civil servants in the definition of a true frontier policy. A nephew of the famous inspector José de Gálvez, he had spent the 1770s as a captain in the campaigns against the hostile Indians of Nueva Vizcaya and Sonora. He drew on those past experiences to define the best way of waging war against the

Apaches, which led him to acknowledge that they had a number of advantages against the Spanish soldiers: their temperament, their strength and agility, their ability to adapt to their environment, the conviction that their fighting was "an act of religion," and their almost compulsive mistrust, which pushed them into an almost continuous state of movement.[28]

Galvéz described the way they would attack the settlements and the presidios as well as how the chief named for the expedition was the most daring, wisest, and the most respected and that they would follow him during the campaign until death if need be. He explained that the Apaches rode excellent horses and travelled by night to avoid being seen; and before attacking a region or a village, they carefully checked the resources and routes of access. Hidden among high weeds, they got as close as they could to their target, so close in fact that they were able to search "the bodies and the clothing of the sleeping soldiers." After reaching a place in which they felt secure in silence, at the moment of attack they launched themselves with fury, yelling at the top of their lungs, not leaving anyone time to defend themselves, creating chaos and panic. "From all those refined ruses comes the fact that they never err in their campaigns," Gálvez said.[29] He then proposed that the best military tactic would be to go out and look for them in their own lands, imitating their strategies as much as possible.

In his explanation of the way the Apaches waged war, Gálvez showed a certain amount of admiration and, in a way, justified his own approach:

> The Spaniards accuse the Indian of cruelty. I do not know what their opinion would be of us: maybe it would not be any better and maybe with more basis in reality. What is certain is that they are as grateful as they are vengeful, and that we should forgive the latter to a nation that has not learned the philosophy of how to tame a natural feeling, which even though it may appear vicious is indeed a heroic cause, that of having a sensitive heart. The Spaniards should be impartial and recognize that if the Indian is not our friend, it is because he does not owe us anything, and that if he is vengeful, it is for the simple reason of wanting to get even for the ill treatment he has received.[30]

Gálvez, as we will see, was only one of the soldiers who, from their closer relations with and their better knowledge of the Indians and their attitudes, abilities, and symbolic ways, started to develop a less simplistic view and ideas about less aggressive ways to deal with them.

The Marqués of Rubí, inspector of the military posts and troops of the north, took quite a different tone. He described the perils represented by the Apaches along the border. In Coahuila, he proposed "the total extermination of the Lipanes," whose character was "depraved," who practiced "the trade of the thief and who used to take refuge in the presidios while at the same time never ceasing to attack the Spanish possessions." He affirmed that if they have been offered peace, it was because they had offered "their treacherous friendship and their supposed desire to be brought into the fold and converted," but in fact they have never been proved truthful in reality.[31] Agreements with the Apache had a way of falling apart (this had been the case since at least the 1750s), and officials such as Rubí and Teodoro de Croix continued to ponder whether the Lipanes or others, given their ways of life and actions, indeed deserved peace.

To get a better idea of the situation, it is necessary to consider the attitudes of the various military commanders. In front of the presidio of San Carlos in 1779, Captain Domingo Díaz received the claim for peace presented by two Apache groups, the Mescaleros and the Natagés.[32] The Commandant General Croix put Lieutenant Colonel Manuel Muñoz in charge of the formalizing of the agreement. We know that during the conferences held in October of that year, nine Indian chiefs arrived to renew their peace promises. They also asked for food as well as for an escort to accompany them to a buffalo hunt, or *carneada*. The Indian captain Alonso asked to be allowed to settle near the village, and two others said they would do so upon returning from the hunt. They all got gifts of clothing, food, and tobacco.[33]

Juan de Ugalde, the governor of Coahuila, did not agree with these efforts. A soldier, he had acquired quite a reputation from his constant campaigns against the Indians as well as his disdain and lack of respect for the instructions coming from the commandant general. Ugalde gave his superior many reasons for dissatisfaction, among which the most significant was his conduct vis-à-vis the Indians, which was totally out of control. Just a few days before, he had sent Croix information about several murders and thefts committed, according to him, by the Mescaleros from the community of a chief named Juan Tuerto. He asked Croix to call back the Indians in order to prohibit them from entering Coahuila without safe conduct. In a threatening tone, he said that if he found Mescaleros in Coahuila, he would treat them harshly. He would execute those who had committed murder, and he would send their ears to Tuerto. Those who had robbed would be flogged and sent to forced labor. Those who had done nothing wrong would be put in jail until their chiefs paid ransom for them.[34]

Croix does not seem to have paid much attention to Ugalde's dramatic pronouncements, since in the first months of 1780 he still appeared enthusiastic about the prospect of an agreement. During those first months of 1780, a few Lipanes had come down to the presidios of Coahuila, seemingly fearful of Comanche attacks. Close to the presidio of Monclova, Juan Ugalde met with Chief Boca Tuerta (Twisted Mouth) and his son, treating them well and offering a few gifts. Ugalde tried to provoke dissension among the Lipanes, whom he considered to be perverse and liars. In his correspondence with Croix, Ugalde made a revealing admission about how to treat the Lipanes: "[T]ruth when talking to them, gifts in due time, punishment when needed should be the three antidotes against that venomous nation; what is important is to know how to apply each one, as too much or too little a dose will not give the effects expected from such medicine."[35] From the documents that describe the events of that year, one gets the impression that keeping peace with the Mescaleros was a complex affair and that the situation was quite confused, even for the military authorities of the area. On the one hand, there were several Mescalero groups, each with its own chief, who was acknowledged as the main authority. Getting all the groups under one authority proved to be impossible, as no one could effectively represent all the bands. In the end, the agreements were partial or weak. Then there were the obvious differences in the aims of each military command, to which one must add the difficult task of communication among provinces, all of which contributed to local conflicts and conduct at times at odds with the terms of the accords.

Thus, Croix reported in June 1780 that Chief Patule had to leave his own people as he could not maintain control over them, while Chiefs Alegre, Volante, Alonso, Bigotes del Bolsón, and El Natagé were being pacified. But at the same time, those chiefs were manifesting their discontent at seeing that peace had also been granted to Chief Juan Tuerto. Croix also commented, "[T]he consequence of the differences between the Indians is that those who are now in peace have asked for our help in punishing and subduing the [rebel ones] of their nation."[36]

On December 29, Ugalde, having learned that some Indians were marauding close to the Valley of Santa Rosa, went out after them to punish them. Tenaciously, he followed some traces among fields of reeds and other inhospitable places, but he never could find them. Having tired himself so much in that endeavor and after having written more than fifty pages of a report, Ugalde had a change of heart and expressed some serious doubts as to his own actions. "I can only confess to your highness that my head is no longer following what my pen has put down, since, the way things have been going, I don't understand myself anymore, but I must also assure [you] . . . that to do my work I have never been more able nor more willing."[37]

According to Captain Muñoz, it was smallpox as well as the lack of meat that led many Mescaleros to commit thefts and other crimes.[38] Teodoro de Croix tried to take advantage of the opportunity and ordered Muñoz to immediately attack the bands of Patule, Bigotes, and Juan Tuerto, which were camping near the hacienda of Sardinas, in the province of Coahuila. De Croix also sent word to Ugalde so that the latter could bring his assistance to Muñoz.[39] That time, though, curiously, Ugalde resisted and did not take part in the action. Perhaps he resented the fact that he had received the Mescaleros peacefully in the northern presidio and had not been given the high command in that Indian campaign. In the end, it seems the attack was not carried out, but Muñoz managed to have his men kill Juan Tuerto.[40]

The declaration of war on various groups and the many hostile actions ultimately achieved new kinds of rapprochement. In his report of June 1781, Croix commented, "Today we have reached the point where we either treat [the Mescaleros] with the deepest amity, in spite of their bad faith, or we openly wage war on them."[41] In September Muñoz convened a meeting with various Mescalero captains to inform them that whoever would not settle in the villages or serve as auxiliaries in the presidios would be considered as an enemy. Given subsequent events, one can conclude that Chiefs Alegre, Volante, and Manuel Cabeza did indeed accept those conditions.[42]

The alliance, however, was shaky and violence kept increasing. In October, Muñoz again fought, campaigning with 109 men and 13 Indian auxiliaries against Mescalero settlements. The auxiliaries were Mescaleros themselves under the command of Chief Alegre. In the course of three different actions, attacks were launched against Apache settlements, resulting in the capture of some fifty prisoners and a large number of cattle. Alegre asked Muñoz to take the families that had surrendered as captives, but before any decision was taken, Alegre ran away to his settlement with nineteen of the prisoners. In the months that followed, hostilities spread.[43]

By the end of 1782, the conflict between Croix and Ugalde had become unbearable. Ugalde openly defied the orders of the commandant and even went as far as talking in public about the incompetence, ignorance, and "lack of religion" of his superior. Croix above all resented the fact that his orders had no effect and that Ugalde "led ruinous campaigns four months long, which rarely gave any result." This was the reason why Croix decided finally to relieve him from his command in November 1782.[44]

PERSEVERANCE AND FAILURE, 1787–1788

In 1787, the opportunity arose again to start peace negotiations with the Mescaleros. The soldiers posted on the frontier had in mind the concepts included in the royal order of 1779 as well as those of Bernardo de Gálvez in his instruction of 1786.[45] Contrary to what he had expressed a few years before, Gálvez considered the Apaches to be the principal enemy along the border but thought that war should not be waged indiscriminately. Rather, it was to alternate with negotiations; strong campaigns were supposed to force the Indians into asking for peace, which would then be conceded, as they would be treated with "sweetness" via trade agreements. But the Indians would have to be punished if they caused damage, and they would be made to understand that if they broke the peace, war would be declared against them. Contrary to the proponents of full-out war, Gálvez repeated the well-known principle that "in the state in which the frontiers are, a bad peace with all the nations that will ask for it will be better than the efforts needed for a good war."[46] He affirmed that special care was to be taken not to upset the Comanches. This was a change in strategy and was designed to favor the participation of the Indians in trade exchanges for Spanish products, thus creating a dependency that would force them into respecting peace.

In January 1787, a detachment of troops under the command of Lieutenant Juan Francisco Granados got in contact with a settlement of Mescaleros who were asking for peace. After much discussion, they promised they would go to the northern presidio on February 10 to negotiate.[47] Commandant General Jacobo de Ugarte immediately ordered captains Domingo Díaz and Juan Bautista Elguezabal to come to the presidio and sent the Indian chiefs the message that they could come with the assurance that they would not be hurt in any way. He proposed conditions for capitulation that involved ceasing hostilities along the border, freeing all captives, and turning over any Indians, mulattos, or *castas* (those of mixed race) who had "gone over to their side." The Mescaleros were told to settle close to the presidio, make a living from cultivation and cattle breeding, and reside in villages led by a governor. They would have to agree to ask permission to hunt or collect mescal, to allow Spaniards to enter their villages at will, and to provide accountings of the settlements committed to peace, the names of their chiefs, and the numbers of people in and cattle held by those villages. They would not, however, be obliged to convert to Christianity and they would be allowed to hold trading fairs in their villages and in the presidio. If the nation was not completely pacified, those Indians who were had to invite the others to join them and war would be waged against the holdouts. The conditions were to be given to the Mescalero chiefs "with great firmness," but Ugarte added that he would listen to proposals from the Indian leaders.[48]

Ugarte came into power in April 1786. In spite of Bernardo de Gálvez's precise instructions, he was alone in making those decisions as the viceroy passed away in November of that same year. To make the situation even more complicated, Ugalde had been vindicated by the Council of the Indies and, by order of Gálvez, had been entrusted with the provinces of Texas, Coahuila, Nuevo León, and Nuevo Santander.[49] The old interim commandant José Rengel remained in charge of Nueva Vizcaya and New Mexico. Toward the end of March, Chiefs Alegre, Ligero, Patule, Zapato Tuerto, El Quemado, Montera Blanca, Cuerno Verde, and Bigotes el Bermejo arrived at the northern presidio and said they were also almost sure of the favorable disposition of the missing chiefs, El Calvo and El Natagé. Without discussion, they accepted the conditions and even offered to prevent the other Apache bands from launching hostilities in the settlements and villages of Nueva Vizcaya and Coahuila.

Captain Díaz commented that those Mescaleros were in the most abject state of poverty, having practically no horses and drought having almost destroyed their harvest of mescal plants, so that he had to host growing groups of women and children and feed them as they came daily to the presidio. He demanded that the Mescalero prisoners held by the military authorities be placed under his authority and that hostilities be avoided with Indians desirous of entering into peace agreements.[50] Ugarte agreed with the treatment given by Díaz to the Indians and said that the most important thing was for the Indians to settle in fixed places, till the earth, and forget about their hunting parties.[51] Some days later, the commandant of the presidio reported that the Mescalero chiefs had asked to be allowed to settle near the *aguajes* (water holes) and ranges immediately to the north. As a sign of good faith, Alegre and Patule proposed that one of them stay in the presidio to offer his help in case of a military campaign.[52]

However, in the first days of April, just as the pact seemed to become more solid and formalized, news came of an attack by troops from Coahuila against Zapato Tuerto's settlement at the time when the Indians were harvesting their mescal. During that action, three Indians were killed, the settlement lost all its horses, and the Spaniards left with some prisoners. The first to learn of those events had been Captain Elguezabal, who immediately sent Lieutenant Granados and sixteen men to make clear to the leader of that troop that those Indians were living in peace, that they had indeed received permission to grow mescal in the sierra, and that they should be given back their horses and the men who had been taken prisoner.[53]

Upon his return, the lieutenant reported that Ugalde had cast a disdainful eye on the order sent by Elguezabal and commented that he would "challenge it in due time."[54] Elguezabal decided to immediately and personally deal with Ugalde, considering that the Indian leaders "were worried" and knowing that Ugalde was ready to continue launching attacks against the neighboring settlements.[55] Chief Inspector Rengel was apprised of the situation but decided not to try to convince Ugalde, whom he knew only too well. Wishing to lessen tensions, he ordered an offer to be sent to the Mescaleros to invite them to come and negotiate with him in El Paso so that he could offer to settle them in the immediate vicinity of that town.[56] In May, Elguezabal reported that he had met with Ugalde, who had stated that "his ultimate decision was to go out and wage war on them wherever he would find them" to the north of the Río Grande.[57]

The settlements of Volante, Alegre, Quemado, and Patule were obliged to settle close to the confluence of rivers where the northern presidio was located. Ugalde paid no attention to the order he received to cease hostilities against peaceful Mescaleros and to return the prisoners and goods he had taken. Patule complained to Elguezabal that he had freed two captives in order to secure the release of fourteen prisoners taken by Ugalde, but in the end, the latter had refused to comply. The Mescalero chiefs lost all trust because they did not understand the delays in implementing the resolutions and the lack of respect for the accords.[58]

In spite of the problems, Captain Domingo Díaz insisted on propping up the peace process. From his conversations with Indian leaders, Díaz summarized the way they understood peace in the present circumstances. They wanted to be allowed to live in the sierras and near the aguajes closest to the presidio, which were the places they knew best. They proposed an end to all hostilities with the Spanish but expected the Spanish to act accordingly. They promised to not let the Gileños camp on their lands and to try to prevent them from crossing the border and agreed that any from their nation who committed robberies could be pursued and punished, saying they would hand over robbers and their loot if they ever went to their settlements. To lessen the Indians' unhappiness because of the lack of respect regarding the return of the prisoners, Díaz offered them an escort to accompany them to the buffalo carneada that was to be organized in December of that year or the following January. Because of the great risk of confrontation with the Comanches, the Indian chiefs accepted that promise with enthusiasm.[59] Just a month later, on July 30, Rengel showed his irritation with the new agreement, which he thought gave the Apaches "the same freedom and use of the same lands as until now." The only difference from the preceding years was that hostilities were supposed to stop and trade would be allowed with the presidio. He had many objections to the promised escort for the hunting party and left the clarification of that point to the commandant general.[60]

On August 9, Ugalde declared his campaign against the Mescaleros finished. He said he had worked on it for 203 days, traveled 1,011 leagues, and found 125 Apache water holes and 31 settlements. Ugalde wrote that he had gotten rid of forty-seven enemies, between "dead, captives and recovered slaves," and had also accumulated a good amount of loot, consisting of animals, pelts, and other objects.[61] On August 12, he answered Ugarte's orders on the peace treaties with the Mescaleros. He emphasized that his campaign had been a total success and that the enemy had almost reached the point of extermination and was by then submitting to his will. He asserted that had the peace offerings in the northern presidio not been made, he would have finished the job and argued that the Mescaleros had been pressured into proposing peace thanks to the campaign led by the troops from Coahuila, emphasizing the fact that the prisoners had been captured during a "good and just war."[62] One senses from Ugalde's writings his feelings of superiority, obstinacy, and vanity. He insisted that if peace had not been set with the Mescaleros in the northern presidio, he would have achieved "the extermination of such fierce people," and that the results would have been comparable to Cortés's conquests.[63]

Faced with such arrogance, Jacobo de Ugarte could not stay silent. He felt he had to answer and correct the falsehoods contained in the material that Ugalde proposed to send the new viceroy, Manuel Antonio Flores. In a letter dated October 15, Ugarte recounted what had happened with the Mescaleros and affirmed that Ugalde was indeed apprised of his orders to respect the peace agreement with the Mescaleros before he left to attack the settlement in Cuerno Verde. Paying no heed, Ugalde carried on with his campaign and now wanted the viceroy to believe that the Mescaleros had begged for peace as a result of the military pressure of the Coahuila troops and that the prisoners had been taken during a "just war." Even if Ugalde's actions were justifiable, it was unfair to keep Indian hostages, since the Indians had respected their own promise to free all their captives. Ugarte commented to the viceroy that the way Ugalde was presenting events served only his purposes, to hide the truth "and mask his insubordinate actions."[64]

In October, Ugarte sent details of the new conditions with which to receive the Mescaleros. He ordered Díaz to make inquiries about the degree of kinship existing between the Indians and the prisoners as well as the amount and type of possessions taken from them, "so that he could adopt a way of compensating them and leave them satisfied," since, according to Ugarte, "conjugal [and filial] love was not so strong in them that it could not be replaced by other objects." He ordered that "each Indian who had lost his wife" would be given "another one to be chosen among the women taken from the enemies," and "as for their sons, fathers, brothers, parents," and goods lost, they would be given "satisfaction through the gift of horses, mules, or other belongings, with the understanding that they would in no way receive goods worth more than what they had actually lost."[65]

Contrary to Ugarte's opinion about the importance given by the nomads to the love relations they had with their wives and children, Díaz later reported in a letter that Chief Zapato Tuerto was currently prisoner in Coahuila. When his settlement had been attacked, the troops had captured his wife, and, even though he had managed to escape together with three other men, "having seen that the woman he loved so much had been taken prisoner," he decided to give himself up voluntarily.[66]

Given the practical impossibility of changing their ways of life, Ugarte agreed to lift the mandates for the Mescaleros to live within close proximity of the presidio, to cultivate the land and raise cattle, as well as to name one sole governor for all of them. They were allowed to settle wherever they chose, but with the following conditions: to report on the place where they were settling, as well as on any change of residence; to stay within the limits of the presidio, unless otherwise authorized; to give up the Mapimí Valley; and to push their sons toward agricultural activities. He also ordered them to wear a distinctive blue and white cloth, to better identify them. He aimed for constant control and indicated to Díaz that he wished to encourage the formation of a "dominant party among them, composed of those who seem of the best faith, so that they can moderate the others by their own example." Ugarte advised him to employ them as auxiliaries in the war against rebel settlements.[67]

In spite of the complex situation, the plan set forth by Ugarte in November constituted a viable project, assuming it would be followed by Colonel Ugalde. In order to achieve this, Ugarte needed the support of the new viceroy, but the latter was more receptive to the fiery warlike discourse of Ugalde. Viceroy Flores thought what was needed was to stimulate the jaded spirit of the colonists along the border "and that cannot be achieved if the commandants do not go ahead and attack the Indians; Ugalde is the only one to go this way."[68]

Having received the reports of both Ugalde and Ugarte on the pacification of the common border and thinking it was impossible for a single chief to manage such an extended territory, Flores decided to split the Interior Provinces between two commands, one to the west, under Ugarte, which included both Californias, Sonora, Nueva Vizcaya, and New Mexico, and one to the east, under Ugalde, with Texas, Coahuila, Nuevo Santander, and the Nuevo Reino de León, also annexing the districts of Saltillo and Parras, which until then had belonged to Nueva Vizcaya. Flores thought he could thus put an end to the disputes between his military chiefs and make Ugalde free to launch his campaigns. In fact, he ordered him to "maintain your troops in constant war operations against the declared enemies and to defend the settled territories" as well as to move to Chihuahua to personally see to the threat of the Indians in Nueva Vizcaya.[69]

In the first days of December, the viceroy sent details of the way the two commanders were to treat the Mescaleros. Before any negotiations, they were to oblige them to accept the humiliation of surrendering. It did not matter if they had shown any proof of good faith, the mere suggestion of asking for an escort or to live without subjugation was a clear indication of "their bad and treacherous dispositions." In spite of the fact that he did not find any good reason to grant them peace, he nevertheless agreed to a "test of their willingness," obliging them to settle down along the Salinas River under the strict command of Ugalde. He also pointed out that now that the two commandants were of the same hierarchical level it was necessary that they work in harmony.[70]

In spite of the disgust that Ugarte must have felt, losing part of his jurisdiction and power, it seemed that the viceroy's instructions at least brought some clarification as far as the Mescaleros were concerned, but in reality things were quite different. As Ugarte was receiving the orders from the viceroy, he also was being apprised of the good conduct of the Indians during and after the buffalo hunt. Captain Díaz reported that the Indians behaved quite respectfully and that apparently all the chiefs were ready to pursue the peace process. Díaz was so confident that, in addition to asking for funds to make gifts to the Indians or to compensate them for their losses, he went so far as proposing they should be trusted with transporting the salt loads sent to the mines of the region.[71] It seemed wise to try to transform those Apaches into carriers, given their wandering way of life and knowledge of the tracks and territories. Ugarte said that it would be an efficient way to incorporate them into the trade activities of the area, but in the end he did not judge it appropriate to put the idea in practice.[72]

In the last days of 1787 and the first of the following year, Ugarte again described and explained to Flores the conditions under which peace had been granted to the Mescaleros and the events that followed, including examples of Ugalde's careless manipulations. He affirmed that the Mescaleros were already in a weakened position when they received that peace and that modifications were later made as it was not fair to demand conditions they could not fulfill. As to his relationship with Captain Ugalde, he expressed his doubts as to the possibility of achieving real agreements because of Ugalde's "less than amenable character" and evidenced incredulity that Ugalde would reach a durable peace with the Mezcaleros.[73] Conscious of the difficulties that might arise from not immediately obeying the orders of the viceroy, Ugarte sent a letter to Díaz in the first days of January, saying nothing was more important than to preserve the peace with the Mescaleros, "in such conditions that they cannot fool us." It was necessary for the Indian leaders to follow the Spanish troops without fail while Ugarte was trying to influence the viceroy.

In a letter he wrote back on January 20, Díaz reported that ever since the buffalo hunt, Chiefs Alegre, Volante, and Joseph were staying close to the presidio; Cuerno Verde had just arrived; and within three days Montera Blanca and Bigotes el Bermejo would be arriving. He also reported that he had sent Alegre to the settlement of El Calvo in the arid lands, "since this captaincillo seems like a god to all of them and they all obey him." A few days later, Díaz wrote to Ugarte of the coming through the presidio of two Mescaleros bearing a safe conduct signed by Ugalde. It seemed that both military bands stationed on the border were trying to strengthen their positions by courting the strongest and most respected Indian leader.[74]

The Apache messengers sent by Ugalde were also supposed to talk to the Mescaleros settled around the northern presidio and tell them they had two months to move to Santa Rosa. The Indian chiefs were thunderstruck, not so much by the implied threat as by the fact they did not know who was giving orders between the two presidios.[75] As if to further contribute to the confusion and growing tension, in this period Ugarte received approval for the peace agreement he had managed to achieve with the Mescaleros from Charles III. Thus, he insisted to the viceroy that there could not be any change in the peace agreements until a definitive order had arrived. He emphasized that the change in Coahuila would augment the number of enemies and that if peace were compromised and promises broken, including that of the king himself, "their mistrust would be eternal" and so would war. Ugarte urged him to put an end to the imprudent conduct of Ugalde, which could only make things worse.[76]

In February and March 1788, Ugarte strove mightily to gather documents demonstrating that the Mescaleros were behaving in strict accordance with the agreements and that the provinces were free of the threat of attacks.[77] He also wrote Ugalde to offer him his sincere friendship and his desire to collaborate and to propose that inasmuch as the Mescaleros were giving clear proof of their faithfulness, it did not matter whether they lived all together or not, and suggested that some of them should stay close to the northern presidio and others along the Sabine River.[78]

But it was in that period that events occurred that would put an end to any possibility of an enduring good relationship with that Indian nation. On April 8, all Mescaleros living in Santa Rosa fled, leaving behind several dead soldiers and civilian neighbors. In the presidio, an Indian woman reported that the rebels were traveling toward the northern sierras, where they would surely unite with the Gileños. She also said that they had many "altercations" with Ugalde since they had gone to that province to recover their captive members. Not only had the captives not been turned over, but the representatives were "kept under strict supervision, with shouts and threats," and were forbidden to return to the northern presidio. That was the reason why they had waited for the best occasion to get away.[79]

On April 15, the viceroy, without knowledge of what had happened in Coahuila, sent an unconditional order to Ugarte to launch a full-scale war against the Mescaleros of Nueva Vizcaya. Finally, after other last-minute efforts to maintain a certain balance, Ugarte ordered captain Díaz, on May 8, to force the Mescaleros out of the presidio, telling them that from then on they would be treated as enemies in Nueva Vizcaya. But at the same time, in a long letter to the viceroy, written in strictest confidence, he confirmed that he had followed his orders to the letter but added with "emotion" that he had decided to renounce his post since his documents and reports had not managed to convince the viceroy.[80] The viceroy refused Ugarte's resignation, and Ugarte continued in his post until 1790.

The history of negotiations along the border continued for many years. We stop our narrative here when, thanks to the support of the viceroy, Juan de Ugalde managed to prevail through intolerance and by constant confrontation with the Mescaleros. In the following months, Ugalde tried time and again to countermand the power of Chief Picax-andé (El Calvo) by setting him against the other Mescalero chiefs. The high point came in March 1789, when, having gathered several Mescalero chiefs in Santa Rosa for purported peace talks, Ugalde ordered them all imprisoned, resulting in the capture of five chiefs, among whom were Zapato Tuerto, Patule, and El Quemado; twenty-three warriors; twenty-nine women; and nineteen children, with two warriors killed while resisting arrest. Flores praised the action and ordered the hostages to be taken to Mexico City prior to their deportation.[81]

FINAL REFLECTIONS: THE NEGOTIATIONS IN PERSPECTIVE

The Spanish Crown tried during the eighteenth century, in accord with Enlightenment ideas of the time, to rationalize the exploitation of its overseas possessions, which implied a better use of their resources and potential, a strengthening of the political structure, and the secularization of religious administration and the actions of its government. Following the cultural transformations of that century, the objectives of the Crown were defined anew in relation to the border regions of the extended empire and the Indian peoples who refused direct subordination. The adoption and execution of that policy was a slow, measured, and, in many ways, erratic process. The eradication of the culture forged by the conquistadors together with the religious orders from the sixteenth century was a painful, even traumatic, process.

If during the first centuries of Spanish domination the idea was that the nomadic Indians' way of life was the result of Satan's influence and it was a Christian duty to free those captive souls from the influence of evil to bring them into the fold of Christianity, in the eighteenth century this process of evangelization was losing ground to a policy aimed at promoting trade and keeping peace and tranquility, which in turn would allow the development of commercial activities and the exploitation of natural resources.[82] In the long run, as far as the treatment of the Indians was concerned, this transition implied a diminishing role for missions and the rising importance of military posts.

The militarization of the borders led to the disappearance of many nomadic peoples whose way of life was associated with the use of the agüajes, hunting, and gathering. According to Cecilia Sheridan, the extermination of some of the nomads in the northern territories must be seen as resulting from the difficult conditions in which they were forced to live, the military campaigns and taking of prisoners by the soldiers, as well as the interethnic wars promoted by the Spaniards. Other nomadic peoples saw their ethnic and cultural identity disappear through their assimilation into more powerful peoples or nations.[83] The warriors of the north managed to survive, adapting to the use of horses and firearms and forging regional and ethnic alliances. One can say that at the end of that century, it was possible to promulgate and manage a border policy that distinguished among nomadic groups who were then more easily defined and contained.

From the point of view of the soldiers and public servants who elaborated that policy, negotiations and alliances were useful in trying to define a point of equilibrium that could guarantee peace and allow the development of agriculture, cattle ranching, mining, and trade. In order to find that point, far-reaching explorations were undertaken, the most experienced soldiers were consulted, and the men living on the border submitted many reports on their own campaigns and experiences in dealing with the Indians. Rapprochement was tried and channels of communication opened to promote a better understanding, using mainly those who had direct contacts and knew the languages and mores of the Indians.

Obviously, the negotiations had to adapt to the circumstances, the strength, and abilities of all parties. It is thus difficult to establish a single pattern for the forms of negotiation. According to the ruling of February 20, 1779, the king wished to limit military actions to defense, attract the

Indians to civilization through gifts, and promote trade to make them dependent on Spanish articles. The Instruction of 1786 is based on the same principles but details the way to deal with the Apache groups and the other frontier nations. However, taking into account the complex and varied situations in which each negotiation had to be held, no matter how detailed those instructions were, they were in the end no more than vague indications and had to be adapted to each case.

As we have seen in the pact with the Comanches, the first negotiators had to look for the Indian chiefs and then try to resolve a number of points of contention that existed among them. The negotiation with the Mescalero Apaches, on the other hand, was presented to the captain of the northern presidio as a previous agreement among the chiefs of the various settlements who were looking for peace. It is clear that the peace achieved with the Comanches was seen as a threat by the Mescaleros, which then pushed them into looking for the Spaniards' protection.

The case of the Mescaleros set off a raging conflict of the highest order between the military commanders. This was a classic situation in which a representative of the old war tactics, intent on annihilating the Indians through frontal attacks, opposed someone who wanted to reach a political agreement with the Indians and who had a better knowledge of the Apaches, their ways of living, divisions, and customs. This clearly shows that the "spirit of conquest" still existed within part of the Bourbon bureaucracy.

Clearly, a number of Spaniards made the argument that, given the divisions between the various Apache settlements and bands as well as the inability of the chiefs to maintain the discipline necessary among their people to avoid hostilities, peace agreements were impossible. But the sources discussed here demonstrate that the Spanish military authorities lacked the capacity to develop a unified policy, whereas the chiefs of the various bands were relatively stable. Inasmuch as they would have respected the given conditions, it could have been possible to achieve a lasting peace with a considerable decrease in the attacks on and thefts of Spanish properties.

Comparing the texts of the various peace agreements, one finds many differences. The tone of the pact with the Comanches indicates a friendly negotiation, but the proposals made to the Mescaleros have an unmistakably threatening tone. The Mescaleros were obliged to settle near the presidio, to learn to till the land, and to give notice when they wanted to hunt or go on foraging expeditions. It was explicitly said that they would not be given any provisions. The Comanches were offered gifts and fair treatment in trade, although they could not allow "strangers" into their settlements.

In the latter case, a special emphasis was also placed on the desire of all parties to wage war on every Apache group. The only similarities between both agreements were the commitment to remit captives and to engage in commerce with the Spanish settlements.

Force and military capacity were undoubtedly a determining factor in dealing with the Indians and in the negotiations. The success of the accords was also influenced by the knowledge, tact, and attitude of the intermediaries. In an apparent contradiction, military leaders promoted the naming of a single chief for the Mescaleros and at the same time tried to use the divisions that existed among the chiefs. In the end, neither occurred because of the profound divisions between, and opposed positions of, the military commanders. In the case of the Comanches, the Indians named an ambassador who enjoyed general recognition. This is important, as it shows that the various forms of integration and organization of the Indian peoples were influenced by their interaction with other Indian groups and with the Spaniards and, as a consequence, by the results of negotiations. The existence of hostile Indians and the form with which negotiations were undertaken with them were fundamental in the strategic decisions taken along the border. In fact, in the capital city the preoccupation with the border had to do with the potential danger of other European powers, but in the direct management of the American institutions along the border the main concern was always the hostile bands of Indians.

Scholars have credited the tranquility achieved along the border in the last decades of the colonial period as resulting from the administrative and military reorganization under the Bourbons. After having examined multiple documents from that period, it is obvious that peace was primarily the result of negotiation with the nomadic groups of the north rather than the product of better organization of the troops or the installation of presidios and other war materials. It is obvious that a stronger military presence worked in favor of stable agreements, but it is also undeniable that the fortifications and the troops by themselves were not enough to sustain a constant state of war against the more powerful Indian nations.

Recent studies have shown that the Indian peoples of the north were participants in the regional geopolitical activities and were actively fighting for the preservation of their ways of life. The nomads were not the bloody and irrational barbarians painted by legend but organized groups who knew their environment well and were constantly on the move in well-defined territories in order to make better use of the natural resources according to the seasons. They were defending their freedom and world-view as well as their forms of government and social organization because those were essential to their survival as hunting and gathering groups.

NOTES

1. Historical studies done in the United States have evolved somewhat as far as the history of Indian peoples, subject of the present study, is concerned, but it is worth isolating the facts about the negotiations in order to better understand cultural exchange and the real meaning of those treaties. Two with particular relevance for this article are Elizabeth John, *Storms Brewed in Other Men's Worlds: The Confrontation of Indians, Spanish, and French in the Southwest, 1540–1795* (College Station: Texas A&M University Press, 1975); Max L. Moorhead, *The Apache Frontier: Jacobo de Ugarte and Spanish-Indian Relations in Northern New Spain, 1769–1791* (Norman: University of Oklahoma Press, 1968). Both follow the relations between the nomadic peoples of the border and the military forces based there. For another vision of Indian culture and politics, see Pekka Hämäläinen, *The Comanche Empire* (New Haven, CT: Yale University Press, 2008).

2. Anthony Pagden, *Señores de todo el mundo, ideologías del imperio en España, Inglaterra y Francia (en los siglos XVI, XVII Y XVIII)* (Barcelona: Península, 1997), 141–145.

3. Joseph de Campillo y Cosío, *Nuevo sistema de gobierno económico para la América* (México DF: Facultad de Economía, UNAM, 1993 [1789]), 16, 210–213.

4. Pagden, *Señores de todo*, 146.

5. Luis Navarro García, *Don José de Gálvez y la Comandancia General de las Provincias Internas del norte de Nueva España* (Sevilla: Escuela de Estudios Hispano-Americanos de Sevilla, 1964), 198.

6. Hugo de O'Conor, *Informe de Hugo de O'Conor sobre el estado de las Provincias Internas del norte, 1771–76* (México DF: Editorial Cultura, 1952), 110.

7. Navarro García, *Don José de Gálvez*, 293–305.

8. "Informe del Gobernador de Texas don Domingo Cabello sobre paces de los apaches lipanes en la colonial del Nuevo Santander, Ano de 1784," Monclova, December 11, 1777, Archivo General de la Nación (hereafter, AGN), Provincias Internas, 64, exp. 2, fols. 2–6v, 12–14. The groups considered to be Indians of the North were named in that meeting and included the Texas, Vidais, Taguayaces, Tahuacanes, Iscanis, Gitchas, Tancahues, Orcoquisaes, Ayses, Aguages, Xaranames, and Comanches.

9. John, *Storms Brewed*, 509–511, 516–519; Atanasio de Mézières al Comandante General de las Provincias Internas, Real Presidio de San Antonio de Béxar, February 20, 1778, AGN, Historia, 28, fols. 226v–243v.

10. Navarro García, *Don José de Gálvez*, 351–357.

11. Moorhead, *Apache Frontier*, 120–123; José de Gálvez to Teodoro de Croix, El Pardo, February 20, 1799; AGN, Provincias Internas, 170, fols. 341–342.

12. "Informe del Gobernador de Texas," fol. 143.

13. Ibid., fol. 119.

14. Phelipe de Neve to Joseph de Gálvez, "Relación concisa y exacta del estado en que ha encontrado las provincias Internas y los divide en los cuatro ramos de Justicia, Policía, Hacienda y Guerra," Arizpe, December 1, 1783, Archivo Franciscano, 3/28, fols. 45–47v (draft); Archivo General de Indias (hereafter, AGI), Guadalajara 268, 50ff (definitive original).

15. Navarro García sees the rampant instability as well as the absence of any real unifying project as characteristic of the period from 1783 to 1793; *Don José de Gálvez*, 427–429; see also Donald E. Chipman, *Spanish Texas, 1519–1821* (Austin: University of Texas Press, 1992), 198. .

16. In the documents, "güichitas" refers to the same Indians that in the nineteenth century were known as "huecos." I do not use "huecos" because it could be confused with the name of one of the communities that spoke Wichita, of which three are recognized: the Tahuayaces, Tahuacanos, and Huecos.

17. John, *Storms Brewed*, 655–661.

18. "Artículos de paz concertados y arreglados en la Villa de Santa Fe y Pueblo de Pecos entre el coronel don Juan Bautista de Anza, governador de la provincial de Nuevo México y el capitán Comanche Ecueracapa, diputado general de esta nación en los días 25 y 28 de febrero de 1786," Santa Fe, July 14, 1786, Juan Bautista de Anza, Archivo General de Simancas (hereafter, AGS), Secretaría de Guerra, 7031, fols. 323–325.

19. Pedro Vial and Francisco Chávez included in a report an interesting "Descripción de la nación Cumanche," November 15, 1785, AGS, Secretaría de Guerra 7031, exp. 9, fols. 98–103; John, *Storms Brewed*, 655–657.

20. Vial and Chávez, "Descripción de la nación Cumanche," November 15, 1785, AGS, Secretaría de Guerra 7031, exp. 9, fols. 98–103.

21. Ibid., fols. 105–106.

22. Ibid., fols. 109–110.

23. Ibid., fols. 125–127.

24. There is no reference to this word or any other similar one in any dictionary, but from the context it may be understood as a kind of military jacket.

25. Domingo Cabello to José Antonio Rengel, Béxar, November 25, 1785, AGS, Secretaría de Guerra, 7031, exp. 9, fols. 86–95.

26. Ibid.

27. The description of the agreements in New Mexico is based on the "Relación de los sucesos ocurridos en la provincial de Nuevo México con motivo de la paz conceded a la Nación comanche y su reconciliación con la yuta, desde 17 de noviembre del año último hasta 15 de julio del corriente," Pedro Garrido y Durán, Chihuahua, December 12, 1786, AGS, 7031, fols. 234–304. See also John, *Storms Brewed*, 668–673.

28. "Noticias y reflexiones sobre la guerra que se tiene con los apaches en las provincias de Nueva España," Biblioteca Nacional, México DF, Fondo Reservado, Manuscrito 626 LAF, sin lugar ni fecha, firmado "B.d.G" (with an annotation that says these letters signify Bernardo de Galvéz), fols. 1–2. Luis Navarro García notes that the date when the document was written is not known, citing two versions that exist at the Naval Museum in Madrid; *Don José de Gálvez*, 196–197.

29. "Noticias y reflexiones sobre la guerra que se tiene con los apaches en las provincias de Nueva España," Biblioteca Nacional, México DF, Fondo Reservado, Manuscrito 626 LAF, sin lugar ni fecha, firmado "B.d.G," fols. 4–6.

30. Ibid., fol. 2.

31. "Dicatámenes que de orden del Emo. Sor. Marqués de Croix, virrey de este reino, expone el mariscal de campo Marués de Rubí en orden a la major situación de los presidios para la defense y extension de su frontera a la gentilidad en los confines al norte del Virreinato," Tacubaya, April 10, 1768, in María del Carmen Velázquez, *La frontera norte y la expereiencia colonial* (México DF: Secretaría de Relaciones Exteriores, 1982), 54–56.

32. Domingo Díaz to Brigadier Don Jacobo Ugarte y Loyola, Guajoquilla, April 28, 1787, Expediente: "Carpeta 1. Contiene las órdenes comunicadas a los capitanes dos Domingo Díaz y don Juan Bautista Elguezabal y los partes que han dado en derechura a esta comandancia sobre las paces de los apaches mezcaleros en el presido del norte," Biblioteca Pública de Jalisco, Ramo Civil; Navarro García, *Don José de Gálvez*, 372.

33. Caballero de Croix, "Extracto de providencias y novedades ocurridas con motivo de las paces de mezcaleros en la provincial de Nueva Vizcaya, según avisos del teniente coronel Manuel Muñoz," Arizpe, May 23, 1780, AGI, Guadalajara 278.

34. Juan de Ugalde to Teodoro de Croix, Santiago de la Monclova, October 13, 1779, AGI, Guadalajara 243.

35. Juan de Ugalde to Teodoro de Croix, Santa Rosa, March 1, 1780, AGI, Guadalajara 243.

36. Caballero de Croix to Joseph de Gálvez, Arizpe, June 23, 1780, AGI, Guadalajara 267; Caballero de Croix to Joseph de Gálvez, Arizpe, July 23, 1780, AGI, Guadalajara 267.

37. Juan de Ugalde to Caballero de Croix, Santiago de la Monclova, January 14, 1781, AGI, Guadalajara 243, fols. 69–72.

38. Navarro García, *Don José de Gálvez*, 374.

39. Teodoro de Croix to Juan de Ugalde, Arizpe, February 8, 1781, AGI, Guadalajara 243.

40. Juan de Ugalde to Teodro de Croix, Monclova, March 29, 1781, AGI, Guadalajara 243; Navarro García, *Don José de Gálvez*, 375; Teodoro de Croix to Joseph de Gálvez, Extracto, Arizpe, June 30, 1781, AGI, Guadalajara 267.

41. Teodoro de Croix to Joseph de Gálvez, Extracto, Arizpe, June 30, 1781, AGI, Guadalajara 267.

42. Navarro García, *Don José de Gálvez*, 375.

43. Caballero de Croix to Joseph de Gálvez, Arizpe, January 26, 1782, AGI, Guadalajara 268.

44. Caballero de Croix a Joseph de Gálvez, Arizpe, November 4, 1782, "Da cuenta de los motivos que le obligaron a separar del gobierno de Coahuila a don Juan Ugalde y conferirlo internamente a don Pedro Tueros," AGI, Guadalajara 283.

45. Bernardo de Gálvez, "Instrucción formada en virtud de Real Orden de S.M., que se dirige al Señor Comandante General de Provincias Internas Don Jacobo Ugarte y Loyola para gobierno y puntual observancia de este Superior Jefe y de sus inmediatos subalternos," Mexico, August 26, 1786 (firmado como Conde de Galvéz), AGN, Ramo Provincias Internas, 129, exp. 1, fols. 92v–93.

46. Ibid., fol. 73v.

47. Moorhead, *Apache Frontier*, 208.

48. Jacobo de Ugarte y Loyola to Domingo Díaz, Chihuahua, February 12, 1787, Expediente: "Carpeta 1. Contiene las órdenes comunicadas a los capitanes dos Domingo Díaz y don Juan Bautista Elguezabal y los partes que han dado en derechura a esta comandancia sobre las paces de los apaches mezcaleros en el presidio del norte," Biblioteca Pública de Jalisco, Ramo Civil.

49. Navarro García, *Don José de Gálvez*, 453–455.

50. Domingo Díaz to Jacobo Ugarte y Loyola, Presidio del Norte, March 29, 1787, Expediente: "Carpeta 1. Contiene las órdenes comunicadas a los capitanes dos Domingo Díaz y don Juan Bautista Elguezabal y los partes que han dado en derechura a esta comandancia sobre las paces de los apaches mezcaleros en el presidio del norte," Biblioteca Pública de Jalisco, Ramo Civil.

51. Jacobo Ugarte y Loyola to Joseph Antonio Rengel, Arizpe, April 19, 1787, ibid.

52. Domingo Díaz to Jacobo de Ugarte y Loyola, Guajoquilla, April 13, 1787; Domingo Díaz to Joseph Antonio Rengel, Guajoquilla, April 13, 1787, ibid.

53. Domingo Díaz to Jacobo de Ugarte y Loyola, Guajoquilla, April 13, 1787, ibid.

54. Elguezabal to Jacobo de Ugarte y Loyola, Norte, April 27, 1787, ibid.

55. Juan Bautista de Elguezabal to Domingo Díaz, Norte, April 21, 1787, ibid.

56. José Antonio Rengel to Domingo Díaz, El Paso, April 27, 1787, ibid; José Antonio Rengel to Jacobo de Ugarte y Loyola, El Paso, April 27, 1787, ibid.

57. Juan Bautista de Elguezabal to Jacobo de Ugarte y Loyola, Norte, May 1, 1787, ibid.

58. Ibid.

59. Domingo Díaz to Joseph Antonio Rengel, El Norte, June 30, 1787, ibid.

60. Joseph Antonio Rengel to Domingo Díaz, Paso del Norte, July 30, 1787, ibid; Joseph Antonio Rengel to Jacobo de Ugarte y Loyola, Paso del Norte, July 31, 1787, ibid.

61. "Carpeta 1a. Con el sumario original de las operaciones y resultas de la campaña ejecutada por el Coronel don Juan de Ugalde," Juan de Ugalde, Santa Rosa, September 15, 1787, AGN, Provincias Internas, 112, fols. 124–124v.

62. Juan de Ugalde to Jacobo de Ugarte y Loyola (three letters), Santa Rosa, August 12, 1787, AGN, Provincias Internas, 112, fols. 95–95v, 101–104.

63. "Carpeta 1a. Con el sumario orginal de las operaciones y resultas de la campaña ejecutada por el Coronel don Juan de Ugalde," Juan de Ugalde, Valle de Santa Rosa, September 13, 1787, AGN, Provincias Internas, 112, fols. 120–125v.

64. Jacobo de Ugarte y Loyola to Manuel Antonio Flores, Arizpe, October 15, 1787, AGN, Provincias Internas, 112, fols. 16–17; ibid., November 12, 1787, AGN, Provincias Internas, 112, fol. 114v.

65. Jacobo de Ugarte y Loyola to Domingo Díaz, Arizpe, November 12, 1787, AGN, Provincias Internas, 112, fols. 152–153v.

66. Domingo Díaz to Jacobo de Ugarte y Loyola, Presidio del Norte, January 20, 1788, AGN, Provincias Internas, 112, fol. 186v.

67. Ugarte to Díaz, November 12, 1787, AGN, Provincias Internas, 112, fols. 155v–158.

68. Manuel Antonio Flores to Antonio Valdés, Mexico, October 23 and 27, 1787, AGS, Guerra Moderna, 7041, citied in Navarro García, *Don José de Gálvez,* 461–462.

69. Manuel Antonio Flores to Antonio Valdés, Mexico, November 23, 1787, AGN, Correspndencia de Virreyes, 1st series, 142, fols. 179–188; Manuel Antonio Flores to Jacobo de Ugarte y Loyola, Mexico, September 21, 1787, AGN, Provincias Internas, 112, fols. 7–9; Manuel Antonio Flores to Antonio Valdés, Mexico, November 23, 1787, AGN, Correspondencia de Virreyes, 1st series, 142, fols. 179v–187; Navarro García, *Don José de Gálvez,* 462.

70. Manuel Antonio Flores to Jacobo de Ugarte y Loyola, Mexico, December 4, 1787 (draft), AGI, Provincias Internas 112, fols. 306–307v. The same orders are contained in a letter from Manuel Antonio Flores to Juan Ugalde, Mexico, December 5, 1787 (draft), AGI, Provincias Internas 112, fols. 310–312.

71. Domingo Díaz to Jacobo de Ugarte y Loyola, Presidio del Norte, November 30, 1787, AGN, Provincias Internas, 112, fols. 172–173v; Domingo Díaz to Jacobo de Ugarte y Loyola, Presidio del Norte, December 31, 1787, AGN Provincias Internas, 112, fols. 177–177v.

72. Jacobo de Ugarte y Loyola to Manuel Antonio Flores, Arizpe, January 28, 1788, AGN, Provincias Internas, 112, fols. 174–175.

73. Jacobo de Ugarte y Loyola to Manuel Antonio Flores, Arizpe, December 24, 1787, AGN, Provincias Internas, 112, fols. 161–163; Jacobo de Ugarte y Loyola to Manuel Antonio Flores, Arizpe, January 5, 1788, AGN, Provincias Internas, 112, fols. 165–168, 170–171.

74. Domingo Díaz to Jacobo de Ugarte y Loyola, Presidio del Norte, January 20, 1788, AGI, Provincias Internas, 112, fols. 190–191; Domingo Díaz to Jacobo de Ugarte y Loyola, Presidio del Norte, January 31, 1788, AGI, Provincias Internas, 112, fols. 194–197v.

75. Ibid.

76. Jacobo de Ugarte y Loyola to Manuel Antonio Flores, Arizpe, February 16, 1788, AGN, Provincias Internas, 112, fols. 192–193v. He sent his letter together with a copy of the royal resolution, Valdés to Jacobo de Ugarte y Loyola, San Ildefonso, December 18, 1787, AGN, Provincias Internas, 112, fol. 198.

77. Jacobo de Ugarte to Manuel Antonio Flores, Arizpe, March 18, 1788; Domingo Díaz to Jacobo de Ugarte y Loyola, February 28, 1788; Juan Antonio González Bracho to Jacobo de Ugarte y Loyola, Saltillo, February 1, 1788; Pedro Joseph de Padilla to Jacobo de Ugarte y Loyola, Parras, February 8, 1788; Diego de Borica, February 29, 1788, AGN, Provincias Internas, 112, fols. 199–203.

78. Jacobo de Ugarte y Loyola to Juan de Ugalde, Hacienda de Encinillas, April 7, 1788, AGN, Provincias Internas, 112, fols. 213–218.

79. Domingo Díaz to Jacobo de Ugarte y Loyola, April 27, 1788, AGN, Provincias Internas, 112, fols. 227–228; Moorhead, *The Apache Frontier,* 245.

80. Jacobo de Ugarte y Loyola to Manuel Antonio Flores, Chihuahua, May 8, 1788, AGN, Provincias Internas, 112, fols. 238–241v.

81. Moorhead, *The Apache Frontier*, 253–254.

82. Carlos Lázaro Ávila proposes the hypothesis that the Bourbon reformers took on the "policy of consensus" of the Old Regime, as far as the frontier Indians were concerned, adapting it to their own needs. But existing documents suggest that, in reality, the treatment of the latter was substantially different in the eighteenth century. See "El reformismo borbónico y los indígenas fronterizos americanos," in *El reformismo borbónico: Una visión interdisciplinario*, ed. Agustín Guimerá (Madrid: CSIC, Alianza Editorial, Fundación Mapfre América, 1996), 283–288.

83. Cecilia Sheridan, *Anónimos y desterrados: La contienda por el "sitio que llaman Quauyla," siglos XVI–XVIII* (México DF: CIESAS, 2000), 354–356.

8 | JOSÉ MANUEL A. CHÁVEZ-GÓMEZ

Waterways, Legal Ways, and Ethnic Interactions

*The Ríos District of Tabasco during the
Seventeenth and Eighteenth Centuries*

The purpose of this essay is to examine part of the colonial period history
of the peninsular Maya who lived in the southwestern area of the Yucatán
Peninsula, an area interlaced with rivers, focusing in particular on their
varied interactions with the Spanish, the English, and other Maya groups.
It is clear from some sources that the southern limits of the Yucatecan
Maya extend in a westerly direction, as far as the banks of the Usumacinta
River; while to the east they go beyond the Petén, reaching into the area of
Verapaz. A subgroup of the peninsular Maya, the Mopanes—whose way of
life was rather different from that of the groups to the north—live in this
region. Yet, such differences notwithstanding, the indigenous population
of Tabasco's Ríos district appears to have ties both to the Petén and to the
northern part of the peninsula.

This chapter demonstrates the role of the Spanish imperial state in
influencing emerging ethnic identities, or ethnogenesis, of several Maya
groups and examines how that role was influenced by Spanish political and
legal practices as well as the presence of English pirates. It also illustrates

ways Maya leaders sought to negotiate with and navigate between the two powers and between the Spanish and their own people.

THE UNCONQUERABLE MAYA OF NOHÁ

During the first half of the seventeenth century, the Spanish organized an expedition that headed in the direction of the Ríos district of Tabasco. This area contained indigenous settlements that still remained outside the control of the Spanish Crown and its local administrators. The purpose of the expedition was to reverse this situation. The operation followed two routes to enter the region: one starting in the province of Chiapas, and passing through the region of Ocosingo; the other traveling along the Usumacinta River, with a beach head in the pueblo of Tenosique.

The driving force behind the expedition was Diego Ordoñez de Villaquirán, who, in addition to serving the interests of the Spanish monarchy, wanted to be granted an *encomienda* (grant of tribute and labor). Ordoñez de Villaquirán gave the region the name El Próspero. The expedition ended in complete failure because Ordoñez had no more than personal enrichment in mind. He was accompanied by a *mestizo* (person of indigenous and Spanish origin) who pushed ahead of the rest of the party and interceded with the Maya, mistreating them and forcing them to work for his own interests. The foreign presence was expanded by a pair of Franciscan missionaries who had gone out to evangelize the Maya. The latter seized on this development to rebel against the mestizo, while also warning the friars to stay away from the area. Following this sequence of events, the Indians proceeded to flee into the jungle.[1]

This particular group of Maya has caused a certain amount of confusion. In the eyes of some scholars, they were apostate Maya—intermixed with Kejache Maya—and had reached the area after fleeing Christianized pueblos in Campeche and the Yucatán. In the opinion of Eric Thompson and Jan de Vos, however, they were not apostate Indians at all but rather formed a different and uncolonized group, which came from the northwestern part of the Petén, having decided for some reason to move in the direction of the Usumacinta River.[2] This latter view seems plausible, if only because the Kejaches were not a homogeneous, unitary indigenous group. Instead, they were composed of different peoples, each of whom had their own way of referring to themselves. Moreover, each people used a distinctive patronymic that was related either to the oldest lineage within the settlement or to the place-name of its specific site. Thus, there is no clear evidence that the Kejaches considered themselves part of those unpacified Indians. Rather, they distinguished themselves through the use of their own names. Furthermore, Kejache settlements were dispersed, independent of each other, and maintained either friendly or warlike relations depending on the prevailing circumstances. At the same time, however, they did have certain features in common, which caused other groups of Maya in the surrounding areas to see them as a single collection of people who were called Kejache. The territory that they occupied was extensive, running from the Hondo River, in Belize, up to the banks of the Usumacinta.

Across the broad region in which they lived, their settlements were separated from each other by large stretches of unoccupied land. Some Kejache pueblos were small in physical size and in population. The larger settlements were located in the heart of the Petén, to the north of the Itzá region. It is therefore likely that the Maya of Nohá were among the most peripheral of Kejache subgroups, having settled as far westward as the Usumacinta River. Thus, because of illness, the passage of time, and the increase in the population of apostate Maya moving in from such places as Sahcabchén, the Nohá groups were slowly assimilated with other groups that arrived from the north.[3]

THE UNPACIFIED *MAYEROS* OF THE JUNGLE PUEBLO OF YUCUM[4]

When, in 1697, the conquest of the Itzá was being consolidated in the heart of the Petén, an expedition—headed by militia from the Ríos district of Tabasco—set off along a series of jungle trails in a southerly direction, intent on finding a group of runaway Indians who had rebelled against their Spanish overlords, in order to bring them back to their home community. In the midst of their travels through the jungle, the members of the expedition accidentally stumbled upon another settlement of Indians who had yet to be subjugated to Spanish authority. These Indians, who spoke peninsular Mayan, lived near the Usumacinta River, in a place called Yucum. Their scattered dwellings—lying eight days away from Palenque—contained a dozen families, all of them apostate Maya, who, adults and youth together, numbered fifty-three.[5]

Upon encountering the Spanish soldiers, the Maya immediately took flight toward Palenque. When they reached the *pueblo* (community), some Indians brought them before the priest, who first baptized them and then designated a place on the outskirts of Palenque where they could reside. Around September 1697, the priest, Francisco de Andrada, informed the *alcalde mayor* (chief political and judicial officer) of Chiapas, Francisco Badillo, that the pacification of this group of fugitive Indians was now an accomplished fact.[6]

The Yucum Maya were also asked whether there were there other communities of apostate Indians living in the jungle, to which they replied that they had heard of just one such settlement, located deeper into the jungle than Yucum, that contained four or five families. At one time, according to their testimony, there had been more settlements, but these had fallen victim to the ravages of the Itzáes, who set upon the pueblos, brutalizing them and eating their inhabitants. It seems that many of the Indians interrogated by the Spanish had been children when the Maya of the Ahitzá committed these atrocities. For this reason, their elders had decided to uproot themselves and find a new place to live where such danger did not exist.[7]

In comparing registries of names, Jan de Vos observed that Couoh was the dominant surname among the mayeros both of Yucum and of another settlement, Petenacté.[8] This surname was connected to one of the most illustrious governing lineages, or family lines, of the Petén Itzá. Its members, who lived in Chakan Itzá, were bitter rivals of the Canek.[9] De Vos also notes that the Yucatecan Maya of Petenacté and Yucum were dissident groups who—suffering persecution at the hands of the Itzáes—chose to flee the Petén Itzá. They settled in small, peripheral communities that fell under the jurisdiction of the *batabil* (political leader) of the Couoh of Chakan Itzá, and that—for reasons connected to the cyclical change in governing lineages—when the Canek assumed power, they instantly attacked the Couoh settlements. The war that ensued thus displaced the Couoh, causing them to move away in the direction of the Usumacinta River, far from the marauding Ah Caneko'ob.[10]

RETURNING TO THE ANCIENT *PUEBLO*: THE FUGITIVE MAYA OF XICALANGO

Around the year 1694, four or five Mayan families fled from the community where they were settled, Atasta de la Real Corona, located in the province of Tabasco. Initially, these runaways numbered only fourteen, including both adults and children, but in time their number increased, as they were joined by extended family. Apparently, eight years passed before the Spanish colonial authorities became aware of this group of Maya. In all likelihood, after leaving their community, the Maya families traveled along the coast of the Gulf of Atasta, adjacent to the Laguna de Términos, attempting to locate the site where the community of Xicalango had previously stood.[11] From there they headed into the jungle, stopping at a place that was distant from both the rivers and the lagoon but close to the site of Xicalango. Among other considerations, they needed to situate themselves where English pirates would not be able to make landfall and raid their settlement.

The runaway Maya apparently received assistance from various neighboring Indians as well as family relations at the time they made their escape and set out for Xicalango. Furthermore, it is possible that the escape plans had been hatched well in advance and that the abandonment of Atasta was carried out in stages, so that the ancient settlement could be repopulated little by little, before the Spanish got wind of what was happening. Although it would have been naïve of the Indians to believe such a strategy would ultimately work, the Spanish civil authorities were in fact quite careless, and it was only when the absence of the natives affected the amount of tribute they were collecting that the Spanish organized expeditions to pull the Indians back into their communities. In addition, the presence of the English and their continual movement up and down the rivers represented an ever-present danger for the Maya. Indeed, if the Maya had been able to avoid contact with the English, they might have managed to remain longer in Xicalango before facing recapture by the Spanish.

Documentation from the period makes reference to several English settlements that were established with the purpose of cutting down and collecting much sought-after *palo de tinte* (logwood). Since the coastal area around the Laguna de Términos was crawling with foreigners, the Spanish placed very little trust in the Maya, who—they feared—might form an alliance with the English and help them "to gain access to [the province of Tabasco] . . . through unknown and out-of-the-way places, such as the by-ways of streams, lagoons, and estuaries that feed into the rivers which crisscross the entire province."[12] This suspicion on the part of the Spanish was unremitting, though misplaced. The Maya likely saw little value in allying themselves with the English, whom they in fact viewed with distrust, since it was well-known that many of the pirates kidnapped the Maya in order to sell them as slaves.

I therefore find little credence in the notion that the Maya sought friendly relations with the English in order to transport them into the hinterland. On the contrary, they coexisted with them solely for the purpose of exchanging raw materials for particular goods that they wanted and needed. The reality is that the two problems—the predilection of the Indians to flee and the presence of the English navigating the estuaries and rivers—were independent of each other. The lackadaisical policy followed by the provincial government of Yucatán toward guarding its coasts permitted the number of Englishmen in the area to grow steadily, and it was this development that posed the real danger to the Spanish. The English filibusterers took advantage of their freedom of movement to steal into the jungle and cut down and carry off the logwoods.

The Spanish increasingly believed that their evangelizing mission would be subverted if the Maya continued to have contact with the pirates. Such contact would inevitably turn them into heretics, because "being ignorant simpletons and lacking in faith, and deprived of the teachings and ministrations of the doctrine, they would fall into idolatry or into practicing heretical rites and dogmas out of their communication and dealings with the English."[13] While the Spanish may have entertained such fears, it is unlikely that the Maya would have embraced the Anglican religion as their own. Having received the sacrament of baptism, they were indeed in a position to abandon or become apostates to the Catholic faith; nevertheless, the native groups were ignorant of the beliefs held by the English, who had neither the time to preach their own religion to them nor an interest in doing so.

In June 1702, alarmed over the drift of events, the alcalde mayor and military commander of Tacotalpa, Pedro Gutiérrez de Mier y Terán, organized a punitive expedition, with the intention of capturing and reconcentrating the runaway Maya as well as engaging the English interlopers, who had been cutting the logwoods and wreaking havoc along the banks of the Usumacinta. The expeditionary party, consisting of fifty well-armed and provisioned men accompanied by Indian guides, set off from Tacotalpa, heading down river in four *piraguas* (canoes), until reaching the Laguna de Términos and adjacent estuaries.[14] The party managed to capture all of the Maya, who were found to be dwelling in the ancient settlement of Xicalango. Their number was small, just thirty in all, and they had few possessions, among which were discovered five *espingardas* (muskets).[15]

As soon as the escaped natives had been brought back, the Spanish authorities decided to keep them under close guard in "secure houses," because the jail was full of Englishmen who had also been taken captive during the operation. After being returned to captivity, the Indians were subjected to an intensive questioning by Gutiérrez de Mier y Terán. The interrogation began on June 20, 1702, with the Spanish attempting first to understand why the Indians had chosen to flee. The first person to testify was one of the leaders of the indigenous community, Pedro García, an Indian of some sixty years of age and a native of Atasta. The questioning of García was done through a Spanish interpreter, Captain Diego de Cervantes, "because he possessed a keen understanding of the Yucatecan language, which is what the said Indian speaks."[16] According to García, the Indians' main reason for fleeing was that they were "being mistreated mentally, and even physically," by the chief political administrator of

Villahermosa, Tomás Laureano. Laureano, so García related, asked that female Indians grind corn for him and male Indians serve as workers on his lands and around his house.[17] Although the Maya complied with his request, the Spaniard was not satisfied. Furthermore, the Indian community was required to fulfill other tributary obligations in the village.

Apart from this situation, however, there was another, stronger motive behind the Indians' decision to set off from Atasta. An extended measles epidemic had plagued the area, resulting in the death of many within the indigenous population. Furthermore, García insisted in his testimony that neither he nor his family had intended to communicate or deal with the English. What precipitated such contact, the Mayan leader maintained, was that during the trip downriver toward the Campeche coast, he and his party suddenly came upon an English piragua and, to avoid being taken prisoner, they offered to trade the English some plantains and fruits. A kind of trade agreement grew out of this unexpected encounter between the Maya and the English, by which the runaway Indians promised to supply the English on a "regular basis" with different types of fruit. As García related the story, however, the Maya failed to honor the agreement, because the leader and his band managed to hide their whereabouts from the logwood cutters. Their dwellings were located in the middle of the jungle, four or five miles in from the main opening of the Laguna de Términos and surrounded on all sides by dense vegetation. There was no river, estuary, or lagoon that could be navigated to reach the site.[18]

One day, when Don Pedro and others were out hunting, they reached a place along the shore of the lagoon where they spotted a great number of boats belonging to the English woodcutters, "anchored in shallow water." This, they assumed, was the mooring point for the woodcutting operation. The English had been felling trees in two places, San Francisco and Laguna Dulce. The Indians' leader mentioned that on several occasions shots fired by the pirates could be heard as faraway as their own settlement.[19]

The shoulder-mounted firearms found by the Spanish when they recaptured the Maya had apparently come into the latter's possession through an exchange that took place between the Maya and an English boat, a *balandra*, that sailed along the coast near Xicalango.[20] In return for tools that they needed, such as hatchets and machetes, the Maya gave the boat's captain items in high demand on the part of the English—parrots, yucca, plantains, and sweet potatos.[21] They used the firearms to hunt game, which served as a complement to their basic diet. Carrying the espingardas, the Maya tracked and shot pheasant, wild turkey, deer, wild boar, jaguar, and mountain lions. The latter two animals likely attacked the Indians or, at the very least, were spotted pacing near their dwellings.[22]

During the questioning, Pedro García also stated that the settlement in Xicalango was purely temporary, because neither he nor his family planned to remain there for long; rather, they wanted to return to their pueblo, to be regathered into the fold of the Church, but two things were "stopping them, their fear" of reencountering both Tomás Laureano and the measles epidemic.[23] Don Pedro likewise confided that he imparted the teachings of the Church to the young children of his community, instructing them in "the doctrine and in making the sign of the cross." Similarly, he proceeded to baptize the adult Maya, invoking the words—pertaining to the Catholic religion—that they had all been taught. The Spanish, not altogether convinced about this Indian's supposed fervor for the Church, asked him to recite the words, which he managed to do "clearly and distinctly." At this point in the questioning, which continued to focus on the religious practices of the runaway Maya, García declared that in the Xicalango settlement the Indians kept the *hechura* (image) of a holy Christ on an altar in a tabernacle where they went to pray. With this statement, García's testimony came to an end.[24]

The answers and explanations that he gave can be accepted as only partially truthful, as he would have introduced various details in order to stave off more severe punishment and avoid the accusation of having committed heresy or some equally egregious wrong. The placement of the image of Christ on the tabernacle altar can be seen in two lights: first, that the Maya were indeed good Catholics and, although finding themselves far from their church and priest, tried to maintain their observance of the Christian faith so as not to fall into the lap of evil; or second, that they had perhaps incorporated some Christian rituals into their ancient beliefs, amalgamating the two sets of practices, and thus producing a kind of pseudo-religion. As I see it, Don Pedro García tried to show that neither he nor members of his family had fallen into any error, that they were not apostates but continued being sincere and devoted Catholics, as demonstrated by the Christ figure to which they prayed. The Maya had also tried to avoid having contact with the English enemy but ultimately were forced by circumstance to deal with them, given the proximity of the English, whom the Indians might perchance run into at any moment. Moreover, the main reason for their taking flight was the mistreatment and abuse that they had received at the hands of Tomás Laureano. The Spaniard demanded a great deal, and the service that he exacted was beyond their capacity. In addition, a dreaded disease had struck down their comrades and neighbors in Atasta; to avoid incurring a similar fate, García and his family fled the pueblo.

In retrospect, it would seem that Pedro García had summoned quite intelligent and well-structured arguments to defend the actions that he and his family had taken. Even in a region far from any center of Spanish political and legal authority and institutions, as a person of authority in his community, García possessed an impressive degree of knowledge of the political and judicial workings of the Spanish colonial administrative system, which he put to good use. When questioned, therefore, he was able to answer effectively and to marshal arguments that would demonstrate his blamelessness or innocence. At bottom, however, García had fled Atasta out of fear of the measles pandemic and because the cycle of change, which in the Mayan cosmology signaled a period of renewal and reordering, impelled him to return to his community's ancient settlement.[25] The Mayan leader had given his version of events; the Spanish, however, were not through with their interrogations.

On the same day, they subjected Juan García, the son of Don Francisco, to a round of questioning. A native of Atasta, Juan García was approximately twenty-two years of age. From the time he was a young boy, Juan had heard his parents and other adult members of the community complain of the mistreatment they suffered at the hands of the Spanish, and he felt the sting and injustice of such mistreatment in his own flesh. For this reason, he testified, he decided to follow his father to Xicalango, a place that he knew only through the stories that his father had told him.[26] He also mentioned that because they were in need of metal tools, members of the group decided to go off in search of someone who might be able to offer them. Consequently, they left their settlement and navigated through the estuaries of the lagoon up to a place known as the "the Spaniards' jetty." From there, he related, they continued rowing until coming around to the front of the mouth of the Laguna de Términos, from where—at a short distance—they could see the boats of the English anchored in the water. Knowing full well the violent disposition of the English and anxious to prevent a confrontation, Juan, his father, and their companions decided to raise a white flag. Thus, it was that they came upon the piragua of the pirates, with whom they offered to exchange birds and fruit for the rifles, machetes, and hatchets that they needed. The rifles would be used to "hunt land animals and game birds."[27]

The Mayas' strategy worked, and the English did not inflict any harm on them. On the contrary, the agreement concluded between the two parties, whereby the Indians were to provision the English with food, enabled the pirates to devote themselves fully to ransacking the forest for logwood. According to García's testimony, the English pursued their surreptitious cutting throughout the year, while maintaining enough artillery on their fleet to respond to any encounter that might arise with the Spanish. The English maintained their own settlements toward the southern end of the opening of the Laguna de Tris; it was there that they piled the cut logwood branches in order later to transfer them—so it must have followed—in their balandra to an area they held that was more secure. In stating that their dwellings lay some four or five leagues in from the Laguna de Términos, Juan García's testimony accorded with his father's. Although the filibusterers tried to figure out the location of the indigenous settlement, the Atastan natives—having little trust in the English—eluded them and kept their location secret by moving with stealth and a cautious eye.[28]

During the course of his questioning, Juan García mentioned that he was subject to the will of his father, that whatever decision his father might make, he would respect it and carry out its dictates. On the surface, this detail appears trifling, but underneath it reveals just who the leader of the family was and why all of its members fled from Atasta—they, like Juan García, deferred to the authority of Don Francisco. He was a person of special standing and possessed special knowledge, which he transmitted to his son; in addition, he was the religious leader of the group.[29] This latter fact played a critical role. Because Pedro García understood why his family and the larger group must return to Xicalango, they were obliged to respect him and to follow his lead.

Finally, Juan García corroborated his father's testimony on one further point; namely, his "vehement" desire to return to Atasta with his family to see how his relatives in the pueblo were coping, perhaps worried about them all the more owing to the pernicious effects of the measles epidemic.[30] In similar fashion, he professed ignorance regarding his position before the law as a result of having run away from his pueblo and having interceded with the English. It is likely that the son was following his father's example and pretending to be ill-informed or unaware of things in order to minimize his punishment. This was a wise precautionary stance; feigning ignorance left the annoyed and weary interrogators empty-handed, anxious to be through with questioning the supposedly dim-witted natives.

Around June 21, 1702, still another member of the García family—a thirty-year-old adult by the name of Sebastián García, appeared before Gutiérrez de Mier y Terán. His testimony by and large paralleled that already given. In reconstructing events, it appears likely that all of the adult members of the García family had gathered to discuss the situation and reached an agreement that they would reduce the severity of their punishment, first, by mentioning nothing that would fault them, and second, by providing the same or very similar information under questioning.

In his declaration, Sebastián indicated that the population of Atasta was dying out because of the measles epidemic and that the García family—alarmed by the prospect that one or more of its members would succumb to the disease—decided to set off in search of a new site, a place faraway, like Xicalango, that was free of the plague. After crossing swamps, low-lying areas, and tributaries of the river, the group decided to settle down in a place that was encircled by extremely dense vegetation. The men cut down trees and brush to build their huts. They prayed and set fire to the grass in order to prepare the ground for planting corn and cotton.[31] This site, as García related it, had to be inaccessible to the English pirates. Nevertheless, since they were in need of serviceable machetes and hatchets, they met up with the English, who were themselves looking for the Maya, because they knew the Maya could provide them with a ready supply of fruit and parrots. As concerned the filibusterers, Sebastián García mentioned that they spent considerable time on land, combing the interior of the jungle. It was clear, he testified, that the English went about cutting down and hauling off the logwood without any fear of being threatened or disturbed by the Spanish. On this matter, García was probably in error since it is likely that the English kept lookouts hidden in certain strategic sites that the Maya had not detected. He likewise assured Gutiérrez de Mier y Terán that the English had neither fortified their settlements nor dug trenches for their defense.

According to García, the group did not possess even a single piragua but had only small boats, canoes more than likely, in which to make their way through the lagoon and along the rivers feeding into it. Like the two interviewed before him, he also referred to his strong desire to return to the community of Atasta. The Spanish would have done well to press García on this point. If the Maya had successfully planted corn in Xicalango, were growing cotton to make their clothes, found ample game for hunting, and easily collected the fruits and birds that allowed them to barter with the English, why would they want to leave such favorable surroundings—where they were free of the Spanish and of the obligation to perform any kind of service or pay any form of tribute—to live once again in the company of disease?

Along these same lines, Sebastián García stated that he did not know whether by fleeing from Atasta and trading with the English he had committed a crime. He had fled the pueblo, he maintained, only to escape the humiliations that he suffered at the hands of the Spanish, and he exchanged goods with the English purely as a matter of survival. Furthermore, in stating that he harbored fears that the English would drag him away to Jamaica, García revealed—perhaps unwittingly—that he knew about the pirates' movements and sailing routes around the Gulf of Mexico and the Caribbean. It followed that he knew what the English were up to and where it was that they transported the logwood. He likewise knew the risk that he and the others were running when they approached the English, although he pretended otherwise, maintaining that it was all the outcome of a chance encounter.

The statement of a fourth Atasta runaway, a twenty-eight year old by the name of Mateo Chan, confirmed all of the preceding testimony. Repeating what the others had said, Chan declared that they had fled the community because of mistreatment by Tomás Laureano, who forced them to work to an unreasonable extent in his sugar mill and cornfields. Out of desperation, the group fled in the direction of the Laguna de Términos in search of the abandoned pueblo of Xicalango. The overriding need for tools, however, "forced the group to reveal itself to the English."[32]

All of the testimony given to Gutiérrez de Mier y Terán had therefore sketched out a clear and consistent picture. The Maya had run away from Atasta, to their ancient pueblo, in order to escape two things: the oppressive treatment meted out to them by the *encomendero* Laureano (holder of an encomienda grant) and the ravages of the measles epidemic. After settling in the vicinity of Xicalango, their need for tools drove them to approach the English, with whom they exchanged goods on a fairly regular basis. The Indians' story—consistent though it may have been—was not terribly convincing to the Spanish authorities, who held a meeting on June 21, 1702, to decide the legal fate of the Maya in relation to their evident apostasy and to their dealings with the English, who had been frequenting the shores of Xicalango in the Laguna de Términos.

Gathered under the leadership of Gutiérrez de Mier y Terán, the Spaniards weighed different options for returning the Maya to their settlements. The group could be broken up, with small numbers placed in different communities, or it could be resettled, en masse, in the pueblo of Atasta. The authorities also endeavored to provide the Indians some type of assistance, to be financed out of tax revenues, from the royal treasury, that were allocated for needs in the province. The use of such revenue could be justified for this purpose and would keep the amount expended to a reasonable limit. To this end, it was decided that each of the runaway Maya would receive a piece of clothing, because the men each wore only an *e'ex* (loincloth), while the women kept their chests bare. Moreover, each male would be given a hatchet and a machete. Very likely, the tools that they had obtained from the English were left behind in Xicalango or appropriated by the Spanish soldiers. In similar fashion, each of the Maya was to receive "some corn" for his daily sustenance.[33]

During the meeting, the authorities made two further decisions: to inform the viceroy about what had transpired and to form a committee composed of the more important Spanish citizens of Tacotalpa and its environs, functionaries of the royal treasury, and other municipal officials led by the alcalde mayor. The committee would meet two days hence, in the village's *casa real* (royal office), to determine what course of action to take with respect to the apostate Maya and to evaluate the security needs of the area in light of the English presence in the Laguna de Términos and along the rivers of the Xicalango and Atasta territory. The Tacotalpa residents and community leaders were notified by letter of the impending meeting so that they could participate.[34]

The committee, presided over by alcalde Gutiérrez de Mier y Terán, met at the casa real on the appointed day. The alcalde was joined by Agustín de Zavala, Antonio de Flores, Pedro Álvarez de Miranda, Diego de Cervantes, and Andrés Gordillo—all local encomenderos and patrons of different festivals—as well as by three of the leading citizens of Tacotalpa, Juan Rodríguez de la Gala, Diego Calderón Díaz, Jacinto Refoxo; and a high-ranking member of the town council, Gabriel Gil. After discussing the matter, the Spanish agreed that the fugitive Maya—since they numbered so few—should not be split up or resettled in a newly-founded pueblo but instead should be taken back to the familiar surroundings of Atasta, where they had extended family and plots of land. The authorities also decided that the Indians should incur certain work obligations and be required to perform some services to the community. They also judged that with the passage of time, the erstwhile runaways—if treated well—could succeed in reintegrating themselves into the community, "forming a very good settlement on the site [of Atasta] where said pueblo exists, [and is] a very useful part of the trade and movement of people in [the region] of la Chontalpa."[35] It is clear from these words of the Spanish that a vibrant local trade existed among different settlements along the Usumacinta River from the Chontalpa region all the way to the Gulf of Atasta. The various river ports were the spokes that connected the wheel of this activity, to the extent that they remained free of English filibustering.

When the committee met, Atasta's indigenous leaders—the alcalde and councilors of the Indian *cabildo* (governing council)—came before it to negotiate on behalf of the onetime runaways, arguing that they could effectively monitor their conduct and actions. Very likely blood relations of the fugitives, the native authorities had apparently journeyed to Tacotalpa, hoping to reduce the severity of any punishments that the Spanish handed down. Pointedly, the Maya alcalde and councilors requested that the Indians who had fled be allowed to return to their community "as natives and tribute-paying subjects of the crown."[36] By so designating the runaways, they were attempting to protect their legal and economic security and prevent them from being reduced to the level of slaves or common prisoners who might be exiled to some outlying area and consigned to unremunerated, forced labor. To possess the status of those who paid tribute or tax to the king, and whose contribution therefore went directly into the royal treasury, meant that they would be free of the clutches of the encomendero, who would no longer be able to exploit, mistreat, and plunder them.

After listening to testimony rendered by both the Spanish officials and residents of Tacotalpa as well as the Maya authorities from Atasta, the committee ruled that all of the men who had been captured in Xicalango were to be given a length of cotton cloth, and all of the women a traditional embroidered skirt. The children were to be treated likewise. So that they could work their cornfields and build their huts, the men were also to receive a machete and a hatchet. Finally, for their sustenance and perhaps also for planting, the Indians were to be provided with a small amount of corn and beans.[37] The spread of disease in Atasta had prevented many of the Maya from working in the fields, thus producing a local shortage of food.

The cost of the tools, clothing, and seeds and grain were charged to the tax used to fund provincial outlays. In the final accounting, of course, it was the Indians themselves—via the tribute exacted from them—who paid for the provisioning and other necessities of the expedition while the Spanish literally spent nothing. The same tax was used to pay for the employment of lookouts and the readying of firearms. All of these decisions taken by the committee concerning the resettlement of the runaway Maya in Atasta were formalized on June 26, 1702.

As soon as the case of the Atastan Maya was resolved, the committee turned its attention to a related matter, the capture and removal of the English who had been camped around the lower part of the Usumacinta River, where it emptied into the Laguna de Términos. The Spanish—encomenderos and soldiers alike—repeated their fear of a possible alliance between the runaway Maya and the English, since the latter had gained a beachhead in the area of the logwoods and had come to be "informed about all of the rivers, estuaries, and lagoòns which crisscross this province." Although such fears were probably misplaced, they could at least be laid to rest for the time being, since the same expedition that recaptured the Maya from Atasta had also managed to take prisoner a number of the English who were cutting down the logwood and imperiling the coastal waters. The soldiers who had been in charge of the operation against the English gave the committee a colorful description of their exploits.

The contingent of Spanish military who faced the British enemy comprised 128 men, all of them armed and well-supplied with munitions.

Divided among seven piraguas and a larger boat, this group was recon-
noitering a part of the Laguna de Términos, including the mouth of the
Usumacinta River, the Xicalango area, and the Gulf of Atasta, with the
mission of locating, engaging, and capturing the filibusterers. The Spanish
troops apparently managed to spring a surprise attack upon the English.
They began cautiously, by surrounding an enemy ship "that had some
Englishmen in it who they set about questioning."[38] From this party, the
Spanish soldiers found out where the English settlements were located and
how they were set up, which enabled them to lay out a strategy of attack.
In order to get into the area where the logwood cutters had their saw mills,
the Spanish "would need to work their way up to a fortification in which
the English had placed a piece of artillery and had posted a sentry and some
guards."[39] Thus, armed with this information, the Spanish moved up and
launched a surprise attack upon the enemy. In the resulting confusion, a
good many of the English scattered and disappeared into the jungle.

The Spanish first took possession of the fort and the canon that it
housed. After the commotion died down, they demolished the walls of the
fort, then dismantled the canon and carried it off to Tacotalpa. A group of
soldiers chasing after the fleeing English, who had headed in the direction
of their jungle encampments, managed to capture sixteen of them, as well
as four Irish Catholics (who had been taken prisoner by pirates and sold as
slaves to the English to work in the logwood forests) and nine blacks. The
Spanish also took control of twenty-eight espingardas, six piraguas, and
two barges, which had been used to transport the wood from the mainland to large sailing vessels anchored in the lagoon.[40]

The Spanish also set fire to several boats and burned the Englishmen's
tools and buildings. The expedition had taken a total of fifteen days to
fulfill its objectives, ending with the transference and incarceration of the
English, who now filled up the jail in Tacotalpa. This military operation
was one of the few that succeeded against the settlements established by
the filibusterers around the Laguna de Términos. As such, it stood as a
victory for the Spanish Crown over the British heretics. It likewise represented a triumph for the Catholic missionary enterprise in bringing back
into the Church's fold a group of Maya who fallen away from the faith and
fled their community. The satisfaction felt by the Spanish authorities, however, may have been short-lived, since over the whole of the eighteenth
century, these and other Maya continued to desert the reductions and flee
from imperial control.

It is interesting to note how this particular group of Maya returned
to an ancient coastal settlement, located in Xicalango, on the Laguna de
Términos. Perhaps Pedro García knew that long ago this site had been one

of great importance and that a period of cyclical change had to be fulfilled now; that is, that this particular time, katún 8 ajaw, marked the time of return to this settlement, as it had for his ancestors, the Itzáes. On the other hand, it is worth emphasizing that these peninsular Maya no longer kept their Yucatecan surname but instead bore a Spanish surname, García. The explanation for this anomaly is that at some juncture there appeared in the Lacandon jungle a group of peninsular Maya-speaking people whose family line had the patronymic Karsía—that is, a "Mayanized" version of the surname García.[41] It is likely that they were the direct descendants of the Maya who had come from Xicalango and had worked their way up the banks of the Usumacinta River. They had thus become one of the Lacandon subgroups found near the end of the eighteenth century and all through the nineteenth around Palenque, Tenosique, and neighboring regions. Such a chain of events would clear up part of the mystery surrounding the origin of one of the present-day Lacandon lineages.

THE "LEGENDARY ENEMIES" OF THE LACANDONES

De Vos uses this appellation to describe a group of Maya known as *petenactes*. The Spanish captain Gaspar Raimundo de Baraya had come across these Maya in the year 1708, while carrying out a routine exploration in the jungles around the military establishment of Dolores Lacandon.[42] In fact, this indigenous settlement had existed since at least the second half of the seventeenth century, when it was noted by the Próspero expedition and the Franciscan friars who accompanied it. During the last three decades of the century, these Maya had moved upland, to the north, trying to find the missionaries who were evangelizing both apostate Maya and a group of Kejaches settled in a pueblo called Tzuctok. The Petenacté Maya sought the protection of the friars, while also managing—from the safety of their missionary settlements—to coexist with both the apostate and unevangelized Maya.[43] One of the Franciscans in the area walked down through the hills to visit Tzuctok's mission church, which had been abandoned by its secular priest. Shortly thereafter, however, it seems that the Franciscans abandoned the settlement to its own fate. The Spanish came through the area again in 1680, during the course of a military operation aimed at capturing apostate Maya, but they apparently ignored the Pentenacté settlements, which then remained free of Spanish contact until de Baraya came across them in the early eighteenth century.

The Petenacté, it seems, were not an entirely peaceful group. According to the testimony offered by Diego de Rivas—a Mercedarian friar who spent time evangelizing in the Lacandon jungle and the Laguna del Itzá region—they had caused considerable harm to the Lacandon Indians. The Petenacté Maya lived in the mountainous areas above the Lacandon River and along its banks, which were also home to another indigenous group, the Cholties (or *cholanos*). The Cholties settlements were periodically attacked by the peninsular Maya, leaving their inhabitants victimized by "destruction and fire."[44]

The peninsular Maya community found by de Baraya was located a little more than fifty leagues from Dolores, along the edge of the Usumacinta River, some five days' journey to the northeast. Its population—consisting of several family groups—lived in a series of small, dispersed settlements. According to de Vos, the community was formed by Indians from the Petén who had broken away from serving the Spanish, mixed with apostate Maya, who were from missionary settlements located in the jurisdiction of Los Ríos, which lay in the easternmost part of the province of Tabasco.[45] These Maya struck the Spanish as rather untrustworthy. Furthermore, they were accustomed to living independently, outside the orbit of Spanish influence and control. In light of these factors, de Baraya decided to transfer twenty-five families to a "Christian" pueblo, located near a garrison that the Spanish maintained, although somewhat distant from Dolores itself. The small settlement, it seems, had as its patron saint San Miguel Arcángel. Ideally, the Spanish captain would have preferred to send these Indians to the Petén, "since they were of that nation and language."[46]

As the years went by, the Maya population near Dolores began to find itself in a precarious situation. Numbering 131 in all, the Petenactés could barely produce enough food to sustain themselves, surrounded as they were by dense, impenetrable vegetation and subject to a year-round climate of intense heat and humidity. Illness and disease were taking their toll on the population, and it did them no good to flee into the mountains, since they encountered the same sicknesses there as well.[47] Consequently, de Baraya and the Dominican friar who ministered to the Lacandones and the Petenactés decided to move the Dolores settlement to a more salubrious location. The friar's preference was to send the Yucatecan-speaking Maya to the Petén, but de Baraya now thought differently and resolved to keep them with the Lacandones, because they had, by this point, learned the Choltí language and established a functioning system of *compadrazgo* (family-based loyalties and social bonds) with the other group. The Dominican missionary would later come around to the captain's position, asserting that the Yucatecan Maya "profess to be great friends of the Lacandones, with whom they deal affably and have formed social ties, priding themselves on speaking the Lacandon language and having abandoned their own."[48]

The move from the Dolores site to a new settlement along the Aquespala River took place in 1714. The resettlement, however, was not permanent. Six years hence the Lacandones were twice moved to other locations, until they were finally placed in a part of Santa Catarina Retalhuleu, on Guatemala's coast of San Antonio Suchitepequez. As a result of being moved about in this way, a good many of the Lacandon fled; others fell sick and died en route, the victims of various illnesses brought on by the change in climate. Thus, by 1712, the Choltíes had all but disappeared.[49] The Petenactés very likely experienced similar misfortune. In their case, however, virtually the entire group fled into the jungle. Such escape and flight was a constant in their way of life. Some of the peninsular Maya must have died along the way, while others—above all those who had formed family ties—would have accompanied the Lacandon to the coast.

THE YUCATECAN "LACANDONES" OF
SAN JOSÉ DE GRACIA REAL

Jan de Vos has studied this topic more fully than anyone else, because he consulted primary source material, managing through his research to identify this group as being the direct ancestors of the present-day Lacandon. What follows is only a brief outline, based on the writings of the Belgian historian and on some further data, aimed at providing a broad historical overview of the Maya from the northern part of the peninsula, Maya of Yucatecan affiliation who established themselves in the Lacandon region.

The first Spanish contact with these heretofore unpacified, uncolonized Maya occurred late in the colonial period in 1786, when a settlement was founded eight leagues south of Palenque. An Indian servant of the secular priest of Palenque engaged in trade with these people, exchanging tools for wax and uncultivated cacao. On the basis of these interactions, the priest wanted to speak personally with them, and—to this end—invited the Maya to attend a religious celebration, the festival of Santo Domingo. On August 4, 1786, they appeared in Palenque and were treated with considerable care and kindliness by the chief authorities of the pueblo, such as the priest, Manuel Calderón, and the resident judicial administrator. The Indians had not expected to be welcomed in such warm fashion. Now confident of the good intentions harbored toward them, they promised to live, henceforth, in a new community under the missionary tutelage of the Spanish.[50]

In the meantime, both the priest and the civil authorities attempted to secure economic and legal assistance from the audiencia of Guatemala and the Spanish Crown in order to implement plans for establishing a reduction. Because Chiapas was in the throes of administrative change (becoming an intendency, whereas previously it had held the status of an *alcaldía mayor*, or official district) and because of opposition from the bishop of Chiapas, however, the project had to be suspended for three years. At that point, officials of the newly created intendency displayed interest in the initiative, and Calderón—still serving as the priest—completed the necessary steps required by the diocesan authority. Nevertheless, bureaucratic procedures caused the process to be delayed for three more years.

It was not until June 1793 that Manuel Calderón, accompanied by his father, several relatives, and some young Spanish-speaking Indian servants, could set off into the jungle to pick up the trail of the apostate Maya. In time, the Spanish located their settlement and remained in it for a period of forty days. The servants in the party proceeded to construct a church and shed for ironworking, so that—depending upon the Indians' preferences—the blacksmith could make them hatchets, machetes, and knives. In similar fashion, the Maya women received sweets, underskirts, mats, blankets, and other domestic items such as bags, ribbons, and glass beads. Showered with this cornucopia of gifts, the Indians swore loyalty to the king and to the Catholic Church.

Around July 23, 1793—or some six weeks after the indigenous settlement had been founded—the priest returned to Palenque with his party in tow. Clearly, he took great satisfaction in having congregated forty-three people in a peaceful community, which was given the name San José de Gracia. Moreover, the Maya had assured him that another 123 people would settle in the community once the time for harvesting had passed. In August 1793, a royal official, responsible for carrying out inspections, passed through the reduction and certified that all was proceeding smoothly within it. Nonetheless, the welfare of the settlement was impaired by a critical problem, namely, the lack of a resident priest. In the long run, this failing necessarily had to affect the ability of the mayeros to be integrated into the colonial system. An indigenous *fiscal* from Palenque, the lay assistant to Calderón, had been placed in charge of the religious administration of the settlement. This individual, however, did not know the Yucatecan language. Its early successes notwithstanding, neither the civil nor the episcopal authorities attached the slightest importance to the reduction nor did any of them bother to pay it even one visit.[51]

Around 1797, Manuel Calderón passed away, and with his death, the recently congregated Maya lost the only person who took an interest in their way of life. Deserted as they were, the Indians faded back into the jungle, although they continued to sow the fields near the once-active settlement of San José de Gracia Real. From time to time, these "Caribes" (as they were sometimes called) were seen in the vicinity of Palenque, where they engaged in trade, exchanging both agricultural products and items from the wild, such as cotton, honey, wax, cacao, and tobacco, in return for ornaments and metal implements.

Over an eight-year period, from 1799 to 1807, the lack of attention paid to them by the Spanish religious and civil authorities caused these Maya to revert to their old ways of life. Little else is known about these people, other than in 1799, a mulatto endeavored to reinstruct them in the teachings of the Catholic faith. Not knowing Yucatecan Maya, however, he was compelled to do so in Spanish and Chol. It is further known that in 1800 they engaged in active trade with the mestizo population of Palenque and that some of their children came to the local church to take the catechism. Twelve of the Maya children were baptized but continued—at the same time—to practice their ancient rites. Concerned over the Indians' lapsed state, the Dominicans offered to renew their work of evangelization. But the bishop of Chiapas—asserting that only the secular clergy could fulfill this responsibility—rejected the offer. Subsequently, no further word ever emerged about this indigenous group.[52]

The episcopal authorities in Chiapas attested to the fact that these Lacandones were peaceful and should therefore be placed in a reduction. At the same time, however, there were other groups of Maya known to be living in the mountains that adjoined the Petén, Maya who spoke the same language but were thus far unpacified.[53] In all likelihood, these Indians were Kejaches and Itzáes who had fled from the Petén lagoon and, over time, also been given the name Lacandones.

FINAL OBSERVATIONS ON THESE EPISODES

From all of the information provided above, along with the research results of various scholars, among whom Jan de Vos stands out, it is possible to gain a picture of the movement, settlements, and territorial distribution of the peninsular Maya—who later came to be known by some as Lacandones and by others as Caribes—during the colonial period and into part of the nineteenth century. The picture yields some understanding of the multiple displacements of people across an immense stretch of untamed and rugged jungle land, displacements that are linked to well-defined peninsular ethnic and linguistic groups, in particular the Itzáes, Kejaches, and unpacified apostate Maya from the north. All of these people, in their totality, gave rise to the present-day Lacandones.[54] The displacements and cycles of community and ethnic formation, displacement, and decline were powerfully influenced also by Spanish interaction or lack thereof. Bourbon policies were not particularly effective for institution building, civil or religious. Local authorities, often adept at negotiation and using the characteristic blend of threat and leniency, could not always influence the more rigid decision making of higher-up officials.

Nevertheless, this picture—informative as it might be—offers only a glimpse of the rich mosaic of Mayan jungle settlements and the mobility of these "men of corn," who possessed a deep knowledge of the land and could thus move from one place to another with relative ease. Their command of the rivers, mountains, and jungle paths enabled them to travel freely, unobstructed, and to choose—each group on its own—a site that was concealed behind the thick wall of jungle, a site far removed from the Spanish presence, from disease, and from their own Mayan enemies. Even as they interacted intermittently with Spanish political and legal authorities, the jungle continued to be theirs, but the flow of time and the policies adopted by liberal-minded creoles in the nineteenth century would eventually alter the situation.

NOTES

1. A more detailed description of the Próspero expedition is found in Grant D. Jones, *Maya Resistance to Spanish Rule: Time and History on a Colonial Frontier* (Stanford, CA: Stanford University Press, 1998); Jan de Vos, *La paz de Dios y del Rey: La conquista de la selva Lacandona por los españoles, 1525–1821* (México DF: Fondo de Cultura Económica, 1988); Pedro Bracamonte y Sosa, *La conquista inconclusa de Yucatán* (México DF: Miguel Angel Porrúa, 1997); and José Manuel A. Chávez-Gómez, *Intención franciscana de evangelizar entre los mayas rebeldes* (México DF: Conaculta, 2001).

2. De Vos, *La paz de Dios*, 218.

3. Chávez-Gómez, *Intención franciscana.*

4. When present-day peninsular Mayans identify another Mayan who speaks the same Yucatecan language, they refer to that person as a *mayero*, that is, one who speaks Mayan.

5. De Vos, *La paz de Díos*, 220.

6. Ibid.

7. Ibid.

8. Ibid., 224.

9. Jones, *Maya Resistance to Spanish Rule*, 88; José Manuel A. Chávez-Gómez, "En busca del maíz perdido: La rebellion Itzá de 1699," *Mexicon* 25 (2003):16–23.

10. Thus, as the conquest of this area took place in March 1697, the Couoh lineage allied itself with the Spanish in order to defeat its enemy, the Canek; the lineage would subsequently seek a way to establish its own territorial autonomy in alliance with the Kejache Chan lineage and with the settlements of Tipu; ibid.

11. The settlements of Xicalango and Atasta had been important places since pre-Hispanic times. Large-scale sites, such as El Aguacatal and Santa Rita, have been found on the Xicalango Peninsula. These communities had played important political and economic roles since the Late Classic period (600 CE), although their high point occurred in the middle of the Postclassic period, between the twelfth and fourteenth centuries. By this time, another site—given the name Atasta—had also appeared. The claim is made that Santa Rita was the ancient port of Xicalango, where there existed an important regional market. Xicalango drew people from as faraway as the Mexican altiplano, the north, and present-day Central America. For the Maya, it thus served as one of the most important maritime entry points along the Gulf of Mexico basin. Atasta, on the other hand, was apparently founded for strategic purposes, to protect the port. Even when the two settlements had long fallen into decay, their fame lived on, acquiring in the collective memory a kind of supernatural aura in place of the commercial, worldly virtues that they embodied in their heyday. See Lorenzo Ochoa, *Renunciar al paraíso: Paisaje y arqueología en las Tierras Bajas pantanosas de la Cuenca del San Pedro y San Pablo y Xicalango, Campeche* (Campeche, Mexico: Instituto Campechano, Gobierno del Estado de Campeche, Instituto de Cultura de Campeche, 1997).

12. Documentos relativos a la reducción de indios apóstatas que vivían en Xicalango y aprehensión del enemigo inglés en la boca de la Laguna de Términos, Archivo General de Indias (AGI), Audiencia de México 1010, June 1702, fol. 767v; photocopy in the document collection of the Instituto de Investigaciones Antropológicas (IIA), Universidad Nacional Autónoma de México (UNAM).

13. Ibid., fols. 767v–768.

14. A *piragua* is a long, narrow craft, larger than a canoe, and generally constructed in one piece out of wood or cane. It is operated by both sail and oar. *Enciclopedia Universal Ilustrada Europeo-Americana* (Madrid: Espasa Calpe, 1989), vol. 44.

15. The *espingarda* was a firearm that in the middle of the fifteenth century replaced a smaller handheld pistol or firearm. The most important improvement that it offered over the earlier weapon was a modification to the butt end, which enabled the person using it to rest it on his shoulder while taking aim and firing; ibid., vol. 22.

16. Documentos relativos a la reducción, AGI, fol. 769.

17. Ibid.

18. Ibid.

19. Ibid.

20. The *balandra* is a covered boat with only one mast and a single sail. Balandras were used mainly for fishing and coastal navigation; *Enciclopedia Universal*, vol. 2.

21. In this period, many of the Maya no longer manufactured their own stone tools, made from obsidian or flint. Furthermore, there was a shortage of silica in the region of Xicalango, for which reason these Indians had need of machetes and hatchets to carry out their agricultural work and daily tasks.

22. Documentos relativos a la reducción, AGI, fol. 769.

23. Ibid.

24. Ibid.

25. It was at this same time that the last Itzá rebellion broke out in Lake Petén, led by batabes, who were rivals to the Canek. The campaigns had begun shortly after the Isla de Noh Petén was taken; the insurgent batabes—composed of Itzá-Couoh, Kejach-Chan, and Tipu Maya lineages—wanted to form their own Kuchkabal. In the cosmology of the peninsular Maya, these events were occurring during the time of katún 8 ajaw (a katún was a time designation of 7,200 days, and "8 ajaw" refers to a day in the sacred 260-day count). This designation of time referred to a cyclical period of great change. See Chávez-Gómez, *Intención franciscana*; and Jones, *Maya Resistance to Spanish Rule*.

26. Documentos relativos a la reducción, AGI, fol. 771.

27. Ibid.

28. Ibid.

29. It has already been mentioned that Pedro García baptized the children in his family and taught them the principles of the faith and that he also looked after the image of Christ and recited various prayers. It is likely, given his knowledge of Catholic ritual, that he had held the position of sacristan in the Atasta church and at the same time was an *ajmen*, or healer (*curandero*), who prophesied and practiced folk medicine. Such individuals knew many prayers by memory, prayers that had been taught to them by the *doctrineros* (regular clergy who served Indian parishes) and were passed down from one generation to another. Since in the colonial period the majority of the Maya did not know how to read or write, they memorized prayers and later taught them to their fellow Indians. Many of the prayers that are recited today by ajmen may be the same prayers that some Franciscans taught their ancestors.

30. Documentos relativos a la reducción, AGI, fol. 771.

31. Ibid., fol. 772v.

32. Ibid., fol. 774.

33. Ibid., fol. 775v.

34. Ibid., fol. 776v.

35. Ibid., fol. 777v.

36. Ibid.

37. Ibid.

38. Ibid., fol. 778v.

39. Ibid.

40. Ibid.

41. On the meaning of the time period, see note 25. On the Garcías, see de Vos, *La paz de Dios*, 227–231.

42. Ibid., 204.

43. Chávez-Gómez, *Intención franciscana*, 317–329.

44. De Vos, *La paz de Dios*, 388.

45. Ibid., 204.

46. Ibid., 388.

47. Ibid., 206.

48. Ibid., 389.

49. Ibid., 210.

50. Ibid., 224–225.

51. Ibid., 226.

52. Ibid., 227.

53. Chávez-Gómez, *Intención franciscana*, 378–379.

54. Robert D. Bruce, *El Libro de Chan Kín* (México DF: Instituto Nacional de Antropología e Historia, 1982), 45–62; Phillip Baer and William R. Merrifield, *Los Lacandones de México: Dos estudios*, trans. Carmen Viqueira (México DF: Instituto Nacional Indigenista, 1972), 91–94; and Alfred M. Tozzer, *Maya y Lacandones: Un estudio comparativo* (México DF: Institutio Nacional Indigenista, 1982). Note also that although the Lacandon communities coexisted, their relationships were not entirely peaceful. Among them existed groups who had come down from the northern part of the region who displayed a suspicious nature and were disposed toward violence. Several researchers mention that the Lacandones were caught up in warring upon each other, the principal motive for which was to capture women in order to ensure that families produced descendants. These aggressive, bellicose Lacandones are likewise described in the mythical accounts collected by Robert Bruce, which have survived in the oral tradition of the region. The emblematic animal of the family groups to which these people belonged was the deer.

SUSAN KELLOGG

Afterword

The Consequences of Negotiation

The essays in this volume demonstrate that negotiation was a vital component of the colonial legal system. They support Tamar Herzog's notion
that what was "political" and what was "legal" in early modern states cannot necessarily be clearly distinguished, nor can formal and informal legal
practices. These domains and practices were not wholly separable. In her
words, "[j]ustice was not imposed by an absolutist state on a subjected
people but was instead a multilayered, reciprocal, and negotiated system."[1]
In colonial New Spain—and throughout the Spanish empire—just as law
was a component of and kind of politics, politics was a component of and
kind of law, with royal officials and institutions at all levels intermingling
their judicial, administrative, and political roles throughout the colonial
period.[2]

The authors provide highly detailed readings of colonial indigenous
behaviors and beliefs relating to the political and legal realms across a variety of regions. Some authors emphasize negotiation as empowering (Baber
and Oswoski), some emphasize the ways negotiation and innovation could

229

ultimately make indigenous communities and groups more dependent on Spanish legal and political institutions (Ruiz Medrano, Romero Frizzi, and Yannakakis), and others show that both empowerment and dependency could result (Velasco Ávila and Chávez-Gómez). A combination of geography, population density, and historical events (especially in the case of the Tlaxcalans) may help to explain these variable outcomes. For indigenous peoples, negotiation might result in the preservation of limited spaces of autonomy, a notion not dissimilar from the concept of *mediated opportunism* as defined by Susan Deeds.[3] Describing mediated opportunism as the "crossroads between cultural and environmental opportunism on the one hand and moral boundaries and biological barriers on the other,"[4] I would also emphasize political and legal constraints. But disease, ecology, and environment all played roles in shaping the spaces of autonomy carved out by indigenous peoples in all the regions discussed in this book. Other consequences of colonial negotiation processes include the redefining of roles of indigenous leaders and the creation of new leadership positions as well as the growing complexity of imperial bureaucracy as some positions and institutions were reshaped or enhanced and new positions and institutions were created.

While sharing certain ideas and concerns, the scholars contributing to this volume certainly have neither identical theoretical orientations nor projects. Their approaches, nonetheless, suggest ways that scholarly interest has focused on indigenous engagement with law and negotiations between Spanish and native officials. The investigation of the latter's creative deployments of Spanish legal and political institutions and officials has led ethnohistorians from both sides of the border to consider much more deeply the interplay of cultural, political, material, and environmental factors in order to explain the development of the colonial legal culture. For example, the development of colonial indigenous legal discourses, whether in native or Spanish languages, used traditional political and kinship concepts, rhetorics, and symbols in new ways and depended on ecological frameworks for the production of material resources that made legal participation possible. The essays also demonstrate that diverse regional and temporal cultural expressions of negotiation existed. While indigenous allusions to war and the emphasis on social hierarchy are apparent in both Ruiz Medrano's and Osowski's essays, the urban milieu and Mexico City as the seat of Spanish power certainly shaped the range of responses possible in that area. In Oaxaca, indigenous conceptions of kinship and the sacred relationships between land and people remain evident in the legal documents of the eighteenth century. In the northern border area, native patterns of political decision making are easily discernible, and in the south, the complex patterns of movement that contributed to eth-nogenesis prior to the arrival of Europeans can be seen to have influenced Maya interactions with the loose, but still meaningful, network of Spanish judicial authority in the region.

While the influence on colonial studies of Edward Said's *Orientalism* has become obvious in works that show how colonial powers constructed colonial subjects, the continuing influence of Ranajit Guha's *Elementary Aspects of Peasant Insurgency in Colonial India* also is evident in the essays in this volume. The authors aim to perceive and analyze the consciousness of subjects, almost always through the opaque, official forms of documenta-tion that the legal system has bequeathed us, even as colonial authorities sought to remake that consciousness in part through the legal system and its practices and forms of documentation.[5] The research indicates that even the cogs of Spanish empire, whose energies so often were spent producing wealth for that empire, learned about and developed innovative ways to negotiate with the representatives of that empire.[6] They did so in order to protect shared identities, ways of life, and modes of autonomy, trying to keep these out of the reach of Spanish officials and a bureaucratizing empire and state in formation operating according to an abstract logic far removed, spatially and ideologically, from the villages, towns, and cities of indigenous New Spain.

Future scholarship might examine in greater depth the legal and political dealings of seventeenth-century native communities and regions, which receive less attention here.[7] Because the intense crises of cultural clash created in the sixteenth century had subsided and the Hapsburg state was maturing, although Bourbon officials had not yet imposed their distinct and more absolutist pattern of rule that undermined processes of negotiation, the legal culture of indigenous communities during those years deserves further study. Nonetheless, as the essays here show, even in the eighteenth century, negotiation within domination was still possible and remained fundamental to the workings of colonial law and politics.

NOTES

1. Tamar Herzog, *Upholding Justice: Society, State, and the Penal System in Quito (1650–1750)* (Ann Arbor: University of Michigan Press, 2004), 258.

2. This intermingling would prove difficult to disentangle during the nine-teenth and even twentieth centuries. While recent historical studies of the evolu-tion of the Mexican criminal legal system slight the legacy of the colonial system in the shape and functioning of that system's development, it could be argued that, even today, the multiple sources of power within and around and the "story-telling" aspects (i.e., the narrative component of written legal cases) of the legal

system, characteristics that are clearly colonial, play a role in impeding current efforts at reform (including efforts at creating an oral, adversarial trial system instead of a written system). On crime and justice in the late nineteenth and early twentieth centuries, see Robert Buffington, *Criminal and Citizen in Modern Mexico* (Lincoln: University of Nebraska Press, 2000); Pablo Piccato, *City of Suspects: Crime in Mexico City, 1900–1931* (Durham, NC: Duke University Press, 2001); Cristina Rivera Garza, "The Masters of the Streets: Bodies, Power and Modernity in Mexico, 1867–1930" (Ph.D. dissertation, University of Houston, Houston, 1995); Elisa Speckman Guerra, *Crimen y castigo: Legislación penal, interpretaciones de la criminalidad y administración de justicia (Ciudad de México, 1872–1910)* (México DF: El Colegio de México and UNAM, 2002); and Beatriz Urías Horcasitas, *Indígena y criminal: Interpretaciones del derecho y la antropología en México, 1871–1921* (México DF: Universidad Ibero-Americana, 2000). On the role of narrative in early colonial legal cases involving indigenous litigants, see Susan Kellogg, *Law and the Transformation of Aztec Culture, 1500–1700* (Norman: University of Oklahoma Press, 1995), chap. 2. On reform, see Sergio López Ayllon, *Las transformaciones del sistema jurídico y los significados sociales del derecho en México: La encrucijada entre tradición y modernidad* (México DF: UNAM, 1997).

3. Susan Deeds, *Defiance and Deference in Mexico's Colonial North: Indians under Spanish Rule in Nueva Vizcaya* (Austin: University of Texas Press, 2003), 6–7. Also see Cynthia Radding's discussion of the concept of "social ecology" in her book *Wandering Peoples: Colonialism, Ethnic Spaces, and Ecological Frontiers in Northwestern Mexico, 1700–1850* (Durham, NC: Duke University Press, 1997), 3–4.

4. Deeds, *Defiance and Deference*, 6.

5. Edward Said, *Orientalism* (New York: Pantheon, 1978); Ranajit Guha, *Elementary Aspects of Peasant Insurgency in Colonial India* (Delhi: Oxford University Press, 1983). Studies that analyze how imperial powers construct their subjects include Nicholas Thomas, *Colonialism's Culture: Anthropology, Travel, and Government* (Princeton, NJ: Princeton University Press, 1994); and Nicholas B. Dirks, *Castes of Mind: Colonialism and the Making of Modern India* (Princeton, NJ: Princeton University Press, 2001). For a comparative overview of studies of colonialism, see Frederick Cooper, *Colonialism in Question: Theory, Knowledge, History* (Berkeley: University of California Press, 2005).

6. The colonial legal system could be seen as "a school in interethnic relations"; Kellogg, *Law and the Transformation of Aztec Culture*, 4. Also see Brian P. Owensby, *Empire of Law and Indian Justice in Colonial Mexico* (Stanford, CA: Stanford University Press, 2008), 41.

7. The seventeenth century is taken up in a general way in Owensby, *Empire of Law and Indian Justice*. Showing how indigenous people and communities used law as a practical tool of political, moral, and social negotiation during the seventeenth century, the book spans widely across central and parts of northern Mexico yet leaves room for more community-, culture-, and region-specific examinations of colonial legal practices.

Bibliography

Note: Archival citations can be found in the endnotes of the individual chapters.

Alcina Franch, José. *Calendario y religión entre los zapotecos.* México DF: Universidad Nacional Autónoma de México, 1993.

Altamira, Rafael. *Manual de investigación de la historia del derecho indiano.* México DF: Instituto Panamericano de Geografía e Historia, 1948.

———. *Técnica de investigación en la historia del derecho indiano.* México DF: J. Porrúa e Hijos, 1939.

Anales Antiguous de México y sus contornos. *Anales antiguos de México y sus contornos.* Trans. Faustino Chimalpopoca Galicia, ed. J. Fernando Ramírez, 4 vols. México DF: Editor Vargas Rea, 1948.

Angulo, Mercedes Meade de. *Erección de Tlaxcala en Ciudad de el año de 1525 por el Papa Clemente.* Tlaxcala, Mexico: Gobierno del Estado de Tlaxcala, 1981.

Anzoátegui, Victor Tau. *El poder de la costumbre: Estudios sobre el derecho consuetudinario en América hispana hasta la emancipación.* Buenos Aires: Instituto de Investigaciones de Historia del Derecho, 2001.

Armendares, Teresa Lozano. *La criminalidad en la ciudad de México, 1800–1821.* México DF: UNAM, 1987.

Assadourian, Carlos Sempat. "La despoblación indígena en Perú y Nueva España durante el siglo XVI y la formación de la economía colonial." *Historia Mexicana* 38, no. 3 (1989): 419–454.

———, and Andrea Martínez Baracs, eds. *Tlaxcala, textos de su historia: Siglo XVI*, 16 vols. Tlaxcala: Gobierno del Estado de Tlaxcala, 1991.

Ávila, Carlos Lázaro. "El reformismo borbónico y los indígenas fronterizos americanos." In *El reformismo borbónico: Una vision interdisciplinario*, ed. Agustín Guimerá. Madrid: CSIC, Alianza Editorial, Fundación Mapfre América, 1996.

Baber, R. Jovita. "The Construction of Empire: Politics, Law and Community in Tlaxcala, New Spain, 1521–1640." Ph.D. dissertation, University of Chicago, Chicago, 2005.

Baer, Phillip, and William R. Merrifield. *Los Lacandones de México: Dos estudios*, trans. Carmen Viqueira. México DF: Instituto Nacional Indigenista, 1972.

Bakhtin, M. M. *The Dialogic Imagination*, ed. Michael Holquist, trans. Caryl Emerson and Michael Holquist. Austin: University of Texas Press, 1981.

Barrientos Grandón, Javier. *La cultura juridica en la Nueva España*. México DF: UNAM, 1993.

Baudot, Georges. *La pugna franciscana por México*. México DF: Alianza Editorial-Conaculta, 1990.

———. *Utopia and History in Mexico: The First Chroniclers of Mexican Civilization (1521–1569)*. Boulder: University Press of Colorado, 1995.

Bautista, Juan. *¿Como te confundes? ¿Acaso no somos conquistados? Anales de Juan Bautista*, trans. and ed. Luis Reyes García. México DF: CIESAS, Biblioteca Lorenzo Boturini y Nacional Basílica de Guadalupe, 2001 [1560s].

Beezley, William, Cheryl English Martin, and William E. French, eds. *Rituals of Rule, Rituals of Resistance: Public Celebrations and Popular Culture in Mexico*. Wilmington, DE: Scholarly Resources, 1994.

Benton, Lauren A. *Law and Colonial Cultures: Legal Regimes in World History, 1400–1900*. Cambridge: Cambridge University Press, 2002.

Berlin, Isaiah. *El sentido de la realidad: Sobre las ideas y su historia*. España: Taurus, 2000.

Bernal, Beatriz. "Estudio crítico al cedulario de Alonso Zorita." In *Leyes y ordenanzas realizes de las Indias del Mar océano*, ed. Alonso Zorita, 31–142. México DF: Miguel Ángel Porrúa, 1985 [1574].

Bierhost, John. *Cantares Mexicanos: Songs of the Aztecs*. Stanford, CA: Stanford University Press, 1985.

Bloch, Marc. *Los reyes taumaturgos*. México DF: Fondo de Cultura Económica, 1988.

Bonfil Batalla, Guillermo. *México profundo: Una civilización negada*. México DF: SEP and CIESAS, 1987.

Boone, Elizabeth Hill. "Migration Histories as Ritual Performance." In *Aztec Ceremonial Landscapes*, ed. Davíd Carrasco, 121–151. Niwot: University of Colorado Press, 1991.

Borah, Woodrow. *Justice by Insurance: The General Indian Court of Colonial Mexico and the Legal Aides of the Half-Real*. Berkeley: University of California Press, 1983.

———. "The Spanish and Indian Law: New Spain." In *The Inca and Aztec States, 1400–1800,* ed. George A. Collier, Renato I. Rosaldo, and John D. Wirth, 265–288. New York: Academic Press, 1982.

Bracamonte y Sosa, Pedro. *La conquista inconclusa de Yucatán.* México DF: Miguel Angel Porrúa, 1997.

———. *La memoria enclaustrada: Historia indígena de Yucatán 1750–1915.* México DF: CIESAS, 1994.

Brading, D. A. *Church and State in Bourbon Mexico: The Diocese of Michoacan, 1749–1810.* Cambridge: Cambridge University Press, 1994.

———. *Miners and Merchants in Bourbon Mexico, 1763–1810.* Cambridge: Cambridge University Press, 1971.

Braswell, Geoffrey E. "Introduction: Reinterpreting Early Classic Interaction." In *The Maya and Teotihuacan: Reinterpreting Early Classic Interaction,* ed. Geoffrey Braswell, 1–43. Austin: University of Texas Press, 2003.

Bruce, Robert D. *El libro de Chan K'in.* México DF: Instituto Nacional de Antropología e Historia, 1982.

Buffington, Robert. *Criminal and Citizen in Modern Mexico.* Lincoln: University of Nebraska Press, 2000.

Buhle, Paul, ed. *History and the New Left: Madison, Wisconsin, 1950–1970.* Philadelphia: Temple University Press, 1990.

Burkhart, Louise M. *Holy Wednesday: A Nahua Drama from Early Colonial Mexico.* Philadelphia: University of Pennsylvania Press, 1996.

———. "Pious Performances: Christian Pageantry and Native Identity in Early Colonial Mexico." In *Native Traditions in the Postconquest World,* ed. Elizabeth Hill Boone and Tom Cummins, 361–381.Washington, DC: Dumbarton Oaks, 1998.

———. *The Slippery Earth: Nahua-Christian Moral Dialogue in Sixteenth Century Mexico.* Tucson: University of Arizona Press, 1989.

Buzzanco, Robert. *Vietnam and the Transformation of American Life.* Malden, MA: Blackwell, 1999.

Cahill, David. "Popular Religion and Appropriation: The Example of Corpus Christi in the Eighteenth Century." *Latin American Research Review* 31 (1996): 67–110.

Campillo y Cosío, Joseph de. *Nuevo sistema de gobierno económico para la América.* México DF: Facultad de Economía, UNAM, 1993 [1789].

Cañeque, Alejandro. *The King's Living Image: The Culture and Politics of Viceregal Power in Colonial Mexico.* New York: Routledge, 2004.

Carey, Elaine. *Plaza of Sacrifices: Gender, Power, and Terror in 1968 Mexico.* Albuquerque: University of New Mexico Press, 2005.

Carlos V. *Documentos y Reales Cédulas de la Ciudad de Tlaxcala,* ed. Mercedes Meade de Angulo. Tlaxcala: Gobierno del Estado de Tlaxcala a través del Instituto Tlaxcalteca de la Cultura, 1984.

Carmagnani, Marcello. *El regreso de los dioses: El proceso de reconstitución de la identidad étnica en Oaxaca, siglos XVII y XVIII.* México DF: Fondo de Cultura Económica, 1988.

————. "Local Governments and Ethnic Governments in Oaxaca." In *Essays in the Political, Economic and Social History of Colonial Latin America*, ed. Karen Spalding, 107–124. Newark: University of Delaware, 1982.

Castañeda, Carlos E. "The *Corregidor* in Spanish Colonial Administration." *Hispanic American Historical Review* 9, no. 4 (1929): 446–470.

Castañeda de la Paz, María. "El plano parcial de la Ciudad de México: Nueva aportaciones en base al estudio de su lista de tlatoques." In *Símbolos de poder en Mesoamérica*, ed. Guilhem Olivier, 393–426. México DF: Instituto de Investigaciones Antropológicas, Instituto de Investigaciones Históricas, UNAM, 2008.

Castro Gutierrez, Felipe. *Nueva ley y nueva rey: Reformas borbonicas y rebelión popular en Nueva España*. Michoacan: UNAM, 1996.

Celestino Solís, Eustaquio, Armando Valencia Rios, and Constantino Medina Lima, ed. *Actas de Cabildo de Tlaxcala, 1547–1567*. México DF: AGN, CIESAS, and Instituto Tlaxcalteca de la Cultura, 1985.

Chamberlain, Robert S. "The *Corregidor* in Castile in the Sixteenth Century and the *Residencia* as Applied to the *Corregidor*." *Hispanic American Historical Review* 23 (1943): 222–257.

Chance, John K. "The *Barrios* of Tecali: Patronage, Kinship, and Territorial Relations in a Central Mexican Community." *Ethnology* 35, no. 2 (1996): 107–140.

————. "The *Caciques* of Tecali: Class and Ethnic Identity in Late Colonial Mexico." *Hispanic American Historical Review* 76, no. 3 (1996): 475–502.

————. *Conquest of the Sierra: Spaniards and Indians in Colonial Oaxaca*. Norman: University of Oklahoma Press, 1989.

————. "The Noble House in Colonial Puebla, Mexico: Descent, Inheritance, and the Nahua Tradition." *American Anthropologist* 102, no. 3 (2000): 485–502.

————, and William B. Taylor. "Cofradias and Cargos: An Historical Perspective on the Mesoamerican Civil-Religious Hierarchy." *American Ethnologist* 12 (1985): 1–26.

Chávez de Orozco, Luis, ed. *Códice Osuna*. México DF: Ediciones del Instituto Indigenista Interamericano, 1947 [1565].

Chávez Gómez, José Manuel A. "En busca del maíz perdido: La rebelion Itzá de 1699." *Mexicon* 25 (2003): 16–23.

————. *Intención franciscana de evangelizer entre los mayas rebeldes*. México DF: Conaculta, 2001.

Chevalier, François. *La formación de los latifundios en Mexico*. México DF: Fondo de Cultura Económica, 1982.

————. *Land and Society in Colonial Mexico: The Great Hacienda*, trans. Alvin Eustis. Berkeley: University of California Press, 1963.

Chilam Balam de Chumayel. *Chilam Balam de Chumayel*, ed. Mercedes de la Garza. México DF: Secretaría de Educación Pública, 1988 [1700s].

Chipman, Donald E. *Spanish Texas, 1519–1821*. Austin: University of Texas Press, 1992.

Códice Franciscano. *Códice Franciscano*, ed. Joaquín García Icazbalceta. México DF: Editorial Chavez Hayhoe, 1941 [1500s].

Colección de documentos inéditos para la historia de Ibero-América. *Colección de documentos inéditos para la historia de Ibero-América* Madrid: Archivo de Indias, 1927.

Colección de documentos inéditos relativos al descubrimiento, conquista y organización de las antiguas posesiones de ultramar. *Colección de documentos inéditos relativos al descubrimiento, conquista y organización de las antiguas posesiones de ultramar,* 21 vols. Madrid: Real Academia de la Historía, 1885–1932.

Collier, Jane F. "El anhelo de conserver y la necesidad de perderse 'Cortacabezas' en San Pedro Chenalhó, Chiapas, México." In *Estudios sobre la violencia: Teoría y práctica,* ed. Witold Jacorzynski. México DF: CIESAS, Miguel Angel Porrúa, 2002.

Concilios Provinciales Primero y Segundo, Celebrados en muy Noble y Muy Leal Ciudad de Mexico, Presidiendo el Illmo. y Rmo. Señor D. Fr. Alonso de Montufar, en los años de 1555 y 1565: Dalos a Luz el Ill.mo Sr. D. Francisco Antonio Lorenzana, Arzobispo de esta Santa Metropolitana Iglesia. *Concilios Provinciales Primero y Segundo, Celebrados en muy Noble y Muy Leal Ciudad de Mexico, Presidiendo el Illmo. y Rmo. Señor D. Fr. Alonso de Montufar, en los años de 1555 y 1565: Dalos a Luz el Ill.mo Sr. D. Francisco Antonio Lorenzana, Arzobispo de esta Santa Metropolitana Iglesia.* México DF: En la imprenta de el Superior Gobierno, 1769.

Contreras, Jaime. N.d. "Dios, casa y reynos: Felipe II; Católico pero no romano." Unpublished ms. Copy in Ruiz Medrano's possession.

Cooper, Frederick. *Colonialism in Question: Theory, Knowledge, History.* Berkeley: University of California Press, 2005.

Cope, R. Douglas. *The Limits of Racial Domination: Plebian Society in Colonial Mexico City, 1660–1720.* Madison: University of Wisconsin Press, 1994.

Córdova, Fray Juan de. *Vocabulario en lengua çapoteca,* edición facsimilar. Oaxaca, México DF: Ediciones Toledo, INAH, 1987 [1578].

Cornelius, Wayne A. *Mexican Politics in Transition: The Breakdown of a One-Party-Dominant Regime.* La Jolla: Center for U.S.-Mexican Studies, University of California, San Diego, 1996.

Covarrubias Orozco, Sebastián de. *Tesoro de la lengua castellana o española.* http://www.cervantesvirtual.com/servlet/SirveObras/80250529545703831976613/index.htm, 1611.

Crespo, José Antonio. *PRI: De la hegemonia a la oposición; Un estudio comparado, 1994–2001.* México DF: Centro de Estudios de Política Comparada, 2001.

Cruz Hernández, Deborah. 1998. "Lo que dicen los viejos." Unpublished ms. Copy in Angeles Romero's possession.

Curcio-Nagy, Linda. "Giants and Gypsies: Corpus Christi in Colonial Mexico City." In *Rituals of Rule, Rituals of Resistance,* ed. William Beezley, Cheryl English Martin, and William E. French, 1–26. Wilmington, DE: Scholarly Resources, 1994.

———. *The Great Festivals of Colonial Mexico City: Performing Power and Identity.* Albuquerque: University of New Mexico Press, 2004.

————. "Native Icon to City Protectress to Royal Patroness: Ritual, Political Symbolism and the Virgin of Remedies." *The Americas* 52 (1996): 367–391.

————. "Saints, Sovereignty and Spectacle in Colonial Mexico." Ph.D. dissertation, Tulane University, New Orleans, 1993.

Cutter, Charles R. *The Legal Culture of Northern New Spain, 1700–1810.* Albuquerque: University of New Mexico Press, 1995.

————. *The Protector de Indios in Colonial New Mexico, 1659–1821.* Albuquerque: University of New Mexico Press, 1986.

Dalí, Ross Roland. "Vasco de Quiroga's Thought on War: Its Erasmian and Utopian Roots." Ph.D. dissertation, Indiana University, Bloomington, 1975.

Dean, Carolyn. *Inka Bodies and the Body of Christ: Corpus Christi in Colonial Cuzco, Peru.* Durham, NC: Duke University Press, 1999.

Deans-Smith, Susan. "Culture, Power, and Society in Colonial Mexico." *Latin American Research Review* 33, no. 1 (1998): 257–277.

Deeds, Susan. *Defiance and Deference in Mexico's Colonial North: Indians under Spanish Rule in Nueva Vizcaya.* Austin: University of Texas Press, 2003.

Derrida, Jacques. *Writing and Difference.* Chicago: University of Chicago Press, 1978.

De Vos, Jan. *La paz de Dios y del Rey: La conquista de la selva Lacandona por los españoles, 1525–1821.* México DF: Fondo de Cultura Económica, 1988.

Dirks, Nicholas B. *Castes of Mind: Colonialism and the Making of Modern India.* Princeton, NJ: Princeton University Press, 2001.

Domínguez Ortiz, Antonio. *The Golden Age of Spain, 1516–1659,* trans. James Casey. New York: Basic Books, 1971.

Elliott, John Huxtable. *Imperial Spain, 1469–1716,* rep. ed. New York: Penguin Books, 1990.

Enciclopedia universal ilustrada Europeo-Americana. *Enciclopedia universal ilustrada Europeo-Americana.* Madrid: Espasa Calpe, 1989.

Encinas, Diego de, and Alfonso García Gallo. *Cedulario indiano: Reproducción facsimilar de la edición única de 1596,* 4 vols. Madrid: Cultura Hispánica, 1945–1946.

Esparza, Manuel. *Conflictos por límites de tierras, Oaxaca.* Oaxaca: Archivo General del Estado de Oaxaca, 1991.

Esquivel Obregón, Toribio. *Apuntes para la historia del derecho en México.* México DF: Editorial Polis, 1937.

Fago, Charles. "Philip II and the Cortes of Castile: The Case of the Cortes of 1576." *Past and Present* 109 (1985): 25–43.

Florescano, Enrique. "El canon memorioso forjado por los Títulos Primordiales." *Colonial Latin American Review* 11 (2002): 183–230.

————. *El nuevo pasado mexicano.* México DF: Cal y Arena, 1991.

————. *Historia de las historias de la nación mexicana.* México DF: Taurus, 2002.

Fragmento de la visita hecha a Antonio de Mendoza. "Fragmento de la visita hecha a Antonio de Mendoza." In *Colección de documentos para la historia de México,* ed. Joaquín García Icazbalceta, 2:72–140. México DF: Antigua Librería, 1866.

García Ayluardo, Clara. "Confraternity, Cult and Crown in Colonial Mexico City, 1700–1810." Ph.D. dissertation, Cambridge University, Cambridge, 1989.

———. "A World of Images: Cult, Ritual, and Society in Colonial Mexico City." In *Rituals of Rule, Rituals of Resistance*, ed. William Beezley, Cheryl English Martin, and William E. French, 77–93. Wilmington, DE: Scholarly Resources, 1994.

García Cook, Angel. *Tlaxcala: Una historia comparada, Los orígenes arqueología*, 16 vols. Tlaxcala, Mexico, and México DF: Gobierno del Estado de Tlaxcala and Consejo Nacional para la Cultura y las Artes, 1991.

García Gallo, Alfonso. "Cedulario de Alonso Zorita." In *Leyes y ordenanzas reales de las indias del Mar océano*, ed. Alonso Zorita, 15–26. México DF: Miguel Ángel Porrúa, 1985 [1574].

García Icazbalceta, Joaquín, ed. *Colección de documentos para la historia de México*, 2 vols. México DF: Antigua Librería, 1866.

García Martínez, Bernardo. *Los pueblos de la sierra: El poder y el espacio entre los indios del norte de Puebla hasta 1700*. México DF: El Colegio de México, 1987.

Garibay K., Ángel María. "Un cuadro real de la infiltración del hispanismo en la alma india en el llamado *Códice de Juan Bautista*." Dos conferencias sobre transculturación. *Filosofía y Letras* 9 (1945): 213–241.

Garza, Mercedes de la, ed. *Libro de Chilam Balam de Chumayel*. México DF: SEP, 1985 [1700s].

Gasco, Janine. "Recent Trends in Ethnohistoric Research on Postclassic and Colonial Central Mexico." *Latin American Research Review* 29, no. 1 (1994): 132–142.

Geertz, Clifford. *Local Knowledge: Further Essays in Interpretive Anthropology*. New York: Basic Books, Harper Collins Publishers, 1983.

Gerhard, Peter. *A Guide to the Historical Geography of New Spain*, rev. ed. Norman: University of Oklahoma Press, 1993.

Gibson, Charles. *The Aztecs under Spanish Rule: A History of the Indians of the Valley of Mexico, 1519–1810*. Stanford, CA: Stanford University Press, 1964.

———. *Tlaxcala in the Sixteenth Century*. New Haven, CT: Yale University Press, 1952. Reprint, Stanford, CA: Stanford University Press, 1967.

Giddens, Anthony. *The Constitution of Society: Outline of the Theory of Structuration*. Berkeley: University of California Press, 1984.

Gillow, Eulogio. *Apuntes históricos sobre la idolatría e introducción del cristianismo en Oaxaca*. México DF: Ediciones Toledo, 1990 [1889].

Gitlin, Todd. *The Sixties: Years of Hope, Days of Rage*. New York: Bantam Books, 1993.

Goldberg, Stephen B., Nancy H. Rogers, Sara Rudolph Cole, and Frank E.A. Sander. *Dispute Resolution: Negotiation, Mediation, and Other Processes*. Frederick, MD: Aspen Publishers, 2007.

González-Hermosillo Adams, Francisco, ed. *Gobierno y economía en los pueblos indios del México colonial*. México DF: INAH, 2001.

———, and Luis Reyes García, eds. *El codice de Cholula: La exaltación testimonial de un linaje indio*. México DF: INAH, 2002 [late 1500s].

Goody, Jack. *The Logic of Writing and the Organization of Society*: Cambridge: Cambridge University Press, 1986.

Gosner, Kevin. *Soldiers of the Virgin: The Moral Economy of a Colonial Maya Rebellion*. Tucson: University of Arizona Press, 1992.

Greenleaf, Richard E. "The Inquisition and the Indians of New Spain: A Study in Jurisdictional Confusion." *The Americas* 22 (1965): 139–165.

———. *La Inquisición en Nueva España siglos XVI*, 3rd ed. México DF: Fondo de Cultura Económica, 1995.

———. *The Mexican Inquisition of the Sixteenth Century*. Albuquerque: University of New Mexico Press, 1968.

———. "The Persistence of Native Values: The Inquisition and the Indians of Colonial Mexico." *The Americas* 50 (1994): 351–376.

Gruzinski, Serge. *The Conquest of Mexico*. Cambridge: Polity Press, 1993.

Guardino, Peter F. *The Time of Liberty: Popular Political Culture in Oaxaca, 1750–1850*. Durham, NC: Duke University Press, 2005.

Guha, Ranajit. *Elementary Aspects of Peasant Insurgency in Colonial India*. Delhi: Oxford University Press, 1983.

Gulliver, P. H. *Disputes and Negotiations: A Cross-Cultural Perspective*. New York: Academic Press, 1979.

Haliczer, Stephen. *The Comuneros of Castile: The Forging of a Revolution, 1475–1521*. Madison: University of Wisconsin Press, 1981.

Hall, Frederic. *The Laws of Mexico: A Compilation and Treatise Relating to Real Property, Mines, Water Rights, Personal Rights, Contracts, and Inheritances*. San Francisco: A. L. Bancroft, 1885.

Hämäläinen, Pekka. *The Comanche Empire*. New Haven, CT: Yale University Press, 2008.

Hampshire, Stuart. *Justice Is Conflict*. Princeton, NJ: Princeton University Press, 2000.

Harvey, Neil. *The Chiapas Rebellion: The Struggle for Land and Democracy*. Durham, NC: Duke University Press, 1998.

Haskett, Robert. *Indigenous Rulers: An Ethnohistory of Town Government in Colonial Cuernavaca*. Albuquerque: University of New Mexico Press, 1991.

Haslip Viera, Gabriel. *Crime and Punishment in Late Colonial Mexico City, 1692–1810*. Albuquerque: University of New Mexico Press, 1999.

Hemming, John. *La conquista de los incas*. México DF: Fondo de Cultural Económica, 1982.

Hernández Castillo, Aída. *Histories and Stories from Chiapas: Border Identities in Southern Mexico*, trans. Martha Pou. Austin: University of Texas Press, 2001.

Herrera y Tordesillas, Antonio de. *Historia general de los hechos de los castellanos en las Islas y Tierra Firme del mar oceano*. 8 vols. Madrid: En la Emprenta Real, (1601).

Herzog, Tamar. *Upholding Justice: Society, State, and the Penal System in Quito (1650–1750)*. Ann Arbor: University of Michigan Press, 2004.

Historia Mexicana. Special Issue: En Su Vigesimo Aniversario, *Historia Mexicana* 21, no. 2 (1972).

Hodges, Donald Clark. *Mexico: The End of the Revolution*. Westport, CT: Praeger, 2002.

Horcasitas, Fernando. *El Teatro Náhuatl: Épocas novohispana y moderna*, vol. 1. México DF: UNAM, 1974.

Icaza, Francisco A. "Miscelánea histórica." *Bibioteca de la Revista Mexicana de Estudios Históricos de los Pueblos*, Appendix 2 (1928): 5–112.

Indigenous Human Rights Declaration. http://www.un.org/esa/socdev/unpfii/en/drip.html. Accessed 2007.

Instituto Nacional Indigenista. *Sierra Juárez: Trabajo comunitario; Identitdad y memoria histórica de los pueblos*, 2 vols. México DF: Instituto Nacional Indigenista y Centro de Estudios Históricos del Agrarismo en México, 1994.

Isserman, Maurice, and Michael Kazin. *America Divided: The Civil War of the 1960s*. New York: Oxford University Press, 2000.

Jacorzynski, Witold. *Estudios sobre la violencia: Teoría y práctica*. México DF: CIESAS, Miguel Angel Porrúa, 2002.

Jaffary, Nora E. *False Mystics: Deviant Orthodoxy in Colonial Mexico*. Lincoln: University of Nebraska Press, 2004.

Jansen, Maarten. "La serpiente emplumada y el amanecer de la historia." In *Códices, caciques y comunidades: Cuadernos de Historia Lantinoamericana*, 5:11–64. The Netherlands: Asociación de Historiadores Latinoamericanistas Europeos, 1997.

John, Elizabeth A.H. *Storms Brewed in Other Men's Worlds: The Confrontation of Indians, Spanish, and French in the Southwest, 1540–1795*. College Station: Texas A&M University Press, 1975.

Jones, Grant D. *The Conquest of the Last Maya Kingdom*. Stanford, CA: Stanford University Press, 1998.

———. *Maya Resistance to Spanish Rule: Time and History on a Colonial Frontier*. Albuquerque: University of New Mexico Press, 1989.

Joseph, Gilbert M., ed. *Reclaiming the Political in Latin American History: Essays from the North*. Durham, NC: Duke University Press, 2001.

Kagan, Richard L. *Lawsuits and Litigants in Castile, 1500–1700*. Chapel Hill: University of North Carolina Press, 1981.

Karttunen, Frances. *Between Worlds: Interpreters, Guides, and Survivors*. New Brunswick, NJ: Rutgers University Press, 1994.

Keen, Benjamin. "Main Currents in United States Writings on Colonial Spanish America, 1884–1984." *Hispanic American Historical Review* 65 (1985): 657–682.

Kellogg, Susan. "Encountering People, Creating Texts; Cultural Studies of the Encounter and Beyond." *Latin American Research Review* 38, no. 3 (2003): 261–274.

———. "From Parallel and Equivalent to Separate but Unequal: Tenochca Mexica Women, 1500–1700." In *Indian Women of Early Mexico*, ed. Susan Shroeder, Stephanie Wood, and Robert Haskett, 123–143. Norman: University of Oklahoma Press, 1997.

———. *Law and the Transformation of Aztec Culture, 1500–1700*. Norman: University of Oklahoma Press, 1995.

Kicza, John. "Recent Books on Ethnohistory and Ethnic Relations in Colonial Mexico." *Latin American Research Review* 30, no. 3 (1995): 239–253.

———. "The Social and Ethnic Historiography of Colonial Latin America: The Last Twenty Years." *William and Mary Quarterly*, 3rd ser. 44 (1988): 453–488.

Kirchoff, Paul, Lina Odena Güemes, and Luis Reyes Garcia, eds. *Historia tolteca-chichimeca*. México DF: INAH, 1976 [ca. 1550].

Konetzke, Richard. *Colección de documentos para la historia de la formación social de Hispanoamérica, 1493–1810*. 3 vols. Madrid: Consejo Superior de Investigaciones Cientificas, 1953.

Langer, Erick D., ed. *Contemporary Indigenous Movements in Latin America*. Wilmington, DE: SR Books, 2003.

"Las Representaciones Teatrales de la Pasión." *Boletín del Archivo General de la Nación* 5, no. 3 (May–June 1934): n.p.

Lazarus-Black, Mindie. *Legitimate Acts and Illegal Encounters: Law and Society in Antigua and Barbuda*. Washington, DC: Smithsonian Institution Press, 1994.

León Portilla, Miguel. *La filosofía náhuatl*. México DF: UNAM, 1993.

Levene, Ricardo. *Introducción a la historia del derecho indiano*. Buenos Aires: V. Abelardo, 1924.

Lira González, Andres. *El amparo colonial y el juicio de amparo mexicano (antecedentes novohispanos del juicio de amparo)*. México DF: Fondo de Cultura Económica, 1972.

Lledó, Emilio. *La memoria del logos: Estudios sobre el diálogo platónico*. Madrid: Taurus, 1996.

Lockhart, James. "Charles Gibson and the Ethnohistory of Postconquest Central Mexico." In *Nahuas and Spaniards: Postconquest Central Mexican History and Philology*, by James Lockhart, 159–182. Stanford and Los Angeles: Stanford University Press and UCLA Latin American Center Publications, 1991.

———. "Encomienda and Hacienda: The Evolution of the Great Estate in the Spanish Indies." *Hispanic American Historical Review* 49 (1969): 411–429.

———. "A Historian and the Disciplines." In *Of Things of the Indies: Essays Old and New in Early Latin American History*, by James Lockhart, 333–367. Stanford, CA: Stanford University Press, 1999.

———. *The Nahuas after the Conquest*. Stanford, CA: Stanford University Press, 1992.

———. *Nahuas and Spaniards: Postconquest Central Mexican History and Philology*. Nahuatl Studies Series, no. 3. Stanford, CA: Stanford University Press, 1991.

———. "Some Nahua Concepts in Postconquest Guise." *History of European Ideas* 6, no. 4 (1985): 465–482.

———. "A Vein of Ethnohistory: Recent Nahuatl-based Historical Research." In *Nahuas and Spaniards: Postconquest Central Mexican History and Philology*, by James Lockhart, 183–200. Stanford and Los Angeles: Stanford University Press and UCLA Latin American Center Publications, 1991.

———, Frances Berden, and Arthur J.O. Anderson. "Preliminary Study: Some Themes in the Actas." In *The Tlaxcalan Actas: A Compendium of the Records of the Cabildo of Tlaxcala, 1545–1627*. Salt Lake City: University of Utah Press, 1986.

————, ed. *The Tlaxcalan Actas: A Compendium of the Records of the Cabildo of Tlaxcala, 1545–1627*. Salt Lake City: University of Utah Press, 1986.

López Austin, Alfredo. "Los reyes subterráneos." II Congreso Internacional de Cultura Maya, N.d. Copy in Ruiz Medrano's possession.

López Ayllon, Sergio. *Las transformaciones del sistema jurídico y los significados sociales del derecho en México: La encrucijada entre tradición y modernidad*. México DF: UNAM, 1997.

López García, Ubaldo. "Las elecciones tradicionales y los cambios actuales." In *Memoria de la Tercera Mesa Redonda de Monte Albán*, 371–404. México DF: INAH, 2004.

Lorenzana y Butrón, Archbishop Francisco. "Reglas para que los naturales de estos reynos sean felices en lo espiritual, y temporal," June 20, 1768. Condumex, México DF.

Losada, Teresa. *Rebelion desde la cultura*. México DF: Editorial Joaquin Mortiz, 1988.

Lundberg, Magnus. *Unification and Conflict: The Church Politics of Alonso de Montúfar OP, Archbishop of Mexico, 1554–1572*. Lund, Sweden: Lund University, 2002.

Lunenfeld, Marvin. *Keepers of the City: The Corregidores of Isabella I of Castile, 1474–1504*. Cambridge: Cambridge University Press, 1987.

Lynch, John. *Bourbon Spain: 1700–1808*. Cambridge: Basil Blackwell, 1989.

————. *Spain under the Hapsburgs: Empire and Absolutism, 1516–1598*. 2 vols. New York: Oxford University Press, 1981.

MacLachlan, Colin. *Criminal Justice in Eighteenth-Century Mexico: A Study of the Tribunal of the Acordada*. Berkeley: University of California Press, 1974.

MacLeod, Murdo J. "Mesoamerica since the Spanish Invasion: An Overview." In *The Cambridge History of the Native Peoples of the Americas*, vol. 2, part 2, Mesoamerica, ed. Richard E.W. Adams and Murdo J. MacLeod, 1–43. New York: Cambridge University Press, 2001.

Magallon Ibarra, Jorge Mario. *Los sonidos y el silencio de la jurisprudencia mexicana*. México DF: UNAM, 2004.

Margardant S., Guillermo Floris. *Introducción a la historia del derecho mexicano*. México DF: UNAM, 1971.

Martin, Cheryl English. *Governance and Society in Colonial Mexico: Chihuahua in the Eighteenth Century*. Stanford, CA: Stanford University Press, 1996.

Martínez, Hildeberto. *Codiciaban la tierra: El despojo agrario en los señoríos de Tecamachalco y Quecholac (Puebla, 1520–1650)*. México DF: CIESAS, 1994.

————. *Tepeaca en el siglo XVI: Tenencia de la tierra y organización de un señorío*. México DF: CIESAS, 1984.

Martínez Baracs, Andrea Guadalupe. "El gobierno indio de la Tlaxcala colonial, 1521–1700." Ph.D. dissertation, El Colegio de México, México DF, 1998.

Martínez Martínez, Juan Carlos. "El expediente judicial desde una perspective dialógica: Heteroglosia o monoglosia?" *Cuadernos del Sur* 19 (2003): 43–50.

Maybury-Lewis, David, ed. *The Politics of Ethnicity: Indigenous Peoples in Latin American States*. Cambridge, MA: The David Rockefeller Center Series on Latin American Studies, Harvard University, 2002.

McBride, George. *The Land Systems of Mexico*. New York: American Geographical Society, 1923.

Meade de Angulo, Mercedes. "Introducción." In *Documentos y Reales Cédulas de la Ciudad de Tlaxcala*, ed. Mercedes Meade de Angulo, 1–4. Tlaxcala, México: Gobierno del Estado de Tlaxcala a través del Instituto Tlaxcateca de la Cultura, 1984.

Mendieta, Fray Gerónimo de. *Historia eclesiástica indiana*, 3rd facsimile ed. México DF: Editorial Porrúa, 1980 [1596].

Mendoza, Don Antonio de. "Fragmento de la visita hecha á don Antonio de Mendoza." In *Colección de documentos para la historia de México*, ed. Joaquín García Icazbalceta, 2:72–140. México DF: Antigua Librería, 1866.

Menegus Bornemann, Margarita. *Del señorío indígena a la república de indios: El caso de Toluca, 1500–1600*. México DF: Consejo Nacional para la Cultura y las Artes, 1994.

———, and Rodolfo Aguirre. *Los indios, el sacerdocio y la universidad en Nueva España, siglos XVI–XVIII*. México DF: Centro de Estudios sobre la Universidad, UNAM, Plaza y Valdés, 2006.

Merry, Sally Engle. *Colonizing Hawai'i: The Cultural Power of Law*. Princeton, NJ: Princeton University Press, 2000.

———. *Getting Justice and Getting Even: Legal Consciousness among Working Class Americans*. Chicago: University of Chicago Press, 1990.

Metcalf, Alida. *Go-Betweens and the Colonization of Brazil, 1500–1600*. Austin: University of Texas Press, 2005.

Miceli, Paola. "El derecho consuetudinario en Castilla: Una crítica a la matriz romántica de las interpretaciones sobre la costumbre." *Hispania* 63/1, no. 213 (2002): 9–28.

Mills, Kenneth. *Idolatry and Its Enemies: Colonial Andean Religion and Extirpation, 1640–1750*. Princeton, NJ: Princeton University Press, 1997.

Miranda, José. *El tributo indígena en la Nueva España durante el siglo XVI*. México DF: El Colegio de México, 1980.

———. *Evolución cuantitativa y desplazmientos de la población indígena de Oaxaca en la época colonial*. *Estudios de Historia Novohispana* 2 (1968): 129–147.

Mirow, M. C. *Latin American Law: A History of Private Law and Institutions in Spanish America*. Austin: University of Texas Press, 2004.

Moore, Sally Falk. *Social Facts and Fabrications: "Customary" Law on Kilimanjaro, 1880–1980*. Cambridge: Cambridge University Press, 1986.

Moorhead, Max L. *The Apache Frontier: Jacobo de Ugarte and Spanish-Indian Relations in Northern New Spain, 1769–1791*. Norman: University of Oklahoma Press, 1968.

Motolinía, Toribio. *Historia de los indios de la Nueva España*, ed. Claudio Esteva Fabregat. Madrid: Historia 16, 1985 [1530s–1540s].

———. *Memoriales o Libro de las cosas de la Nueva España y de los naturales de ella*, 2nd ed., ed. Edmundo O'Gorman. México DF: UNAM, 1971 [1530s–1540s].

Murdock, George. *Social Structure*. New York: The Free Press, 1949.

Nader, Helen. *Liberty in Absolutist Spain: The Habsburg Sale of Towns, 1516–1700*. Baltimore, MD: Johns Hopkins University Press, 1990.

Nader, Laura. *The Life of the Law: Anthropological Projects.* Berkeley: University of California Press, 2002.

Navarro García, Luis. *Don José de Gálvez y la Comandancia General de las Provincias Internas del norte de Nueva España.* Sevilla: Escuela de Estudios Hispano-Americanos de Sevilla, 1964.

Nutini, Hugo G. *Ritual Kinship: The Structure and Historical Development of the Compadrazgo System in Rural Tlaxcala.* 2 vols. Princeton, NJ: Princeton University Press, 1980–1984.

Obregón. Luis G. *Rebeliones indígenas y precursores de la independencia mexicana: En los siglos XVI, XVII y XVIII,* 2nd ed. México DF: Ediciones Fuente Cultural, 1952.

Ochoa, Lorenzo. *Renunciar al paraíso: Paisaje y arqueología en las Tierras Bajas pantanosas de la Cuenca del San Pedro y San Pablo y Xicalango, Campeche.* Campeche: Instituto Campechano, Gobierno del Estado de Campeche, Instituto de Cultura de Campeche, 1997.

O'Conor, Hugo de. *Informe de Hugo de O'Conor sobre el estado de las Provincias Internas del norte, 1771–76.* México DF: Editorial Cultura, 1952.

Olivera, Mercedes. *Pillis y macehuales: Las formaciones sociales y los modos de producción de Tecali del siglos XII al XVI.* México DF: CIESAS, 1978.

Orozco, Luis Chávez de. *Códice Osuna.* México DF: Ediciones del Instituto Indigenista Interamericano, 1947 [1565].

Orozco y Berra, Manuel. *Noticia histórica de la conjuración del Marqués del Valle: Años de 1565–1568; Formada de nuevos documentos orginales y seguida de un extracto de los mismos documentos.* México DF: Edición del Universal, Tipografía de R. Rafael, 1853.

Osborne, Wayne. "Indian Land Retention in Colonial Metztitlán." *Hispanic American Historical Review* 53 (1973): 217–238.

Ots Capdequí, José María. *El estado español en las Indias.* México DF: El Colegio de México, 1941.

———. *Manual de historia de derecho español en las Indias y del derecho propiamente indiano.* Buenos Aires: Talleres Gráficos de A. Baiocco, 1943.

Oudijk, Michel R. "Espacio y escritura: El Lienzo de Tabaá." In *Escritura zapoteca, 2500 años de historia,* ed. María de los Ángeles Romero Frizzi. México DF: CIESAS, INAH, 2003.

———. *Historiography of the Bènizàa: The Postclassic and Early Colonial Period.* Leiden, The Netherlands: Research School of Asian, African and Amerindian Studies, 2000.

———. "La toma de posesión: Un tema mesoamericano para la legitimación del poder." *Relaciones* [El Colegio de Michoacán] 91 (2002): 97–131.

———. "The Zapotec City-State." In *A Comparative Study of Six City-States,* ed. Mogens Herman Hansen, 73–90. Copenhagen: Copenhagen Polis Centre, The Royal Danish Academy of Sciences and Letters, 2002.

Ouweneel, Arij, and Simon Miller, eds. *The Indian Community of Colonial Mexico: Fifteen Essays on Land Tenure, Corporate Organization, Ideology and Village Politics.* Amsterdam: Center for Latin American Research and Documentation, 1990.

Owensby, Brian P. *Empire of Law and Indian Justice in Colonial Mexico*. Stanford, CA: Stanford University Press, 2008.

Pagden, Anthony. *Señores de todo el mundo, ideologías del imperio en España, Inglaterra y Francia (en los siglos XVI, XVII Y XVIII)*. Barcelona: Península, 1997.

———. *Spanish Imperialism and the Political Imagination: Studies in European and Spanish-American Social and Political Theory, 1513–1830*. New Haven, CT: Yale University Press, 1990.

———. "Translator's Introduction." In *Hernán Cortés: Letters from Mexico*, trans. and ed. Anthony Pagden, xxxix–lxxi. New York: Orion Press, 1971.

Paso y Troncoso, Francisco del, ed. *Epistolario de Nueva España*. 16 vols. México DF: Biblioteca Histórica Mexicana de Obras Inéditas, 2nd ed., Antigua Librería Robredo de José Porrúa e Hijos, 1939–1942.

Patch, Robert W. "Indian Resistance to Colonialism." In *The Oxford History of Mexico*, ed. Michael C. Meyer and William H. Beezley, 183–211. New York: Oxford University Press, 2000.

———. *Maya Revolt and Revolution in the Eighteenth Century*. Armonk, NY: M. E. Sharpe, 2002.

Peñafiel, Antonio. *Ciudades coloniales y capitales de la República mexicana*. 2 vols. México DF: Impr. y Fototipia de la Secretaría de Fomento, 1908.

Piccato, Pablo. *City of Suspects: Crime in Mexico City, 1900–31*. Durham, NC: Duke University Press, 2001.

Poniatowska, Elena. *La noche de Tlatelolco: Testimonios de historia oral*. México DF: Ediciones Era, 1971.

Preston, Julia, and Samuel Dillon. *Opening Mexico: The Making of a Democracy*. New York: Farrar, Straus and Giroux, 2004.

Radding, Cynthia. "Cultural Dialogues: Recent Trends in Mesoamerican Ethnohistory." *Latin American Research Review* 33, no. 1 (1998): 193–211.

———. *Wandering Peoples: Colonialism, Ethnic Spaces, and Ecological Frontiers in Northwestern Mexico, 1700–1850*. Durham, NC: Duke University Press, 1997.

Recopilación de Leyes de los Reynos de las Indias. *Recopilación de Leyes de los Reynos de las Indias*, 4 vols., 3rd ed. Madrid: Mandadas Imprimir y Publicar por la Magestad Católica del Rey Don Carlos II, 1774 [1681].

———. *Recopilación de Leyes de los Reynos de las Indias*, 3 vols. Madrid: Imprenta Nacional del Boletín Oficial del Estado, 1998 [1681].

Restall, Matthew. "A History of the New Philology and the New Philology in History." *Latin American Research Review* 38, no. 1 (2003): 113–134.

———. *Maya Conquistador*. Boston: Beacon Press, 1998.

Reyes García, Luis, ed. and trans. *¿Como te confundes? ¿Acaso no somos conquistados? Anales de Juan Bautista*. México DF: CIESAS, 2001 [1560s].

———, ed. *Documentos nauas de la Ciudad de México del siglo XVI*. México DF: CIESAS y Archivo General de la Nación, 1996.

———, ed. *Documentos sobre tierras y señorios en Cuauhtinchan*. México DF and Puebla: Fondo de Cultural Económica and Estado de Puebla, 1988.

Ricard, Robert. *La conquista espiritual de México*, trans. Angel María Garibay. México DF: Editorial Jus, 1947.

"The Rights of Indigenous Peoples." Fact Sheet No. 9 (Rev. 1), Office of the High Commissioner for Human Rights, 1995. http://www.unhchr.ch/html/menu6 /2/fs9.htm. Accessed March 3, 2005.

Rivera Garza, Cristina. "The Masters of the Streets: Bodies, Power and Modernity in Mexico, 1867–1930." Ph.D. dissertation, University of Houston, Houston, 1995.

Romero Frizzi, María de los Angeles. *El sol y la cruz: Los pueblos indios de Oaxaca colonial.* México DF: CIESAS, 1996.

———. "Los cantos de los linajes en el mundo colonial." *Memorias de la Academia Mexicana de la Historia* 43 (2000): 41–60.

———, and Juana Vásquez. "Memoria y escritura: La Memoria de Juquila." In *Escritura zapoteca, 2500 años de historia,* by María de los Ángeles Romero Frizzi, 393–448. México DF: CIESAS, INAH, 2003.

Ruiz Medrano, Ethelia. "Las primeras institucions del poder colonial." In *Gran historia de México ilustrada,* 4 vols., ed. Bernardo García Martínez, 2:41–60. México DF: Planeta de Agostini, CONACULTA, INAH, 2002.

———. "Los negocios de un arzobispo: El caso de fray Alonso de Montúfar." *Estudios de Historia Novohispana* 12 (1992): 63–83.

———. *Mexico's Indigenous Communities: Their Lands and Histories.* Boulder: University Press of Colorado, 2010.

———. *Reshaping New Spain: Government and Private Interests in the Colonial Bureaucracy, 1531–1550.* Boulder: University Press of Colorado, 2006.

Sahagún, Fray Bernardino de. *Florentine Codex,* Book 7, Part 8, trans. Arthur J.O. Anderson and Charles E. Dibble. Santa Fe, NM, and Salt Lake City: School of American Research and the University of Utah Press, 1977 [1569].

———. *Historia general de las cosas de la Nueva España,* 2 vols. México DF: Consejo Nacional para la Cultura y las Artes, Alianza Editorial Mexicana, 1989 [1570s].

Said, Edward. *Orientalism.* New York: Pantheon, 1978.

Salvatore, Ricardo D., Carlos Aguirre, and Gilbert M. Joseph, eds. *Crime and Punishment in Latin America: Law and Society since Late Colonial Times.* Durham, NC: Duke University Press, 2001.

Sánchez, Enrique, ed. *Derechos de los pueblos indígenas en las constituciones de América Latina.* Santa Fé de Bogotá: Disloque Editores, 1996.

Sánchez Bella, Ismael, Alberto de la Hera, and Carlos Díaz Rementeria. *Historia del derecho indiano.* Madrid: MAPFRE, 1992.

Santos, Boaventura de Sousa. *Toward a New Common Sense.* Evanston, IL: Northwestern University Press, 2003.

Sarabia, María Justina Viejo. *Don Luis de Velasco, virrey de Nueva España, 1550–1564.* Sevilla: Escuela de Estudios Hispano Americano, 1978.

Sarmiento, Sergio. *Conflictos agrarios y perspectivas del campo oaxaqueño.* Oaxaca: CIESAS, Institutio de Investigaciones Sociológicas, UABJO, INI, 1999.

Scardaville, Michael C. "(Hapsburg) Law and (Bourbon) Order: State Authority, Popular Unrest, and the Criminal Justice System in Bourbon Mexico City." *The Americas* 50, no. 4 (1994): 501–525.

Schäfer, Ernst. *El Consejo Real y Supremo de las Indias: La labor del Consejo de Indias en administración colonial*, 2 vols. Madrid: Marcial Pons Historia, 2003.

Scholes, France V., and Eleanor B. Adams, eds. *Documentos para la historia colonial de México (Cartas del Licenciado Jerónimo de Valderrama y otros documentos sobre su visita al gobierno de Nueva España, 1563–1565)*, vol. 7. México DF: José Porrúa e Hijos, 1961.

Schroeder, Susan, ed. *Native Resistance and the Pax Colonial in New Spain*. Lincoln: University of Nebraska Press, 1998.

Seed, Patricia. *Ceremonies of Possession in Europe's Conquest of the New World, 1492–1640*. Cambridge: Cambridge University Press, 1995.

Sheridan, Cecilia. *Anónimos y desterrados. La contienda por el "sitio que llaman Quauyla," siglos XVI–XVIII*. México DF: CIESAS, 2000.

Sierra Juarez. *Sierra Juárez: Trabajo comunitario; Identidad y memoria histórica de los pueblos*, 2 vols. México DF: INI and CEHCAM, 1994.

Silva Prada, Natalia. *La política de una rebelión los indígenas frente al tumulto de 1692 en la Ciudad de México*. México DF: El Colegio de México, 2007.

Simpson, Lesley Byrd. *The Encomienda in New Spain: The Beginning of Spanish Mexico*. Berkeley: University of California Press, 1950.

Skinner, Quentin. *The Foundations of Modern Political Thought*, 2 vols. Cambridge: Cambridge University Press, 1998.

Snow, Dean R. "Ceramic Sequence and Settlement Location in Pre-Hispanic Tlaxcala." *American Antiquity* 34, no. 2 (1969): 131–145.

Solórzano Pereira, Juan de. *Politica Indiana*. Amberes: H. y C. Verdussen, 1703.

Spalding, Karen. *Huarochirí: An Andean Society under Inca and Spanish Rule*. Stanford, CA: Stanford University Press, 1984.

Speckman Guerra, Elisa. *Crimen y castigo: Legislación penal, interpretaciones de la criminalidad y administración de justicia (Ciudad de México, 1872–1910)*. México DF: El Colegio de México and UNAM, 2002.

Spicer, Edward. *Cycles of Conquest: The Impact of Spain, Mexico and the United States on the Indians of the Southwest, 1533–1960*. Tucson: University of Arizona Press, 1962.

Starr, June, and Jane F. Collier. *History and Power in the Study of Law: New Directions in Legal Anthropology*. Ithaca, NY: Cornell University Press, 1989.

Stavenhagen, Rodolfo. *Derecho indígena y derechos humanos en América Latina*. México DF: El Colegio de México and Instituto Interamericano de Derechos Humanos, 1988.

———, and Diego Iturralde, eds. *Entre la ley y la costumbre: el derecho consuetudinario indígena en América Latina*. México DF: Instituto Interamericano de Derechos Humanos and Instituto Indigenista Interamericano, 1990.

Stern, Steve J. "Feudalism, Capitalism, and the World-System in the Perspective of Latin America and the Caribbean." *American Historical Review* 93 (1988): 829–872.

———. *Peru's Indian Peoples and the Challenge of Spanish Conquest: Huamanga to 1640*. Madison: University of Wisconsin Press, 1982.

Suárez de Peralta, Juan. *Tratado del descubrimiento de las Indias: Noticias históricas de la Nueva España.* Preliminary note by Federico Gómez de Orozco. México DF: Secretaría de Educación Pública, 1941 [1588].

Tanck de Estrada, Dorothy. *Pueblos de indios y educación en el México colonial, 1750–1821.* México DF: El Colegio de México, 1999.

Tau Anzoátegui, Victor. *Nuevos horizontes en el estudio histórico del derecho indiano.* Buenos Aires: Instituto de Investigaciones de Historia del Derecho, 1997.

Tavárez, David. "Idolatry as Ontological Question: Native Consciousness and Juridical Proof in Colonial Mexico." *Journal of Early Modern History* 6, no. 2 (2002): 114–139.

————. "Invisible Wars: Idolatry, Extirpation Projects and Native Responses in Nahua and Zapotec Communities, 1536–1728." Ph.D. dissertation, University of Chicago, Chicago, 2000.

Taylor, William B. "Between Global Process and Local Knowledge: An Inquiry into Early Latin American Social History, 1500–1900." In *Reliving the Past: The Worlds of Social History,* ed. Olivier Zunz, 115–189. Chapel Hill: University of North Carolina Press, 1985.

————. *Drinking, Homicide, and Rebellion in Colonial Mexican Villages.* Stanford, CA: Stanford University Press, 1979.

————. *Landlord and Peasant in Colonial Oaxaca.* Stanford, CA: Stanford University Press, 1972.

————. *Magistrates of the Sacred: Priests and Parishioners in Eighteenth-Century Mexico.* Stanford, CA: Stanford University Press, 1996.

————. "Santiago's Horse: Christianity and Colonial Indian Resistance." In *Violence, Resistance, and Survival in the Americas,* ed. William B. Taylor and Franklin Pease, 153–189. Washington, DC: Smithsonian Institution Press, 1994.

————. "The Virgin of Guadalupe in New Spain: An Inquiry into the Social History of Marian Devotion." *American Ethnologist* 14 (1987): 9–33.

Ternaux-Compans, Henri. *Voyages, Relations et Mémoires Originaux pour Servir á l'histoire de la Découverte de l'amérique,* 2nd ed., 8 vols. Paris: A. Bertrand, 1837–1841.

Terraciano, Kevin. *The Mixtecs of Colonial Oaxaca.* Stanford, CA: Stanford University Press, 2001.

Thomas, Nicholas. *Colonialism's Culture: Anthropology, Travel and Government.* Princeton, NJ: Princeton University Press, 1994.

Thompson, E. P. *Customs in Common: Studies in Traditional Popular Culture.* New York: The New Press, 1993.

Tira de Tepechpan. *Tira de Tepechpan: Códice colonial procedente del Valle de México,* ed. Xavier Noguez, 2 vols. México DF: Instituto Mexiquense de Cultura, 1996 [1500s].

Todorov, Tzevetan. *Nosotros y los otros.* México DF: Siglo XXI, 1991.

Torquemada, Fray Juan de. *Veinte í un libros rituals í monarquia indiana,* 3 vols. Madrid: Nicoás Rodríguez Franco Impresor, 1724 [1615].

Tozzer, Alfred M. *Mayas y Lacandones: Un estudio comparativo.* México DF: Instituto Nacional Indigenista, 1982.

Trachte-Huber, E. Wendy, and Stephen K. Huber, eds. *Mediation and Negotiation: Reaching Agreement in Law and Business.* Cincinnati: Anderson Publishing Co., 1998.

Tutino, John. *From Insurrection to Revolution in Mexico: Social Bases of Agrarian Violence, 1750–1940.* Princeton, NJ: Princeton University Press, 1988.

Ulloa, Moddesto. *La hacienda real de Castilla en el reinado de Felipe II,* 3rd ed. Madrid: Fundación Universitaria Española Seminario "Cisneros," 1986.

Urías Horcasitas, Beatriz. *Indígena y criminal: Interpretaciones del derecho y la antropología en México, 1871–1921.* México DF: Universidad Ibero-Americana, 2000.

Van Cott, Donna Lee. *From Movements to Parties in Latin America: The Evolution of Ethnic Politics.* Cambridge: Cambridge University Press, 2005.

Van Young, Eric. "The New Cultural History Comes to Old Mexico." *Hispanic American Historical Review* 79, no. 2 (1999): 211–247.

———. *The Other Rebellion: Popular Violence, Ideology, and the Mexican Struggle for Independence, 1810–1821.* Stanford, CA: Stanford University Press, 2001.

———. "Two Decades of Anglophone Historical Writing on Colonial Mexico: Continuity and Change since 1980." *Mexican Studies / Estudios Mexicanos* 20, no. 2 (2004): 275–326.

Velásquez, María del Carmen. *La frontera norte y la experiencia colonial.* México DF: Secretaría de Relaciones Exteriores, 1982.

Vinson, Ben. *Bearing Arms for His Majesty: The Free-Colored Militia in Colonial Mexico.* Stanford, CA: Stanford University Press, 2001.

Viqueira Albán, Juan Pedro. *Propriety and Permissiveness in Bourbon Mexico,* trans. Sonya Lipsett-Rivera and Sergio Rivera Ayala. Wilmington, DE: Scholarly Resources, 1999.

Volpi Escalante, Jorge. *La imaginación y el poder: Una historia intelectual de 1968.* México DF: Ediciones Era, 1998.

Wachtel, Nathan. *El regreso de los antepasados: Los indios urus de Bolivia, del siglo XX al XVI.* México DF: El Colegio de México, Fondo de Cultura Económica, 2001.

Wagner, Henry Raup. *The Life and Writings of Bartolomé de las Casas.* Albuquerque: University of New Mexico Press, 1967.

Warren, Kay B., and Jean E. Jackson, eds. *Indigenous Movements, Self-Representation, and the State in Latin America.* Austin: University of Texas Press, 2002.

Waterbury, Laura R. "In a Land with Two Laws: Spanish and Indigenous Justice in Eighteenth-Century Oaxaca, Mexico." Ph.D. dissertation, University of Illinois at Chicago, 2004.

Weddle, Robert S. *The San Saba Mission, Spanish Pivot in Texas.* Austin: University of Texas Press, 1964.

Yannakakis, Yanna P. *The Art of Being In-Between: Native Intermediaries, Indian Identity, and Local Rule in Colonial Oaxaca.* Durham, NC: Duke University Press, 2008.

———. "Indios Ladinos: Indigenous Intermediaries and the Negotiation of Local Rule in Colonial Oaxaca, 1660–1769." Ph.D. dissertation, University of Pennsylvania, Philadelphia, 2003.

Yashar, Deborah J. *Contesting Citizenship in Latin America: The Rise of Indigenous Movements and the Postliberal Challenge.* Cambridge: Cambridge University Press, 2005.

Zaid, Gabriel. *Adios al PRI.* México DF: Oceano, 1995.

Zamora, Lois Parkinson. *The Usable Past: The Imagination of History in Recent Fiction of the Americas.* Cambridge: Cambridge University Press, 1997.

Zamora, Stephen, José Ramón Cossío, Leonel Pereznieto, José Roldán-Xopa, and David Lopez. *Mexican Law.* New York: Oxford University Press, 2004.

Zápata y Mendoza, Juan Buenaventura. *Historia cronológica de la noble Ciudad de Tlaxcala,* trans. Luis Reyes García and Andrea Martínez Baracs. Tlaxcala and México DF: Universidad Autónoma de Tlaxcala, CIESAS, 1995 [late 1600s].

Zavala, Silvio. *De encomiendas y propiedad territorial en algunas regiones de la América española.* México DF: Antigua Libreria Robredo, de J. Porrua e Hijos, 1940.

———. *La encomienda indiana.* México DF: Editorial Porrúa, 1973.

Zermeño, Sergio. *México: Una democracia utopica; el movimiento estudiantil del 68,* 2nd ed. México DF: Siglo Veintiuno Editores, 1981.

Zorita, Alonso de. *Leyes y ordenanzas reales de las Indias del Mar océano.* México DF: Miguel Ángel Porrúa, 1985 [1574].

———. *Relación de la Nueva España,* ed. Ethelia Ruiz Medrano, 2 vols. México DF: CONACULTA, 1999 [1585].

Contributors

ETHELIA RUIZ MEDRANO (coeditor) is a fulltime professor and researcher at the National Institute of Anthropology and History, Mexico. She is the author of *Shaping New Spain: Government and Private Interests in the Colonial Bureaucracy, 1535–1550* (Boulder: University Press of Colorado, 2006), among other publications. In 2006 she was awarded a Guggenheim fellowship. Her main interests are the relationship between Indians and the colonial and Mexican state and Mesoamerican Indian history.

SUSAN KELLOGG (coeditor) is a professor of history and the director of Latin American Studies at the University of Houston. She is the author of *Law and the Transformation of Aztec Culture, 1500–1700* (Norman: University of Oklahoma Press, 1995) and *Weaving the Past* (New York: Oxford University Press, 2005).

R. JOVITA BABER is an assistant professor of history at the University of Illinois, Champaign-Urbana, with a Ph.D. from the University of Chicago.

Interested in imperial legal and political systems and the daily experience of native peoples in colonial contexts, Baber specializes in the legal and social history of colonial Latin America in the early modern Iberian world and is revising her book manuscript titled "The Construction of Empire: Politics, Law, and Community in Tlaxcala."

JOSÉ MANUEL A. CHÁVEZ-GÓMEZ is a researcher at the National Institute of Anthropology and History, Mexico. He is the author of *Intención franciscana de evangelizar entre los mayas rebeldes* (Mexico City: Consejo Nacional para la Cultura y las Artes, 2001).

EDWARD W. OSOWSKI teaches history at CEGEP John Abbott College in Montreal. He specializes in Mexico's indigenous history, frequently using Nahuatl-language documents in his research. He is coeditor (with Nora E. Jaffary and Susie S. Porter) of *Mexican History: A Primary Source Reader* (Boulder: Westview Press, 2009).

BRIAN OWENSBY is a professor of history and department chair of the Corcoran Department of History at the University of Virginia. He is a specialist in both Brazilian and Mexican history and is author of *Empire of Law and Indian Justice in Colonial Mexico* and *Intimate Ironies: Making Middle-Class Lives in Modern Brazil*.

MARÍA DE LOS ÁNGELES ROMERO FRIZZI is a full-time professor and researcher at the National Institute of Anthropology and History in Oaxaca, Mexico. She is a well-known specialist in the ethnohistory of Oaxaca's indigenous population. Among other publications, she is the author of *El sol y la cruz: Los pueblos indios de Oaxaca colonial* (México DF: CIESAS, 1996).

CUAUHTÉMOC VELASCO AVILA is a full-time professor and researcher at the National Institute of Anthropology and History in Mexico. He specializes in Comanche colonial and nineteenth-century history. Among his work is "Sociedad, identidad y guerra entre los comanches, 1825–1835," in *La reindianización de América, siglo XIX*, ed. Marta Irurozki and Leticia Reina (México DF: Siglo XXI, 1997).

YANNA P. YANNAKAKIS is an assistant professor of history at Emory University. She specializes in the ethnohistory of Oaxaca, with a special focus on legal, political, and social history. She is the author of *The Art of Being In-Between: Native Intermediaries, Indian Identity, and Local Rule in Colonial Oaxaca* (Durham, NC: Duke University Press, 2008).

Index

Absolutism, Bourbon, 162–63
Afro-Mexicans, 6, 79
Aguila, Laureano de, 91
Ahitzá, 208
Alcaldes mayor, 2, 31, 142; land disputes, 118–27; in Sierra Zapoteca, 109–11, 129(n8)
Aldas, Antonio de, 148
Aldas, Francisco de, 154–55
Alegre, Chief, 186, 187, 189, 194
Alliances, with Wichitas and Comanches, 176, 177–78
Alonso, Captain, 185, 186
Alvarado, Miguel de, 52
Alvarado Matlaccohuatzin, Francisco de, 23
Álvarez de Miranda, Pedro, 217
Amealco, 98
Anales de Juan Bautista, 67, 72(n3); on encomendero revolt, 48, 51, 59–61; on

Montúfar, 54–55; on resistance, 70–71; on tribute payments, 61–63, 65–66, 68–69
Andrada, Francisco de, 207
Angeles, Jacinto de los, 139
Anunciación, Domingo de la, 52
Anza, Juan Bautista, 179; negotiations with Comanches, 182–83, 200(n18)
Apaches, 9, 181, 184; relations with, 185–87
Aragón y Alcántara, Joseph de, 140, 141
Arches, Corpus Christi festival, 80, 81, 82–85, 87, 88, 92
Arellano, Felipe de, 36
Arellano, Pedro de, 49
Argueta, Hernando de, 32
Armados, 79–80, 104(n57); economics of, 99–100; Holy Week and Corpus Christi, 96–99